D1236766

Published by Sterling & Ross Publishers
New York, NY 10001
www.SterlingandRoss.com

Cover design by Charmaine O'Saerang

Page composition/typography by Sarah Heath

Photographs courtesy and © of:
The Atlanta Braves and Major League Baseball, Rome Braves, Jim Jones, Nancy Wainwright, John Nelson, David Francoeur, Hiram Davies, Sherry McCann, Jenn LaRoche, Kansas City Royals, Ann Orowski, and Fontaine Lewis

Cover Photo: Andruw Jones, 1999 NLCS, Walk-off Homerun, Courtesy the Atlanta Braves, © 1999 Atlanta Braves

ISBN: 09766372-1-9

FIRST EDITION

10 9 8 7 6 5 4 3 2

Printed in the United States of America.

SCOUT'S HONOR

THE BRAVEST WAY TO BUILD A WINNING TEAM

BILL SHANKS

STERLING & ROSS PUBLISHERS
NEW YORK   TORONTO

-For Charlotte Williams-
Thank you for playing catch with me in the front yard, even
though it ruined your shoulder; for letting me stay up to listen to
the games, even when I had a test the next day;
and for being the best set of parents on the planet.

CONTENTS

Author Preface

I thought I knew baseball. I had watched it on television since 1978. But it wasn't until I got up-close in 2001 that I really found out what the game was all about. As a fan or a casual observer it's easy to believe you know what's going on, but access shines a much brighter light on the reality of the sport.

That was the year I worked out a deal with the Atlanta Braves to produce and host a weekly television show about their minor league system. It was the only show of its kind in the country. Doing a show that focuses on the major leagues is one thing, but the minor leagues are so full of stories that have yet to be told. So it was my duty to tell the stories of these kids who hadn't yet made it to the 'show.'

And of course, I got more than I bargained for. Learning about the players was great, but I also learned about an organization. The Braves have been my team since I was 8-years-old, growing up in Waycross, Georgia, and while I've appreciated the success they've had since 1991, I really didn't understand it until I got close. Then I discovered a much deeper story that was truly incredible.

It's simple to assume that money allocated by Ted Turner and then Time Warner is the prime reason for the Braves' success, but for fourteen straight years? There had to be more to it than just the money, and there is. In covering the minor leagues, I discovered how the Braves develop a certain type of player, not just one that will get to the major leagues, but also one that will succeed in the major leagues. There's a big difference. I learned the importance of a word that you will read time and again in this book: *makeup*.

Then I heard about a book by Michael Lewis called *Moneyball*. It focused on the Oakland A's and their reliance on computer technology in shaping its major league roster and its farm system. Several people in the Braves' organization warned me not to read it. "It'll get your blood boiling," they warned. "They just do things differently than we do." I resisted for a while, but then went ahead and read the book.

The differences outlined in the book were amazing. As someone who had watched a minor league system spit out players using one philosophy, it was incredible to read about a wholly different methodology. Some may say I'm being closed-minded, but the brash disregard for scouting in its truest sense as portrayed in *Moneyball* was just as insulting to me as it was to so many scouts around the game. As it was explained in the book, the A's, and the 'moneyballers,' apparently care more about on-base percentage than the makeup of a player, and even though I knew the Braves paid attention to OBP, it wasn't the telling factor in choosing a draft pick or a possible left fielder. The philosophical differences were staggering.

So I knew the Braves' story, and the story of scouting vs. bean-counting, had to be told. The more people I interviewed, the better the story became. Passion runs deep on the subject. But this story goes beyond the current Braves. You can trace its roots back to people around the Braves almost fifty years ago, the Baltimore Orioles of the 1960's, and the Kansas City Royals of the 70's and 80's. This story is about how baseball operated long before computer wiz kids got involved. It's about instincts, wisdom, and knowledge, not just a Microsoft spread sheet.

As I found out what type of players the Braves wanted on their team, the type of individual they wanted on the field in a crucial situation, I also found out that the makeup of the people implementing this philosophy mirrored the type of players they were looking for. The philosophy was important, but more important were the people doing the work. The individuals, not a computer program, made the Braves the most successful franchise in the game. How can a team win this much and for this long while others can't? Well, it's about the people. This book is their story. And it's about the only way to build a baseball team, if winning's what you seek.

1

"I DIDN'T THINK WE HAD A CHANCE"

Adam LaRoche had the best day of his young baseball career. With his Atlanta Braves down 5-2 to the Houston Astros in Game Four of the 2004 National League Division Series, the rookie first baseman quieted the huge crowd at Minute Maid Park with a mammoth three-run home run over the right field bullpen. The Braves would go on to win to force a deciding fifth game.

"That's about as excited as I can get," said the normally calm LaRoche before Game Five. "To be able to tie it for these guys who have been battling their butts off everyday and give us another chance to come back home for Game Five was the highlight of my baseball career."

LaRoche is one of the many reasons the Braves were where they were. Handed the first-base job at spring training, some wanted him to go back to the minors when he started off slowly. But after missing 31 games with a separated left shoulder in late May, LaRoche came back with a vengeance, hitting .301 with 11 home runs in 196 at bats for the rest of the season. He also hit .345 over his last 28 games.

But neither LaRoche nor his teammates could muster any

magic in Game 5. Despite the second largest and perhaps loudest crowd in Turner Field history chanting and chopping for most of the night, the Houston Astros proved they were the better team, beating the Braves 12-3 to advance to the National League Championship Series.

"It is disappointing," center fielder Andruw Jones said. "To have people celebrate on your own home ground doesn't feel good."

When the Astros celebrated the NLDS win on that field, it was the fifth straight season an opponent had beaten the Braves on their own turf. All but one of the series was the Division Series, meaning it had become very difficult for a team that appeared in the World Series five times in the 1990's to get out of the first round. And despite thirteen straight trips to the postseason, the Braves won the World Series only once.

"I have blocked out the other twelve," says the teary-eyed elder member of the Braves, reliever John Smoltz. "I don't remember anything about the other twelve. All I know is that this was not supposed to happen. We were not supposed to get here. We were not supposed to beat the Houston Astros and we almost did. I know "almost" and "could be" and "what ifs" don't go a long way in this city, but I think when you really break down this team and you really look at what happened, it's a remarkable year."

As you look over the tremendous and historic run of success the Braves have been on since 1991, you can see many similarities from team to team. All had good pitching, and for most seasons the Braves had one of the highest payrolls in the game. But 2004 was drastically different. After winning 101 games in 2003, the Braves needed a makeover that could have required a network reality show.

Time Warner, the corporate structure now in charge of the Braves, forced the team payroll to be cut from around $100 million to the low $80 million range. That mandate coincided with several key players declaring themselves free-agents (specifically half of the starting lineup and the best pitcher). Right fielder Gary Sheffield, who had a career year in 2003 with a .330 average, 39 home runs, and 132 RBI, would sign a long-term contract with the New York Yankees. Third baseman Vinny Castilla, who hit 22 homers and drove in 76 runs, signed with the Colorado Rockies. First baseman Robert Fick, who accounted for 11 homers and 80 RBI in 2003, signed with Tampa Bay. And the best catcher in Atlanta Braves history, Javy Lopez, would take his career-best numbers of 43 homers and 109 RBI to the Baltimore Orioles. That's 115 home runs and 397 RBI that had to be replaced in the Atlanta lineup.

The pitching staff would also undergo a big change as Greg Maddux would leave Atlanta only eleven wins shy of 300 career victories. He would go on to sign with his original team, the Chicago Cubs, and win his 300th in August of 2004. But Maddux's departure signified the huge transition that was taking place. He had won 194 games in eleven seasons in Atlanta, but a budget crunch would send him to another club.

Seeing the Braves ostensibly headed for a fall, the Philadelphia Phillies made moves to try and take control of the National League East. They acquired Billy Wagner from the Astros, Tim Worrell from the Giants, and Eric Milton from the Twins. The New York Mets added outfielder Mike Cameron and Japanese Star Kazuo Matsui. The Florida Marlins, who won the World Series in 2003, had most of their roster back.

Braves' General Manager John Schuerholz never had a bigger challenge. Sure, a lot of teams would die for a payroll of $80 million, but Schuerholz was faced with a 20% payroll cut while still trying to field a competitive team. That was something he never had to do in thirteen offseasons with the Braves.

Schuerholz replaced Maddux with John Thomson, a thirteen-game winner for Texas in 2003 that would make half of Maddux's salary with the Cubs. J.D. Drew was brought in from St. Louis in a huge trade to replace Sheffield, and two young players, LaRoche and Johnny Estrada, would replace Fick and Lopez. For the first time in many years, the Braves would not be the favorites coming out of spring training.

"I didn't think there was any way we could fight for a division title," Smoltz admits. "I thought we would fight for maybe the last two and a half weeks for an outside chance at a playoff spot. But as far as I was concerned with all the changes, it was going to be tough."

Fate would not help the Braves early on in 2004, as several key players went down with crucial injuries. Marcus Giles, arguably the Braves' best player through the first thirty-two games, broke his clavicle on May 15th and missed the next fifty-two games. Chipper Jones missed twenty-five games with hamstring trouble. Horacio

Ramirez, a twelve-game winner as a rookie in 2003, made only nine starts before going down with shoulder tendonitis. And then there was LaRoche's injury, which knocked him out for a month.

On the morning of June 26th, the Braves were six games under .500 (33-39), in fourth place in the National League East, and 5.5 games back of the Philadelphia Phillies. There were even rumors that day that the Braves were talking to the Chicago White Sox about a deal that would send starter Russ Ortiz and center fielder Andruw Jones to the American League. Some of the best moves a GM makes are the trades that aren't made, and John Schuerholz astutely held onto Ortiz and Jones.

The Braves won that Saturday, 6-0 over the Orioles, as Ortiz allowed only seven hits in seven innings. The next day Atlanta trailed 7-1 in the eighth inning, but rallied to win 8-7. Beginning June 26th, the Braves would win thirty of their next thirty-eight games to improve to 63-47. In a span of forty-four days, Atlanta would go from fourth place and 5.5 games behind the Phillies to first place and 5.5 games ahead of Philadelphia.

A number of players who were not even thought of on Opening Day contributed. Paul Byrd, out all of 2003 with Tommy John surgery, returned in late June and went on to win eight games while replacing Ramirez. Nick Green, a career .261 minor league hitter, was called up to replace Giles and hit .283 with 3 homers and 25 RBI in his place. After watching Mark DeRosa struggle as the starting third baseman, Manager Bobby Cox moved Chipper Jones back to third and Jones' production immediately improved. After Chipper vacated left field, the Braves called up a kid from the minors whom no one knew, but would instantly become a hero.

The Braves would finish the 2004 season with a record of 96-66 and finish ten games ahead of the Phillies, thirteen games ahead of the defending champion Marlins, and twenty-five games up on the Mets. That's only five games worse than the 101-win season of 2003 with a 56% turnover in the 25-man roster.

"Florida and Phily definitely had much better teams than we did, and no one can tell me otherwise," Smoltz says. "We did the things in the crucial part of the season that you had to do, and then let everybody else believe that we were the old Braves of the past. You can't talk about it during the season because it's going to come out like you don't believe in your team. But to a man, they're just giving you fake optimism if they really believe that we were that much better, ten games better, than those two teams. It's taught me a lot because in the beginning of the year and a good part of the year I lost confidence in us. I didn't think we had a chance. I would have been lying to you if I thought we did."

When Smoltz joined the Braves in 1988, the team didn't know how to win. Atlanta was in its fifth straight losing season and had had only seven winnings seasons in the first twenty-three years of the franchise. But Smoltz was a key figure in a dramatic overhaul that saw one of the worst teams in baseball become one of the very best. He was a part of a group of players that were part of a plan, part of a blueprint to change the Braves' ways. The philosophy centered on a major league team built around pitching, mainly from high school kids who were groomed and developed by the Braves themselves, not college coaches. The major league team would be built through the farm system, filling in with trades and an occasional free agent when necessary, but relying mainly on a continuous pipeline of homegrown talent.

And many years later, that philosophy is what has kept the Braves in the upper echelon of the National League. How else could a team drop 20% of its payroll, have the second-youngest lineup in the National League, and still win the division by ten games? How can the Braves show so much consistency? Why do other teams win and then fall off?

The Florida Marlins won 92 games and the World Series in 1997, and then won only 54 the next season, averaging only 70 wins for the next five years before winning it all again in 2003. Then after winning those 91 games and the World Series, they fell off to third place and only 83 wins in 2004. The San Diego Padres won 98 games and then the National League Pennant in 1998, but then averaged 72 wins over the next five seasons before finally finishing over .500 again in 2004.

How about the New York Mets? After winning 94 games and losing in the Subway Series to the New York Yankees in 2000, the Mets finished two games over .500 the next season and then averaged only 71 wins between 2002-2004. The Arizona Diamondbacks may be the biggest tragedy. They won the World Series in 2001 after winning 92 regular season games. Three years later the Diamondbacks would go 51-111, 60 games below .500. The Anaheim Angels won the World Series in 2002 and had 99 regular season victories. The next season they would fall to 77-85, twenty-two games worse than their championship year.

How can all of these teams struggle for consistency while the Atlanta Braves just keep winning? Since the 1991 season, the Braves have averaged 95.8 wins per season. Again, the Braves have had relatively high payrolls over the years, but to see other teams outspend them and still finish behind them in the standings, you know there's more to it than money.

It's all about the core philosophy and the people implementing that philosophy. And it all starts with a draft.

2

ROY'S FIRST DRAFT

The Atlanta Braves were the Team of the 90's. They won nine division titles, five National League pennants, and one World Series Championship. It was quite a decade for a team that for years was an unadulterated laughingstock.

Prior to 1991, the Braves won just two division titles in the first twenty-five years since the team moved from Milwaukee to Atlanta. They were not very good. But things have changed.

Roy Clark was in charge of keeping their last decade's success going into the new Millennium. He was named Scouting Director in July of 1999, replacing Braves' icon Paul Snyder. Taking over for a legend is never easy, and Snyder was a very difficult man to replace. He joined the Braves in 1957 and had been involved in the scouting and development of many key Braves players. More importantly, he was partly responsible for turning the franchise into a winner. In many ways, the Braves represented him as much as he represented the Braves. And even though he wasn't going home completely, he was no longer in the first chair when Draft Day rolled around.

This was now Roy's job, but he wasn't going to change a thing. The philosophy that had worked so well for so many years would remain intact.

"It's basically the same thing...emphasize the makeup," Clark said. "The philosophy I've always had is that tools get you drafted, but you've got to be able to play in the big leagues. Radar guns get you drafted, but you've got to be able to pitch to get to the big leagues. So we're looking for guys who not only have the tools and a good fastball, but the makeup that separates minor leaguers from major leaguers."

The Braves are what you call in the game of baseball, an "old school organization." Radar guns and stopwatches are always in use, and of course they'll check out the stats. But there's a personal side that's more important to this gang. They believe in getting to know their potential players. What's he like off the field? Is he a winner? Can he handle adversity? Can he handle winning and losing? Does he hustle? What's his desire? What's his attitude? What's his personality? Is he coachable? Does he have heart?

This is makeup. It defines the character of a ballplayer. It can't always be judged by looking solely at a player's stats. It can only be determined by the work of a scout, someone trained to analyze ability and project future performance by seeing the player in person, spending time with him, and determining whether he fits the mold of what the organization has determined makes a major leaguer successful.

"The best scouts have instincts," Clark (left) explains. "They can tell you 'this guy is a big leaguer.' Maybe they can't even describe it. But they just say, 'hey, I can just tell you this guy is going to be a big leaguer.' The philosophy that they've had here in place before I got here works. We weren't going to change that. If it ain't broke, don't fix it."

So Clark's big day was June 5, 2000. Even though he had been on the job as Scouting Director for eleven months, this would be the day he would be tested. It was an even bigger test than usual considering the Braves had five extra picks. Russ Springer, Jose Hernandez, and Gerald Williams were three Braves' free agents signed by other teams. As part of baseball's rules, those teams had to hand over draft picks to the Braves as compensation. So Atlanta had eight of the first 106 picks in the Amateur Draft. It was a chance to stock up the farm system and prepare for life after Glavine, Maddux, and even Smoltz. It was a chance to acquire talent for the future.

"I was completely relaxed," Clark remembers. "If you've got the right scouts and you've got the right crosscheckers (the scouts who prioritize the prospects) and you've got a good game plan, then you follow that game plan and you'll have success."

Clark's plan going in was simple: Don't go against the strengths of the draft. One of the strengths of the 2000 draft was the tremendous talent in the state of Georgia. For years Georgia had not been a hotbed of amateur talent. It was always California, Texas, and Florida. But as the major league team in Georgia improved, so did the amateur talent. The Braves' success in the 90's made kids want to go out and play baseball again. They wanted to hit like David Justice and pitch like John Smoltz and Tom Glavine.

With the first of their two first-round picks in the draft, Atlanta focused on a home-state player. Adam Wainwright was a tall, lanky kid from Glynn Academy in Brunswick, Georgia. His arm was loose and free and his six-foot-six frame made you wonder how big he might be in another four years. But more important for Roy Clark was the fact that Adam Wainwright wanted to be a Brave.

"Ever since I can remember breathing, I was a Braves fan," Wainwright says.

After his parents divorced when he was seven, Adam spent nights watching the Braves with his brother Trey, seven years his senior. Adam's mom, Nancy, was also around, making sure her two boys were in front of the TV when the Braves were on. "Every night at 7:35," Adam says, "we made sure dinner was scheduled around it so we'd be there to watch."

Adam was always an athletic kid, even though he was almost always a foot taller than his classmates. He played soccer, basketball, and then later football, but baseball was his favorite. Many kids have fathers to help them improve at sports, but Adam had Trey, who was also a baseball player in high school.

"Not to take anything away from my dad, but Trey was my father figure growing up," Adam explains. "He was older and he had been through things. He was real good at making sure there was time for me and making sure I was included."

Trey graduated from Glynn Academy when Adam was in the fourth grade. After he continued his studies at Georgia Tech and then later in law school at the University of Georgia, Trey continued to play a big role in Adam's life. "I tried to stay involved," Trey says. "From time to time I would drive to see him play soccer in Columbus or baseball in Savannah. When I was in Athens he was in high school and I would call him almost every night just checking in, seeing how his day went, how practice was going, and how he was feeling. I'm sure there were times I was just like a nuisance father."

Trey would really be needed in Adam's junior and senior seasons. Adam had become Glynn Academy's best pitcher as a junior, but midway through the season his elbow started to bother him. "My mechanics had been altered," Adam explains. "From throwing the football, I started throwing the baseball like a quarterback would. It wasn't so much an all-of-a-sudden thing. It just kind of got worse every time out."

Adam was diagnosed with a strained ligament in his elbow, the type of injury that can lead to the dreaded Tommy John surgery. Doctors simply told him to rest. The injury caused him to miss several summer showcases, which are important in getting on the radar going into the senior season. In hindsight, it may have been a blessing in disguise.

"Instead of going all out all summer long and peaking at the wrong time and being tired by the time he was in his senior spring, he sat out the whole summer and peaked at the right time," Trey believes.

Adam signed a college scholarship to play at Georgia Tech, but as his senior season approached, pro scouts were again interested in the tall righty. He regained his velocity that had abandoned him when his elbow started hurting. Adam really proved himself at a late spring All-Star game in Valdosta, Georgia.

"My arm had just started to peak," he says. "I was throwing the hardest (95 mph) I had ever thrown. I was on my game. I think that got me drafted."

Paul Snyder was one of ten Braves' scouts to see Adam. Early in the spring he watched Wainwright pitch and immediately called a crosschecker.

"There's a kid down here who you really need to see," Snyder said.

"Is he good enough for me to change my schedule," asked the crosschecker.

"Well, if you don't you might as well keep going the other

18

way because this is our guy," Snyder said.

The Braves tracked him closely, but they were worried about another team picking Wainwright before their twenty-ninth pick in the first round. The Dodgers (#17), Pirates (#19), and Giants (#21) were all interested. Trey Wainwright decided to take matters into his own hands. He had a feeling the Braves wanted Adam, but he wasn't sure what Adam wanted. So the night before the draft Trey had a heart-to-heart with his baby brother.

"Adam, what do you want to do?" Trey asked. "What would be the scenario you most want? If you can be a Brave in slot twenty-nine or a Giant at slot twenty-one, which would you rather be?"

"I'd rather be a Brave," Adam said.

"I knew then that if Adam got picked higher, that would be fine," Trey remembers. "But if he had any control over it he wanted to be a Brave. So I picked up the phone and called Rob English (the Braves' area-scout for Georgia). I told him, 'Rob I can tell you right now that if he's got a chance to be a Brave, he wants to be a Brave. But if that's not possible, or if it's 50/50, then we need to know. If you guys are not going to commit to him, then we're certainly not going to tell everybody else to go away.'"

English asked Trey to give him a half hour and went to speak with Roy Clark and the other Braves' scouts. "We realized Adam wanted us as much as we wanted him," Clark says. "So it was a good fit." English called Trey back and said, "I can't promise you anything. I probably shouldn't be telling you this, but the way the board is setting up now, there are only a couple of guys that we're going to take ahead of Adam, and we don't think they're going to be there when we pick."

That was all Trey and Adam needed to hear.

After not sleeping much that night, Adam, his brother and mother, waited for the draft. The Giants called that next morning, only to wish Adam luck. But they gave no indication he would be their pick. So with no big communication from any of the other teams, they believed there was a good chance Adam would make it to pick number twenty-nine. One by one, the Dodgers, Pirates, and Giants all passed on him. Then the Braves were up.

"Alright, here it comes," Nancy Wainwright said. "Here it is. It's the Braves' pick."

Adam was leaning on his pool table, but moved in a bit to listen to the Internet.

"Atlanta selects player number 0997, Wainwright."

"At that moment, that was probably in the top two or three moments of my life," Adam remembers.

Wainwright celebrates his first-round draft choice with 350 neighbors, friends, coaches and family (including his mother, far right.)

Scott Thorman always preferred baseball to hockey. He lived in Canada, so that decision wasn't always popular. At ten years old he was forced to make a choice. His hockey coach wanted him to make a year-round commitment, but Thorman chose baseball. The sport just came easier to him. His dad was his coach, at least until he passed away from cancer when Scott was twelve. But then his mom took over. She drove him to practices, workouts at the Skydome in Toronto, and then when Scott was sixteen she started driving him all over the United States to play ball.

"She was unbelievable," Thorman says. "We went everywhere together. It was kind of like 'my mom and I against the world' type of thing. When it was dads and their sons going to scouting camps, it was my mom and I. When we were doing interviews with universities and professional teams, it was my mom and I. We'd drive fourteen hours and she'd drive the whole way, before I could drive. I'd stay awake and be up with her. So we had some great times from baseball and traveling."

As the Thormans traveled, one thing became clear: Scott was pretty good. He was on a Connie Mack team that played in Ohio, Michigan, and even Tennessee. Then he went to the Area Code Games in California and another showcase in Florida. He played on as many as five or six teams during one summer, simply getting exposure to scouts and colleges that might be interested in him in a few years. Jim Kane was the Braves scout in Canada. Kane, who has since passed away, spotted Thorman when he was fifteen years old. "He was always around during our workouts and he'd watch me pitch and watch me hit," Thorman says. And that was the question: Was Scott going to be a hitter or a pitcher? He played third base, and like most team's best players, he also pitched. But pitching was more than just a secondary position.

"I threw a fastball, curveball, and a change-up," Thorman admits. "I wasn't polished at all. I'd just rare back and fire. The hardest I've ever thrown was when Paul Snyder was there. I touched 95 mph. I had a decent idea of where it was going, but basically it was a chuck- and-duck type thing."

But the always pitching-hungry Braves saw something else. They saw a left-handed hitting six-foot-three, 215-pound kid that looked like a linebacker and who swung the bat hard. Thorman reminded the Braves of another kid who had been a good pitcher in high school, Ryan Klesko, whom they had drafted in the sixth round back in 1989 as a first baseman. Many teams wanted Klesko as a pitcher. He threw hard just like Thorman, but the Braves believed Klesko could hit. And an appearance at their spring training complex in Orlando convinced them that Thorman might be the same type player.

"Scott had come down to Florida (in 1999) with the Canadian team and had worn out our Extended Spring Training team with the wood bat," Roy Clark says. "We felt like he certainly had a big upside."

"I was in Orlando in 1999 and 2000," Thorman says. "We'd work out at Disney (Atlanta's training complex) and the Braves had as good a look as anybody at me. I showed I could hit well with the wood bat in high school. I think that alone had more of an impact on the Braves taking me than anything else."

The Braves made him (at the time) the highest high school player taken out of Canada, with the thirtieth overall selection. "I was very happy," Thorman admits. The Braves had him at third base after he signed, but an injury to his shoulder, suffered right before the draft, kept bothering him. The Braves brought him back down to Orlando to work on his shoulder in January of 2001, but then something happened. "I was playing long toss and my shoulder popped out again," Thorman explains. "When it popped out, it got stuck above my head. There was clearly something wrong with it."

Thorman had reconstructive surgery on his left shoulder and missed all of the 2001 regular season. "When I got back (in the 2001 Instructional League) they had some kid named (Andy) Marte (now a top-rated Braves prospect) over at third who had done pretty well for himself," Thorman says. "I needed some at bats since I had missed the whole season, so they gave me a first baseman's glove. I would have been a big third baseman, so I'm very happy at first base."

First base was where the Braves wanted him all along. Just like Klesko.

Thorman's first full season was in Macon in 2002. He hit .292 with 16 home runs and 82 RBI. Then in 2003 he went to a hitter's nightmare, Myrtle Beach, South Carolina. The ballpark there is a mile and a half from the ocean, and deep fly balls can become infield pop-ups. Scott's production dipped to a .243 average with 12 homers and 56 RBI. It wasn't until 2004 that Thorman really became a serious prospect. He went back to start the year at Myrtle Beach and hit .299 with 4 homers and 29 RBI in 43 games. Then he went to AA Greenville and hit .252 with 11 home runs and 51 RBI in 345 at bats. That's a combined 15 home runs and 80 RBI in 499 at bats.

"I thought he came a long way in 2004," says his AA Manager Brian Snitker. "Scott's not there yet, but he's getting better. He became really dangerous with two strikes. He slowed his swing down and started going to other way."

That's the key for Thorman. He's very aggressive. His swings are sometime so hard that he looks like he's going to corkscrew into the ground. Just like Klesko. But Thorman's only twenty-three years old and he's still got a chance to become a pretty good pitcher-turned-first baseman. Just like Klesko.

"Obviously, I'm honored to be compared to him," Thorman admits. "Whenever you're compared to a big leaguer, it's not a bad thing. We both swing hard. We both play hard. Yea, there are a lot of similarities. But I'm Scott Thorman and he's Ryan Klesko. I'm going to go out there and play as hard as I can."

Just like Klesko.

Kelly Johnson was a surprise. Not many people expected his

name to be called when the Braves picked him thirty-eighth overall in the 2000 draft. The Orioles had mentioned the twelfth round to Johnson, and other teams said somewhere between rounds ten to fifteen.

"The Braves were really the only team that expressed that much interest in me as far as taking me early," says the left-handed hitting Johnson.

John Flannery was the Braves' Midwest Regional Scouting Supervisor in 2000. He didn't live too far from Westwood High School in Austin, Texas, and would drive by their batting cages and watch Johnson hit.

"He just had a sweet swing," Flannery says. "A lot of times I would stop in on my way home just to see who was at the ballpark that night. He was always at the ballpark."

"I'd be in the cage and I'd see him drive by and wave," Johnson says. "He'd stop by the curb and didn't say anything. He'd just watch. Every single day I'd see him driving by."

Flannery told the area scout, Charlie Smith, to keep a watch on Johnson. Smith had met Johnson prior to his sophomore year, so he was well aware of his talent. Johnson quickly became tops on the Braves' draft board from that area, higher even that Adrian Gonzalez, who was the number one pick in the draft by the Florida Marlins. Johnson didn't go to any showcases, so he was under the radar a bit. But he was in a very competitive area and played summer-ball with many high-profiled players.

"I was playing right there with them, but all the other teams didn't have the interest the Braves did," Johnson explains. "The Braves sent like eight or nine guys out just to watch a game here and there. The other teams didn't have that much interest."

"Charlie Smith and I were really sweating it out on whether we'd be able to get him," Flannery says. "We were trying to strategize the draft so we could get as many good players as we could."

The Braves did get him and were rewarded in his first full season of pro ball. Johnson hit .289 with 23 home runs in Macon and was voted the best prospect in the South Atlantic League by its managers. The next two seasons he struggled a bit, perhaps due to a defensive change in the field. The Braves moved him from shortstop to third base and he hit 19 home runs and drove in 97 between 2002 and 2003. They switched him again in 2004, this time to the outfield, and his bat responded by hitting .282 with 16 homers and

50 RBI in 479 at bats in AA. His defense in the outfield was very impressive, and Johnson is now very close to getting a shot in the big leagues.

"The saying goes 'if you can hit, it's easier to hit in the big leagues,'" Flannery says. "I think he's going to be one of those guys. I don't know what position he'll end up playing. I could see him at third base or one of the corners (in the outfield). He's so confident in his ability. I think he's going to be one of those guys that when he gets to the big leagues he's going to be a .300-plus hitter and hit 20 home runs consistently."

Johnson has a little extra incentive to prove the Braves were right in taking a chance on him that high when all the other teams were telling him he'd slip out of the top ten rounds. He's matured now into a solid prospect, one that might play anywhere in the infield or the outfield. "Defensively, being out in right field I've gotten comfortable out there now," Johnson says. "I still take ground balls everyday. I feel comfortable at five or six positions now. They're starting to write articles now in major magazines about the super utility guys that play all these positions, like Ryan Freel. I can see where that versatility is only going to help me. The best part about it is that I know that I ever get called up I could go up there and they could put me in anywhere."

J.J. Picollo was in his first year as a Braves' scout in 2000. He covered a very important area: Virginia, West Virginia, Maryland, Delaware, and Pennsylvania. Both Roy Clark and Paul Snyder had covered the Atlantic region in the past, so Picollo knew this was an area the Braves would scout heavily.

One of the first names on Picollo's list was Aaron Herr. It was a familiar name, since Aaron's dad Tommy had played in the major leagues for thirteen seasons, becoming a star with the Cardinals in the 1980's. Aaron was very similar to his father. He was a middle infielder, but more than that he was Tommy's son. "If they are walking next to each other, you know it's father and son," Picollo says. "They carry themselves the same way. They are almost clones of each other."

When Aaron was just a young kid, he spent many days with his dad at the big league ballpark. "Constantly," he says. "Ever since I was old enough to walk I was out shagging balls during BP, throwing with all the major league guys, and being a batboy for all the teams. So I had a great experience as a young kid that most kids don't have."

Scouts often target sons of major league players, and Picollo knew Aaron Herr would have some bonuses because of his history. "It was very important," Piccolo says. "The advantage those kids have over those who haven't been exposed to it is that they know what to expect everyday. I wouldn't want a player to sign and to expect what they see on TV and in the movies. I want them to know what it's like. With Aaron or any other player's kid that's been through it, he's seen all that. That's not a shock to them. And if they were too young to remember it, then their dad is going to prepare them for it."

Picollo first saw Herr in the East Coast Showcase in Wilmington, North Carolina, and then in the Area Code Games. His superiors told him to keep up with Aaron closely. "We were going to be patient with him," Picollo says. "We were going to go see him, and if he didn't perform well, we were going to give him another chance because we had seen him perform well leading up to that spring. With the exception of one day, he performed exceptionally well."

Herr had many of the same characteristics as his dad, but Picollo also saw some differences. "Tommy Herr was a guy who could steal bases, hit for some average, and he was a switch-hitter in an organization that emphasized speed," Picollo says. "Aaron's more of a Bret Boone-type. He's got power. He's an offensive player. The makeup was very good. He plays hard and rose to the occasion when the game was on the line. He wouldn't only get a big hit; he'd hit a home run."

Picollo and the Braves had to sweat it out; worrying that Texas might take Herr with the thirty-fifth or thirty-ninth overall pick in the sandwich round. Atlanta grabbed him with pick number forty. "It was my first draft," Picollo says. "I was real excited. I knew Aaron wanted to be an Atlanta Brave, so it was fun to make that call."

No sooner had Picollo hung up from telling Aaron Herr he had been drafted by the Atlanta Braves, did he get another call about one of his other prospects. With Atlanta's very next pick, number fifty-one overall, the Braves selected right-handed pitcher Kenny "Bubba" Nelson out of Riverdale Baptist High School in Fort

Washington, Maryland.

"I first saw him when he was about sixteen years old pitching for a fall scout team," Picollo says. "He just always carried himself with that competitiveness and solid mound presence that you want to see out of pitchers."

Kenny Nelson started his baseball career as a four-year-old shortstop in T-ball, but when he was nine years old two important things happened: he started pitching, and his dad gave him a nickname.

"He would get to the ballpark and forget his bag and we'd have to turn around and go get it," says John Nelson, Kenny's dad. "He wouldn't remember to take his books to school and we'd have to go get his books. He just did things like a Bubba. I just looked over at him one day and said, "You know what? You do things like a Bubba. I'm going to call you Bubba."

John Nelson started taking Bubba to play baseball all around the country. When he was nine, Bubba played for the Delaware Diamonds and played in the Continental Amateur Baseball Association's World Series in Iowa. Then at twelve, Bubba traveled to Mexico, Ohio, New Jersey, and Pennsylvania.

"It was always good to have my dad around pushing me along," says Bubba. "He was always there to hit me in the back of the head when I needed a little extra drive."

Along the way, the Nelsons met Hank Allen, a former major leaguer with John Nelson's favorite team, the Washington Senators, and the older brother of Richie Allen, the 1964 Rookie of the Year with the Phillies and 1972 AL Most Valuable Player with the White Sox. Allen, a scout for the Milwaukee Brewers, lived about a half hour from Bubba in Maryland.

"I knew who he was as soon as I saw him," says John Nelson. "I told Kenny, 'If this guy tells you something, you listen to him. He's played at the highest level you can play.'"

Allen soon became a mentor to Bubba. He saw him play in many high school and amateur games. Allen was in pro scouting, not amateur scouting, so he acted more like a friend than someone scouting Nelson. "He helped me out tremendously," says Bubba, "not so much physically, but the mental part of the game. I think that's given me an edge in a lot of areas. He always had confidence in me. Whatever I did, he always knew I could do better. He demanded nothing but better than what I gave the last time I played."

As Nelson reached sixteen and his sophomore season, he started to do pretty well. When he wasn't playing third base, he was pitching, and started to get a reputation as having a good arm. Nelson went 11-0 in his tenth grade season, and then 9-2 as a junior.

When Nelson started his senior season, the Braves zeroed in on him as a possible pick. Picollo went to the Nelson's house to express formal interest and left a video prepared by the Braves for potential draftees.

"The video was called 'Turning Young Men Into Champions,'" says John Nelson. "It had Tom Glavine, Greg Maddux, John Schuerholz, and it explained the Braves' way of baseball. It talked about the Braves' way of pitching. Bubba and I sat down and watched the video. Actually I think I watched it about ten times and I was like, 'I don't want Bubba to play for anybody else. I just want him to play for the Braves.'"

Bubba did his part with a great senior season, going 12-1 with an ERA under one. But there were a few things that kept him from being a higher pick. "The hard part with Kenny was he was not the six-foot-five prototypical right-hander that a lot of teams want to draft," Picollo says. "So you had to kind of see through that a little bit. The more you saw Kenny pitch, the more you saw his stuff. He's a pitcher. When you have a guy that is six-foot-one, he's got to have some pitchability and that's what Kenny had to prove to us his senior year, and he did. He did it in front of everybody, we had go in there and scout him. So he kind of took care of the guesswork by performing well when they were there."

On draft day, Nelson had to travel fifteen miles into Washington, D.C. to accept an award from *The Washington Post*. He was on his way back home when his dad gave him a call on his cell phone.

"Kenny you got picked by the..." John Nelson said, only to be interrupted by static as Bubba lost his signal going over the Wilson Bridge.

"I said, 'Well I think I got picked in the eleventh something,'" Bubba remembers. "I didn't know. All I could hear was joy in my dad's voice, so I knew it had to be good. I walked in the house and my dad was crying. I had never seen him cry before. My mom was crying too."

"Well where did I go?" Bubba asked his parents.

"You got picked eleventh in the second round, fifty-first overall," John told his son. "It's the Braves."

"Awesome," Bubba said.

Bryan Digby was a little different than Adam Wainwright. He really didn't care if the Braves drafted him or not. Sure, as a kid from Georgia, he grew up watching the Braves and rooting for Dale Murphy. But when it came to being drafted, he just wanted to play pro baseball.

Digby was a hard-throwing righty at McIntosh High School in Peachtree City, Georgia, about twenty miles southwest of Atlanta. Paul Snyder and Dayton Moore, one of Roy Clark's chief lieutenants in 2000, both came to see Digby, who dazzled them with a mid-upper 90's fastball. But the Braves were one of twenty-eight teams that came to Digby's house before the draft, so he had no idea if the Braves would get him.

"I really wasn't gung-ho Braves when I was in high school," Digby explains. "I just wanted to play for anybody who drafted me. When they draft you and after you get in the organization, then you get a little more pro-Braves because that's where you want to play and there's not a better organization around."

Digby is your typical hard thrower who was almost destined to battle arm injuries. He had only 166.2 innings in his first three and a half seasons in the Braves' system, mainly due to shoulder trouble. But before the start of the 2004 season, with Digby finally fully healthy, the Braves told him that he was going to be a starter for their Low-A team in the South Atlantic League. Most of the players he was drafted with were already at a higher level, but the Braves wanted Digby to get the one thing he didn't have much of in his career: innings.

"They said, 'we don't care how you throw or if you throw a no-hitter in spring training,'" Digby explains. "They sent me to Rome to get as many innings as possible. They said, 'we want you to go there and learn a little bit about pitching. Learn how to go through a full year and see what happens. We don't care if your ERA is a thousand.'"

It's one thing to be a hard thrower, but sooner or later all young pitchers have to learn how to pitch. The higher you go up the minor league ladder, the harder it is to just get by on just your fastball. So the minor leagues allow young pitchers to work on other pitches so they can be more refined as they pitch against better competition. With the Braves having so much pitching in their system, there was no need to rush Digby. He could progress on his own schedule and develop what was needed to improve. While on the surface some of his numbers looked shaky, the organization was pleased. Digby went 8-9 with an ERA of 5.94 in 27 starts. He allowed 189 hits in 144 innings along with 71 walks and 107 strikeouts. Again, for what his goals were, Digby had a solid developmental season.

"Everything's working a lot better," says Digby. "All my pitches are working a lot better. I'm running pretty much anywhere from 91 to 97 mph on my fastball, but the big thing was learning how to pitch. It's basically like they're saying, 'you've got a great fastball that allows you to overpower guys. So now go pitch.'"

"That's the good thing about this organization," says his pitching coach in Rome and one of the most important men in the farm system, Kent Willis. "We don't have to rush them. Anytime that you've done well at the major league level, that gives you some room at the bottom half of the organization to give guys that don't get it right away some time. He's had arm problems, but he has a tremendous amount of ability. It gives those guys an opportunity to continue to develop. He was able to go out and make twenty-seven starts for us and then he finished healthy. He developed his changeup, which he's never been able to use. Instead of trying to be a max effort guy, he learned to try to pitch a little bit. He got more of a feel for pitching. One thing is if you've never pitched and you've always been a thrower, then there's a transition to learn how to do it."

Now that Digby has logged those innings, anything's possible. With his talent, a mid to upper 90's fastball and an improving changeup, Digby's the type that if the light bulb fully comes on, the Braves will have another top-flight pitcher. But it's that patience shown by the organization, even four years after Digby was drafted, that has allowed the youngster to develop at the correct rate.

Blaine Boyer was a center fielder for Walton High School in Marietta, Georgia in 2000. He was a few weeks from being drafted by the San Francisco Giants in the fifth round as a third baseman. But then a strange thing happened that changed Boyer's life forever. Walton High School was in the Region Championship against Lassiter. Their best pitcher, Mike Gross, came down with back spasms right before the game. None of the other regular pitchers were able to throw, so the center fielder stepped up.

"Hey, I'll do it," Boyer told his coach. "Let me throw."

Boyer had never pitched before in his life. The coaches knew he had a good arm from the outfield, so they let him go at it. They really had no other choice. Talk about starting off with a bang. Boyer threw a one-hitter, touched 96 and 97 mph on the radar gun, and struck out fifteen.

Mr. Boyer, you are now a pitcher.

"It was nuts," he says. "I mean it was ridiculous. From then on, they turned me into a pitcher in the state playoffs."

Word spread quickly of what Boyer had done. The next time he pitched, in the state playoffs, there were fifty scouts in the stands. He did well the second time out, too, beating Clarke County.

The damage was done. "Yeah, from then on, there was no chance at being a position player," Boyer says. "They told me, 'no more. You're going to pitch.'"

The Braves had certainly taken notice. Walton High School is only five minutes from Roy Clark's house. Clark's son and the son of Walton's coach, Dennis Jordan, played on the same amateur team. Jordan called Clark and told him, "Roy, this guy is going to throw about 95. We haven't really used him yet. He's our center fielder and our best hitter."

So Clark and the area scout for Georgia, Rob English, went to see Boyer throw on the side after one of the playoff games when he didn't pitch.

"When I finished, Rob and Roy came up to me," Boyer says. "Roy said, 'We want you to come down to Turner Field and throw a little bit.' I was just shocked. I said, 'You've got to be kidding?'"

Well, the Braves don't kid about pitching. They wanted to see more of this raw arm and determine if Boyer was someone they could mold into a pitcher. It would be a project, but there was little doubt the stuff was there. But Boyer had one more tryout.

"The workout at Turner Field was...I remember I was sick. I had the flu prior to going to Turner Field. I had lost weight, and I was out of it. I remember getting on the mound and I was hyperventilating. I was so nervous. I had all these big dogs around me. There were like six scouts back there with radar guns. I did not know what to do. They said, 'throw a curveball.' So I did. I acted like I knew what I was doing, but I was just out there throwing, just as hard as I could, just trying to wing it. They had me throw like fifteen pitches. You can picture an eighteen-year-old kid on the diamond at Turner Field, throwing for the team of his dreams. It was amazing. It was surreal. I was right there in the middle of the stadium with all these guys watching me. I started hyperventilating and Paul Snyder brought me out some water 'cause he thought I was going to throw up on the mound."

The nausea didn't deter the Braves.

Clark walked up to Boyer, careful of not getting too close, and asked, "Do you want to play for the Braves?"

"Just draft me," Boyer instructed. "That's all you've got to do, just draft me. I don't care where. Just draft me." And Clark did just that. It was in the third round, and Clark reminded Boyer of how much he wanted to play for the Braves when they started negotiating.

The signing was not as hard as what was ahead. Boyer was impressive as a thrower in high school, but now he had to learn how to become a pitcher. He had a lot to learn. "The mental aspect of pitching, staying mentally strong," Boyer says, "is the toughest thing to deal with. As a pitcher, if you get beat up, you've got to come right back. You can't get down on yourself, and I've struggled with that. You can't let your emotions get the best of you. That's something that I really learned besides having to learn how to spot my fastball and throw my curve and changeup for strikes. From the get go, I had to learn a curve and changeup from scratch, along with learning how to throw my fastball mechanically. It's been tough. They had confidence in me. They saw something that they thought they could work with. So far, it's worked out."

But it's taken time, something the Braves can afford to have when it comes to developing young pitchers. Boyer was a reliever in 2002 at Macon, pitching in only forty-three games and getting 70.1 innings. But then the Braves brought him back to Low-A (the affiliate switched to Rome, Georgia) in 2003 and he became a starter. Even though many in the organization believe Boyer might be a reliever one day in the big leagues, it's the Braves custom to have their best minor league pitchers get innings as a starter. Boyer went 12-8 with a 3.69 ERA. In 2004, he moved up to Myrtle Beach and took another step forward, going 10-10 with a 2.98 ERA in twenty-eight starts.

Boyer has developed into a great pitching prospect. Leo Mazzone, Atlanta's pitching coach, was so impressed with Boyer when he threw at "Camp Leo," the annual pre-spring training throwing session, that he went on national radio and compared Boyer to "a young Rob Dibble."

And if Mike Gross had not had back spasms that day back in the Region Playoffs...well Blaine Boyer knows how lucky he's been. "That game basically changed my life," Boyer says. "If he hadn't gotten hurt, I don't know where I'd be. It's crazy how you can go back in your life and pick out a point where if something were to have gone different, there's no telling where you'd be. I'm sure I wouldn't be here. So that was just a blessing."

The Braves were the first professional team to ever talk to Zach Miner. He was a freshman baseball player at Palm Beach Garden High School in Florida. Rene Francisco, one of the Braves' International Scouts at the time, who lived in South Florida, met the young fourteen-year old right-hander.

"Right before a game my coach brought over a card and it was an Atlanta Braves' player information card," Miner says. "I filled it out. I was very excited. I really wasn't pitching much then. I was playing shortstop. I just thought it was cool."

Miner pitched a few games his freshmen season, and by his junior year he was still playing a little shortstop, but not much. The mound was his new home. Scouts started to show up every time Miner pitched. "I started to realize they were going to want me to pitch, so I better start taking this seriously," he says.

After his junior season, Miner played in some summer showcases. He was ranked very highly going into his senior season, with some even predicting he could be a top fifteen pick in the first round. Almost every major league team sent a representative to scout Miner and talk with him in his home. "The most frustrating thing that I went through was them coming in there and no matter what you say they're going to believe what they want to believe whether you say you're signing or not," he says. "You can say, 'I want to play.' But they're going to have their own pre-conceived notions thinking, 'well, you signed with this agent so you're going to be a tough kid to sign.'"

"This agent" was Scott Boras, known as the toughest negotiator for high school draftees. Miner admits having the super agent might have scared some teams off, along with his commitment to play baseball at the University of Miami. But it was all part of a plan to play for the team that called him first.

"I was pretty sure the Braves were going to take me," Miner says. "I just didn't know what round. They were going to take me as late as they thought I would go. Teams would ask me and I would tell them I'd sign for a certain amount of money. Naturally, that's going to scare some teams off that didn't want to pay a lot. I threw for the Pirates' Scouting Director a few days before the draft, so I thought I might go to them."

The six-foot-three, 190-pound right-hander went 9-2 in his senior season with a 0.33 ERA. Miner struck out 107 batters in 63 innings pitched. He did nothing to hurt his stock as a top talent, but the association with Boras and the commitment to Miami had him fall to the fourth round of the draft to the Braves.

"They called me and told me not to worry about it," Miner says. "They said, 'we'll take care of it.' I knew I was just as good as a lot of guys that were taken in the first round. The Braves had to know there were only a couple of teams that could take me there that would pay me enough to forego going to college. They made out pretty good."

Miner was paid the same amount as Adam Wainwright, Atlanta's first pick, but it took a while. "They told me that they needed to sign the other six guys in front of me before they could sign me," Miner explains. "They were planning on paying me more money and it wouldn't look good to a guy drafted in front of me, so it was a little while before I got my first offer."

The Braves pulled it off. They were able to get a pitcher most believed was a first or second round talent, in the fourth round. Four years later, Miner has developed into a solid prospect. He struggled early in 2004 at AA, going 2-4 with a 7.90 ERA in his first eleven games. But after June 1, Miner was 4-5 with a 3.98 ERA in sixteen games (fifteen starts). He finished with 111 strikeouts in 129.1 innings. Miner has an arm that could easily develop into a very important piece of Atlanta's future.

Chris Waters was different in a big way from the other 2000 draft picks. He didn't start playing baseball until he was thirteen years old. But it was an incident three years prior to that which set his baseball career in motion.

Waters's family was on vacation in Atlanta in 1990. They went to a few Braves games, but happened to be in a mall when Chris ran into a rookie Braves' player by the name of David Justice.

"He talked to me like I was his best buddy," Waters says. "I told him I played football and he talked about work ethic and that you've got to work hard to be successful. But he said, 'school's first. School comes before anything. If you work hard and put your mind to it, everything you want will come true.' That kind of stuck with me. He didn't have the big league act toward me."

The conversation Waters had with Justice inspired him to also play baseball, but it wasn't until his family moved to Florida that he really began his baseball career. Then, when he was sixteen, he started playing AAU baseball for Southwest Florida on their eighteen-and-under team. Waters played the outfield and would pitch when needed, but his size, or lack of it, kept him from being more of a prospect in high school.

"The Devil Rays, Reds, and Rockies looked at me my senior year," Waters says. "The Rockies wanted me to sign as an outfielder. But they said I needed another year or two to get stronger."

At only five-foot-nine, 150 pounds, Waters took off for South Florida Community College to bulk up and become a better player. "I got to college and started lifting and got up to six feet and 180 pounds," Waters says. "Then my fastball went from 86-87 in high school to 89-93 in college."

Waters still played the outfield, but the more he pitched, the better he got. He threw a perfect game as a sophomore, fanning twenty of the twenty-one batters he faced. The strikeouts started to pile up (he was second in junior college baseball in 2000 with 192), and so did the scouts watching him from behind home plate. The Braves called him the day before the 2000 draft.

"We're going to be aggressive with you," Braves' Florida scout Marco Paddy told him. The next day the Braves drafted Waters in the fifth round.

Later that summer, Waters was in a mall in Orlando when

who in the world did he run into? David Justice. Ten years after their first encounter.

"He remembered me," Waters says. "I told him that I had signed with the Braves. He was like, 'sweet.' I told him hopefully I'll be able to face him one day, and he kind of got a little smirk on his face."

Like Waters, Matt Wright was a football player. He was a tight end and defensive end for Robinson High School in Lorena, Texas. Texas A&M, TCU, and Memphis all wanted Wright to continue playing football in college.

"There's no experience like Texas football playoffs," Wright says. "We made it to the Astrodome with 25,000 people there. There's nothing like that for a high school game. I loved the mentality in football. I set a record for sacks. Some teams wanted me for defensive end and some wanted me for tight end, but some wanted me to redshirt and make me a linebacker."

But there was one problem. This six-foot-four, 230-pound bear of a young man wanted to be a baseball player. Being that big, being a pitcher, and being from Texas means only one thing: you want to be like Nolan Ryan.

"I grew up watching the Rangers," Wright admits. "But as a pitcher I watched Nolan Ryan a lot. I got to see him pitch one time at the Ballpark at Arlington. I grew up watching him and Roger Clemens, the Texas guys. They always say I'm 'the big tall righty from Texas.' I hear that a lot about being tall, being big, and being from Texas."

Ironically, it was another tall (but lanky) Texan who alerted the Braves about Matt Wright. In fact, it was a former Brave. Craig McMurtry was a six-foot-five right-hander who was with the Braves in the mid-1980's. He saw Wright pitch in high school and called Charlie Smith, the same Texas scout who was watching Kelly Johnson. Smith then called his regional supervisor, John Flannery.

"He didn't throw particularly well the day I was there," Flannery says. "But that's a testament to our area scout (Smith) and our associate scout (John Baron) for staying with Matt. Those guys knew they could sign him and they stayed with him. He had a good arm and he could spin the ball."

Wright believed he would be taken as high as the eighth

round or as low as the seventeenth round, but after the first day and the first twenty rounds, he wasn't drafted. The Indians, who knew the Braves were interested in Wright, called the night after the first day of the draft to give him a little advice.

"They said, 'Listen, tell the Braves you want some stupid amount so we can get you,'" Wright says. "By that time, I really didn't care, but I wasn't going to say that to the Braves. They got me the next day in the twenty-first round. I was disappointed in not going earlier, but when the Braves drafted me I knew being a pitcher in their system was going to be a great opportunity. I really didn't want to take that chance of passing that up. There's really not a lot of money in the twenty-first round, so I definitely didn't do it for money. I did it for the opportunity."

It took a few years, but Wright has become a legitimate prospect. He blossomed the second half of 2003 in Rome, going 10-2 with a 1.65 ERA in thirteen starts. Then in 2004 he went 4-6 with a 3.53 ERA and finished second in the Carolina League with 133 strikeouts, despite pitching for almost six weeks with a hairline fracture in his throwing arm.

Now that's a football mentality for you.

Trey Hodges, the seventeenth round draft pick out of LSU, would be the first of the 2000 draftees to help the Atlanta Braves. He made the Atlanta roster out of spring training in 2003 after two straight fifteen-win seasons in Myrtle Beach and Richmond. Hodges pitched in fifty-one games out of the Atlanta bullpen and had a 3-3 record and a 4.66 ERA. A numbers crunch forced Hodges back to AAA in 2004, and he was sold to a Japanese team in May.

Left-handed pitcher Matt Merricks, the sixth round pick, spent a few years bouncing around from Low-A to AA before being traded to the Dodgers in a trade deadline day deal in 2004. Traded for lefty reliever Tom Martin, Merricks was not even considered to be one of Atlanta's top forty prospects when he was dealt, but no doubt was a higher rated prospect when moving on to the Dodgers' organization.

Four of the 2000 draftees (Wainwright, Nelson, Merricks, and Charles Thomas) were traded to help the Atlanta roster, one made the Atlanta roster in his third season (Hodges) and one in his fifth season (Adam LaRoche), and seven were still considered legit prospects almost five years after the draft (Thorman, Johnson, Digby, Boyer, Miner, Waters, and Wright). Compare that to the previous two drafts the Braves had in 1998-99. The 1998 draft produced three players that made it to Atlanta (Ryan Langerhans, John Ennis, Tim Spooneybarger), four players used in trades (Spooneybarger, Matt Belisle, Nick Green and Brad Voyles), and only two from that draft still in the Braves' system in 2004 (Langerhans and Daniel Curtis). The 1999 draft did not produce one player that made it to Atlanta, although three were traded to help the big league club (Andrew Brown, Ben Kozlowski, and John Foster), and only three remained in the system in 2004 (Alec Zumwalt, Angelo Burrows, and Bryce Terveen). So the 2000 draft was very impressive and very productive.

"I think it was probably the best depth of any draft I've been involved with," Flannery says. "When we sat down to line up the players and who we thought we had a chance at we knew we had those extra picks. These were the players we like: the power arms, the hitters, and some of the lower guys who ended up being big leaguers. It's always the saying in baseball: you make your draft in the fourth through tenth rounds. And that was the case in this draft. We drafted good prospects high, middle, and low. Some of those players are in the big leagues and some of them are getting close. We're pulling for them to make a splash here pretty soon."

"We've got a number of guys who are considered prospects and still have a chance," Roy Clark explains. "First of all, I really believe that every guy we draft in the first ten rounds – if they stay healthy – should be a big leaguer. They should be. If we do our homework on their makeup, if we evaluate them properly, and give them an opportunity to play, then they should be a big leaguer. So the success of the 2000 draft is not a surprise. Every scout that's out in the field knows I'm going to ask one question when they present a prospect to me: 'Is he a big leaguer or not?' And that's a combination of ability and makeup. So we expect that to happen."

What a draft that was- and it was only Roy's first.

3
THE BRAVES' OWN
BRANCH RICKEY

Branch Rickey is known as the "Father of Baseball Scouting."
He created the modern farm system when he was General Manager
of the St. Louis Cardinals. Then as GM of the Brooklyn Dodgers
he integrated baseball with Jackie Robinson in 1947. Rickey is also
credited for inventing batting cages, pitching machines, and batting
helmets. There are not many people more instrumental in making
baseball what it is today than Branch Rickey.

Just as Rickey is important to the game of baseball, Paul
Snyder has been just as crucial to the history of the Atlanta Braves.
To see him today is to witness the epitome of an old-time baseball
scout. He's semi-retired but works tirelessly, starting with the whole
month of March at Spring Training, several days scouting amateur
players leading up to the draft, and then spending a few games with
each of the Braves' top four minor league clubs. It's a limited role
now, but it doesn't mean his contribution is not important.

At spring training, Snyder walks around with his old reliable
golf hat shielding the hot Florida sun from his face, his radar gun,
and his trademark cigar. Sometimes it's not lit, but it's just there,

kind of like Paul. His presence is important. Players know who he is, many of them were scouted by him or have simply heard the stories from other players about how great Paul Snyder has been to them. Snyder is afforded a great deal of respect in the Braves' organization as well as in baseball. Age may be part of it, but it's something more. It's an appreciation for what he's accomplished and the friendships he's created.

Pure and simply, Paul Snyder is the Atlanta Braves.

It's a frightening thought really, but Snyder could have easily have been even more like Rickey. The Dodgers wanted to sign him out of his Pennsylvania high school, but Paul's parents, both of whom had gone only through the sixth grade, wanted him to go to college. Paul resisted. He had played in the old Interstate League from the age of fifteen and won a couple of batting titles. School was not for him. "I just wanted to play baseball," he says.

But Snyder went to Lebanon Valley, a small college in Annville, Pennsylvania, eight miles east of Hershey. He only played there one year, and then went back home to work with his dad as a plumbing and heating contractor. Then, Sterling Arnold, who was pitching for a Red Line Team called Snyder to get him to come play. "You know they were making money, so I might as well make some too," Snyder believed. So he played with Red Line as an outfielder and then the Washington Senators offered him a $3,000 contract. Arnold was also a "bird-dog" scout for the Braves, and he called John Ogden, one of the Braves' best scouts at the time, to come see Snyder play. Ogden was impressed with the young outfielder.

"How much do you want to sign with the Braves?" Ogden asked Snyder.

"Well, Washington's offered me $3,000," Snyder shot back.

"You want $3,000?" Ogden asked. "Well, why don't you earn it? I'll give you $500 now and if you have a good year I'll get you $2500 more."

Snyder knew the Senators had a shaky reputation, while the Braves were having a great year in the National League that would lead to a World Series title later that fall. So he agreed to the deal laid out by Ogden and for the rest of the 1957 just worked out for Wellsville. The next season he hit .351 with 106 RBI's. "I got my $2,500 and got me a new car," Snyder recalls.

The next few years Snyder bounced around from Midland, Texas to Cedar Rapids to Eau Claire, Wisconsin, and in 1959 to Winnipeg in the Northern League. "We're riding station wagons up in that league," Snyder says. "Six guys in a wagon, three guys sitting up front and three asleep in the back. Well, it was my turn to be one of the three guys to sleep in the back. So we made the first stop and we went to change and I couldn't get up. I couldn't sit up. My back had finally given out on me."

Snyder spent much of the next six months in traction. The only positive thing that happened was that he met his wife, Petie. Finally, in January 1960 he had spinal fusion, but battled back to play in Wellsville, New York, for the rest of that year. It was in Wellsville that Snyder spent time with a man who would become a huge influence on him.

"I ran into a guy by the name of Harry Minor, a longtime scout and coach in the Braves' organization," Snyder explains. "I had met him at spring training in Waycross, Georgia (the Braves minor league spring training complex) back in 1958. He was the manager in Wellsville and he just had a great way of handling young players. The guys I had played for along the way were hard-asses when you lost. They didn't want you talking, didn't want you doing nothing. Well, Harry knew that we played 140 games a season and we couldn't harbor on one loss. So when the game was over we had to sit in the locker for fifteen minutes and think about what you could have done and what you should have done. He just wanted you to replay the game back and think about the things you could have done to help the team win and then forget it. It was just how he treated people. He never fined anybody. If the police fine was $10, just come on out and give me ten laps without stopping. If the police fined you $30, just come on out and give me thirty laps without stopping. He didn't make little boys out of us. I had never played for a man like that before. I had never met a finer human being than Harry Minor."

Minor had played in the minor leagues for about seven years with the Braves before becoming a coach and manager in 1957. "When you're not real old, and I was still playing a little bit then, dealing with eighteen-year-olds in most cases is not always an easy situation," Minor says. "You had to treat the boys like men and they're not really men yet. You hoped that you helped develop some characteristics that were going to help them not only in baseball but also in life."

Minor learned that philosophy from his legion coach, who

"treated us like we were professionals, even though we were only sixteen-years old."

"The minute Paul came to our ball club, we were better," Minor remembers. "He brought some maturity to my ball club that was very valuable. He wasn't officially a coach, but he probably was in some occasions. He always had the good baseball mind. He was always thinking. He would ask me questions about why I did this and why I did that. He was managing the game even when he was playing. Paul was a good hitter. He had a real nice swing and he waited good on the ball. He had a chance, but the injuries set him back."

The injuries would keep Snyder from reaching the big leagues. His back gave out again in 1963 when he was playing for Denver. "I was hitting back in the cage and I go down like a heap," Snyder says. "My back went out and I was scared shitless. It wasn't but a couple of days and they had me ready to go again." But he had already spoken with the Braves about managing if his injuries kept him out of the show. His manager in Denver, former big league skipper Jack Tighe, approached Snyder about ending his playing career.

"Paul, Mr. Mullen (Farm Director John Mullen) is ready for you to start your managing career," Tighe told Snyder.

"I'm not ready, Jack." Snyder told his manager. "I'm only twenty-seven years old."

"Hold it. Hold it. You go shower and I'll see you back here." Thirty minutes later, over dinner, the two men broke down Snyder's game and concluded all he could do was swing the bat. The back injury made him a one-dimensional player. Four days later Snyder was managing in Greenville.

"Who are you pitching tonight, skip?" asked outgoing Greenville Manager Jim Fanning, who was becoming a special assignment scout with the Braves. Snyder was still in a haze. Here he was four days removed from playing and he was now the leader of a team only three and a half games out of first place. Snyder did pretty well for a first-year manager. Greenville won the first-half division title and later that summer won the Western Carolinas League title. Then the next year Snyder managed Bimington in the New York-Penn League until John Mullen offered him another assignment.

"We're going to start a baseball complex," Mullen explained

to Snyder. "We need somebody to go in there." It was the birth of the Gulf Coast League, and Snyder took off for Sarasota where the Braves shared the facility with the Cardinals, Yankees, and White Sox for a four-team rookie league. "Then the next year (1965) I got to West Palm Beach in the Florida State League," Snyder says. "Well, here we go again. They needed a manager in the Gulf Coast League." Snyder had managed for three seasons, but he knew the 1966 season might bring a change. The Braves' major league team was moving from Milwaukee to Atlanta.

Paul Snyder

"I knew In 1966 I was going to find a new career or else," Snyder says. He wasn't sure if he wanted to continue managing, only that he wanted to stay in the game. Then John McHale, the President and GM of the Braves, offered Snyder a new job in Atlanta: Director of Stadium Operations for the new Atlanta Stadium. "They had to explain it to me," Snyder says. "I knew nothing about nothing. I went back to Atlanta on the first of November and started to get football coaches to get kids to come out and be ushers, ticket-takers, and all that kind of stuff. I knew nothing about a ground crew. I hated that job. We didn't have a cleaning contract. We were trying to clean the stadium ourselves. We got winos to come in to sweep. I'd sleep in the first aid room. It was horrible."

Snyder knew that he had no future in Stadium Operations. Meanwhile, Jack Tighe, his old Manager in Denver, had left his scouting job with the Braves. Tighe covered Ohio, Michigan, and Indiana. That was something Snyder knew he could do. "Honey," he told his wife Petie, "I'm going to get my ass to the ballpark tomorrow and ask Mr. Richards for that job."

"Mr. Richards" was Paul Richards, a former manager with the Orioles and White Sox and the first General Manager of the Houston Colt 45's (later changed to Astros). Richards had replaced John McHale as the Braves' GM. "He got to the ballpark and said, 'Well, what have you done son?'" Snyder recalls. "I told him what my past was. He said, 'Let me see about this.' So he asked if I could come back in after lunch. So I did and he said, 'The job's yours.' It was like I was flying. It had to be better than the job I had. The

43

biggest thing about when I went to be in Stadium Operations, was that I got a $3000 raise. But my wife and I figured it out and it came out to like $1.08 per hour when you figure all the time you put in. I can't tell you how bad I hated it."

Snyder would scout for three years until Richards called on him to manage once again, this time in Twins Falls, Idaho. Rod Gilbreath was the Braves' third round pick in June of 1970. An infielder out of Mississippi, Gilbreath was signed and put on a plane for Twin Falls and met by his new manager.

"He was very, very understanding, and an old-school type manager," Gilbreath says. "He was a very good teacher. We did the little things. We would get to the ballpark at ten o'clock in the morning and we would have two workouts before we even played the ballgame. That's the way you get better. He knew how to bring up young players. He always treated me like a son."

Snyder went back to scouting in 1971, and then managed in A-ball in Greenwood the next season. Richards was fired and replaced by his assistant, Eddie Robinson, and he promoted Bill Lucas to Minor League Administrator. Lucas wanted Snyder as his top assistant. "I told him I'd come in on one condition," Snyder says. "I wanted to manage the rookie club that summer in 1973. I didn't know if I was going to like that and I didn't know if they were going to like me. But that was the last year of that managing."

Bill Lucas started his baseball career selling peanuts in Jacksonville back in the 1940's. Then he attended Florida A&M before playing in the Braves' farm system for several years. Lucas played with Snyder in 1962 when he jammed his knee in a game against Tulsa. "He would have played in the big leagues if not for that accident," Snyder says. Lucas went to Atlanta and worked in the Public Relations department before becoming an Assistant to Eddie Robinson in Player Development.

Both Snyder and Lucas learned a lot from Richards and Robinson. "Well, you did," Snyder admits. "You had to – especially Mr. Richards. If you were around him at all – Paul was probably one of the few General Managers that almost everyday would stop by the minor league clubhouse at the end of the day and just sit there and BS with the guys, and most of the time talk about the rules of the game. He was good to me. Eddie was good to me."

Richards stressed pitching. He was a little different from Snyder and Lucas in that he had an ego. Richards liked to see players many times before signing them, not fully trusting his scouts to make the evaluation and the recommendation. He and Robinson had a track record with their work together in Baltimore and Houston that demanded respect.

As the Hank Aaron era ended in Atlanta and the home run champ was traded to Milwaukee to end his career, the Braves were trying to get younger, and Lucas and Snyder were the architects of the entire blueprint. But then Snyder almost lost it all.

In 1975, Snyder had been on a carnation diet, drinking four cans one day and then three the next, with celery and carrots. "Needless to say, the weight started falling off," Snyder says. "Then I started to get the sweats. I had quit dieting but the weight kept falling off." Snyder was getting ready to go out west on a hunting trip with Braves pitcher Phil Niekro and his brother Joe. He decided to get an upper and lower GI before he left.

"We were leaving 6:00 am Saturday morning," Snyder explains. "Friday night I asked the doctor, 'Would you stay or would you leave if you were me?' He said, 'Medically, I'd stay, but if I were you I'd probably go too.' They warned me that the higher altitude would cause the chills and sweats to get more frequent. When I came back two weeks later, my wife said I looked like death warmed over."

Snyder's wife took him to Piedmont Hospital the morning after he got back from his hunting trip. Doctors found an infection and a defect in his heart.

"Your aortic valve has three main chambers going out of it and I was born with only two," Snyder says. "I guess in the use and abuse of athletics one of the valves had calcified shut and the other had to hold it. I was out there for six weeks walking around with an IV pole stuck in my arm. They wanted to replace the valve then and I said, 'No we can't do that. We've got the January draft. And then we've got spring training and we've got the June draft. How about setting me up for the first of July?'"

The doctors agreed. Snyder made it through the January draft, spring training, and the June draft. But then on the night the draft had been completed, Snyder awoke in the middle of the night.

"I told my wife that my right arm was asleep," he says. "She said, 'Why don't you get up and walk around a little bit?' Well, my right leg was asleep too. She called Dr. David Watson and they got me into the back end of the station wagon and to Piedmont Hospital. Next thing I know I see my wife and David at the end of my bed in the emergency room. He said, 'I think Paul's had a slight stroke. This is as bad as he's going to get.' Then the lights went out. I don't remember anything until waking up with a turban on my head after the surgery."

Snyder, in fact, had a major stroke. He was only forty years old. He lost use of his entire right side and had to learn how to walk and talk all over again.

"I stayed in the hospital for about two weeks with the therapy and stuff," he says. "Then my wife said she could do that. A lot of nights we went to bed and I didn't know if she loved me and I didn't know if I loved her, because she was relentless. Thank god she was. I've lost about 35% feel of the right side. If I take your hand I've got to watch my hand into yours. If I shake your hand I've got to watch it go in so I won't miss. I don't have fine motor tuning to this day. I lost a couple years of memory. It's just some things I don't remember."

His friend and old teammate, Bill Lucas (left), stood by Snyder. There were some in ownership who wanted to let Snyder go, but Lucas said, "I could do that, but you'd have to replace me too."

So around the same time Snyder returned to work the team was sold to a television station owner by the name of Ted Turner. Turner didn't know much about baseball, but he wanted the Braves to be a part of his television schedule on WTCG (which later became WTBS). He had big dreams of taking that station national, putting it up on a satellite for cable companies to receive. Turner was a loud-mouthed southerner with big dreams and big ideas. "I didn't know what the hell to think," Snyder admits on Turner's arrival. "You just had to prove yourself all over again. He kind of emulated the Dodgers because they were successful. Ted had a little trouble figuring out that he couldn't go and get baseball players like he got cameramen."

Not long after Turner took over, he fired Eddie Robinson and brought in John Alevizos, a former Administrative VP with the Red Sox, as the GM. But he lasted only four months. In the meantime,

Turner was listening to Snyder and Lucas and soon developed a trust with both of them. "There's one person Ted Turner believed in and that was Bill Lucas," Snyder believes. "They hit it off. It was somebody that Ted believed in."

Lucas became the de-facto GM, even though Turner had the title. Lucas was the one making the trades and setting the tone for the organization, and Snyder was now running the scouting department. Even though he wasn't given the title of General Manager, Lucas became the first African-American to run a major league franchise.

"Bill was the General Manager," Snyder says. "He was the first one."

Lucas hired Pat Nugent, an executive with the Yankees, to be Paul's assistant in the Scouting Department. "Bill Lucas was a wonderful person," Nugent says. "He had a way with people. He let you do your work. He'd scrutinize it pretty closely, but he'd let you do it. He had a wonderful relationship with the players. They all really loved him. He would be able to get the most out of our players. He had a great eye for talent. He could envision other things. He was just a natural at it."

As the late 70's approached, the game plan executed by Lucas and Snyder was starting to show results. The Braves were developing talent, mainly with position players like Dale Murphy, Bob Horner, Glenn Hubbard, Rafael Ramirez, and Bruce Benedict.

"It was always pitching with us," Nugent says. "We always just had so much bad luck with pitching. I think we had as good scouts as anybody. We had the proper flow of information, but we just had a string of bad luck in developing pitchers. Now the Braves seem to have a Midas touch with developing pitching. But on the players side we were starting to develop some folks in the late 70's. You could see it starting to form."

The Braves had hired a young manager in Bobby Cox, had a young GM in Bill Lucas, and a young nucleus of talent. Of course, Lucas had to deal with Turner going after the hot free agent every winter. And while Turner succeeded in getting Andy Messersmith and Gary Matthews, it didn't deter the plan the brain trust had in place. Then in May of 1979, another medical emergency befell one of the Braves executives as Lucas suffered a brain aneurysm.

"Rubye (Lucas's wife) and Bill were watching Johnny Carson," Snyder says. "At that time Ted was showing the ballgames at 1:35 in the morning where you could see it again. Something happened in the fourth inning and Bill wanted to see it again. His wife talked to him and he didn't answer. She called his name louder and he didn't respond. So she just reached over and kind of flipped him on the cheek. She said normally it was something that would have ticked him off. There was no response."

Lucas was rushed to the hospital, but "for all intent and purposes I think he was dead right then," Snyder says, of the passing of Lucas.

The team of young players that Bill Lucas had helped get to the big leagues was crushed. Ted Turner was crushed. "Bill was like a son to Ted," Nugent says. "We had a good philosophy. It really did start with Bill. He knew what to do and how to do it. A plan like that takes time to develop. If Bill had lived, he would have gotten a tremendous amount of credit. He'd be there today. He had a plan. It doesn't vary any more than what is going on today. The same things being done today were all laid out when Bill was there."

Snyder had lost his friend and boss. "Bill was an excellent evaluator," he says. "He had great communication skills. He had the guts of a burglar. And the players loved him. I thing there's no doubt about that."

The search for a replacement did not begin with Snyder. "I didn't want it," he contends. "I told Ted that I'd do whatever needs to be done here until he found somebody. I just wanted to go back to my little scouting and player development job."

So Turner hired John Mullen, the man who first hired Snyder as a manager back in 1963. Now Mullen would lead Snyder and Hank Aaron, back in the organization as the Farm Director, in the new front office. This allowed Snyder to concentrate more on scouting. He started hiring more people, with Ted Turner's confidence, including his former infielder at Twin Falls, Rod Gilbreath.

"I don't know how to explain it to you other than he was my mentor," Gilbreath explains. "We would talk about different things like how to recognize players, what to do with players that couldn't play, and what to do with players that could play. Paul always appreciated the people he was around."

Hep Cronin was a high school baseball coach in Cincinnati when he became an Associate Scout for Snyder in the late 60's. Then in 1980 Snyder hired Cronin as a full-time scout. "I don't think he's changed much in the 37 years I've known him," Cronin says. "He was Paul Snyder from day one. The amazing attribute he's got...I could be an Associate Scout, a nobody, and he's going to treat me the same as he does someone who might be Scouting Director. He's not going to walk into a ballpark and migrate to a General Manager or something because he's the bigger wig. He'd rather migrate over and talk to the area scout from Tennessee or something. That's just Paul Snyder. Everybody's equal. He's the architect of this all."

The one thing that Gilbreath and Cronin both learned was the trust Snyder had in his scouts. "He trusted the people he hired to do their job," Gilbreath says, "and if you didn't do your job he would let you know that too, but in a calm way. He was never the type to come out and just blast you for not doing your job. He got his point across every time."

"I hear other people that crosscheck talk about how their boss calls them every day and how their boss asks them this or that," Cronin says. "I started crosschecking for Paul, he'd rarely call. He just assumed I knew what I was doing. I'd be headed for Florida and he'd call and ask, 'where you at?' I'd say, 'I'm heading to Florida.' He'd say, 'Ok, call me if you need me.' He'd just let you do your job. He figures you know what you're doing."

"You go away from your interaction with Paul knowing he heard everything you said," according to Dayton Moore, who joined the Braves in 1994 as a scout in the Mid-Atlantic States. "Paul has a great ability when you're talking with him to be there and to engage in conversation where you know it's you and him. It's a tremendous skill. The relationships are what are important in every aspect of society. Paul has the ability to make relationships work. That's what has ultimately enabled him to remain successful in this game over a long period of time."

John Flannery joined the Braves as a scout in 1988. "Paul Snyder is the prince of baseball," Flannery says. "He is somebody who is probably the most personable, most hospitable, and the best listener I've ever met. To this day, he hasn't changed at all. He still works as hard as he ever did. He could probably work a lot of us into the ground. You always felt like when he came in to see your players and you talked about them that he just really cared and he really listened."

"If you're not going to listen to them, why have them?" Snyder asks. "All we ask is you just have to get as many guys that work as hard as you work. If they don't, they've got to go."

A few years ago, *Baseball America* awarded Snyder its

Excellence in Scouting Award for the period of 1982-2001. "There was another Scouting Director as I was coming down from receiving it, and he said, 'If I had Bill Wight, Fred Shaffer, and Lou Fitzgerald (three of Snyder's veteran scouts during that period) I could have gotten that Goddamn thing too.' I said, 'You probably could have but you're not smart enough to listen to them.'"

Snyder's scouts knew exactly what type of players he was looking for. It was no secret. He preferred high school kids to college players, and was always on the lookout for good young arms.

"I liked projectable high school pitchers that don't have any hickeys," he says. "If you're sitting in a chair and heaven forbid you have a heart attack, do you want me to get a GP or you want me to get a cardiologist? What do you want? You want a cardiologist. Hell yes you do. That's why I always had gray-haired pitching coaches who have seen many mistakes in pitchers. They can correct anything. You look at Bill Fischer, Bill Slack, Eddie Watt, and Bruce Dal Canton. Damn, their hair, what they had left, was all gray. Johnny Sain was here. I look at a pitcher being three years younger than a player. It's going to take him three years to become a pitcher. We've got to get him to that point without him getting hurt. Why let someone else groom your kids? Mold them the way you want them to play."

"We focused on high-ceiling athletic baseball players with good makeup," says Brian Kohlscheen, who was with the Braves as a scout from 1991 to 2000. "We felt if we could get the high school kid in particular, into the system, our player development people could take this piece of clay and mold them into the type of player and person to have success on and off the field. Paul is real good about picking up things like that."

It's not more than a coincidence that a man whose makeup was unquestioned would also focus so heavily on players with solid makeup. "In scouting, if you don't have the right makeup, it's easy to be average," Kohlscheen explains. "Paul would always say in meetings, 'which players are going to seek their level? Which scouts are going to seek their level?' In order to seek your level you have to have good makeup. They'll be enough people that will tell you that you aren't good, whether you're a player or a scout or whatever. The people that are made right, that are able to overcome that, and to keep that focus on the goal, are the ones that put rings on your fingers."

Snyder stayed on as Scouting Director until 1990, when the

new GM brought in his own Scouting Director and made Paul a Special Assistant to the General Manager. "I was hurt," he admits. But five years later, in 1996, Snyder was named Director of Scouting and Player Development once again. "I felt good again," he says. Snyder was once again in charge of molding the Braves' future, a job he cherished. He had put his mark on pennant winning teams and a World Series winner in 1995. But whether Snyder is sitting in the main chair or not, his mark on the Braves' organization is indelibly woven into its fabric. The philosophy is in place, and its success only makes it natural to continue. When Snyder moved back out of the Scouting Director's position after the 1999 draft, it was important to keep the ball rolling with someone who would stay the course and continue the excellence.

4

LEARNING FROM PAUL SNYDER

Roy Clark was almost born for his job. It's not that he couldn't have been a coach or a General Manager. He'd certainly be a good one. But a Scouting Director only has to wear a tie about three times a year. Roy prefers it that way. He likes instead to be out in the field, dressed only in a polo shirt and slacks with maybe a dip in his bottom lip.

Before Clark became the Braves' Scouting Director in 1999, several other teams had approached him about the same position. But Clark wanted to stay with the Braves, so the plan that was put in place was similar to Conan O'Brien biding his time in the wings waiting for Jay Leno to retire. When Paul Snyder decided to step down, Clark would take over. In the meantime, Clark would spend time with Snyder and learn from the old master.

"It was kind of a smooth transition," Clark says. "I knew he was going to retire. He's the hardest working man I know. Paul's the best Scouting Director in the history of baseball, in my opinion."

John Flannery, now a National Crosschecker for the Braves, believes Clark had big shoes to fill when he replaced Snyder.

"I don't think there was anybody but Roy who could have replaced Paul," Flannery says. "I think the brilliant thing was that

Roy was the National Crosschecker for Paul, so they worked closely together. They were in the draft room together. It was just like they traded seats. When Roy took over he just kept it going. It was a seamless transition with the same kind of effort and attention to detail. They both have different styles and they're both different people. The results and the style of effort are very similar though."

"The benefit Roy got coming into this job is that he came with us and was under Paul," says Hep Cronin, Braves' Crosschecker. "He learned under the guy and kept 90% of us. Thank God. Roy has done some things a little different. He will try to get a college guy or two in those first few rounds, where Paul might take eighteen straight high school guys. Roy might try to get a college guy in a little earlier than Paul did. I think Roy's still 90% high school."

Stability is important to the Braves. They've had the same GM since October of 1990 and the same Manager since June of that same year. Clark believed in the same basic principles as Snyder when it came to the draft: go after the best player available with a slant on high school players, projectable young arms, and always stress *makeup*. The makeup part he learned from his own experience. Clark was an All-ACC middle infielder at the University of North Carolina in the late 1970's and was drafted by the Seattle Mariners in the twenty-fourth round of the 1979 draft. He put up good numbers in rookie ball, AA, and in two years of AAA, but then the Farm Director with Seattle wanted him to repeat AAA the next year and backup one of the Mariners' top prospects, Harold Reynolds.

"I realized that if I couldn't compete for a job...if I was going to be delegated to a utility role then I didn't want any part of it," Clark says. "So I went back and finished my degree at North Carolina. Then I got a job in the real world and it didn't take me long to realize that it wasn't my cup of tea."

So instead of being a salesman for the American Furniture Company, Clark went to work on the grounds crew at the ballpark in Martinsville, Virginia, for minimum wage.

"Then I sent a letter to Jeff Scott, my old Farm Director, saying that if he had anything in coaching or in scouting open up to give me a call," Clark remembers. "He called me the next day after he got the letter. I went to work for $6,000 a year as a coach, an infield and outfield instructor, in the Midwest League. Then, the second year our scout in the Carolinas got sick. So I left spring training and scouted through the draft and then went and coached.

I realized then that was what I really wanted to do."

Clark scouted for the Mariners for the next two years before leaving for the Cleveland Indians in 1988. Then, in the fall of 1989, an opening came up in the Braves' organization. He had met Paul Snyder at the North Carolina state games, but the two really got to know each other one night in a bar, where a lot of the business of scouting gets done. "We hit it off from the time we sat down and talked in Martinsville, Virginia," Clark says. "They had a scout, Smokey Burgess, in the Carolinas who was in declining health. So they were looking for a full-time scout in that area. I was recommended to him. I started working there in October of 1989."

"I was looking for someone to make a damn difference," explains Snyder. "When I go to see a ballplayer play, I see the player, make my notes in my little book that I carry, and then see who is scouting. I'm seeing how alert they are. I'm really scouting the scouts right then. But I knew after watching Roy that with his tenacity and his energy he could help make a difference."

It didn't take Clark long to make a difference. One of the big things that impressed Snyder was Clark's belief in tryout camps. "He just kind of turned me loose," Clark says. "He just kind of let me do my thing. I signed a lot of guys that first year. We had a lot of clubs and I signed a lot of guys. Brian Bark and Brian Kowitz, two guys that got some big league time, were signed out of those early tryout camps."

Tryout camps used to mean a last chance for players who were looked over in the draft. But that's not the true meaning in Roy's eyes. "Well, the most important reason you have tryout camps is not to sign players, but to get to know the young players at an early age and then watch them progress each year," he says. "So if you get to know a kid as a sophomore, and then you see him the next year getting better and better, and you see him and you know him and you're talking to him and you feel good about him, that's when you get a real feel for whose coming and who are the strong-makeup kids."

But along the way, Clark also found a few diamonds in the rough at his camps. In 1991 the Yankees spent over a million dollars (when that was a lot of money) on Brien Taylor, a projectable high school left-handed pitcher taken out of South Carolina with the first pick in the draft. The Braves got their own lefty out of South Carolina that year, but it all started at a tryout camp, something that very few other teams ever bothered with. A high school coach called Clark and told him he had to see a big, tall pitcher named Hiawatha Terrell Wade.

"I look over and we've got a radar gun on him and this kid looks like Brien Taylor," Clark says. "So we stopped everything and went over and saw him throw about ten pitches, and that was it. I called Chuck Lamar (the Scouting Director at the time) and said, 'Chuck, I'd like to sign the guy.' So by then I had talked with his momma and Terrell said if I met him that night we'd sign a contract. So I went over in the pouring rain. He had me meet him in a grocery store that was also a pool hall. I walked in with two of our part-time scouts and he's shooting a game of pool. So he looks at me and says, 'can you hold on a minute?' And he ran the table. He knocked in about six balls, got his money, and then he came over and we signed the contract."

In a few short years, Wade would become the Braves' best prospect. He spent parts of three years with Atlanta, with his best season coming in 1996 (5-0, 2.97 ERA in 44 games, 79 strikeouts in 69.2 innings pitched). Conversely, the Yankee prospect Brien Taylor got into a bar fight, hurt his arm, and never played in the big leagues. Terrell Wade wasn't even drafted, yet Clark found him and he contributed mightily to the Braves' 1996 season. How does that happen?

"He was a basketball player," Clark says. "He wasn't drafted at all. If a kid plays basketball and goes right into baseball there's a period, a month or six week period, where you just are not going to see them at their best. Kevin Millwood (another Clark signee) was the same way. Kevin came out of the shoot real slow his senior year because he was playing basketball. Those basketball coaches don't like you to work out in baseball when they're trying to win a championship. So the same thing happened with Wade and Millwood. I caught them at the right time. Timing is everything."

Millwood was another tryout camp kid for Clark. He came to the camp as a junior and Clark got a good look at a tall country boy from North Carolina with a good arm. "There were twenty, twenty-five scouts there to watch him the first part of his senior baseball season," Clark says. "I knew what he could do because of the tryout camp. So he came out slow? So what? I remember going to his last game of the year and he was throwing 92, 93 mph in a championship game. He had gotten into shape. There was *one* other scout there. That's how you make good drafts. You stick with guys. You see them and stay with them. At the end, right before the draft, you have to make that call. You don't have to make it in February. You make that call right there before the draft."

As a result of the camp and their belief in sticking with guys from an early stage, Atlanta took Millwood in the eleventh round in 1993. He debuted in 1997 and spent the next five and a half years in the Braves' rotation before being traded to Philadelphia.

While he was with the Indians in the late 80's, Clark scouted and signed Greg McMichael, a seventh round pick out of the University of Tennessee. He was a low three-quarters pitcher with a sinker and a slider. His changeup was not great, but he could pitch. McMichael dominated the Carolina League in 1988. "He went from A ball to AA and somehow, someway, somebody got a hold of him and instead of him being a two-seam sinkerballer guy, they tried to make him a four-seam fastball guy," Clark says. "So they changed his mechanics. He was straight over the top and was very readable. He was at 93 mph but couldn't get nobody out, plus he had some knee problems."

"So he got released by Cleveland and he called me up. I went and met him in Bristol and I couldn't put my finger on what it was 'cause I hadn't seen him in a couple of years. So I talked with him. Greg's a great guy. He's one of the greatest people I've ever met on the face of the Earth. His mechanics were out of whack. So I'm riding down the road and it just clicked. I said, 'I know exactly what we need to do.' So I called Greg up and said, 'Here's what we want to do. I want to sign you. But I want you to call Mark Connors (the head coach at Tennessee at the time and a former Yankees' pitching coach) and for two weeks I want you to just get back to your old delivery. I want you to just get back to what you did right and not this over-the-top four-seam fastball stuff.'"

Connors worked with McMichael and got his mechanics back in order. The Braves sent him to Extended Spring Training and then to High-A Durham. Two springs later he won a job in the Atlanta bullpen and wound up as the Braves' closer, saving 19 games with an ERA of 2.06 in 74 games and finishing second in the voting for National League Rookie of the Year behind Mike Piazza. McMichael spent four seasons in Atlanta before playing for the Mets, Dodgers, and A's and finishing up with the Braves in 2000.

The McMichael story is a classic example of what scouting is really all about. It's about knowing what kind of person you're dealing with, the work ethic of the player, and knowing their makeup. It's not sabermetrics or bean-counting or number-crunching. It's instinct and gut and intuition and experience. It's makeup.

Clark learned a lot about makeup when he was in the minor leagues himself. "When you're in the minor leagues and you spend two weeks with your teammates, you can ask anyone of them in the clubhouse and they'll tell you who the big leaguers are," Clark says. "It's something that separates them, but most of the time it's going to be the makeup. They can have plus-tools (a player strong in the five tools: hitting for average, hitting for power, speed, arm strength and fielding) across the board, but if they don't have the makeup...I mean, there are a lot of guys stuck in the minor leagues who have great tools."

Clark learned what separated great ballplayers as he continued to scout and see players like Wade, Millwood, and McMichael make the majors. It helped that he worked for an organization that already emphasized makeup, but he also developed his own ideas about what to look for in a player.

"The most difficult thing to define is 'what is makeup?' Well, it's the guy that you want at home plate with the game on the line and he wants to be there. Or it's the guy who's on the mound in a tough situation and you know that he is thriving in the moment. To get a good read on a kid's makeup you can't just see him one game or one time and see him perform one time. You might see something there, but I like to see a guy at his best and I like to see a guy at his worst. I want to see how he handles adversity. I like to see him play other sports. I like to see him in crucial situations, game on the line, title on the line, state championship on the line. I want to see how they react. They ones that have the strong makeup, the ones that we're looking for, are the ones that thrive in that situation."

As the 1990's progressed, so did Clark's career with the Braves. He became the Southeast Regional Supervisor in 1995 and then a National Crosschecker in 1996. "The job of the National Crosschecker is to basically front your Scouting Director," Clark explains. "In other words, I'd go out to the West Coast and see all the top guys and we'd call Paul and say, 'Paul you need to see this guy and that guy.' You're in the airports a whole lot more than I was used to. But I really felt like Paul Snyder was a Hall of Famer, and it was my job to prove he was the best Scouting Director in all of baseball.

To do that, myself and our staff, we had to do the little things to continue to produce. Paul would never ask us to do what he wouldn't do himself. Paul was a workaholic. For years he would be down in Spring Training, for example, and he's there first thing in the morning, through the day, and he's working with those kids, and then at night he'd drive three hours to go see a kid play, and then get back at one or two in the morning. He did that for twenty-five, thirty years."

As the National Crosschecker, Clark would be at Paul Snyder's side on draft day. He was able to see how Snyder juggled the draft board, one of the most challenging jobs for any baseball executive. "He was outstanding," Clark says. "He had done it for years. He had his style. It was good. We had some long hours. We did a lot of research and watched a lot of tape. Paul obviously emphasized pitching."

So Clark knew all about makeup and the type of player the Braves were looking for. His arrival as Scouting Director came as more teams were moving toward a reliance on statistical analysis in scouting, relying more exclusively on stats instead of allowing the scouts to use their instincts to project potential ability. This trend has also seen more teams pursue the college player, cutting down the time between their draft date and their big league debut. But with the plan Snyder had put in place over many years, Clark wasn't about to change the Braves' philosophy.

"We've been drafting predominantly high school players since Bobby Cox and Paul Snyder and Stan Kasten all got together and said, 'This is the route we want to go,'" Clark says. "So it's been going on for some time now. But there are more teams that are taking the college type kids now. So what happens is more and more of these high school kids have been falling to us the last four or five years, that we thought would be long gone. It's worked out for our benefit the last several years."

While the Braves do add more of a personal touch with their potential players, getting to know them and determining their makeup, it doesn't mean stats aren't examined. "We use a number of different tools to evaluate a player," Clark explains. "The radar gun is just one tool. The radar gun can get you drafted, but you've got to be able to pitch to get to the big leagues. The same thing with a stopwatch and it's the same thing with stats. Obviously you don't want to get a guy who's hitting .230 in high school. I think that you look at stats and you don't totally dismiss them, but we trust our scouts' instincts. We trust our philosophy. We feel that every guy we bring in we can help them reach their ceiling. There's a long history of guys who did not have good stats in their draft year for some reason, maybe they're nicked up or coming out late because of basketball, so you've got to trust your scouts."

Once again, Clark has been able to use his experience as a player and relate it to his scouting philosophy.

"The stats can be misleading," he believes. "In high school I played with this guy who wasn't real big and strong. I out hit him. I was the MVP on our high school teams. If you go by stats alone, I should have been in the big leagues instead of him. You may have heard of this guy. His name is "Sweet" Lou Whitaker, and he played eighteen years in the big leagues. I may have had better stats, but the tools made the difference. If you went totally by stats- stats don't play the game, people do."

"But we do look at stats," he continues. "Brad Clontz is a guy we signed in the early 90's. Brad was right in my backyard. He went up to the Cape Cod League and had an ERA of 0 and set a record at that time for saves. There are certain times when you're looking at a kid and if you know he's set a record for saves, you're going to take a look at him. So we do look at stats, but it's is just a tool just like a radar gun is a tool and just like a stopwatch is a tool. But there are other things that come into play that make a guy a big leaguer."

Over the last five years, Clark has assembled a group of scouts that mirror his image: hard-working and committed to the philosophy that's been in place for so long. Former Oakland A's pitcher Tim Conroy is now an Assistant to General Manager John Schuerholz and was the National Crosschecker for Clark.

"Roy sets the bar for all of us, for the whole staff," Conroy says. "Nobody works harder than him. He's out there seeing as many players as he can, running around the country. He's very aggressive. All of us are aggressive and try to keep up the pace. I think we're as well prepared of a staff as there is in baseball."

J.J. Picollo was the Braves' scout in the Atlantic states for several years before moving into the front office in 2004. He says Clark's patience is very important for the area scouts working for him.

"Roy has said on many occasions, 'I don't care what you have in February, just get them right come June,'" Picollo says. "He'll be patient with you. There is a level of expectation as a Braves' scout because we're still high school oriented and now we're also looking at college players. We're still open on both fronts. We have to be thorough in our evaluation and in our process, and our process includes things like the tryout camps that Roy likes so much. I've had summers where I've had twelve tryout camps. Anthony Lerew (one of the Braves' top pitching prospects) came out of a tryout camp. I saw him at a tryout camp as a junior. He just read about it in the paper and showed up. He didn't go to a Perfect Game or Area Code showcase, so he was a little bit of an unknown. It's Roy and Paul educating us and letting us go about it in a certain way that allows you to develop as scouts."

Dayton Moore (left) was hired by Clark and is now the Braves' Director of Player Personnel. "When I spoke to him about coming over to the organization, I wanted to be apart of his passion for baseball and his expertise," Moore says. "All you've got to do is stay in his wake and you're going to get pulled along and you're going to get better. But he has great focus, a strong desire to be the best, and a relentless commitment to this philosophy that's in place."

Perhaps Clark's biggest fan is the man he replaced.

"I didn't know how good he was as an evaluator," says Paul Snyder. "I thought he was good, but I didn't know until I got him over here. He's probably the quickest evaluator I've ever been around. He loves to work and loves his job."

The biggest motivation for Clark is to keep the Braves' run of success going. Compared to other important people in the organization, he's the new kid on the block. So he doesn't want the team to be unprepared to win or to not be able to improve because of a deficiency in his scouting department. The goal is consistency – not just getting a team ready to win for one year, but to continue the streak of thirteen straight division titles.

"I relate that to my alma mater and the coach, Dean Smith, at North Carolina," says Clark. "The one thing that they did as long as he was there was that they had a chance to win every year because of the plan they had in place. Our goal with the Atlanta Braves is to have a chance to win a championship. To do that you've got to have a plan and stick with it. The credit belongs to Bobby Cox and Stan Kasten and Paul Snyder for starting this. Then

John Schuerholz took it up a notch. We're just continuing that trend. Our goal is to have a chance to win every single year and the only way to do that is to fill up this organization with prospects."

5
NURTURE vs. NATURE

Bill Wight was a left-handed pitcher in the big leagues for twelve seasons, starting in 1946, for eight different teams. Wight was 77-99 in his career. After his playing days were over, Wight became a scout, working for Paul Richards in Houston before joining the General Manager in Atlanta in 1967.

Wight became one of Paul Snyder's chief lieutenants. Even though he was a pitcher, Wight seemed to scout position players very well. One of his biggest finds for Houston was a small second baseman named Joe Morgan. Snyder thought it was a true gift of scouting that a former pitcher had a great eye for position players, and he was able to see it first hand when he visited Wight in California.

"We were sitting out there the first year I went out to California to scout with Bill," Snyder says. "This foul pop goes back over the stands. It was way up there. And Bill says, 'Well that answers that.' And I thought, 'What the hell is he talking about?' So I didn't say anything. I was smart enough to keep my mouth shut. I got to the car and said, 'Bill, that foul ball went back over and you said 'that answers that.' What was that all about?' He said, 'Paul, did you ever see a banjo (weak) player hit one back over like that? The ball doesn't have to be hit to the field, it can go anywhere for an indication of power.'"

"This was a guy who was a pitcher," Snyder says. "This guy spent a dozen years in the big leagues. But he ended up being a better player scout than he was a pitcher scout. He had to study those hitters to survive in his own career, so he had an eye for hitters and position players who had talent."

So it should be no surprise that in 1973, when Wight was scouting up in Oregon, a young catcher caught his eye. Dale Murphy was a junior at Woodrow Wilson High School in Portland. Murphy's American Legion coach was a lookout guy for Wight; paid a percentage if the Braves signed anyone he told them about. The coach knew Murphy and his family well, and told Wight to take a look at him.

"I got to look at him as a junior," Wight remembers. "He had a little history of knee trouble, even in high school. Second year of high school he played first base, but he was a catcher and I knew he had a great arm. As a senior he was catching all the time."

Dale Bryan Murphy was quite an athlete. He was six-foot-five, 190 pounds and full of athleticism. Woody Hayes, the legendary football coach at Ohio State, recruited Murphy to play football, even though Murphy didn't play high school football. He was a catcher, and quickly became one of the top prospects in the nation.

"The potential was great," Wight says. "But the productivity wasn't all that great. You had to project him. But you can do that with a high school player. His arm was tremendous. He had a lot of power. But he'd swing through balls. Usually those big guys have a little trouble with those high inside pitches since they have big swings. But he was just a big, physical specimen."

Murphy remembers the scouts showing up to see him when he was a junior. Then they came more frequently his senior season. The Phillies even flew him to Philadelphia for a pre-draft workout. He was there with Lonnie Smith, and even ran a sixty-yard dash against Willie Wilson. "I didn't do too well," Murphy says. Then when the draft rolled around, even though he thought the Phillies were interested, he didn't know what to expect. There was no *Baseball America* or Internet around back in 1974.

"We had no idea what was going on," Murphy admits. "We just kind of sat around and waited."

Then Bill Wight called to tell Dale and his parents the Braves had selected him with the fifth overall pick in the first round.

Murphy had committed to play in college at Arizona State (ironically where he would have played with his future Braves' teammate Bob Horner), but really wanted to play pro ball.

"We basically didn't know what we were doing," Murphy says. "We started talking about money and what they were offering. We had no idea what other guys were getting and what other guys had gotten in the past. Now it's more sophisticated. Bill came up with an offer. I think it was $52,500. We thought, 'Man, that sounds pretty good.'"

The Braves sent Murphy to Kingsport, Tennessee for his first stop on the minor league ladder, but the first few months of pro baseball were tough for the young man. He was desperately homesick. "I was like, 'I don't care how I'm doing,'" Murphy says. "I just wanted to go home. It was just uncomfortable. Here I was eighteen-years-old and I was pretty skinny. I was playing with college kids that were mature and strong. I was like, 'Well, why was I drafted? These guys were pretty good.'"

Murphy also ran into some pressure of being a first round draft pick.

"It was an uncomfortable feeling for me," he says. "The whole thing, number one this, number one that. I wasn't really too clued in to as to what was going on, where I was going, and who these guys were. You just didn't know anything. I was playing with college guys, all stars in their respective leagues. The league was tough. I was like, 'Man this is challenging.' I know I was ready to get home. I was glad that rookie league season was only a couple of months long."

Murphy hit .254 with 5 homers and 31 RBI in 181 at bats (54 games) in that first season of pro ball at Kingsport. The next season, 1975 in Greenwood, he hit .228 with 5 home runs and 48 RBI in 443 at bats (131 games). He struggled with his defense, often throwing the ball past the second baseman and into center field when opponents would run on him, and that often affected his offense. There are a lot of expectations on first rounders, and early on in his career, Murphy didn't live up to the hype. But Paul Snyder and Bill Lucas had faith in him. They inspired Murphy to keep at it by telling him they had confidence in his ability.

"My whole feeling about my experience in minor league baseball was I felt a really unique personal relationship," Murphy explains. "It wasn't that it was a deep relationship or that we talked all the time. They couldn't do that as our bosses. But I felt they cared about me. They did care about me. They were patient with me. I felt like kind of a lost kid away from home. They were just there. I felt a caring from people in a real tough business that really helped me out. They helped me get through a lot of things. If I had been in another organization with another group of people, I just don't think I would have made it. I know there were times when Paul Snyder and Bill Lucas probably had to stick up for me and say, 'No, stick with this guy a little longer.'"

Snyder and Lucas did stick with Murphy, even though his confidence was ruptured. Murphy went to AA in 1976 in Savannah. Now twenty years old, he started getting a little stronger and started hitting better. It helped that Savannah had a short left field porch, and he hit 12 homers in 352 at bats, a big improvement over his first two seasons. Then for three weeks the Braves sent him up to AAA Richmond, where his manager was Jack McKeon, who would go on to win a World Series as the Florida Marlins' Manager in 2003.

'We had a funny team," Murphy says. "We had Jim "Bo Bo" Breazeale and Al Gallagher, guys that I felt were ancient, guys who had been in the big leagues and were trying to get back. It was an eye-opener for me."

What was even more of an eye-opener for Murphy was when Lucas sent him to the big leagues to finish the 1976 season.

"To be honest with you, I was scared to death," Murphy admits. "I would have been fine going home. I just was not confident. I would have been fine ending the year in AA. You're out of your comfort zone. Gosh, I know they were trying to do me a favor, but I didn't do anything (to warrant a promotion). I was a number one pick I guess. I look back and know that they just did things for me. They wanted me to succeed."

The next year Murphy went to spring training with a chance to make the Atlanta roster. He was only twenty-one years old, but the Braves were not a very good team, and they could take a chance of putting a young, unproven player on their roster. But Murphy struggled at the plate and again at catcher. Sometimes his return tosses to the mound would end up in center field, and he'd either throw baserunners out with ease or sail the ball to his center fielder, thirty feet behind the second base bag.

"I was really struggling," Murphy says. "I was supposed to make the team and didn't. It was not pretty. I was about as down as

I could ever be."

Murphy was sitting in the clubhouse that spring after another rough game. He knew he was struggling both with the bat and in the field. He was crying, wondering if he would ever be a major leaguer, and even wondering if he ever wanted to play baseball again. He was that discouraged. Paul Snyder saw Murphy sitting in front of his locker and walked over and sat down.

"He told me that I couldn't quit," Murphy says. "He was very encouraging. He had just had his stroke the year before, and he was basically trying to tell me to count my blessings. He said, 'Dale you've got your health. You can't give up. You've got a lot of things that you can't take for granted.' I'll never forget him sitting there and talking to me and taking a personal interest in me and helping me. He would try to see the bright side of the thing that would have no bright side. I thought my career was over. I'll just never forget that act of concern for a young kid wondering if he was ever going to play again. This was a good man. I was supposed to make the big league team and I didn't know where I was going. The way I was playing I thought I might go home."

Murphy didn't go home. Instead, he went back to AAA Richmond. His catching was still a problem, but his offense turned the corner. He hit .305 with 22 home runs and 90 RBI. The Braves called him back up to the Show in September of 1977 and he hit .316 with 2 homers and 14 RBI in 76 at bats. Then, after the season, Murphy went to play in the Dominican Winter League, and his defensive struggles continued. But again, the Braves gave him every reason to believe they still had confidence in him.

"I'm down in the Dominican playing winter ball and Bill Lucas calls me," Murphy explains. "I was really struggling. I had some kind of bonus, a performance bonus. I wasn't even thinking about the bonus. Bill called me and said, 'Hey, we're going to give you the bonus.' I told him, 'No way.' I was crazy, but I was like, 'what? Are you sure?' He said, 'No, you've earned it. We're happy with your progress.' That was just Bill. He treated you with kindness and respect. I think there was a respect you felt from him no matter who you were. I think that's one of the things – you just instantly had respect for him as well."

The bat came around in 1977, so that was less of a concern, but his struggles behind the plate gave the Braves reason to think he'd have to move to another position. So at the end of the 1977 season, he played a handful of games at first base in AAA. Then after struggling again at catcher in the Dominican League over the winter, Murphy was met with a new manager in spring training, and a new position: first base.

"Bobby Cox (the new manager) and Bill and everybody said, 'Well let's try it,'" Murphy says. "I started to show a little bit of power, so they must have thought they needed to get me in the lineup. But again, I just felt like they bent over backwards for me to give me an opportunity to succeed."

Murphy's 1978 rookie season was impressive, even though he only hit .226. He managed 23 home runs and 79 RBI. Defensively, he played 129 games at first base and 21 games at catcher. He was not very comfortable yet at first base. Then in May of 1979 he was catching veteran knuckleballer Phil Niekro, not an easy job for even the best catcher in the league. Murphy tore cartilage in his knee and missed almost two months. When he returned he played solely first base. His catching career was officially over.

The 1979 season was memorable for another reason. Bill Lucas's death from a brain aneurysm hurt Murphy deeply. He was in Pittsburgh when Lucas's secretary called his hotel room with the news.

"It was shocking, devastating," Murphy says. "I spoke at the funeral. It was very emotional. He had such a good sense of humor, and he had a care and concern for you. It was just a close-knit feeling that kept me with the Braves for a long time. I just felt part of that organization and I didn't want to leave when other opportunities throughout my career possibly could have come up. There was a feeling there that I was part of his family. Bill Lucas had a way of creating that feeling of friendship and loyalty. I know he was pulling for me. You want to play well and perform well for somebody that believes in you. That's just who he was. That's what he did and that's the kind of person he was."

Lucas created a sense of pride in Murphy that pushed him to succeed even more, so when his manager called that next winter with another new challenge, he didn't blink.

"Come to spring training as an outfielder," Cox told his young star.

"Ok," Murphy responded humbly.

The Braves acquired Chris Chambliss from the New York Yankees to play first, and Murphy had to learn to play his second new position in three years. Left field was his new home.

"It was the safest place for everybody," Murphy says with a chuckle. "It was kind of a last chance deal. Again, they just hung in there with me. They believed in me."

Murphy looked at home in the outfield. He ran well, so he covered a lot of ground and wasn't afraid to make diving catches. His arm, from all those years of catching, was still good, so runners didn't take chances on him. With his defense in order, his offense went to another level. He hit .281 in 1980 with 33 home runs and 89 RBI.

But it wasn't until two seasons later that Murphy's career took off. Joe Torre had replaced Bobby Cox as Braves' manager. Torre was very similar to Murphy in that he had also started his career as a catcher but was then moved to first. But Torre's interest in Murphy centered on his offense. Torre knew Murphy had tremendous talent, but he also knew Murphy had so much more to give.

"Joe and I really clicked," Murphy says. "He really helped me as far as my hitting."

Torre's first season with Atlanta was magical. The Braves won their first thirteen games of the season, and held off the Dodgers to win the National League West by one game. Murphy was a major reason for the Braves' success. He hit .281 with 36 home runs and tied for the league lead with 109 runs batted in. But with the Braves winning, they became a national story. With the games on a national cable channel, the team was not just a southern team, but also a national team. They even got the nickname of "America's Team," and Murphy, a twenty-six-year old who looked like 'John Boy' from the "Waltons," was the fan favorite.

As a result of all the attention Murphy started doing his share of endorsements. Known for his squeaky clean image, Murphy endorsed Kinnet Milk. He also became spokesman for several charitable causes in the Atlanta area. Murphy became a 'rock star,' unable to go anywhere without being recognized as the Braves' best and favorite player.

"It was overwhelming," Murphy explains. "Just over five years from wondering how you were going to be able to keep playing, to having success like that was overwhelming. It kind of hits you and you don't know what's going on. It was a time you didn't know how to handle or how to react because we hadn't had success like that as a team and I hadn't had success like that as a player. It was all kind of unexpected, but it was a fun, fun time. That's probably what made it more fun. It just all kind of happened. It was overwhelming trying to deal with the notoriety and the popularity. It was a challenge for Nancy (his wife) and I and our young family to try to figure it all out and to try to maintain our privacy without being hermits."

In response to his fantastic season Murphy was named the 1982 National League Most Valuable Player. He also won a Gold Glove for his tremendous season in left field, but Joe Torre still believed Murphy could get better. He wanted Murphy to hit the ball the other way, to right field and believed Murphy would be a better hitter if he didn't pull everything. So after the Cardinals eliminated the Braves in the playoffs, Torre made a suggestion to his willing pupil.

"I want you to come down to the Instructional League," Torre told Murphy.

"What?" Murphy asked in amazement.

"Just for a week," Torre replied. "Just come down for a week. I want to get some thoughts in your head."

Here's a kid who was in the process of winning an MVP award, and his manager wanted to send him to the place he had gone after his first season of pro ball. The Braves' best player would be down in "Instructs" with eighteen-year olds and lower level minor leaguers. But Murphy says the extra sessions were needed. "The way I ended made the MVP voting pretty close," Murphy believes. "You look at my stats and you wonder how an MVP could wind up with those kind of stats. They weren't anywhere near what they're doing now. I struggled a bit late in the season."

So the MVP of the National League went to Florida to get some extra innings in the Instructional League. Torre brought in his brother, Frank, himself a former big league hitter, and the two Torres worked with Murphy on his hitting.

"Look, here's what we want you to think about all winter," Joe Torre told Murphy. "We just want you to kind of end on a better note."

"I went down there and took some BP and things just kind of clicked," Murphy says. "Then I had a better year in 1983."

Murphy followed up his MVP season of 1982 with another one, but the stats were even better. He hit .302 with 36 home runs and 121 RBI and 30 stolen bases. He became the youngest National League player ever to win back-to-back MVP Awards and was just the sixth major leaguer to join the 30 (homers) /30 (stolen bases) club.

The same player who sat in front of his locker six years earlier crying and wondering if he was even going to be a big leaguer, had become the game's best player. Murphy combined with another young slugger, Bob Horner, to form the best young hitting tandem in the National League.

Dale Murphy in stride.

"It was fun," Murphy says. "I felt we were a good combination. Bob was the best hitter I've ever seen. What a great guy. I had some great teammates like Hubby (Glenn Hubbard) and Bruce (Benedict). We also had Chris Chambliss and Claudell (Washington) was there too. We had a good team. It was fun playing. We could score some runs."

In 1984, the Braves brought up a kid to add to that good group of players. Brad Komminsk was Atlanta's number one pick in the 1979 draft (fourth overall). He was a tall, power-hitting outfielder who put up tremendous numbers in the minor leagues. Komminsk won a Triple Crown in 1981 by winning the Carolina League batting title (.322), the home run title (33), and RBI crown (104). After his 1983 season in AAA Richmond, where he hit .334 with 24 home runs and 103 runs batted in, the Braves believed he was ready for a spot next to Murphy in the Atlanta outfield.

Late in the 1983 season, with the Braves battling the Los Angeles Dodgers in the National League West, team owner Ted

Turner made a trade. The Dodgers had just acquired left-handed pitcher Rick Honeycutt from the Texas Rangers. The Braves had also been in the hunt for Honeycutt, but the Dodgers won the auction by putting Dave Stewart and Ricky Wright in the deal. So after losing one pitcher to the Dodgers, Turner felt the Braves had no chance but to acquire a starter.

Atlanta then entered discussions with the Cleveland Indians about right-hander Len Barker, who was best known for his perfect game in 1981. Barker was also known as a strikeout pitcher, leading the American League both in 1980 and 1981. The Braves agreed to give the Indians three players for Barker: outfielder Brett Butler, pitcher Rick Behenna, and minor league third baseman Brook Jacoby.

"It was always our thought that we needed another pitcher," says Pat Nugent, the Braves' Assistant GM at the time. "Barker had thrown that perfect game previously. Our scout, Bill Wight, followed him forever that summer and thought he'd put us over the hump."

"Pat Nugent called me at home that night and told me we had gotten Barker," says Wayne Minshew, Public Relations Director for the Braves from 1978-1987. "He kept on reading off all these names of who we were giving up for him. I remember thinking at the time that it was a little much to give up for Barker."

"The Len Barker deal was pure panic," remembers Gerry Fraley, Braves' beat writer for the *Atlanta Constitution* at the time and now a columnist for the *Dallas Morning News*. "The Braves were in on Honeycutt, but the Dodgers beat them to him. The Rangers wanted Brad Komminsk and Albert Hall. Ted (Turner) got so mad that he ordered GM John Mullen to get another pitcher within seventy-two hours. The result was Barker. Cleveland also wanted Komminsk and Hall, but the Braves convinced them to take Butler, Jacoby, and Behenna."

Barker did not help the Braves for the rest of the 1983 season. He went 1-3 in six starts. Atlanta signed him to a five-year contract before the 1984 season, but Barker only pitched two seasons with the Braves. He battled elbow troubles and was a big disappointment. Barker was 10-20 in 47 games (44 starts) with a 4.64 ERA. After averaging 215 innings in the three full seasons prior to coming to Atlanta, Barker would pitch in only 233 innings for his Braves' career.

To make matters worse, Jacoby and Butler went on to have great careers. Jacoby was a tremendous prospect in his own right. He had hit .299 with 18 home runs and 58 RBI in AAA in 1982 and then had a .315 average with 25 homers and 100 RBI in AAA at the time of his trade in 1983. The Indians made him their starting third baseman in 1984 and he went on to start for them for nine seasons, collecting 1220 hits and 120 home runs.

Atlanta fans were outraged when Butler was included in the deal. He was as much a fan favorite as Murphy was at the time. The speedy outfielder played with Cleveland, San Francisco, Los Angeles, and the New York Mets over the next fourteen seasons. He finished his career with 2375 hits (2137 after his trade from the Braves) and 558 stolen bases (489 after the trade).

The Braves were comfortable in dealing Butler because of Brad Komminsk. They were convinced he was the next Dale Murphy, and even home run champion Hank Aaron, the Braves' Farm Director at the time, had no trouble making the comparison.

"I sure did think he would be another Dale Murphy," admits Paul Snyder. "His minor league numbers were tremendous."

The Braves wanted Komminsk to take over left field in 1984, but he struggled in spring training and got sent back to AAA. Joe Torre was forced to use a platoon of Jerry Royster and Gerald Perry in left. When the Braves called Komminsk up in late May, he had hit .257 in Richmond with 5 home runs. But instead of going to left, Komminsk replaced the injured Claudell Washington in right field.

Komminsk had a miserable rookie season. He hit only .203 with 8 home runs and 36 RBI in 301 at bats. He not only had the pressure of being the player the Braves said was going to replace the very popular Brett Butler, but there was still that label he had to live up to. Dale Murphy had become an icon in Atlanta, and being compared to him was not easy for anyone to match.

"I think that was kind of right at the height of my career," Murphy remembers. "I think it's one thing to say some things about players and compare him to other players, but gosh, while you're sitting there playing with the guy, it's not easy. I just came off two MVP's. It's a hard enough game to play without trying to measure up to other people's expectations and the pressures. It's not that easy to predict things. People just tried to be complimentary but it probably added to the pressure of being out there with me and having these comparisons. I think that happened to Brad a little bit."

The Braves gave Komminsk the left field job in 1985, but his performance didn't improve. He hit only .227 with 4 home runs and 21 RBI. Komminsk played only five games in Atlanta the next season, and the Braves traded him to the Milwaukee Brewers before the 1987 season. He would also see major league time with the Indians, Giants, Orioles, and A's, mostly as a backup outfielder. Komminsk would retire after the 1991 season at the age of 30 with a .218 career average, 23 home runs, and 105 RBI.

Who knows whether the pressure of living up to comparisons to Murphy killed Komminsk's chances of being a solid major leaguer. Some people say that Joe Torre and Bob Watson, a backup first baseman with the Braves when Komminsk was a rookie, pushed Komminsk to change his swing once he arrived in the big leagues. The failure of Komminsk to develop into a solid player really hurt the Braves, especially since Butler turned out to be one of the best leadoff men in the game during the mid-80's.

But perhaps an even bigger setback for the organization, albeit in the short-term, was the firing of Torre following the 1984 season. The Braves had won the division in 1982, and then finished second in both 1983 and 1984. Torre's dismissal touched Murphy directly as a result of the strong bond the two had developed.

"Yea, I never really understood it," Murphy admits. "I wasn't getting involved and asking a lot of questions. It was a weird time for me. Personally I had success with him and as a team we were having success."

Eddie Haas, Murphy's hitting instructor when he was in the minor leagues in the mid-70s', replaced Torre as Atlanta's manager but lasted only two-thirds of the '85 season. Atlanta would go on to average only 65 wins between 1985 and 1990. By the time the 1988 season rolled around, the Braves were in a full rebuilding mode.

"I wish I had gotten a little more involved in the late 80's and just asked what was going on," Murphy says. "But I kind of felt like I was a player and I was not really one to talk too much. I wish I would have."

What Murphy may not have realized was that the Braves were putting together the pieces of the puzzle that started the tremendous run the team is still on today. But as a player in his prime, it was tough to accept the fact that the team was not going to win for a couple of years. At the end of the 1988 season, Murphy was almost a casualty of the rebuilding process. He was going to be thirty-three years old in 1989, and for a team that was adding young players in their early twenties, the guy who had always been the kid was suddenly the elder statesman of the team.

The New York Mets, still in their heyday after winning the 1986 World Series, were interested in acquiring Murphy. With the 1988 Winter Meetings in Atlanta, the Mets made getting Murphy a priority. Bobby Cox, back then as the Braves' GM, placed a high price on his star player. He asked the Mets for young outfielder Lenny Dykstra, third baseman Howard Johnson, and minor league pitching star David West. The Mets balked, wanting to hold on to West, but Cox, always out for pitching, demanded West be included. The talks lasted several months, and Braves fans and Murphy himself had to think about an Atlanta outfield without number 3.

"The rumors were kind of interesting," Murphy says. "They really didn't bother me. It was part of the job. Those two guys and that big left-hander like that would have been a good deal for the Braves."

But the deal with the Mets could never get done. Some criticized Cox for not pulling the trigger on the trade, especially as Dykstra and Johnson became solid players. But as Stan Kasten, the Braves President at the time says, "It was Dale Murphy. The thought of ever trading him was hard to swallow."

"I don't know if I would have been able to handle New York," Murphy says. "It would have been a challenge for me cause I think I benefited in my career by playing in Atlanta in relative obscurity at the time. Guys play in the eras that fit them, and I played when I think it was best for me and Atlanta."

But as the 1980's ended and as Murphy moved into his mid-30's, he started to wonder how long he could last as a Brave. In the middle of the 1990 season, with his contract up at the end of the season, Murphy made the decision that he would not re-sign with the Braves for 1991.

"I told Bobby that I was going to be a free agent and I had decided I was going to move on next winter," Murphy says, "and if there's a trade that you think could work or that you wanted to do and I think I could go to that team and it would be a good team for us then we'd look at it. We felt it was time to move on. We had probably felt like that for a while. I think probably since the trade talks to New York I had been thinking about the possibility that I might not end my career here. They had talked about trading me, so it was something that they had thought about. I just decided it was time to move on."

Cox started talking to teams around baseball, and the Phillies, Padres, and Astros were interested. Since Murphy was not signed past the 1990 season, the Braves were not going to get a lot for him. On August 3, 1990, Murphy was traded to the Phillies along with young pitcher Tommy Greene for reliever Jeff Parrett, infielder Victor Rosario, and outfielder Jim Vatcher.

Murphy knew a trade was inevitable. After all, he had asked for it. But when the word finally came on that Friday night in August, it was a shock. He had been a Brave all his life. It was almost surreal for Braves fans as well, who simply couldn't imagine a Braves team without Murphy.

"I think Nancy and I felt the same way," Murphy says. "It was like, 'Oh no. What in the world is going on?' There were a lot of tears shed, but there was kind of a sense of excitement. Guys kind of need a little jumpstart sometime. I don't know if guys like to admit it. I was kind of in the doldrums and the team was kind of in the doldrums. It got kind of awkward with "Knucksie" (Phil Niekro) at the end of his career. I just thought, 'Well, I'm going to force the issue. I'm going to make the decision and move on.' But it was a shock even when we knew it was coming."

The Braves moved David Justice from first base, where he had been playing for the vertigo-stricken Nick Esasky, to right field, his natural position. In hindsight, the move was almost symbolic. It was the end of one era, the Murphy era, and the beginning of a new era of Braves baseball. Justice went on to hit .301 with 11 home runs and 29 RBI in the last 30 games of the season to capture the National League Rookie of the Year award. He was also one of the most important pieces of the Braves' resurgence in the early 90's, capping it off by hitting the game winning home run in Game Six of the 1995 World Series against the Cleveland Indians.

The reality of the trade still hadn't hit Murphy upon his arrival in Philly- even after he put on the uniform for the first time. Instead, it happened late one night when he flew back to Atlanta on an off day for both the Phillies and the Braves. His car was still at Atlanta-Fulton County Stadium. Before leaving, he decided to walk though the outfield tunnel and look at the field. The stadium was empty, but Murphy's heart was full of emotion. He decided to go a little further, walking onto the field, but seeing it only in the moonlight.

"I had a few tears remembering all the things that happened in that stadium and now being with a different organization," Murphy admits.

Murphy had a decent season in his first full year with the Phillies, hitting .252 with 18 home runs and 81 RBI. But the 1991 season was difficult. He had to watch the Braves win from another dugout. It's somewhat ironic that the first year of the Braves' run was Murphy's first full year away from the team. Murphy played in only three playoff games with the Braves, but the team made it all the way to the World Series in 1991.

"I was really wishing I could be part of it," Murphy says. "I was really thinking, 'Boy that would have been fun.' You're always second-guessing yourself. It was challenging still living in Atlanta and not being part of all that excitement. Talk about excitement. I thought 1982 was exciting, but 1991 was tremendous."

It was even more difficult for Murphy since he was the one that instigated the trade from the Braves. "It probably would have been easier if the scenario had been different, like the Braves just traded me, as opposed to me just making the decision and getting the ball rolling," he says. "But since I felt like I was the guy, that kind of got the whole trade thing going, I did a lot of second-guessing."

In a historical perspective, it's almost as if the Dale Murphy era of the Atlanta Braves had to end in order for the Braves to do what they've been able to accomplish since 1991. He was such a hero for the fans and the city that it's almost inconceivable that he would have to leave before they could win, but the fact is the team did start its incredible run after his trade.

"Maybe I was sensing that," Murphy admits. "Maybe everybody was sensing that. I think that's why I forced the issue. Let's say I stay there, (John) Schuerholz does come in, and he sees that we've got to move Murph. It would have gotten real sticky. I didn't want to go through that. Dave Justice was coming up and (Ron) Gant was out there. Let's say they make that trade for Otis (Nixon, in the spring of the 1991 season) and I'm still there. They wanted to go with the young guys. It sure felt like it was time to leave. I felt I was very loyal to the team, but it was time for me to move on."

Hank Aaron may be the most famous player to ever wear

a Braves' uniform, but he started his career in Milwaukee before playing in Atlanta. But Dale Murphy was Atlanta's first baseball hero. He had come a long way from sitting in front of his locker wondering if he would ever be good at the game. The patience shown by Snyder and Lucas was rewarded with the best player ever developed by the Atlanta Braves. That trait would become the trademark of an organization that would rely more on homegrown players as the years progressed. "Murph" became the perfect prospect, and before there was a Chipper Jones or a battery of great pitchers, Dale Murphy was the Atlanta Braves.

6

SEARCHING FOR A LEFTY

Every team has a position that is hard to fill. The Cubs tried for years to replace Ron Santo at third base. The Reds have tried for years to replace Hall-of-Fame catcher Johnny Bench. The Mariners have been looking for a left fielder since their inception. The Atlanta Braves are no exception; they, too, historically, had a bug-a-boo position:

Left-handed starting pitchers.

It's ironic that the franchise that had the most successful southpaw in the history of the game had trouble finding productive lefties. Warren Spahn won 363 big league games, more than any other left-hander. 356 of those wins came in a Boston Braves or Milwaukee Braves uniform. Even when Spahn was with the Braves, pitching was rarely the strength of the team. "Spahn and (Johnny) Sain and Pray for Rain" is a slogan dating back to the 1940's. Boston's pitching in the late 40's wasn't as bad as Atlanta's pitching in the late 70's, but it did represent the lack of superior pitching depth compared to other teams.

It would be unfair to say the Braves were looking for another Warren Spahn, for that was never the goal and certainly would have been unrealistic. The team was simply looking for a consistent left-handed starting pitcher. In the first sixteen years the Braves were in Atlanta, only seventeen different left-handers started games. Seven of those seventeen pitchers started less than ten games in their Atlanta career (three of those seven started only once). There was even one season, 1974, when the Braves had no left-hander start a single game. In the 1,609 games started by Braves' pitchers in the 1970's, left-handed pitchers started only 14% of them.

Don't believe that the team wasn't trying to grow left-handed pitchers. The same year the Braves didn't have a game started by a lefty they took fifteen left-handers in the draft. Only one, Larry McWilliams, would pitch in a Braves uniform. In 1983, the Braves signed eighteen lefties. Only one, Paul Assenmacher, made it to the big leagues, and he was signed at a tryout camp.

"I wish I could tell you why we haven't had more success from our left-handers," Paul Snyder told the *Atlanta Constitution* back in 1984, "but I can't. We have made an effort."

George Stone is considered the first homegrown Atlanta left-handed starter. Stone came up late in the 1967 season and would go 43-44 in 101 starts through the 1972 season. He was traded in 1972, along with infielder Felix Millan, to the Mets for Gary Gentry and Danny Frisella, two right-handed pitchers. There were phenoms, like Jimmy Freeman and Mike McQueen, but they were flops. Jamie Easterly was another possibility. He debuted in 1974, but would only become an average reliever after starting only twenty-eight games over a six-year period. For whatever reason, the team didn't acquire many lefthanders in trades.

McWilliams debuted in 1978 and was magical. He won his first seven decisions and finished 9-3 in fifteen starts, but McWilliams will always be remembered as helping reliever Gene Garber stop Pete Rose's forty-four-game hitting streak in Atlanta on August 1, 1978. Rose was trying to pass Wee Willie Keeler for the National League record of hitting in consecutive games, and he was only twelve away from Joe DiMaggio's fifty-six-game record. McWilliams walked Rose on his first at bat and then got him to ground out in the fifth inning before turning the game over to Garber. The event would be the highlight of the 1978 season for the Braves, who were suffering through another disappointing season.

McWilliams was the Braves' first round draft choice back in 1974 out of Paris Junior College in Paris, Texas. He was a slinger; pure and simply he slung the ball from the left side of the pitching rubber. It would prove costly though, as he would battle elbow problems for most of his five seasons in Atlanta. McWilliams would finish with a 25-23 overall record in 65 starts before being traded to Pittsburgh for Pascual Perez and Carlos Rios in June of 1982. He would go on to win 53 more games in his career, finishing out with the Royals in 1990.

At the same time the Braves were trading McWilliams, their latest left-handed hopeful was debuting in the major leagues. Ken Dayley was a six-footer out of Oregon. He attended the University of Portland when the Braves drafted him in the first round of the 1980 draft (third overall pick). "He was the best free agent pitcher I ever scouted," Snyder says. "Some guys threw harder, but I thought he was the most complete pitcher I've ever scouted. He had four quality pitches. His mechanics were very good."

"I struck out quite a few," Ken Dayley recalls of his college seasons. "I think my freshman year I ended up fifth in the nation in strikeouts, and then my junior year I led the nation. I want to say it was something like 14.6 strikeouts per nine innings."

The Braves signed Dayley and immediately sent him to AA Savannah in 1980.

His minor league numbers were dazzling: 29-14 with a 3.08 ERA. His numbers once again gave the Braves hope that they had found their elusive left-handed starting pitcher.

Dayley was aware of the Braves' huge need for a lefty. "I knew they were always searching and looking," Dayley says. "I just knew that the road in front of me looked like it was wide open. It was a matter of me getting things done on my level too."

Dayley was the highest rated Braves' pitching prospect in many years. He didn't throw very hard, which bothered Atlanta's pitching coach at the time, Hall-of-Fame flamethrower Bob Gibson. Dayley soon became the centerpiece of a philosophical difference in the Atlanta organization, one that would limit Dayley and perhaps keep the Braves from getting over the hump in the early 80's.

When Bob Gibson was a pitcher for the Cardinals in the 1960's, he was one of the hardest throwing pitchers in the game. He was famous for pitching inside with a devastating fastball that paralyzed batters. "That's the way he pitched and that's the way he wanted everybody to pitch," Dayley explains. "He was about being a power pitcher with a good slider and very few people have that combination. We had guys like Rick Mahler and Larry McWilliams, some of these guys who were more of the Johnny Sain type pitcher. They used their off-speed stuff to set up their fastball, and Gibby's philosophy was the fastball to set up all your off-speed stuff."

Sain, part of the Braves' lethal pitching combo with Warren Spahn in the 40's, was the pitching coach at AAA Richmond in the early 80's. He believed in his pitchers throwing between starts and changing speeds on the mound – hitting the corners with off speed pitches and the fastball. "Johnny was from the mold that the tougher the situation the slower you throw it," says Craig McMurtry, Dayley's teammate in the minors before joining him in Atlanta in 1983. "He said when he got into a bind he just kept throwing it slower and slower and slower because the hitters just kept getting more anxious. Bob Gibson was of the mindset that you just rare back and throw it as hard as you can."

There was little doubt in the minds of most baseball observers that the twenty-three-year-old Dayley would succeed when he debuted on May 13, 1982. But from the time he left Richmond and got to Atlanta "there were some problems there with trying to understand how (Manager) Joe (Torre) and them wanted me to pitch versus how I was used to pitching," Dayley explains. He was feeling even more pressure since the Braves had turned it around that spring and were competing for a division title, and now he had to change something as fundamental as his pitching style..

"(Atlanta starter) Rick Mahler was keeping the pitching charts and he came down about the third or fourth inning of one of my starts and asked me why I was throwing so many fastballs," Dayley remembers. "Gibby (Gibson) had said we were going to go with whatever (catcher Bruce) Benedict called, and they were basically calling all of the pitches. I think I threw – I think fifty fastballs and three off-speed pitches. They were trying to prove that they wanted me to use my fastball, move it around, make it effective, and then use off-speed pitches here and there. But they were going to the extreme. Using your fastball, moving it around, works well for a couple or three innings in the big leagues, when you do have a good fastball. After the second time through the lineup major league hitters are going to figure it out."

And in 1982, major league hitters were figuring it out, at least more than the minor leaguers had. He would pitch in twenty games in 1982, starting eleven and going 5-6 with an ERA of 4.54. Torre and Gibson shuffled him to the bullpen late in the year, and he would finish the season effectively as a reliever allowing just one run in five appearances covering six innings.

1983 was a weird season for Dayley. He started the year in AAA Richmond, and again gave the Braves reason for hope with five straight victories to start the year. He was promoted to Atlanta in May, and would have a superb start against Cincinnati, striking out nine players on June 24th. Dayley was back and forth between the rotation and the bullpen for the rest of the 1983 season as Torre would also use Rick Camp and free agent signee Pete Falcone, a lefty, as the bottom-of-the-rotation starters. Dayley would finish with a 5-8 record and an ERA of 4.30 in 24 games (16 starts).

Dayley was still struggling trying to pitch the way Torre and Gibson wanted him to throw, but he still believed he'd turn things around. "I thought I was going to make the adjustment," Dayley says. "Everybody that I had competed against or pitched with when I was coming up through the system was in the big leagues and they were being successful. That was frustrating for me. Why wasn't I being successful? What was going on? Why was I not getting people out the same way I had before? That was the most frustrating part of it. And being young you start carrying that pressure around on your shoulders, and it kind of snowballs, and before you know it you're worrying about the wrong things instead of pitching and getting people out one at a time."

But the Braves still had confidence in Dayley and they knew he needed to get into the rotation full-time. For that to take place, however, important decisions had to be made. The first, and most important, was about veteran right-hander Phil Niekro. The forty-four-year-old was at the end of his contract, and the Braves had to make a decision about his future. Niekro went 11-10 in 1983 with an ERA of 3.97. For a forty-four year old, it wasn't bad. But it clearly was not an easy season for the Braves veteran. Niekro started 33 games, but had become a six-inning pitcher. With Dayley on board and the twenty-three-year old McMurtry establishing himself as a solid pitcher, youth was being served on the pitching staff. Unfortunately, Niekro was not in the Braves' plans for 1984.

Pat Nugent was the Braves Assistant Vice President for Baseball at the time. "It wasn't that we didn't believe Phil couldn't get hitters out, but there was a great concern that he couldn't protect himself on the mound," Nugent remembers. "The belief was that his legs were gone and that teams might bunt him to death."

The Braves were a bit coy about Niekro's future. They really wanted him to retire, so they could retire his number 35 jersey and name him as a minor league manager. But Niekro still wanted to pitch, despite being forty-five years old on Opening Day of 1984. The Braves' brass had a meeting in late September and decided Niekro would not return in 1984, but he wasn't told until October 7th.

That period of time in between was almost surreal. It was as if the Braves were afraid, or possibly ashamed, to tell Niekro he was gone. Team owner Ted Turner told Joe Torre that he would tell Niekro, so Torre avoided Niekro for several weeks. But then Turner went out of town, causing a delay in the official announcement.

Niekro clearly saw the writing on the wall. He told the media he expected to be released, but was adamant about his desire to continue pitching. Phil's brother, Houston Astros starting pitcher Joe Niekro, blasted Torre in the Atlanta papers. Joe Niekro believed his brother was being used as a "scapegoat" for the Braves' disappointing finish to the 1983 season, and that Torre was threatened by Phil's presence on the club.

Niekro had applied for the Braves' manager's job when Torre was hired in October of 1981. There was always talk that Niekro would one day be Braves Manager. Maybe that did bother Torre, but the real problem might have been with Torre's pitching coach, Bob Gibson.

Gibson was critical of Niekro throughout the 1983 season. The two pitching legends were exact opposites. Gibson was the hard throwing headhunter when he was a pitcher, while Niekro was a soft-tossing knuckleballer who rarely threw above 85 miles an hour. Niekro claimed after he was released "a coach on the staff (all signs pointed to Gibson) believed I should have retired in June."

"Gibson just liked power pitchers," recalls former Braves Public Relations Director Wayne Minshew. "I know that there was inner turmoil all the way around because no one wanted to lose him (Niekro). But Joe (Torre) didn't mind letting him go."

But Dayley was clearly the main reason the Braves wanted to release Niekro. Also, several members of the Braves' staff, especially Gibson, wanted to move Steve Bedrosian from the bullpen to the starting rotation. "Bedrock" had been a starter for his entire minor league career, but mostly a reliever with Atlanta in 1982 and 1983. Bedrosian had great stuff, including a mid-90's fastball that Gibson and others believed would fit great in a starting rotation.

"Bedrosian and Dayley had to have a chance," Nugent says. "Ken was a tremendous competitor, and we didn't need Phil there to shake his confidence. It was always debated about Bedrosian being a starter or reliever. He had all the pitches to do either. Anyone with that talent, you're constantly talking about which way to use him."

So on Friday, October 7th, Phil Niekro cleaned out his locker at Atlanta Fulton County Stadium. The scene was unimaginable for longtime Braves fans who had grown up watching Niekro pitch in an Atlanta uniform. He had been a Brave even before the team arrived in Atlanta, and was synonymous with the team.

"He was Mr. Brave," Nugent says.

The debate about Niekro's release did not only center on the Braves' decision, but on the way it was handled by the organization. General Manager John Mullen defended the tactics, saying Turner was the one who wanted to tell Niekro, causing the delay. Niekro's teammates were shocked. Several showed up the day he cleaned out his locker to wish him well. Some of the players were visibly upset. "I think a lot of people will really examine how this was handled," Braves pitcher Rick Camp said at the time. "I can't imagine him not being around here."

Niekro had no trouble finding teams with interest in him. The Cardinals, White Sox, Athletics, and Yankees expressed the most interest. For almost two months, the Cardinals were considered the favorite. St. Louis manager Whitey Herzog expressed a sincere interest in Niekro, but the two sides could never strike a deal. Niekro signed a two-year contract with the New York Yankees on January 6, 1984.

The Braves immediately declared Ken Dayley a new full- time member of the starting rotation. There was tremendous pressure on him, since he was thought of as "the" replacement for Phil Niekro. The new Yankee would even call Dayley in spring training of 1984 to encourage him to do well in his new role. Dayley admits there was some pressure taking Niekro's place in the rotation.

"That was in the back of your head," he admits. "But I don't think I looked at it that way. I looked at it as they told me I was going to get thirty or thirty-one starts; I was going to get the ball every five days."

Atlanta had a lot of promise in 1984. Third baseman Bob Horner was back after missing the last quarter of the 1983 season.

Len Barker, acquired late in 1983 in the ill-fated trade for Brett Butler, would be with the team in the starting rotation for the entire season. Plus, '84 was the year Ken Dayley was to step up and fulfill his promise.

But it didn't happen. Dayley's first four starts were horrible. He went 0-3 with an ERA of 5.32. Dayley was still trying to please Gibson, but the styles just didn't match. "You want to do things the right way, and you really aren't sure what the right way is at the time," Dayley explains. "You'd have some players come and tell you that you need to tell them to put a sock in it and do it your own way, and then you have other people tell you to bare with them and it'll smooth out this and that. From a player's standpoint you get one side, and from a management standpoint you want to please them because they're the ones who decide what's going on. But I think there was some lack of understanding, or it just wasn't working and why I didn't know."

The Braves felt they had no chance but to send him back to AAA Richmond. Once again Dayley was successful in Richmond, going 5-1 in 9 starts. "When I went down to Richmond that year the first game I pitched I had a no-hitter going into the ninth with two outs and Rafael Santana from the Mets had a little infield base hit and I ended up getting a one hitter. But it made me just sit back and say 'why is it working there and not here?' You do wonder why you're successful here but not there, especially successful at the top of the league. Not just getting by and being ok, but being the best and not being able to make the next step. That was a very frustrating part."

Meanwhile in Atlanta, power-hitter Bob Horner was hurt again. He broke his wrist in May and would miss the rest of the season. General Manager John Mullen scanned the league for an experienced replacement. He spoke with the Twins about Roy Smalley, but settled on St. Louis third baseman Ken Oberkfell, a left-handed hitter who was a valuable member of the Cardinals' 1982 World Championship team. But again, he was a different player from Horner. Oberkfell provided solid defense, but was more of a #2 hitter in the lineup.

To get Oberkfell, the Braves had to do something that they were loath to do: they gave up Dayley and first baseman Mike Jorgenson to the Cardinals. It was clearly throwing in the towel on Dayley, succumbing to the doubts that Dayley would ever adjust to

Gibson's style. Dayley was shocked at the trade at first but "what I thought was going to be the worst thing that could happen turned out to be a blessing in disguise." He would go on to have some solid seasons in St. Louis, relying on an upper-80's fastball and a curve and becoming a quality left-handed reliever for the Cardinals (39 saves in 6½ seasons). Dayley would battle vertigo problems after he signed a three-year contract with Toronto before the 1991 season and retired after the 1993 campaign.

"He was never really the guy I thought he should have been," says a still disappointed Snyder. "I thought he was going to be our number one starter for ten or twelve years. He should've lasted a long time with us. His psyche was beat down."

McMurtry agrees the philosophical challenges bothered Dayley. "I know he was a very demanding player on himself and wanted to really do well," McMurtry remembers. "Sometimes I thought he tried too hard. Ken was a good guy. When he left there and went to St. Louis, shoot, he stood up and had some really good years. Maybe that was the pressure thing where he felt like a new start and a new chance to go in and be one of the pitchers, instead of the one counted on for big things."

Dayley, who admits he got along with Torre and Gibson despite the philosophical differences, believes his time in Atlanta was simply part of the learning experience of baseball. "I didn't succeed to near the level I was wanting to," he says. "They saw in me something that they thought could win a World Series for them. 'You are the guy that can help get us there.' You want to be that guy. As a competitor, there's nothing more I want than to have the ball. You want to do well for them. Obviously, before my time came, I didn't have that opportunity."

As the Dayley era ended quickly in Atlanta, Phil Niekro rejuvenated his career. Niekro would win 50 games after leaving the Braves, finishing with 318 for his career. Atlanta's faith in Dayley and its never-ending quest for a left-handed starting pitcher would cost the team those wins. Niekro was inducted into the Baseball Hall of Fame in 1997, after coming back in 1987 to finish his career in a Braves' uniform.

The philosophical difference that caused trouble with Dayley and Niekro was solved after the 1984 season when Torre and Gibson were both fired. Johnny Sain replaced Gibson as Atlanta's pitching coach.

With Dayley gone, the Braves again looked to their minor league system for another left-handed pitcher. The same week the Braves traded Dayley, they promoted left-handed starting pitcher named Zane Smith to AAA Richmond. It was a quick minor league trip for the six-foot-two southpaw, who was drafted in the third round of the 1982 draft out of Indiana State University. The school where Larry Bird became famous for basketball became a baseball school after he left, and Smith was 9-3 in his junior season, attracting interest from major league scouts.

Braves Scout Stu Cann saw Smith pitch several times during the 1982 season, and after Paul Snyder put out an SOS for his scouts to find left handed pitchers, Cann called in with a good report. "If they can walk or stumble, if they're ready to go out and play, let's go get them," Snyder told his scouts. Cann had found one whose left-handed arm "worked so easy. He had a big league arm, even maybe a first round arm."

But Smith's stock suddenly fell when rumors surfaced questioning his competitiveness. "At a game I was not at," Cann explains, "and I'm glad I didn't see it, Zane supposedly looked at the dugout and wanted out of a tough situation. That's one of those things that won't show up in the statistics. But I didn't see it, and I didn't interview him before we drafted him." In the early 80's, third round picks were not investigated like they are in today's market. Kids who are drafted in the third round now sometimes get half a million dollars, so teams are usually careful in determining the makeup of such a costly draft pick.

"I saw Zane, and then Paul saw him, and then Paul sent in a couple of his trusted sergeants to go and see him," Cann says. "They all liked the way he delivered the ball."

Atlanta would draft right-handers Duane Ward and Joe Johnson in the first two rounds, and then spend their third round pick on Smith. But then the team discovered some of the worries the other scouts had about his makeup.

Cann met with Smith and his family in a hotel room for five hours to iron out a contract. "Zane came up with a comment as to where he would be playing after we signed him. I said, 'Well, it seems that Paul wants to send you to Durham, which is pretty good baseball right off the bat in High-A ball.' And he wanted to know whom he'd be replacing. Now, I spent seven years in the minor leagues and saw guys come and go all the time. I said, 'I don't know. They might put a guy out of the rotation and put him in the bullpen. They might ship him down south. They might send him home.' Then Zane said, 'Will the guy beat me up?'"

Cann got up from the Smith family and went into the hallway with Bill Wight, one of the senior members of the scouting staff there to help with negotiations. Even though the deal with Smith was done, the pitcher was unnerving Cann with his comments. "Billy, I don't know if I want this guy anymore," Cann told Wight, who was equally concerned. "We've got to sign him," Wight said. "We haven't signed our top two guys (Ward and Johnson) and the negotiations aren't going well with those two. We've got to take him and go with it."

Smith had not even played high school baseball. Growing up in North Platte, Nebraska, he instead played for a legion baseball team. You weren't on a high school baseball team unless you were in a big city in Nebraska, and at the time North Platte had a population of only 28,000. He had a chance to play football and baseball at the University of Nebraska, but Bill Hayes, another kid from North Platte who became a first round pick of the Cubs in 1979, convinced Smith to attend his alma mater Indiana State.

But Smith admits he really didn't learn much about pitching in college. "Granted they taught me how to throw a slider, but that might not be the best pitch to learn," Smith says. "I was a thrower. I wasn't a pitcher back then. A good fastball does wonders and I had movement on my pitches which was a bigger plus."

Instead of Durham, the Braves sent him to Anderson in the South Atlantic League in the summer of 1982. He would struggle there (5-3, 6.86 ERA) and at Durham the next season (9-15, 4.90 ERA) under the watchful eye of Leo Mazzone. But then, in 1984, things turned around for Smith. He won his first seven decisions with AA Greenville. The Braves could see he was maturing, on and off the field.

"He just started getting a little confidence in himself," explains Bruce Dal Canton, the pitching coach with the 1984 Greenville team. "We didn't want to put him over his head. He was very low key and very easy going. He got better and better with each start and his confidence got higher and higher. He started attacking the hitters more. You could see the confidence."

Smith agrees. "As a young pitcher, facing better hitters, that does more for your confidence than anything else, when you know you can get them out."

His great start in 1984 might have given the Braves even more reason to trade Dayley to the Cardinals. Smith knew the Braves were an organization needing a lefty, and the Dayley trade gave him his chance.

"Obviously, when Dayley got traded I knew there was a great opportunity for me," Smith says. "But I really didn't feel any pressure. I knew they didn't have many lefties in the organization, but it's not like I had the coaches say, 'Ok, you're it.' I was more of a thrower when I came up. I still wasn't a pitcher yet. But when I had my good stuff, yea, I don't think I had too many problems."

Smith split the 1985 season between the Atlanta rotation and bullpen, finishing the year with 9 terrific starts (4-1, 1.32 ERA). New Atlanta manager Chuck Tanner would name Smith a permanent member of his starting rotation in 1986, and his record would reflect the poor record of the team. Smith went 8-16 on a team that won only 72 games, but with a respectable 4.05 ERA. Then in 1987 he would go 15-10 on a team that won only 69 games. He was clearly learning how to pitch. Ted Simmons, a former All Star catcher with the Cardinals and Brewers who was mainly a bench player with the Braves, helped Smith tremendously. "It took Ted to teach me how to pitch," Smith confides. "He became my personal catcher. Ted just got tired of watching me throw, so he went out there to teach me how to pitch."

Dal Canton, who by 1987 was Smith's pitching coach in Atlanta, said the Braves purposefully put Simmons with Smith.

"We felt we had to have a veteran guy catch him," Canton says. "Whenever Ted put down a sign, Zane had confidence that was the right thing to do. Zane developed a better changeup because Ted wanted him to throw it. At that time we were losing a lot of games and it was hard on everybody. I would tell him 'you just got to go out there and do as much as you possibly can.'"

But it was difficult with a porous defense that led the National League in errors. Plus, Smith was a sinkerball pitcher, who gave up a lot of ground balls and relied on his defense.

"Those guys were doing the best they could," Smith says. "When I had my good stuff, I'd do well. When you're on a losing team, it's every man for himself. I wasn't a big strikeout pitcher, but I learned early on that the fewer pitches I threw, the better."

1988 was a tough season for every Braves player as the team

went 54-106 and Smith won only five games. He battled injury problems and would finally have surgery on bone chips in his elbow in September. He also battled trade rumors. As one of two Atlanta players with significant value (Dale Murphy being the other), Smith was also wanted in trade talks. The Indians offered Brett Butler back to the Braves for Smith, but General Manager Bobby Cox said no. The Yankees floated around names like Al Leiter, then a young pitcher in New York's farm system, and Jay Buhner, who would later go on to be a star for Seattle. Cox resisted trading Smith, mainly since he was the only dependable starter. The other Braves' pitchers were either not very good or too young to make a difference. In the summer of 1989 with Smith struggling at 1-12, Cox finally traded his "veteran" lefty to the Montreal Expos for pitchers Nate Minchey and Sergio Valdes and outfielder Kevin Dean. Smith says the trade rumors were not distracting. "When I finally did get traded, I didn't think I was going to be traded. I wasn't doing very well, but I wasn't getting that much help either."

Smith would leave the Braves as the most successful left-hander in two decades. His record: 39 wins and 58 losses. But it should be noted that he pitched for Atlanta between 1985-1989, five of the most horrible seasons in franchise history (324-480).

"Atlanta was a good place to play," Smith says. "I feel I was better than a below .500 pitcher."

Dal Canton agrees. "He was a tough competitor once he got in the ballgames," Dal Canton says. "I think the defense and the field (conditions at Atlanta Fulton County Stadium) did affect everybody. I would tell him that he couldn't field for them and couldn't hit for them. All he could do was his job, and I think he did a great job for us."

Zane Smith would go on to have several successful seasons with Pittsburgh, then one year in Boston, before returning back to the Pirates to end his career in 1996. He would finish with a career record of 100-115 in 288 games started with an ERA of 3.74. The numbers were pretty decent considering the lean years in Atlanta. Smith just missed being apart of winning seasons in Atlanta. "Sure I would've loved to have been apart of it," Smith says. "I think I could have helped them, but I can't complain. It was weird to play against them." Smith would pitch against the Braves twice in the 1991 National League Championship Series. He was 1-1 with an ERA of 0.62 (1 ER in 14.2 innings pitched).

George Stone, Larry McWilliams, Ken Dayley, and Zane

Smith were all counted on to be the Braves' left-handed ace. All four were college pitchers. It would take a high school hockey star from Billerica, Massachusetts to finally become the pitcher the Braves were looking for.

His name was Tom Glavine.

7
BOBBY COMES HOME

It's funny how one baseball season can dramatically change the history of a franchise. 1985 was clearly a pivotal year for the Atlanta Braves.

Ted Turner fired Manager Joe Torre in October of 1984 despite the team winning a division title in 1982 and finishing second the next two seasons. The differences in pitching philosophy between Bob Gibson and Johnny Sain became counterproductive, and Torre refused to fire his former Cardinal teammate.

"That was a rough one," Dale Murphy says of the Torre firing. "It kind of started things going in the wrong direction."

Turner was also convinced Torre could not coach the young Braves players like Brad Komminsk, Gerald Perry, and young veterans like Murphy and Bob Horner. So he brought in the man who coached many of them in the minor leagues

Eddie Haas was an organization patriot. He played in the big leagues with the Chicago Cubs and the Milwaukee Braves and had coached or managed in the Braves' system since 1965, the year before the Braves moved to Atlanta from Milwaukee. Haas was a quiet man, a teacher who had the reputation of helping young players reach their potential.

The Braves were labeled favorites by many in 1985, mainly due to the addition of free agent reliever Bruce Sutter, who was the premiere name on the market over the offseason. But Sutter battled injuries and saved only 23 games, and three pitchers who were expected to be the centerpiece of the Atlanta rotation (Pascual Perez, Craig McMurtry, and Len Barker) combined for a 3-25 record.

Haas never gained the respect of the veteran players. His quiet demeanor was a stark contrast from the vocal and public Torre, and he never seemed to communicate well with the players or the media. "This is a dead ball club," outfielder Claudell Washington said at the time. "This is not a AAA ball club. You can't manage it like one."

So after the team had lost six in a row and twelve out of its last thirteen games, Turner fired Haas with the Braves at 50-71 on the season, 22 games out of first place. Bobby Wine was the Interim Manager for the rest of the 1985 season, but it was obvious that Turner had to bring in someone to fix the club and its subsequent dismal ratings on TBS.

Turner's first choice was Toronto Manager Bobby Cox, whom he had fired as Braves Manager after the '81 season. But Cox was tied up managing the Blue Jays in the 1985 American League playoffs against the Kansas City Royals (General Managed by John Schuerholz), so Turner was going to have to wait until the Blue Jays were finished with their postseason.

Afraid that he might not be able to get a qualified candidate, Turner turned to Chuck Tanner, who had just been fired by the Pittsburgh Pirates as their manager. Tanner himself was a former Brave, having played in Milwaukee in 1955 and even played with the Atlanta Crackers minor league team in 1954. He was also a very respected manager with a 1979 World Series victory under his belt.

Tanner was hired on October 10, 1985. The Blue Jays were eliminated from the playoffs on October 16th. The next day, Turner called to ask for permission to speak with Cox to become his General Manager, and five days later Bobby Cox came home.

Atlanta became home for Robert Joe Cox in 1978, when Bill Lucas hired him to be the Braves Manager. That itself was a homecoming as Cox played for the Richmond Braves in 1967 after being acquired in a trade from the Dodgers the previous year.

Cox never played in Atlanta, as the Braves traded him to the New York Yankees after that 1967 season. The next spring Cox beat out Mike Ferraro for the Yankees' third base job and was on the Topps' All-Rookie team. But then the next season his roommate, Bobby Murcer, supplanted Cox as Yankees third baseman. He spent one more full season in the minor leagues before knee troubles forced him to retire at the age of thirty.

After Cox's playing career ended, Yankees General Manager Lee MacPhail asked him if he was interested in becoming a manager. Not knowing what else he would do, Cox accepted the skipper's job in Fort Lauderdale. He would then go on to coach six years in the Yankees system, winning the Eastern League title with West Haven in 1972 and the International League's Governor's Cup in 1976.

Pat Nugent was the Yankees Farm Director and Cox's boss for two years in the mid-70's. "I just thought he was going to be the next Yankees Manager," Nugent recalls. "There was just no doubt he was going to do that. When you're a Farm Director you deal with problems a lot. There were just never any problems with Bobby's teams. They were well coached and very professional. He knew what his job was and he just did it."

Cox spent the 1977 season as New York's first base coach, and then after the season, Braves GM Bill Lucas hired the thirty-six-year old Cox as Atlanta's new Manager.

"We wanted a young man, one who was not recycled," Lucas said in 1978. "We wanted someone who was a good teacher and worked well with young players, who had a winning record and could lead the Braves to play a different brand of ball. Observing Bobby over a period of years – first when he was a player and then when he was a minor league manager – I got to learn that he's aggressive and wants an aggressive team. That's what Ted and I want. That's what Bobby wants. That's why he's here."

Dale Murphy learned quickly about what kind of manager he'd be playing for with an incident during spring training in 1978. The Braves were in Fort Lauderdale playing the Yankees in a Grapefruit League game when Atlanta pitcher Mickey Mahler threw a pitch up and in on star player Reggie Jackson. Mahler was just going by the scouting report, but it got a little too close for Reggie's liking.

"The next pitch Reggie hits a little ground ball to me at first base and I flip it to Mickey covering," Murphy remembers. "Reggie runs by and tries to wing him with his elbow."

Cox then came up to Murphy and Mahler in the dugout to find out what happened. After the explanation, Cox replied, "That's it. We're hitting him next time up." Murphy was surprised.

"What? It's Reggie Jackson."

Several innings later Mickey's brother, Rick Mahler, came in to pitch for the Braves. "We looked at him and said, 'You've got to hit Reggie Jackson,'" Murphy says. Rick Mahler did what needed to be done. The first pitch was behind him and the second pitch hit Jackson square on the butt.

"Reggie didn't do a thing," Murphy says. "He was mad but I guess he knew Bobby was the manager. The main thing I got from that was that Bobby was not going to put up with anything."

Rookie Manager Cox

But Cox had a lot of losing to put up with in his early days as Atlanta's manager. The Braves went 69-93 in 1978 and 66-94 in 1979. Then in 1980, the Braves finished over .500 (albeit it one game) for only the fifth time in the team's fifteen years in Atlanta with an 81-80 mark. Murphy and Bob Horner were maturing into solid young stars, and players like second baseman Glenn Hubbard, shortstop Rafael Ramirez, and catcher Bruce Benedict were developing into solid regulars. The pitching staff was also developing with young arms like Tommy Boggs, Larry McWilliams, and Rick Matula joining Phil Niekro in the rotation.

"We started showing signs of improving and not losing a hundred games every year," Murphy says. "Bobby made the trade (with the Yankees) to get (Chris) Chambliss. That was huge. Then they signed Claudell (Washington)."

The 1981 season was troublesome for all of baseball. A fifty-day player's strike paralyzed the game and broke the season into two halves. The Braves finished 25-29 in the first half and 25-27 in the second half. They made progress, with players like Brett Butler making his big league debut, but the 50-56 overall record was a disappointment.

After the season, some of Ted Turner's executives convinced him to fire Cox. The ratings on WTBS were down and they believed a bigger name needed to come in to lead the team. The baseball folks, like Paul Snyder, wanted Ted to hire Eddie Haas. But he instead went with Torre, who had played for the Braves in the late 60's and had managed in the large New York television market with the Mets from 1977-1981.

For Bobby Cox, there was sincere disappointment in not being allowed to finish the job he started. The Braves were on the cusp of becoming winners, yet he was pushed out before his plans came to fruition. Cox made the Braves respectable, but his bosses didn't feel he could get the team to the next level. Turner was almost apologetic when he fired Cox, saying in the press conference announcing his firing, "If I hadn't just fired Bobby, he'd be one of the leading candidates."

So Cox had to look for another job. He didn't really want to since he had met Pam Boswell and the two had been married in 1978. Atlanta had become their home. But now he'd have to go manage somewhere else.

"We thought we were doing a pretty good job actually," Cox recalls. "I thought I'd be in baseball. I didn't think I'd be out of it. You never know, but I felt good about it."

The Toronto Blue Jays were very similar to the Atlanta Braves in the early 80's. They had a lot of young talent with players like Willie Upshaw, Alfredo Griffin, Damaso Garcia, Lloyd Moseby, Jesse Barfield, and Dave Stieb blossoming into young stars. The Blue Jays needed someone to get them to the next level. Pat Gillick was the GM of the Blue Jays and wanted Cox as his manager.

"When Coxie got fired down there, we thought, even though our record (37-69 in 1981) didn't show it, that we were headed in the right direction," Gillick says. We thought we needed someone with a background in player development, a background in managing, and someone that we knew could carry on the game plan. At that point Bobby was our only candidate."

Gillick met Cox in the winter of 1972 when he was the Director of Scouting for the Houston Astros and Cox was managing a club in the Venezuelan League. But then two years later Gillick moved on to the Yankees as their Coordinator of Player Development and Scouting and watched Cox manage in the Yankees system. Gillick knew Cox was the man he needed for the job in Toronto.

"He had managed AAA, managed winter ball, coached for the Yankees, and managed the Braves," Gillick explains. "He was originally in the Dodgers chain, which was committed to player development and scouting. He had played with (Ralph) Houk over there with the Yankees. Consequently, he had the kind of background we were looking for and we knew the guy. We thought he was exactly the type of person that we needed."

The Gillick-Cox team worked perfectly. The Blue Jays went from thirty-two games under .500 in 1981 to a 78-84 record in Cox's first season in 1982. After two straight 89-73 seasons in 1983 and 1984, the Blue Jays won the American League East in 1985 with a 99-62 record. The players Cox inherited in 1982 developed into championship caliber ballplayers, and in the ninth season of the franchise, Toronto was a premiere team in the American League.

It shouldn't really be a surprise that the duo of Pat Gillick and Bobby Cox would work so well together. In a way it was a precursor to the type of relationship Cox would have later in Atlanta with John Schuerholz. But the ability of Cox to watch Gillick mold the team would become a huge influence when he returned to Atlanta as GM in 1985.

Gillick pitched in the Baltimore Orioles' farm system from 1959 to 1963 and along the way learned a few things from people like Paul Richards, Eddie Robinson, and Harry Dalton. "Throughout the organization there was a structure and there was consistency in the way that they treated people and the way they went about doing their job," Gillick recalls. "So consequently, wherever you played at in that organization, you could expect the same situation at every level."

After Gillick retired at the age of twenty-six in 1963, Eddie Robinson, his Field Director with the Orioles, asked him to join him and Richards in Houston. Richards had left the Orioles in 1961 to become the first General Manager of the Houston Colt 45's (later renamed the Astros when they moved into the Astrodome in 1965). Robinson joined Richards as his assistant and then became Farm Director in 1963 when he asked Gillick to come aboard as a member of the front office.

"Eddie and Paul taught me a lot about player development and a lot about scouting," Gillick says. "They taught me more on the field stuff, like what you should look for and what you should expect on the field. Even though Harry (Dalton) was still in Baltimore, I talked with him a lot and with Hank Peters, who at the time was in Kansas City with the A's, about the administrative end. Eddie was an excellent hitting instructor and was a good judge of talent, and Paul was a guy who had one of the richest minds in player development and scouting."

"Paul was a guy who was a deep thinker. He could look at a player, especially a pitcher, and say, 'this is what we have to do to make this guy better. These are the adjustments to make this guy better. We have to add this pitch or we have to change his delivery.' Eddie was along the same lines with the hitters. He was an excellent hitting instructor. Eddie would make suggestions to the hitters on how they could be good hitters. So I got a lot of information from them."

Gillick also learned a great deal from Tal Smith, who replaced Richards as the Vice President and Director of Player Personnel for the Astros when Richards left to go run the Braves in 1966. Smith then hired Gillick to join him with the Yankees in 1974.

"I think the guy that really from an administrative standpoint and from just structure, Tal Smith played a very big part," Gillick says. "He played a big part in my thinking. But from learning things on the field, it was Robinson and Richards."

Gillick got an opportunity to show what he had learned from those guys when in 1976 the Labatt Brewery called him to become the first GM in Toronto. He would start a franchise from scratch, a dream for any baseball executive.

"Our ownership in Toronto was committed to player development and scouting," Gillick explains. "They were committed to a ten-year plan. We told them it was going to take about ten years to get this thing up and rolling. Throughout that whole ten-year period, they never wavered at all. They were right on target with us when we were losing a hundred games. They were right there with us. But again it goes back to the fact that we told them we thought we had a good game plan, we thought it was going to work out, but we just had to be patient. It was just consistency. If you think you've got the right game plan just have the guts to stick with it."

Gillick's game plan was simple and was much like the plan in place in Baltimore when he was a player and in Houston with Robinson and Richards.

"We were sort of a high-risk, high-reward type club," Gillick says. "It didn't matter to us if it was a high school or college guy. There's a certain amount of resources that you have to work with. You have the amateur draft, the professional draft (Rule V), you can make trades, six-year professional free agency, minor league free agency, there's Latin America, and there's the Pacific Rim. To me it's like you've got five or six rivers running into the ocean. Consequently, I think you have to look at all of them. I don't really think you're doing right to not only your ownership, but also your fans if you don't try to use every resource. Whatever guy we thought had the best upside, whatever he is (high school, college, or International), that was our philosophy."

Gillick used the Rule V draft perfectly, drafting players like George Bell (from the Phillies), Kelly Gruber (from the Indians), Jim Acker (from the Braves), and Willie Upshaw (from the Yankees). He signed players that had been let go by other clubs like Doyle Alexander and Tom Filer, along with trading for young players who were stuck behind more veteran players like Damaso Garcia, Fred McGriff, and Cecil Fielder. Gillick's scouts, led by former Braves Scout Al LaMacchia, made great choices like Lloyd Moseby (first round, 1978), Jesse Barfield (ninth round, 1978), Dave Stieb (fifth round, 1978), and Jimmy Key (third round, 1982).

Even Ted Turner saw what Gillick was putting together in Toronto. When Bill Lucas died in 1979, Turner offered Gillick a chance to be the Braves new GM. He flew to Atlanta and met with the eccentric Turner about joining the Braves.

"Bill and I had been pretty close," Gillick says. "We were both in player development so we were in meetings and things like that. I went down there and met with Mr. Turner. Coxie was managing. I probably would have gone down there but again I felt a responsibility and loyalty to the people of Toronto. They gave me an opportunity. They gave me a chance. Even though it didn't show at the time, we were making progress. I just decided to stay up there."

And it was that consistency in the philosophy that helped Toronto become a great team in the mid-80's. Cox was in the dugout, but he closely watched Gillick build a winner in the front office.

"Pat was a workaholic," Cox remembers. "He scouted himself. He went beyond just being a GM. He was kind of hands on in the entire scouting department. Pat was great. There were a lot of young players coming up, and it was fun to be there at that stage. It was fun to manage them."

But after losing to the Royals in the ALCS in 1985, Cox had

the opportunity to go home. When Turner called, Gillick knew he didn't want to lose the manager that had ushered his team to the playoffs, but he knew the draw to return home was too good for Cox to pass up.

"I think it was natural that maybe he wanted to get back down there," Gillick says. "His wife was from down there and he still lived there. I think from his standpoint he was unhappy that he was terminated (after the 1981 season) and I think he wanted to go back and he had something to prove."

The word in Toronto was that Cox was never completely happy being away from his family in Atlanta. If the Blue Jays had an off day, Cox would occasionally slip away and fly to Atlanta to spend twelve or sixteen hours with Pam and their kids. He supposedly almost missed one game because he couldn't get back to Toronto in time. So it might not have mattered if Turner called wanting Cox to be a parking attendant, the chance to go back to Atlanta was the appeal.

"Ted said, 'Bobby I want you to be the GM,'" Cox says. "It was hard to refuse simply because I lived there in Atlanta."

"I think probably deep down that Ted wanted him as the manager," Gillick believes. Even Cox admits that Turner may have initially wanted him to be the manager again, but "we were in the playoffs and he started running out of time. But he did want me back."

So a man who had been in a pro uniform for 26 years showed up to work at Atlanta Fulton County Stadium wearing a shirt and tie. Bobby Cox was the GM and Ted Turner wanted him to fix his Braves.

The first thing Cox did was meet with John Mullen, whom he replaced as GM and who became his Assistant, Paul Snyder, and Snyder's Assistant Rod Gilbreath. The four went over every player in the organization, from Rookie Ball to AAA and the entire forty-man roster.

"I came out of that meeting with a great feeling that Bobby Cox had a game plan," Gilbreath says. "Between Bobby and Paul Snyder, they had a game plan that we were going to draft as many pitchers as we could. That was our game plan."

The Braves were always known as an offensive team, with one of the best hitter's stadiums in the league and young boppers like Murphy and Horner. There was a perception that the Braves could never be a team built around pitching. Their stadium was nicknamed "The Launching Pad" for obvious reasons. But Cox didn't buy it. "Good pitching will work on an ice rink," he says.

"Even back in the late 70's and the early 80's we could always score runs," says Gilbreath, who was a backup infielder on Cox's teams in the late 70's. "We couldn't keep the other team from scoring. I think they just looked at our tradition and our past history and said, 'hey let's flip-flop this thing around a little bit and see if we can get some pitchers up here and let the hitters fall where they may.' And we're still doing that."

"I've always been a pitching guy," Cox says. "We didn't have a lot. I wanted to sign as many good pitching prospects as we could. We tried to pump as much money as we could into the farm system and scouting department. Having a guy like Paul Snyder made that a simple task."

Snyder was all in favor of changing the philosophy and going after pitching. The team had not neglected pitching, but over the years there had just been a lot of bad luck. So when Cox came back and became GM, it gave Snyder another chance to place a greater emphasis on pitching. He was also convinced this was the way to go by one of his most trusted scouts.

"A lot of this came from my scouting mentor, Bill Wight," Snyder explains. "This was a 'Bill Wight thought'- that everybody's always looking for pitching and if you have pitching you can get players. We'd be sitting in the draft and start arguing about this guy or that guy, well I'd just go for the pitcher, especially if he was left-handed. It goes back to the old Branch Rickey theory: the more shit you throw up against the wall, the better chance they are going to stick."

"If you get the long range pitching established, you've got the nucleus of taking a second division ball club into the first division faster than anything," Wight says, now retired and living in California. "Good pitching will keep you in every ball game. We tried to get quality pitchers with long-range potential. But mainly we tried to get arms that definitely had a chance of getting there. That was kind of a selling point that with our club you might get there a little quicker.

The emphasis was placed on high school pitchers. Cox and Snyder wanted to get young arms that had not been damaged by overwork in college, and allow them to get the appropriate innings so they would develop fully.

"They wanted to draft high school kids and develop them through the organization," Gilbreath explains. "They wanted to bring them up the way we train players. When they go to college, we have to break that training and re-train them. Bring them up in your own organization, train them, teach them your own techniques, and then stay with those theories all the way through the minor leagues."

Cox also made changes in the atmosphere throughout the organization. Bobby Dews was Assistant Farm Director under Hank Aaron. He was headed to the Houston Astros to be their Farm Director when Cox called and intervened. "He called me the Sunday before I was to go to Houston," Dews says. "He said, 'we're going to sign the best players. We're going to go first class. No financial or any other stone will be left unturned to get that player to be the kind of player we want in the big leagues.' It was kind of like they would be our children and this would be our family. We would give them everything they needed to be successful in the big leagues."

Dews subsequently wrote a playbook detailing the new philosophies that were being implemented.

"I wrote 'The Braves' Way' at the top of the book," he remembers. "It was 'the way' we wanted to do everything. We wanted the same bunt plays at the major league level all the way through the minor league level – all the way through to the rookie leagues. It was consistency. If you'd go to Low-A, you'd do the same thing we would be doing in Atlanta. Everything was the same except for the signs. When we sent a ballplayer to Atlanta, all we wanted them to do was to walk up to the manager and ask, 'what are your signs?' They'd know everything else they were going to do."

That consistency was critical. The organization had struggled with consistency for some time, so having people in place that believed their jobs were safe despite how poorly the record may have been at the big league level was crucial. Just like in Toronto, when Labatts believed in Pat Gillick's ten-year plan, the long-term plan in Atlanta was clear and was now led by someone who had Ted Turner's trust.

"Ted had confidence in Bobby," says Paul Snyder. "Bobby had learned so much from when he was in Toronto. It's pretty hard to be around a guy like Pat and not learn something."

"I would think it (Cox's time in Toronto) had some influence on him," Gillick says. "I think the whole thing he was trying to do was the same thing we were trying to do and what we kept telling ownership, and that was, 'Look we have got to collect as many good players as we possibly can, be it Dave Stieb or George Bell or Lloyd Moseby or Jesse Barfield or whoever it is, we have to collect as many young players as we can."

So that was Cox's plan: get as many good young players as possible and give them the time to fully develop and reach their potential.

The plan was in place, and Cox had settled into his role of suit. But there was one more administrative piece missing. The puzzle was still incomplete.

8

"STARTING MONDAY YOU'RE RUNNING THE BRAVES"

With Bobby Cox in place as General Manager, there was still a need for a leader at the top. Ted Turner was a busy man. He was running a worldwide news network, buying movie studios, and trying to buy television networks. Turner had already backed off making some major decisions. He no longer wined and dined free agents like he had done in the late 70's and early 80's. The baseball people were now running the show.

But every organization has the need for a leader. Yes, Bobby Cox was in charge of the on-field operations, but Turner wasn't available to make other decisions that Cox may not have cared about. Cox needed to work on getting the team better, but there's a lot more involved in running a sports franchise.

The best candidate was already inside Turner Broadcasting.

Stan Kasten always loved sports. While getting his law degree at Columbia, he played baseball in the Jersey Shore League. Even though he planned to be an anti-trust lawyer, a career in sports was always in his mind as a possibility. He did a lot of reading, and even took a seminar the NFL offered for aspiring agents.

"I expected to be involved in sports someday," Kasten explains, "but who knew where."

After finishing law school and taking two bar exams, Kasten decided to take a break. He and his wife took off for a ten-day trip around the country driving to different baseball parks. It was the summer of 1976 and Turner, who had recently purchased the Braves, was on the road with his newest toy. Kasten recognized him immediately.

"I was so big a baseball fan that I even knew who the owners were – even the new ones," Kasten says. "Ted was running up and down the stairs like he always did in those days. I told my wife, 'you know I'm going to go up and talk to him after the game.'"

Kasten approached Turner and told him of his love of sports. The two hit it off right off the bat.

"Write me a letter," Turner urged Kasten.

When he got back to New York, Kasten did write Turner a letter expressing his interest in getting into sports. Turner replied with a job offer, "Come on down and we'll see how it works out."

So in October of 1976 Kasten became an in-house counsel for the Braves. His first day on the job he attended a bargaining session where Turner was going over the final details of his purchase of the Hawks NBA team from Tom Cousins and Bud Seretean. Six weeks later, Turner's WTCG became a SuperStation. Turner's dream of putting his sports teams over the cable air to all fifty states was becoming a reality.

At that point, Mike Storen was the GM of the Hawks. He was a former ABA Commissioner and had been a basketball GM for several basketball teams. Storen had arranged a huge deal, where the Hawks obtained Len "Truck" Robinson from Washington. Robinson was a heck of a player, averaging twenty-two points per game for a team that won only thirty-one games. But then after the 1976-77 season, Robinson was lost to New Orleans via free agency. It was a big loss and it really gave Turner a reason to try and make a change with his GM.

Turner was the type of owner that sat on the front row, which enabled him to meet some pretty important people in Atlanta. He became friends with Michael Gearon, who was a retired real estate developer and a huge basketball fan.

"I'm firing Storen," Turner told Gearon. "Mike, I need you to come in and do this for me. Find me a GM."

Gearon agreed to take on the task but had a condition. "I'm not at all a details or a paperwork or a rules guy," he explained to Turner. "I need some help. I hear you have a young lawyer with the Braves who would be a good fit for this. Can I borrow him for two weeks?"

Turner introduced Gearon to Kasten, and the two instantly hit it off. They interviewed a couple of candidates for the GM's job, but couldn't find the right choice.

"Mike was doing the stuff himself and I was helping him," Kasten says. "Things started falling into place. We had cut the payroll all the way down. The team, little by little, started to win games and started to look respectable. So Mike and I just stayed."

The next two years Gearon ran the Hawks as the GM with Kasten's help. The team improved to .500 (41-41) in the 1977-78 season and then went 46-36 in 78-79. In July of '79, Gearon finally found someone to replace him as the General Manager, hiring Lewis Schaffel, who had been with New Orleans and had stolen Truck Robinson away from the Hawks two years before. But Schaffel didn't last six months. He was out by November.

"There was just little ole me left, so I became the GM," Kasten says.

He was twenty-seven years old, the youngest General Manager in the history of professional sports. That season the Hawks won the Central Division and Kasten quickly gained the trust of Gearon and Turner. But the team was getting older, and over the next few years, Kasten would rebuild the Hawks into one of the NBA's best teams. The big move came on September 3, 1982.

Dominique Wilkins had been a star at the University of Georgia. The Utah Jazz selected him with the third overall pick in the 1982 draft. Kasten wanted him badly. He believed the local star would be a big draw and could also be a centerpiece to build around. But the price would be high – Hawks' star forward John Drew and one million dollars.

"That was a lot of money in 1982," Kasten says. "I told Ted what it was going to do for us both on the court and off. Ted had never heard of Dominique Wilkins. That was just not his thing. He turned to the CFO of the company, Bill Bevins, and he said, 'Bill, can we get a million dollars from the bank?'

Kasten says that Bevins responded without flinching, "No Ted, we cannot. It can't be done."

Turner rolled around in his chair and looked at Kasten and

replied in his long southern draw, "Stan, go do it."

The trade turned out to be the best in the history of the franchise. Wilkins became "The Human Highlight Film," the great player Kasten envisioned when making the deal. The next season Kasten added guards Glenn "Doc" Rivers and Randy Wittman through the draft, and then in 1984 Kevin Willis, a seven-foot power forward, was added to the mix. Kasten also traded longtime Hawks' star Dan Roundfield to Detroit for two young players, Antoine Carr and Cliff Levingston. These six players formed a young nucleus that quickly became one of the best teams in the league.

The Hawks went 50-32 during the 1985-86 season and Kasten was named as the NBA's Executive of the Year. He also still dabbled a little bit with the Braves, attending Board meetings since the Braves and Hawks Board of Directors were so similar. As Kasten was fixing one part of Turner's sports empire, the other part was floundering. So it was only a matter of time before the chief asked Kasten to get more involved.

"Stan we need you to do this," Turner pleaded with Kasten to take over the Braves in addition to his duties with the Hawks. "We need you to do this."

"Ted, you just can't do two things," responded Kasten.

"You could be the first guy running two teams. That would be great."

"Ted, do you know why there aren't other people running two teams?"

Turner asked why.

"Because it's such a bad idea," Kasten said, now almost pleading with Turner to drop the issue.

"Nah," Turner said with his trademark scowl, "you can do it."

Turner's not the type to be told no. Kasten had held him off for two years. He wanted to make the Hawks the best NBA franchise before he did anything else. But then in October of 1986, the request to run the Braves turned into a demand.

"We were in Richmond with the Hawks for a preseason game," Kasten explains. "The Braves had just come off another sad, sad season. It was the middle of the World Series. Bob Wussler (the Chairman of TBS and one of Ted's lieutenants) called me and said, "Stan, we'll need you to take over the Braves."

"Bob, we keep having this argument," Kasten told his boss. "I don't want to do it."

Wussler repeated his comment. "Stan, we need you to run the Braves."

"Like I said," Kasten reiterated, "we've been over this before."

Wussler shot back quickly. "No, no, no. You don't understand. Starting Monday, you are running the Braves."

Kasten was a little shocked at the ultimatum and just said, "Bob…"

"I've got to be out of town Monday," Wussler continued, pretending to not hear the incredulity in Kasten's voice. "But you've got to come in Monday. Ted's expecting you in, at which time you're going to be assigned the Presidency of the Braves."

Kasten genuinely did not believe he could handle both jobs. The Hawks were the talk of the NBA. They had just begun a run that would have them win at least fifty games in each of the next four seasons. His mentor, Michael Gearon, thought he could do it.

"You can do this," Gearon told his now experienced protégé. "I'll help you. You can do it."

But Kasten "didn't want to do it. As much as I love baseball, I had built a career in basketball by now. We were the preseason favorite to win it all. We were really flying and I was really involved."

That next Monday Kasten showed up at Turner's office.

"Stan you have to do this," Turner said. "I'm just so tired. They've been bad for so long. They're embarrassing. I need them to be good. I know you can do it."

"I'll tell you how serious I am," Turner continued. "I've been President of the Braves until now. I'm going to step down and you're going to be President. It's not that you're just a guy, you are the guy."

Now that Turner had become serious, Kasten did as well.

"You know Ted, you've been doing things a certain way for so long," Kasten replied. "If I come in and find out what I think is the problem, then I'll want to change things."

"Stan I don't care. Just whatever it takes, just fix it. Please just fix it."

So Kasten's success in building the Hawks landed him the job doing the same for Turner's Braves. The draft was the key to Kasten's Hawks blueprint, and developing young players would soon be his game plan for the Braves.

Dating back to Turner's purchase of the Braves in 1976, he

had always gone after the hot free agent during the offseason. For instance, signing Andy Messersmith right after he took over the franchise. But over the next few years, he struck out landing the big players. Stars like Pete Rose, Dave Winfield, Don Sutton, Reggie Jackson, and Rich Gossage all came to town to be entertained by the entertaining Turner. Yeah, he wanted to improve the Braves, but he also wanted to improve the TV ratings of the SuperStation.

"The problem was the way we had been doing it, because of the imperatives of TV," Kasten explains, "which were critical to the maintenance of our company back then. The Braves were such an important part of TBS programming in the 80's."

Turner did sign two big free agents in the 80's, getting reliever Al Hrabosky in 1980 and signing Bruce Sutter before the 1985 season. Turner finally caught his big fish in Sutter, who was the premiere reliever in the game at the time. But for the first two seasons of Sutter's six-year, $10.125 million dollar contract, he had only 26 saves and battled injuries.

Kasten jumped on that free agent disaster to prove something to Turner.

"If you spend two million bucks, maybe you get one great year out of one player," Kasten told Turner. "Whereas if you take that two million dollars and you buy extra minor leagues teams, hire more instructors at all those levels, hire more scouts, and sign more draft picks, then maybe instead of the one great season out of one great player, maybe you'll get ten major leaguers each of who may give you ten great seasons. That's a difference of 100-to-1. If you do it that way, and you're willing to invest in the long term, your chances for long-term success are much greater."

Kasten says that Turner started paying attention to his theories.

"Contrast that to how we had been doing it before when we'd sign one free agent, then a) you spend two million bucks and you don't have it to use on other people, b) if you have developed anyone coming up from your system, that player can't play because this free agent has to play, and c) and most importantly, you had to give up draft pick compensation. And if a player got injured like Sutter, then all of it had been lost, including your two million bucks, which you couldn't use to get other players."

Turner not only endorsed Kasten's beliefs, but also encouraged him to move forward. So Kasten's next step was to learn more.

He got hold of a Xeroxed copy of a book by Branch Rickey, the legendary baseball executive who was also an inspiration to Paul Snyder.

"Quality out of quantity," Kasten says. "That was Branch Rickey's theory. Just sign more players and you'll wind up finding more players." With that in mind, Kasten knew the Braves needed more minor league teams so the additional players could play.

"I told Ted, 'Let's use the money down below (in the farm system),'" Kasten remembers. "I remember telling him, 'Look Ted, for the next three years I could be the village idiot because fans don't want to hear about how good your young players are in Richmond and Greenville and Durham and Greenwood, South Carolina. They don't care.' But if we believe in it, then we've got to stick with it."

Paul Snyder was eager to do anything to help the organization. He knew he needed more players, more teams, more scouts, and more instructors. Kasten made it happen.

"I remember talking to Paul about a lot of different philosophical things," reflects Kasten. "We talked about whether we could get a tryout camp in every state. We had real possibilities with the reach of our SuperStation. This was all music to Paul's ears. We went ahead and bought another minor league team because we were going to start signing more guys. We needed places for them to play."

"This to me is the turnaround," Snyder says pointing to Kasten's arrival as team President. "We were talking and the Dodgers had just had thirty-six scouting contracts approved. We had our little nine or ten. I said to Stan, 'we're still trying to catch the Dodgers. We're still going after them.' Then we finally started playing catch up. We finally got the manpower. Then we got into the tryout camp machine. Right there is where it all started. I showed that to him and he started getting us money."

This was another change. John Mullen was the GM in the past and the main person dealing with Turner. But as Snyder points out, "John wasn't going to go ask for anything. He didn't have the security himself."

But Stan Kasten did.

"Ted is the single most intimidating guy I've ever had to deal with," Kasten says. "His intellect and his drive are ferocious. But I told him where I thought we were coming up short and why, here's how it can be fixed, and that it can be fixed. At that point, Ted had a lot of confidence in me. So I was maybe able to sell it while

111

a John Mullen might not have been able to."

Again, Turner was busy starting the Goodwill Games, his own Olympics, and building his TBS Empire. "He's the one that concluded that it wasn't right to run an important sports franchise part-time. Those were his words."

So Kasten started working closely with Snyder and with Bobby Cox, who had already been in his job as the General Manager for one season. "What I was able to help him do was turn the dial all the way to the right," Kasten says. "Bobby was a first time team executive, and he was watching what gets done here and what gets done there. I came in and enabled him to turn the dial all the way."

Cox and Snyder had already agreed that pitching would be a priority. Kasten came in and had the same philosophy.

"I remember having a great, long conversation with Frank Cashen (Mets General Manager at the time)," Kasten says. "He spent a long time with the Orioles, and we talked about how important pitching was. He said whenever they drafted pitchers, with those great Baltimore teams in the 60's and 70's, they had one guy who was a specialist with pitchers for the draft. They had lots of scouts and lots of checkers, but if it came down to a group of ten pitchers in the draft, they'd send one specific guy around and do nothing but look at these pitchers. That way, he could get the big picture and compare each guy. We had a guy like that in Freddy Shaffer."

"Whenever we made a trade it was clear that we had to have an arm thrown in. A young arm had to be in the deal, and even if they didn't make it, again quality out of quantity. If we had twice as many pitchers than any organization, then we're going to graduate twice as many pitchers."

So Kasten, Cox, and Snyder had the blueprint in place to change the Braves into a winning franchise:
1. Draft as many high school pitchers as possible.
2. Have more tryout camps to find more players.
3. Be patient with the pitchers.
4. Hire more scouts, instructors, and coaches.
5. Get pitchers in every trade.
6. Stay away from free agents.
7. If a season or two has to be sacrificed, so be it. Don't forget the long-term goals.
8. Don't change the plan.

The last part was tough. Everyone wants to win, and despite the plan to be patient, there were chances to go for that quick fix. Tim Raines and Andre Dawson were both free agents before the 1987 season, and both had interest in coming to Atlanta. This was the era of collusion, when owners backed off from signing free agents and the Player's Association filed suit. Dawson had to present a blank contract to teams so he could leave Montreal. The Cubs put $500,000 on the deal and signed him, but the Braves had the same shot. Dawson expressed an interest in Atlanta, but the Braves stayed true to their philosophy. The same thing happened the next winter, as Detroit outfielder Kirk Gibson said he was interested in Atlanta. He wound up signing with the Dodgers and helped them win the World Series in 1988, but if the Braves had blinked, he could have been in right field in Atlanta instead.

"We were trying to win but we were pumping more money into signing players for the system than we were in the big leagues," Cox says. "So it was hard. It is hard knowing that you're a little ways away."

As the Braves' young pitchers started to mature, more teams came calling for them in trade talks. Reports had the Red Sox constantly calling Cox about Tom Glavine, even floating the names of Wade Boggs and Mike Greenwell in conversations. The Braves could have improved more quickly, but they knew the plan took patience.

"I had the secret ingredient," Kasten says. "If Ted understands what I'm doing, who else's opinion matters? If the media people are getting on me, I couldn't care less. If Ted is OK, and Ted was, then we were fine. And Ted was more than OK. He was the secret ingredient. I didn't have an owner who was going to fire me if we lost ten games in a row. You see that in every city. Here's what people don't understand about Ted, when he wants an answer, he can be the most impatient guy in the world. But when the answer you give him is a plan that requires time, then he can be the most patient guy in the world. He will give you that if the plan makes sense. I knew that. I had the secret ingredient. I had an owner in my corner that would let it happen and would allow it to work."

"It was a commitment Ted made to me and he lived up to all of it. I think it's the biggest reason why we had success. He understood the point we were making that baseball decisions have to be made by baseball people. You should have a guy at the top of the pyramid who understands the way the business of baseball intersects with the on-field strategy, and that happened to be me. Good or bad, we did some right things. You do need the head of your business operation to understand. I had been a GM. That was very useful in working with Bobby. The only success worth having is long-term success. You cannot achieve long-term success without a long-term plan. We had a long-term plan. Long-term plans are exactly that, they take a while to put in place."

For years there had been criticism that the Braves were not run by the baseball people, but that the television executives at TBS made all the important decisions. Kasten admits there might have been some truth in that prior to his arrival, but he quickly diffused any potential trouble.

"I made it a point when I came in of separating that," Kasten says. "This wasn't Ted anymore, and the TV insistence of getting a free agent every year for ratings was over. We decided to build the baseball team with baseball people making baseball decisions. It was the single most important change I was able to institute, with Ted's blessing by the way."

Kasten says the folks at TBS still cried a bit when the team was struggling in the late 80's, but "the buck would stop with me. All blame stops at my desk. That was the way it was. Ted let me do the things I thought we needed to do. Period. Baseball decisions were made by baseball people – period."

The Braves' front office actually believed the plan was starting to click in 1990. Many of the Braves' young pitchers had matured and, by most accounts, were ready to bust out. So Turner OK'd a plan to spend a bit more money on free agents to try and compliment the talent that was in place from the farm system.

"We thought we were finally going to reach .500," Kasten explains. "We should have. But Nick Esasky (signed from Boston to a three-year contract) got vertigo and was out for the season. We lost our closer when Mike Stanton, who was great the year before, went down with a torn labrum in his shoulder. And we lost one of our starters in Pete Smith, who had shoulder trouble. So you lose your cleanup hitter, a starter, and a closer. Well, the year went to hell. I always said that in 1991 we went from worst to first, but we probably shouldn't have been worst in '90. It just worked out that way."

The 1990 Braves got off to a 25-40 start. Injuries were a part of it, but the losing was starting to wear on many of the players and a change needed to be made. Russ Nixon, who had replaced Chuck Tanner midway through 1988, was the manager. He was a solid baseball man, but the team was just not playing well. Kasten started wondering if his General Manager Cox, who was an excellent field manager before he put on the tie, would be interested in getting back on the field.

"I asked Bobby a number of times when we were alone and really, really serious with each other, if he ever saw himself back on the field," says Kasten. "The most he would ever say, and he said this so often it was making me sick, 'Stan, I'll do whatever you and Ted want me to do.' I'd say, 'No, that's not what I asked you, goddamn it. Do you want to get back on the field?' He'd say, 'Stan, whatever you and Ted ask me to do is what I'm going to do.' So that cleared it up for me."

"I always did feel Bobby would be back on the field. I'll tell you what was real important to me though. I really didn't want to put Bobby on the field in June of '90. Everyone has his own capability and their own level of credibility. Credibility with the customers, the fans, and the media is very important in getting a fair shake at doing your job. I was fearful that even if Bobby was the best guy to ultimately be our manager, that if I trotted him out there too early before the team was good enough, and he spent too much time, a year or more losing, his credibility would be burned up. If he gets burned in the community with the media and the fans, that seeps down to your team and you've shot your best opportunity. So I was very, very concerned about pushing the Bobby-button too quickly."

"I was worried. I wanted to wait until the end of the year, but it had gotten so bad. Tensions in the locker room were so bad. People were openly questioning this and that, so I felt I had no choice."

Kasten went away for the weekend to think about what he was going to do. There was no doubt the team was accumulating talent, but how long could he continue with a manager who probably wouldn't be around to see them reach their potential anyway?

"I came back and said, 'Bobby, this is what I'm doing.'"

And with that decision, Bobby Cox was back where Ted Turner wanted him all along: in the dugout.

"I told him, 'For the rest of this year you're going to serve in both roles, with John Mullen basically doing the GM stuff,'" Kasten says. "I told him, 'at the end of the year, I'll make a decision. I will tell you this, you won't be doing both jobs.'"

So Cox finished out the season and the Braves were once again in last place, 65-97, twenty-six games behind the Cincinnati Reds. The plan Cox and Snyder, and then Kasten, had in place was working. The farm system was rated as the best in baseball. Everyone in the game knew the Braves had the best young talent in the game.

The three people mainly responsible for getting the young talent accumulated in the late 80's deserve equal credit. Paul Snyder, Bobby Cox, and Stan Kasten were all on the same page. They were all patient and all believed in their philosophy and in their players. Now as they look back, all three try to spread around the accolades.

"We took the bull by the horns and tried to build something," Cox says. "Paul Snyder was great. I didn't have much to do with building this. Snyder and those guys are the ones who made the hard decisions. And Stan gets overshadowed. He oversaw everything. He was helpful in many, many ways. He was the money guy so he had to approve everything."

"Stan is the unsung hero of the whole thing," Snyder says. "And Bobby came in and that helped us more because Ted had confidence in Bobby."

"Enough can't be said about the role of Paul Snyder," says Kasten. "He's an unsung hero. The guy is a Hall-of-Fame caliber scout. Bobby just put it together beautifully and executed it beautifully."

Cox, Snyder, and Kasten had all done their jobs according to what they believed was the best way to build a winning team. Not through college player stats, not through pricey free-agent additions or by farm-depleting trades, but by patience and home-grown nurturing. The type of nurturing that was only possible from an organization that relied on the instincts of sharp baseball minds and the focus on makeup over math.

The Braves were on the verge of becoming a winning franchise. But there was still something missing. They needed a winner.

9

FINDING THE LEFTY

"If the guy was left-handed and he was in your area,
if you didn't go see him you were in trouble."
– Hep Cronin, Veteran Braves Scout

When Paul Snyder put out the edict to his scouts to find left-handed pitchers, he didn't limit their search geographically. So it was no surprise that the best lefty the Braves found since Warren Spahn came from an area that the Braves had tapped into before.

Some teams don't even bother to scout the Northeast. The belief being players in warm weather states play more baseball, so they'll be more advanced than someone from a cold weather state. But the Braves had found some success up north before. Snyder found catcher Matt Sinatro in Connecticut and took him with a second round pick in 1978. He then followed that selection with Steve Bedrosian, a pitcher out of Massachusetts who was pitching at the University of New Haven, in the third round. By the early 1980's both players were on the Atlanta roster. Then in 1982, Snyder's scouts found Joe Johnson, from Wrentham, Massachusetts. He was pitching at the University of Maine and went in the second round. By 1984, he was one of Atlanta's top prospects.

Since they'd found a few diamonds in the rough from the Northeast, they weren't going to overlook that area in their incessant search for a lefty.

"Once you have a kid from a certain area have success, it stimulates things," Snyder said back in 1984. "It lets people see what can happen. That was really the start of it."

Tony DeMacio was in his first year as a Braves Scout in 1984. Snyder asked him to go up to the Northeast and take over that region. DeMacio felt he had somewhat of an advantage considering Snyder was from the Northeast and had found talent there before. He also knew Snyder believed the pitchers in the Northeast could have fresher arms, since they weren't pitching as much as the kids in warmer states.

"When Paul broke into scouting after his playing career he worked in cold weather areas," DeMacio says. "I think Paul's never been afraid to take a cold weather player."

As a first-year scout, DeMacio wanted to find a player his new boss would be proud of, but since he was brand new it was hard to compare talent. He didn't have the years of scouting experience Snyder and the other veteran Braves' scouts had, so when he saw a player he thought was pretty good, it was hard to know *how* good he really was in relation to everything else out there. DeMacio found a pitcher at Billerica Memorial High School in Billerica, Massachusetts, a suburb of Boston.

"Tommy was good," DeMacio says. "He was a great athlete first of all, and he was an excellent student."

'Tommy' was Thomas Michael Glavine, an eighteen-year old left-handed pitcher. He was a four-time league All Star and All Conference player in baseball, but his talent didn't end there. He was also an outstanding hockey player, winning the same honors in that sport three times. *The Boston Globe* named him their All-Scholastic and Player of the Year for both sports in 1984.

"You could see the athleticism," DeMacio says. "You could see the competitiveness. Tom just had a lot of the extra things that go along with being taken. Of course, he had the stuff. We all knew that. But he had the intangibles that we looked for."

The "stuff" included a decent fastball, decent curve, and a forkball that he used as a changeup. DeMacio liked him immediately, as did his regional supervisor Bob Turzilli. But the first time the Braves brought in Lou Fitzgerald, their national crosschecker, Glavine didn't pitch very well. Fitzgerald's report included the words "no way" on the possibility of drafting Glavine. But DeMacio and

Turzilli knew the kid was good, so they made a phone call to Paul Snyder.

"Paul, Tommy had a bad day," DeMacio told his boss. "It was cold. It's New England. They aren't going to pitch perfect up here every day."

"Don't worry about it," Snyder responded. "Tell me when he's going again and we'll be there."

Snyder turned around and called Fitzgerald.

"Fitz, you didn't see the real guy up there," Snyder told his veteran scout. "I want you to go back up there."

Fitzgerald went back up to Massachusetts. Glavine threw a shutout, pitching like he had for DeMacio much of that spring. The organization's opinion changed quickly.

"That was the first negative report we had on the guy," Snyder remembers. "When someone (Fitzgerald) with that track record says something negative, that carries some weight. But like with anything, you toss out the high and toss out the low, and there was only one negative report. I had known Turzilli since 1965 so I knew he saw something in Tommy. And I trusted DeMacio – if I didn't, I wouldn't have hired him."

"Paul…listening to his scouts like he always does," DeMacio says. "Even a first year scout. We knew what we liked and knew what we saw."

So DeMacio got back into scouting Glavine heavily, but in a rather unorthodox way. Unlike he would learn to do as he grew as a scout, DeMacio did not get to know Glavine personally very well. It was strategic. He felt he had to proceed with caution if the Braves were going to eventually sign him.

"I visited with him as much as you were allowed to," DeMacio says. "I visited with him on more of an informal basis more than a formal basis. I don't think Tommy really knew that we had that much interest in him. I was a young guy in an area with a lot of veteran scouts. I was an outsider. I was not a New Englander. I was trying not to show my hand. When you're competing with the Red Sox for a local kid, you're careful. It was a matter of visiting with him informally, but not showcasing that we had much interest."

The Braves were able to draft Glavine in the second round of the June draft. But a few weeks later, he was also taken in the National Hockey League draft, in the fourth round by the Los Angeles Kings.

"It wasn't easy with him," Snyder says of Glavine's two choices. "But deep down inside, there was a positive feeling there. We thought he wanted to play baseball. We were worried, but we didn't want to have a long negotiation because we wanted to get him down there."

Glavine did want to play baseball and signed with the Braves for $85,000 that summer. The hockey experience was part of the attraction the Braves had with Glavine. They believed he was a tough competitor, fearless on the mound, just like he had to be when he was on the ice.

It didn't take long for him to prove that he was a special pitcher. In his first season in the minors, in Bradenton, he went 2-3 with a 3.34 ERA in 8 games (7 starts), along with 29 hits allowed, 13 walks, and 34 strikeouts in 32 innings pitched. Then in 1985, he was even more impressive in Low-A Sumter: 9-6, 2.35 ERA in 26 starts, 114 hits allowed in 169 innings, 73 walks, and 174 strikeouts.

Zane Smith was just starting to establish himself as a starter in Atlanta, so the Braves knew they had at least one left-hander in the fold. But as Glavine started to develop, they started to believe they had someone special.

"You could just see his makeup," says Bruce Dal Canton, Glavine's pitching coach when he got to AAA Richmond in 1986. "He had everything you look for in a pitcher. It was just the way he handled himself. You could tell he was something special."

Glavine put up more great numbers in Greenville, going 11-6 with a 3.41 ERA in 22 starts before being promoted to AAA Richmond. He struggled a bit there, going 1-5 with a 5.63 ERA, but it didn't alter the Braves' opinion at all.

"He wasn't overwhelmed at being at the AA level and then for a brief bit in AAA," Dal Canton says. "There were probably a lot of pitchers that had better stuff than Tommy Glavine when he first came up. You have to look at what the guy's got inside and what he's got on top of his shoulders. That's what really set him apart."

The Braves soon found out that the hockey mentality had created a very strong baseball player. Glavine was intense on the mound, often staring at the batter like a cowboy in a western movie. He was purely imperturbable. The Braves had found a pitcher who was mature for his age and didn't seem to let a lot bother him. So after putting up solid numbers again in AAA in 1987 (6-12 record but a 3.35 ERA in 22 starts at the age of twenty-one), the Braves believed Glavine was ready for the big leagues.

On August 17, 1987, Glavine made his major league debut at the Houston Astrodome. He was a little shaky, giving up 6 runs and 5 walks over 3.2 innings, but the Braves knew it wasn't going to hurt him. They knew Glavine would be able to overcome any adversity.

"All I know is he kept doing his job," says Dal Canton, who by 1987 had also been promoted to Atlanta as their pitching coach. "That's what he was focusing on. He was making himself better and better as he went along."

When Glavine went to Spring Training in 1988, the Braves were prepared to give him a spot in the starting rotation. He had impressed in his nine-game tryout at the end of the previous season, and with a commitment to a youth movement already in place, they were ready to sink or swim with young pitchers. Snyder asked one of his chief lieutenants, Bill Wight, himself a former big league lefty, to come in and work with Glavine in the spring.

"He got the most out of his ability," Wight says. "His fastball was average. He had a good curveball, but he came up with a changeup. But he knew he had to acquire what he didn't have. He knew his own shortcomings and his own strengths. He was a self-taught guy. That doesn't happen too often. Tom had that hockey mentality. He was just unflappable."

That's exactly what gave the Braves confidence that Glavine could handle whatever happened in 1988. The Braves were not going to be a very good team, so throwing a young pitcher out there in that situation could be a risk. Some might crack under the pressure of knowing they're pitching well but losing games, while the hope is that a pitcher in that circumstance will build on the adversity and become better long-term.

The Braves went 54-106 in 1988 and Glavine went 7-17 with a 4.56 ERA. All of his ancillary numbers were solid, but it couldn't hide that poor record, even if you could blame the Braves poor fielders for part of the trouble.

"My biggest concern when he kept getting loss after loss was that he might get discouraged, thinking that, 'I can't pitch here,'" Dal Canton says. "But you couldn't tell if he won or lost. Every time he pitched he went out and did his job and that's all I can ask him to do. It was just the way he handled himself. I knew we had something special in that kid."

"I think you knew that right from the get go," Snyder says, "the work ethic just made him special. His tenacity on the mound is something you just can't teach."

Over the next two years, Glavine would take his lumps as a solid big league pitcher on a poor team. He was 14-8 with a 3.68 ERA in 1989, even though the Braves went 63-97 that season. Then in 1990, Glavine was 10-12 with a 4.28 ERA, but the team scored only 30 runs in his 12 losses. He had suffered through three tough years with the team while he was earning his stripes as a pitcher, but the Braves knew he could handle it. And no one had more faith in him than his manager, Bobby Cox.

"Bobby had tons of confidence in him," says Stan Kasten, Braves President at the time. "I remember a writer in Atlanta saying, 'He's never going to make it because he doesn't have an out pitch.' Well, Bobby always believed in Tommy. In fact, there were rumors every week about Tommy going to Boston. That was never true. Bobby would never entertain it. There was a very large story that we were trading both Tommy and David Justice for Mike Greenwell, who was a big-time hitter then. Bobby knew Tommy was special."

Glavine finally proved he was special in 1991, when he led the Braves to their first division title in nine years and captured the Cy Young Award with a 20-11 record. The losing from the previous seasons didn't shake him one bit. Glavine's business-like approach came to symbolize the entire Atlanta team. As the 1990's progressed, he became their leader, and when the team needed a victory to win the World Series in 1995, he pitched eight scoreless innings to stifle the Cleveland Indians. Glavine was the World Series MVP with two victories in the series.

The crafty left-hander would go on to finish his Braves' career with 242 wins and only 143 losses. He became the second best lefty in Braves' history, behind only the legendary Warren Spahn. But with the franchise looking for a lefty savior in the mid-1980's, a freckled-face kid from Massachusetts took the leading role in a storybook recovery. The resurgence can be traced right back to that August night in the Houston Astrodome when Glavine first took the mound for the Atlanta Braves. It might not have come to fruition until 1991, and then even more in 1995, but it all started that night, and Tom Glavine was the perfect person to be the fulcrum on which the Braves' fortunes would pivot.

"I think he was the most mature of all of us," says his teammate at the time, Pete Smith. "Just the way his mindset is, the way he carries himself. Not much bothers Tommy. He's just all business."

Glavine was the perfect person and the perfect pitcher to lead a new group of pitchers into a new era of Braves baseball.

Lynchpin of the Braves starters in the 1990's, Tom Glavine.

10
THE YOUNG GUNS

While Tom Glavine may have been the first of the Braves bunch to make it, there were several other arms that formed a solid group of pitching hopefuls in the late 1980's. In keeping with organizational philosophy General Manager Bobby Cox was always looking to acquire a good, young arm in any deal, and his very first major trade was no exception.

The Braves needed a catcher going into the 1986 season, and Cox got All-Star Ozzie Virgil from the Philadelphia Phillies in exchange for pitcher Steve Bedrosian and outfielder Milt Thompson. But Cox demanded that the Phillies "throw in" a young pitcher.

Pete Smith was actually first on the Braves' radar screen back in 1984, when he was a right-handed pitcher at Burlington High School in Burlington, Massachusetts. The Phillies took him in the first round that year, but a year and a half later when they made the Virgil trade, they included Smith in the deal.

"I guess it was a little bit of a shock since I was a number one pick," Smith says. "I figured my first shot would be with the Phillies in the big leagues. The first thing I thought was, 'Well hey, Tommy's there. How cool will that be?'"

Smith had played against Tom Glavine in high school. Burlington was only five miles from Billerica, both being suburbs of Boston. Glavine beat Smith when Billerica won a state tournament, and then Smith beat Glavine in an American Legion game. But the two really never knew each other. They met briefly in Spring Training in 1985, just a quick "Hello" and "Good luck," but it wasn't until Smith's trade that the two became friends. When he heard he was dealt to the Braves, Smith decided to call Glavine.

"Hey Tommy, I got traded to the Braves," Smith told his neighbor.

"Yeah, I heard about that. Cool," Glavine responded.

And with that, the two high school rivals became teammates.

They started working out in the winter of 1986 by going to a nearby gym to set up a Nautilus program. Then when Smith arrived in West Palm Beach for his first Spring Training with the Braves, Glavine showed him the ropes.

Smith battled some arm troubles in his first season with his new team, possibly because in his first two years with the Phillies he was mainly using his fastball. When he arrived in the Braves' system, coaches started helping him throw breaking balls. He developed a slider and learned how to change speeds with his fastball. But along with learning how to pitch, Smith also had to grow up. The Braves coaches helped him with that as well.

"I remember having good talks with Beach (Jim Beauchamp, Smith's Manager in Greenville in 1986 and 1987)," Smith remembers. "He said, 'You're eighteen-years-old, you've got a good arm, but you're not all that. You have all the tools, but if your head's not into it you're going to struggle.' It was kind of like a wakeup call. I was doing okay, but after that talk I ended up going on a pretty good run. I think that's the biggest thing with being young and being in the minors. Everyone to a degree has the physical tools, but it's the mental approach that can take those guys to the next level."

Smith had a much better season in 1987 as he returned to Greenville, going 9-9 with a 3.35 ERA in 29 games (25 starts), 162 hits, 67 walks, and 119 strikeouts in 177.1 innings pitched. That 1987 Greenville team went 70-74 overall, but it was comprised of a pretty substantial nucleus of talent, including Smith and infielders Jeff Blauser, Ron Gant, David Justice, and Mark Lemke, all who later became important pieces of the Braves' puzzle.

"We all kind of clicked and I think we all kind of fed off each other," Smith says. "We had a heck of a team. You go back and look at how many guys from that team made the big leagues. We had a good group. I think they saw something in that Greenville team that was special. I think all of us maybe in the back of our heads knew that we were going to get a chance."

Another member of that Greenville team was Tommy Greene, Atlanta's first round pick in the 1985 draft out of Whiteville High School in North Carolina.

"I was fortunate enough to come up behind some guys in high school that drew scouts into the ballpark and they got a chance to see me from the ninth grade on up," Greene says. "They got to see me develop over the course of my high school career."

What developed was a big ole country boy that could pitch. Greene was six-foot-five right-hander who threw hard. In his first four full seasons in the Braves' minor league system, Greene would be paired with a young pitching coach named Leo Mazzone.

"Leo's never sugarcoated anything," Greene says. "He told me how things were. I was a work in progress. He was trying to get a fire out of me and to get me to kill my laid-back attitude. He was trying to find that fire on the mound, that aggression. When the rough times come during the course of a game, he didn't want me to be laid-back and let them control me but to take the bull by the horns and steer it the way you want to go. So it was that type of fire he was looking for. It took me a while."

In fact, it took three years for Greene to mature from that easy-going country boy to the bulldog Mazzone was trying to develop on the mound. It all changed in one game in 1989.

Greene was pitching a decent game, with some of his best stuff of the season, but then he gave up a bases-clearing double. Greene circled the mound in disgust, and when he turned around he found Mazzone standing there with his hands on his hips.

"What the hell are you doing out here?" Greene asked his coach. "Why don't you march your little ass back to that dugout."

"I've been trying to get you to tell me that for four damn years," Mazzone replied. "Why don't you take that aggression to the damn dish where it belongs?"

Mazzone was, in a way, trying to shape Greene in the mold of Glavine, who had a natural tiger-mentality on the mound. There was no doubt Greene had the stuff, a mid-90's fastball along with a good curveball, but he needed to be more aggressive in his approach.

Greene had a great season in Greenville in 1987, going 11-8 with a 3.29 ERA in 23 starts. He allowed only 103 hits in 142.1 innings of work. Greene joined Glavine and Smith as one of the Braves' top prospects as the youth movement began to take hold.

The emergence of Smith as a prospect had GM Bobby Cox on the lookout for additional young pitchers they could add from other organizations. In May of 1987, Cox re-signed veteran free agent pitcher Doyle Alexander, who had been acquired midway through the 1986 season from Toronto for pitcher Duane Ward. Alexander became a free agent after that season, but didn't sign with anyone and couldn't re-sign with the Braves until May. Even though the Braves were rebuilding with younger talent, there was a reason they brought Alexander back.

"The only reason we signed him, and Bobby (Cox) and I talked about this, was that later in the year someone might need him," says Stan Kasten. "We just didn't have any need for Alexander long-term. That's specifically why we signed him."

Alexander went 5-10 in his 16 starts for the Braves. By August, Atlanta was already out of the race and they promptly put the veteran on the trading block. The Detroit Tigers were battling the Toronto Blue Jays and the New York Yankees in the American League East. They needed a veteran arm to compliment Jack Morris, Frank Tanana, and Walt Terrell. Detroit General Manager Bill Lajoie called Cox to express his interest in Alexander.

"We had a chance to win the division," Lajoie recalls. "Bobby asked for a left-hander named Steve Searcy or righty John Smoltz."

Smoltz was a lanky right-hander the Tigers drafted in the twenty-second round of the 1985 draft. He was a Michigan kid, born in Warren but grew up in Lansing, about an hour and a half from Detroit. Smoltz was a huge Tigers fan as a kid and was even at the clinching game when they won the 1984 World Series. But Smoltz had another connection to the organization. His grandfather worked on the Tigers' ground crew for thirty years.

"All of those things kept playing through my mind that some day I was going to wear a Tigers uniform," Smoltz says. "Obviously getting drafted by your hometown team, you can't imagine how incredibly happy I was."

The Braves scouted Detroit's minor league system and felt either of the two would be adequate compensation for Alexander.

Searcy was a twenty-three-year-old who had made it all the way up to AAA in 1987. He had a good season in Glens Falls the year before going 11-6 in 27 starts with a 3.30 ERA, but his season in AAA was cut short after getting hit on the knee. Smoltz was a twenty-two-year-old struggling in AA.

"I wanted to give them Searcy," Lajoie says. "The Farm Director, the man in charge of the minor leagues and scouting, felt that Searcy was closer than Smoltz and so we should keep Searcy and let Smoltz be the guy since it was one or the other. I was not in what I would call a real strong position there at the time, so I didn't overrule anybody and went ahead with the consensus."

Lajoie says the Braves had no preference between the two pitchers. The only resistance he found in his own organization to trading Smoltz was from John Hiller, one of his minor league pitching coaches.

"I remember him saying, 'Oh, not him. Don't trade Smoltz.'"

But Lajoie and the Tigers did trade Smoltz to the Braves for Alexander, who would go 9-0 for Detroit and help them squeeze by the Blue Jays for the division crown.

"It's funny," says Pat Gillick, Toronto's GM at the time. "We gave the Braves Alexander for Ward and then they turned around and gave Alexander to Detroit for Smoltz. Then Alexander helped Detroit beat us in the race that year."

Smoltz was in the dugout in Glens Falls when he got two notes, one to call his father and one to call the Tigers organization.

"Of course I called home immediately, first thinking something was wrong," Smoltz says. "My dad told me that I had been traded to the Atlanta Braves. He likes to joke around. I threatened him that I pretty much would fly home and beat him up if he was joking cause that wasn't funny. Then I had the other note in my hand and called the Detroit front office and they verified what my dad had said."

Smoltz was no different from any other young player who is traded away from the team he happened to grow up rooting for. He was absolutely stunned.

"I didn't talk," he says. "I didn't think one good thought. I didn't understand what a trade actually meant. I thought I wasn't wanted. Under these circumstances it was different because it was my hometown. As far as I was concerned the Braves were the worst team in all of baseball. I didn't know if I would ever be part of a winning situation. But there were so many bright spots that if I would have just let myself think about the opportunities I would have realized it was tremendous for me. There was no way it couldn't be."

At the time Smoltz was a Double-A pitcher with a 4-10 record and an ERA of 5.68. It was a typical late season deal of a team trying to win a division by acquiring a veteran player in return for a youngster who may or may not pan out.

"First of all, Smoltz had not done anything out of the ordinary to indicate that he would be the pitcher he has become," Lajoie says. "So it wasn't like we were trading a sure thing or a guy who was definitely going to win twenty games. We still had a pretty good ball club and I thought we should try to win if we could. It does result in greater ticket sales, fan appeal, etc. You don't trade to trade. You trade to win and to better your club. But let's say we didn't win that year. You could see from that point to this present day the Tigers haven't won a thing. So if you can't take gambles like that, and it is the job of the scouting department to supply players, you'll never make a trade."

Over the years, Lajoie has occasionally been criticized by the sportswriters in Detroit for trading a pitcher who might eventually make it to the Hall of Fame. But the reason he made the deal was to help the Tigers win the division that season and they wouldn't have won it if Alexander hadn't gone 9-0.

"It doesn't bother me," Lajoie says. "It did what I wanted it to do. I don't have any regrets about it at all."

The trade also did what the Braves wanted it to do. It gave them another arm to add to their stable of prospects. It all goes back to the theory employed by Cox, Kasten, and Snyder: quality out of quantity. The more good young arms they had like John Smoltz, the more that would eventually stick in Atlanta. Smoltz made three starts in Richmond to finish the 1987 season, going 0-1 with a 6.19 ERA. He then went to the Instructional League and was immediately placed under the care of Leo Mazzone.

"I had been through a reconstruction of my whole mechanics with (Pitching Coach) Billy Muffett with the Tigers," Smoltz explains. "When I saw Leo I was just fearful that this whole thing was going to start all over again. I thought I was pretty good and then when I signed with Detroit they changed just about everything. Leo said, 'your delivery is perfect. We're just going to upgrade your pitches.' That was a huge weight off my shoulders. It was from that point that I just kept getting better and we never had to work much on mechanics again. We worked on a throw and turn curveball and commanding my fastball better. I always had a great curveball but I was told that it was too big with Detroit. We went back to it. I developed a throw and turn slider, and the rest is history."

The history really started that next spring when Smoltz would get acquainted with the other young pitchers in the Braves' farm system that were trying to make their mark as super-prospects.

"My first recollection of John Smoltz was when Tommy and I were playing golf down in Spring Training," says Pete Smith. "John was playing in a foursome behind us. We really didn't know him. He said, 'I can hit this five iron 210 yards.' We were like, 'There's no way you can hit this five iron 210 yards.' I think right off the bat we were like, 'This guy's a little competitive.' He got up there and said, 'I'll do it. I'll do it. I know I can do it.' We kind of got the feeling within a week that he was going to fit right in. He's just a big kid, a big, competitive kid."

"We just had pretty much the time of our life," Smoltz says. "We were all young and were trying to find a way to learn how to pitch better. We all liked golf so that was easy. We all had tremendous respect for each other knowing that everybody had something to bring to the table."

Smoltz returned to Richmond in 1988 and was absolutely devastating, going 10-5 with a 2.79 ERA in 20 start. It didn't take him long to realize he had arrived in pitching heaven.

"We never had a pitching coach with the Tigers," Smoltz says. "They only had rovers. There was no pitching coach assigned to any team so I rarely saw a pitching coach. It was a strange situation. The Tigers didn't spend any money in the minor leagues. So I couldn't believe it when I got here. The Braves spent all kinds of attention to the minor leagues. They had a pitching coach at every level. They had roving pitching instructors. So I noticed a major difference in the development of young players."

Smoltz's development had definitely taken his game to another level. The Braves believed he had proven all he could in the minor leagues, so they made the decision to promote him to Atlanta. His big league debut was a Saturday afternoon game at the NY Mets in late July. Ironically, it was "Tom Seaver Day" at Shea, as the first place Mets were honoring an eventual Hall of Famer that

Smoltz had actually been compared to.

"It was numbing," he admits. "It didn't seem real. I've always welcomed and have loved challenges like that. I'll never forget it because the place was packed. That team was loaded and eventually went to the playoffs. It was an incredible roller coaster."

Braves perennial workhorse John Smoltz

Smoltz would go 2-7 in 12 starts with a 5.48 ERA – not great numbers, but like the others, he was just fitting in. He was joined on the 1988 Richmond roster by left-hander Derek Lilliquist, the Braves first round draft choice in 1987 out of the University of Georgia. Lilliquist was a bit different from Smoltz, Smith, Greene, and Glavine in that he had been a college pitcher, just down the street from Atlanta in Athens, Georgia. The Braves believed Lilliquist was too good to pass up picking that high in the draft. He was a stocky lefty that relied on changing speeds and hitting the strike zone with his breaking ball.

"Derek wasn't a power type pitcher," says Bruce Dal Canton, "but he knew how to pitch. He wasn't afraid. If he wanted the ball in, he threw it in. If he wanted the ball away, he'd put it there. That's the biggest asset you can have as a pitcher: you can't be afraid to throw strikes. All of those guys weren't. They kept coming at you and coming at you. As long as you're throwing strikes and you have a little movement on your fastball, you're going to be okay."

By the time Spring Training rolled around in 1989, the Braves' young pitchers were doing fine. Glavine, Smoltz, and Smith were pretty much set in the Atlanta rotation, while Greene and Lilliquist were not far behind in AAA. The Braves, in need of a good public relations gimmick to promote their young and promising pitchers, decided to get all of them together on a sunny afternoon in March of 1989.

"They just kind of called us," says Smith. "I think it was Jim Schultz (Braves Public Relations Director). "He said, 'Hey, we've got a photo shoot we want to do. We're going to go to this ranch.' So we all got in this van and drove for forty-five minutes. We get there and they had all these chaps and hats and vests and all this stuff. They said, 'we just want to take a picture. We're going to set up this new thing called 'The Young Guns.' We were like, 'Oh okay, that's kind of cool.'"

The five pitchers lined up, Lilliquist and Glavine, the left-handers of the group, were on the left, Smith was in the middle with a glove in his left hand, followed by Smoltz and Greene. They all had cowboy hats on, bandanas, the whole works, along with two horses behind them on the ranch. All five had a scowl, looking as tough as the Braves hoped they would all be on the pitcher's mound. *The Atlanta Constitution* used the picture in a preseason article, and then the team had posters printed that were given away during the 1989 season with the words, 'Young Guns' plastered across it.

"It just kind of took off," Smith says. "They thought, 'these guys are going to be the core of our pitching staff, so let's promote them.' They were patting our egos a little bit. I think most of us thought it was pretty cool, a little different. They were just trying to promote something with the team since they had fresh new faces and young kids. We were all young – twenty-two or twenty-three. I think they were looking for something to draw an audience and that was it."

"I remember it being pretty neat, but we also knew that we had to deliver to make it worth it," Smoltz admits. "We didn't want to be known as the "Pop Guns," after so much hype."

"It was fun," Greene says. "To me, it was an honor they considered me a part of that. We had five, but then it became seven with Kent Mercker and Steve Avery."

Kent Mercker was the Braves' first round draft choice in 1986, a left-hander out of Dublin High School in Ohio. He was a bit behind the other five pitchers since he missed almost all of the 1987 season with elbow trouble. Mercker would make his Atlanta debut at the end of the 1989 season, but didn't settle onto the staff for good until 1990.

Steve Avery was one of the most perfect amateur pitching

prospects the Braves ever scouted. He was a six-foot-four, 180-pound left-handed pitcher at John F. Kennedy High School in Taylor, Michigan. Avery's dad Ken was a former pitcher in the Tigers' system, and he was also the Athletic Director at his son's high school. Steve was an athlete; he ran cross-country and averaged 22.4 points in his senior season for the basketball team. But it was baseball where he excelled the most.

Tony Stiles, who had also scouted Mercker for the Braves two years earlier, wrote in one of his first scouting reports that Avery was "better at this age than Mercker." That told the team a lot since Mercker himself was advanced for his age. But Avery was mature in a scary way. When you saw him on the mound he didn't look like a teenager and his outstanding breaking ball attracted a lot of scouting attention.

"I remember Jerry Krause, the GM of the Chicago Bulls and architect of their championship teams, who was a baseball scout before that, and is again a baseball scout, told me about being with our scout, Freddy Shaffer, when he first saw Steve Avery," says Stan Kasten. "He described to me how his face lit up. He was trying not to have his face light up but it was obvious that this was a rare gem in terms of mechanics and capabilities."

Then there's the famous story of when Paul Snyder went to scout Avery. He was behind the screen with the radar gun pressed against the fence right behind the catcher. Avery was pitching, throwing about 93 miles an hour with a nasty curveball. He had a no-hitter going with 15 strikeouts and up to the plate comes a small, young batter.

"The umpire called a bad pitch and rang up the batter on a backdoor curve." Snyder remembers. "It was a ball though. The little guy turned around and told the ump, 'Mr. Ump, this guy don't need no help.' All the scouts just cracked up."

Avery finished his high school career with six no-hitters and a 9-0 record in his senior season. His 0.23 ERA was accompanied by 137 strikeouts in 61.1 innings pitched. Atlanta took Avery with the third overall pick in the 1988 draft, and instead of accepting a scholarship to Stanford, he signed with the Braves. He immediately became a phenom, mowing over hitters in the Appalachian League (7-1 with a 1.50 ERA in ten starts, 80 strikeouts in 66 innings pitched) in 1988. Then in 1989, between Durham and Greenville, he combined for a 12-7 record, an ERA of 2.11, and 163 strikeouts in 171 innings pitched. Less than two years out of high school, Avery found himself in AAA in 1990, and he went 5-5 with a 3.50 ERA in 13 starts. The Braves thought about holding him off until the 1991 season, but decided he had proven enough. He had a 2.34 ERA in 49 minor league starts, and on June 13th, at twenty-three years old, Avery made his big league debut in Cincinnati.

"You just knew there was something special about him," says Bruce Dal Canton. "We were in Cincinnati, which is not far from Detroit, and they sent a lot of press down there to see his first start. But just the way he handled himself through all of that. Again, you knew something was different. With this kid there was something special with just the way he handled himself. Here's a young kid with all this media pressure on him and he went out and pitched okay. You could tell he was something special."

Avery started 20 games for Atlanta in 1990, but his numbers looked worse than he pitched. He was 3-11 with a 5.64 ERA. Those struggles typified what the Braves' young pitchers went through in their early years. From Glavine to Avery, all had poor records early on, but it was partly because of the poor teams they played on. They weren't pitching poorly, but with horrible defense and the worst playing field in the game of baseball at Atlanta-Fulton County Stadium, they didn't get much help. Luckily, (though perhaps self-made luck) the risk of harming their confidence was not a problem considering the solid makeup of the group. The Braves believed even with the losing, the pitchers would improve over time – as long as everyone was patient.

"We knew if we gave up two or three runs we were going to have a tough time winning," says Pete Smith. "But then it started to turn around a little bit and we got some more runs. All the top people (in the front office) said, 'Just keep throwing it. Just keep throwing it. It'll get turned around.' It was almost like we were their kids. They were always very supportive. They didn't want to chew us out. They wanted to kind of take us by the hand and let us know that it was going to be all right. I think all of us appreciated that."

"We had two things going against us," Smoltz believes. "One, I wasn't a ground ball pitcher. I was a fly ball pitcher and we played in the friendliest ballpark in America for fly balls. The other guys relied more on ground balls and we had one of the worst infields and hardest places to field a ground ball. It just made it very difficult to feel like you were going to be able to compete at the level you wanted to."

Luckily, there were some solid veterans on the team that helped show the kids the ropes. One such person was Bruce Benedict, a catcher with the Braves since 1978.

"Bruce Benedict took Tommy and me under his wing," Smith says. "When the plane would land he'd say, 'be in the lobby in twenty minutes.' We'd asked, 'Where are we going?' He'd say, 'don't worry about it. Just be here in twenty minutes.' We'd say, 'Okay Mr. Benedict.' He'd take us out to dinner and we'd just talk baseball. He'd say, 'Keep your head up. Keep your chin up.' We were getting our tails kicked in ninety-eight degree heat and he'd come out and make some crack like, 'Hey, did you see that girl right over the dugout? Okay, now let's get in here and finish this inning.' He just kept it calm and cool. He was the biggest help to us our rookie year. He showed us the way."

Smith says other veterans like Jim Acker, Charlie Puleo, Ed Olwine, and Randy St. Claire also spent time with the young pitchers. They helped keep the kids grounded, especially since the team was struggling so much. But the young pitchers were able to overcome the adversity, and the pitching coach who was with them when they debuted says that all goes right back to what the scouts had been looking for and relying on all along: their makeup.

"I think they handled that very well," says Dal Canton. "It didn't faze them one bit. They still knew they had to go out and do their job, which they did. That's a lot of pressure when you think about it because Atlanta was basing all their hope on their young kids. And they did the job. You couldn't ask for any more than what they did."

"It's never fun to lose," says Brian Snitker, Atlanta's bullpen coach when the young pitchers came up. "I think they had a sense of reality about it. They were smart. They could see the big picture. It didn't make it any easier to not do well or not win in the interim. But they knew if they could weather the storm, then things had a chance of getting better."

When the Braves made the decision to rebuild with pitching, they knew it was going to take some time. They made the commitment to be patient with their young arms, which meant sacrificing the present for the future.

Paul Snyder remembers, "Bobby (Cox), bless his heart, he said, 'they're going to take their lumps for a year or so. But we got to live with them.'"

Smoltz actually believes the struggles the group had in the late 1980's and in 1990 were very important to developing the historic run of success seen in Atlanta ever since.

"We did it in a non-stressful environment," Smoltz explains. "We weren't very good so we got to get our brains beat out and learned from it. The guys now, like Horacio Ramirez or anyone else who has come up in the last five or six years have had to win in a winning environment. They didn't have the time or the luxury to get their brains beat in. But they believed in us. That to me is an amazing quality that Bobby Cox has had. He had it as a GM and he's had it as a manager. It's really easy in this day and age to give up on people and ship them off or basically write them off. They didn't."

"I knew the big league team was struggling, but I didn't think they'd actually put us in as quickly as they did," Smith says.

But that's exactly what the Braves did. Two weeks after Glavine made his debut in August of 1987, Smith was called up from Greenville. He got six starts the rest of that season for Atlanta, going 1-2 with a 4.83 ERA. He was only twenty-one years old. Then in 1988, just like Glavine, Smith had a poor record: 7-15. But it didn't get him down in the least.

"I felt like I threw the ball great," Smith says. "I had a 3.60 ERA and I'm thinking, 'Heck, on a team that scored some runs, I could have had a 15-7 year.' Tommy was 7-17, but he didn't pitch poor enough to lead the league in losses. He was throwing the ball real well. We kind of fed off each other. There was a little bit of 'poor us.' But then again we were twenty-two and were in the big leagues."

Part of the reason the group was able to stay grounded and battle through their early-career struggles was their own competitiveness. They all became good friends, and they also competed heavily with one another. Whether it was golf, playing cards, or baseball, 'The Young Guns' developed a competitive edge. They all wanted their teammates to do well, but they wanted themselves to do a little bit better.

"They're a different breed than anybody else," says Snitker. "That mentality, that inner confidence and dedication of what they want to do and passion for what they were doing is just different than anybody else. They enjoy baseball. They loved competing. It wasn't about just getting my innings and getting to Atlanta in two or three years. It was all about winning that day. They were just a different breed."

"You had to check your ego," Smoltz says. "If you had an ego it was going to get bruised because these guys were going to do enough stuff to make it humiliating if you were worried about being the ace of whatever it was. I just think that the personalities allowed us to pitch as long as we did, compete with each other, and push each other."

"The competitiveness was there," Smith says. "If Tommy threw a great game, John wanted to throw a better game. If John threw a great game, Avery wanted to throw a better game. If 'Ave' threw a great game, I wanted to throw a better game. It just filtered down. It was just a mix of good personalities. If we had a day off, we'd all go play golf together. We'd all go to a movie. We had dinner together and hung out together. We became a family."

Smith started 27 games in 1989, but then missed half of the 1990 season with shoulder trouble. The injury continued into 1991, as Smith pitched in only 14 games (10 starts) during the Braves' magical season. After winning 30 games in parts of seven seasons, the Braves traded Smith to the Mets after the 1993 season for outfielder Dave Gallagher. He would then go on to play with the Reds, Padres, and Orioles before retiring after the '98 season.

Greene pitched in only 9 games (6 starts) with the Braves in 1989 and 1990 before the team traded him to Philadelphia in the Dale Murphy deal in August of 1990. He knew he had been passed over by Steve Avery when he was demoted to AAA Richmond in 1990. Two weeks later, the Braves gave Avery the number 33 Greene had worn in Atlanta.

"You almost knew they were going to use one or two of us in a trade to get some quality big leaguers to better their team," Greene says. "Now that I look back at it, they had us stockpiled to where they could do that."

The big right-hander nicknamed "Jethro" for his country personality thrived when he got to the Phillies. He went 13-7 in 1991 including a no-hitter, and then after missing most of 1992 with arm trouble, Greene bounced back in 1993 to go 16-4 in the Phillies' World Series year. Greene's career was cut short because of his numerous arm injuries and he would pitch in only 20 games after that 1993 season before retiring at 30 years old in 1997 with a

38-25 career record.

Neither Greene nor Smith matched the success of Glavine and Smoltz, and they weren't around much as the Braves became the 'Team of the 90's.' But they still cherish the time they spent as members of 'The Young Guns."

"I wouldn't replace those years for anything in the world," Greene says. "I learned a lot from those guys. Those were some of the best times of my life. It was kind of like high school. If somebody said, 'Do you want to go back to high school?' Hell yeah I'd go. The Braves gave me my opportunity. They gave me a chance."

"I just think it's a neat run and it's kind of cool to say, 'Well, we kind of started that,'" Smith says.

"It's something I'll never forget," Smoltz admits. "To think that I'm the last guy standing is kind of hard to believe."

Smoltz is still standing and is back in Atlanta's starting rotation after three unbelievable seasons as the team's closer. With his injuries over the years, Smoltz has overcome some tremendous obstacles, but the losing seasons he was apart of in his early days in an Atlanta uniform were more influential than anything in developing a player that refuses to lose.

"You just wanted to be a fly on a wall in a winning organization to see what the difference was," Smoltz says. "We didn't feel we were that far away. But you get negative and down on things and the next thing you know you start getting used to it and get accustomed to losing and misery loves company. But fortunately we were able to bring in some experience that shed some light on how to win. That was the only thing we lacked- how to win."

And now, a decade and a half later, John Smoltz knows nothing but.

11

A CHIPPER OR A VAN POPPEL?

With their 63-97 record in the 1989 season, the Atlanta Braves got the chance to pick the first player in the 1990 amateur draft. The Detroit Tigers (59-103) actually had a worse record than the Braves, but it was the National League's turn to pick first. With 'The Young Guns' in place as the future of the franchise, the Braves had the opportunity to add to that depth by selecting the best player in the country.

The consensus top player that year was a tall Texan who threw hard. Todd Van Poppel had numbers that teams drool over: six-foot-five, 185 pounds and a fastball in the upper 90's. When tall Texas pitchers throw hard, there are always inevitable comparisons to Nolan Ryan and Roger Clemens, two of the best pitchers to ever walk on a mound. Sure enough, Red Murff, the Braves scout watching Van Poppel, believed he had a chance to be just as good as Ryan.

"It's like he's playing catch with his little sister," Murff said in 1990.

"Red got fairly close to the kid," says Paul Snyder. "He thought we could sign him. But when you've got the number one pick in the country, you're not going to take that chance."

That "chance" was that despite his size and fantastic stuff and despite his 0.97 ERA in his senior season, Van Poppel had made the decision as a senior at Martin High School in Arlington that he wanted to attend the University of Texas, which for a kid from Texas can be as much of a dream as playing in the majors. He had played in Mickey Mantle World Series and the Connie Mack World Series as a kid, and he was set on going to Texas to try and get to the College World Series. He also was interested in pitching in the '92 Summer Olympic Games.

"It was a situation where my total intent, which I told all twenty-six teams at the time, was that I was going to college," Van Poppel says. "University of Texas baseball is a big deal down there. As big as football is, the University of Texas has a great baseball program. I had full intent to go to school."

Van Poppel was telling everybody who would listen that the plan to attend college was not a negotiating ploy. He genuinely wanted to play college baseball. Snyder saw him pitch twice, and there was no doubting Van Poppel's talent. But mainly through discussions with Van Poppel's parents, the Braves had enough doubts on his signability that they started to look at other candidates. They really weren't in a position where they needed a pitcher, considering the tremendous depth they already had in their system. The team had used their top draft pick on a pitcher in six of the previous eight years. So they felt that if Van Poppel wasn't going to be an option, they might look instead to a position player. They pinpointed five such players to scout heavily, including University of Iowa shortstop Tim Costo and four high school players: outfielder Adam Hyzdu and infielders Shane Andrews, Marc Newfield, and Chipper Jones.

Jones grew up in Pierson, Florida, the "Fern Capital of the World." But his parents, Larry and Lynne, sent him to The Bolles School, a private boarding school in Jacksonville, ninety miles north of home. Chipper had always been a great athlete, but when he got to Bolles he became a star.

The six-foot-three, 185-pound shortstop was compared to both Alan Trammell and Cal Ripken, Jr. He hit .488 with 5 home runs, 25 RBI, 10 doubles, 45 runs scored, and 14 stolen bases in his senior season, and even had a 7-3 record and an ERA of 1.00 as a pitcher. Jones was a three-time Class AA All-State Selection and was the High School Player of the Year in Florida in 1990. He had great size, great fielding ability, great instincts, and he was a switch-hitter. Not a bad combination for an infield prospect.

"That was an exciting time," Jones says. "From the beginning of January right up until the draft there were constant scouts, and I was taking personality tests, eye tests, and physicals. I wasn't able to go to a game without seeing fifty guys with stopwatches in the stands. It was really exciting."

Jones was always a kid to keep an eye on, but it was between his sophomore and junior years in high school when he realized he might have a chance to play professional baseball. That was the summer he played American Legion baseball in Deland, Florida.

"I was playing with a lot of guys who were older than I was," says Jones. "I came home from Bolles and just really excelled that year. I think I hit close to .400 switch-hitting. I went and played in the state tournament that year. It was just the acceptance that I received from guys who had been drafted low and ended up not signing that I could play with them, and they respected me as a ballplayer. We went on to win the state championship my junior year at Bolles. Again, even though I wasn't set to be drafted that summer, you could always see scouts in the stands. I couldn't walk to the bus after the game without scouts giving me their card and telling me they'd like to talk with me."

Dean Jongewaard was a Braves crosschecker and scouted Jones four times.

"He was a good player, a very competitive guy," Jongewaard says. "I just saw leadership qualities in him as well as baseball qualities, which was very important to me."

Jongewaard and Tony DeMacio, the area scout for Florida that year, found that even though Jones had a scholarship offer to attend the University of Miami, he wanted to play pro ball. With Van Poppel hedging, the Braves started closely following Jones as his senior year progressed.

"The first time I saw Chipper I really loved the guy," says Rod Gilbreath, the Braves Assistant Scouting Director in 1990. "You could just see big league all over him. Just the way he walked; he had that cockiness about him. It wasn't an arrogant type, but just the confidence that he could play baseball. He caught everything. He had a plus arm. He was a switch-hitter. Paul, Bobby Cox, myself, Hep Cronin (crosschecker), and we even brought (former Blue Jays Manager) Jimy Williams up from Tampa during this time to look at Chipper. After the game, Jimy came up to Bobby and said, 'If you guys can't make up your mind on this damn guy, you don't need me here at all.'"

"I didn't see Chipper play bad," says Snyder. "I saw him twice at Bolles High School while we were in Spring Training. Then Lou Fitzgerald and I had the benefit of the Tigers workout in Lakeland and Chipper with a wooden bat. They didn't know we were there. They were working him out on one of the back fields. He put on a pretty damn good show. Then at one of his games I was there with Hep Cronin and Jimy Williams. We were sitting there and we were going to talk with Larry, his dad. We were going to head over to the first base side so we could have a good look at his swing. Larry said, 'Stay here guys. He's hitting left-handed tonight.' And the first swing he took, the ball ended up out on the street."

The Braves liked Jones tremendously, but Van Poppel was just so good it was hard to lay off him as their top choice. Murff was adamant about Van Poppel's talent and lobbied hard for the pitcher. But the more they were around Van Poppel, the more they became convinced he was serious about his desire to go to college. Whether he just didn't want to play for the last place Braves or not, the team was not in a position to lose their top pick. They were rebuilding and needed all the help they could get.

"We couldn't afford to draft a guy with the top pick and have him not sign," Snyder says. "Not the way we were. We had to get our guy."

As the Braves continued to scout both players, they backed off from talking to them directly. They were pretty sure Jones would sign and that Van Poppel was still a question mark. So they concentrated on taking their time and making sure their evaluations were complete. The more people that scouted Jones, the more they became enamored with his talent and his potential.

"For me, I just thought it was General Lee up there sitting in a gray uniform on a horse leading the troops," says Jongewaard. "He was a leader. You really get happy when you see that. There's not even one in every draft. You can go two or three drafts and never see that kind of ability. Like a Ken Griffey or an Alex Rodriquez, you can go years without seeing that type of player come along."

The only question the Braves had about Jones was his toughness. He was a superstar at a boarding school, a good-looking kid who seemed to have everything going for him in the world. The Braves wondered if he lacked that inner-city toughness that you see in a lot of kids. It only took one incident a week before the draft to ease those fears.

"Paul loved him and wanted me to stick with him," says Cronin, one of Snyder's crosscheckers. "Bobby Cox was kind of conservative on him. Bobby loved the ability but was worried about his makeup, his toughness. He wore a different T-shirt than the rest of the kids. He wore orange and they wore black. He was kind of aloof. The thing that won Bobby over was when some kid on another team yelled at Chipper's pitcher. Chipper decked him. Bobby said, 'He's my guy.' I mean Chipper just decked him. I know Paul called and said, 'Well, the makeup question about whether or not he's tough enough has just been answered.' That fight settled it."

"Yeah, I broke my hand," Jones remembers. "It was an unfortunate incident. It's something that happens between seventeen and eighteen year olds everyday all over America. It's unfortunate that they had to see that. I would rather that they didn't, but if I didn't react the way I did it would have contradicted the way I was raised. I never would have thought that me getting in a fight would have ever enhanced my chances of being taken number one in the draft. I would have thought it would have been strictly on talent."

A few days before the draft, the Braves decided to take a vote. Which player should they take with the first pick? Van Poppel or Jones?

"We had nine reports from nine different people that had seen both of those guys," Snyder says. "The vote was 5-4 Chipper."

But Van Poppel was a pitcher who was being labeled a potential franchise pitcher. The same month as the draft in 1990, the Braves had a pitcher with similar expectations making his debut in the big leagues. Steve Avery had been considered a franchise type pitcher when he had been drafted two years earlier, but Van Poppel was considered an even better prospect. The thought of having Van Poppel join Avery, Tom Glavine, John Smoltz, and Pete Smith in a rotation was enticing. So two days before the draft, Cox decided to go to Texas one more time to see if there was any way Van Poppel would sign if the Braves picked him.

"Bobby had the idea that if he went out (to Texas), they'd meet with him," Snyder says. "We knew we could sign Chipper. We just didn't know if we could sign Van Poppel. So we're in the draft room and he goes out there. We're putting the board together and Bobby goes out and the kid doesn't show, again. Bobby called back and said, 'Just go the way you're going guys.' He just wanted to find out for sure. Something might happen in the next day or two where Chipper wouldn't sign. So we just had to make sure."

"It really wasn't a situation where we did a lot of talking," Van Poppel admits. "They basically came up and asked me if I was interested and I told them the same thing I basically told every team. 'I'm going to school.'"

With that, the Braves knew what they wanted to do. After Cox called with the directive, Snyder asked the area scout to relay the message. "Call the Jones family and tell them that we would like to make Chipper our number one pick," Snyder told DeMacio, who then turned around and called Larry Jones.

"He said they would be proud to be Atlanta's number one pick," DeMacio said.

Chipper Jones didn't really know where he was going to go in the draft. When the Braves didn't speak to him for a while, he wondered if they were still interested.

"They had contacted me all throughout my senior year, even during football season before baseball season even started," Jones says. "But there was a long period of time where I didn't hear from the Braves. I just got the impression from them that they were going to take a step back and watch from afar. I'm pretty sure they were there. I just didn't have direct contact with them. They were the one team I was keeping track of since quite obviously they had the first pick. I knew that the Tigers (picking second) were dead set on Tony Clark. I knew that the Phillies (picking third) were dead set on Mike Lieberthal. I knew that the White Sox (picking fourth) were dead set on Alex Fernandez. The only question marks were who were the Braves going to take and then five (Pirates), and six (Mariners). So having not heard from the Braves for a long period of time, I really expected to go fifth or sixth, to Pittsburgh or Seattle."

A representative from the Mariners told Jones he would not get past their pick at number six, so he felt confident he was going to be a high pick.

In the days leading up to the draft, Jones had his mind on other things. He graduated on Saturday afternoon and then had his prom later that night. The next morning he was headed to the beach with his friends when his plans suddenly changed.

"Prom was a big deal in Jacksonville," Jones says. "We used

to always go out to the beach, rent a condo out there, and fifteen or twenty of us would stay out at the beach for a couple of days. It was a couple of days thing. We had all this planned. I didn't get to experience any of that because as we were driving out to the beach my father called me and said, 'The Atlanta Braves are in Daytona to meet with us tonight to discuss your signability if they were to make you the number one pick in the draft.' Obviously I dropped what I was doing and hauled butt down to Pierson."

Chipper quickly showered and got ready for perhaps the most important meeting of his life. He was surprised the Braves wanted to see him since there hadn't been much recent contact and most still believed they would take Van Poppel. But then word leaked out about Cox's 'meeting' with Van Poppel in Texas, and it became obvious the Braves had made their decision.

Chipper and his parents met DeMacio and Jongewaard in Daytona. They offered to take the entire family out to dinner before they started negotiations. They just wanted to spend a little time with them, do something nice for a player they were going to draft the next day as the top pick in the entire nation. DeMacio told Chipper they could go anywhere he wanted to go, maybe a fancy restaurant to celebrate what was happening.

"Chipper wanted to go to the Olive Garden," DeMacio says. "I said, 'Anywhere you'd like to go, a place you've never been to, someplace real nice.' Chipper said, 'Oh no. We like the Olive Garden.'"

"Basically, I was so nervous it was the first thing that came to mind," Jones explains. "We were pretty limited in our amount of choices for restaurants where I'm from. We were a pretty simple family. We didn't go to real expensive places. You know a nice night out for us was spaghetti and meatballs at the Olive Garden. It was pretty nice, so that's where we went."

After the meal at the Olive Garden, they all went back to the Jones's house to negotiate a deal. It took only two hours. The Braves offered $250,000, while the Jones countered with $300,000. It was Chipper who finally suggested the two sides simply split the difference. So Sunday night Larry Wayne Jones signed his name on a contract with the Atlanta Braves for $275,000, which at that time was the largest bonus ever given to a high school draftee.

"The kid wanted to play," DeMacio says. "That was the difference. He really wanted to play. He wanted to be a big leaguer."

After DeMacio and Jongewaard left the Jones's house with a contract in hand, DeMacio called Snyder, who was back in Atlanta preparing the draft board.

"It's done," DeMacio told his boss.

"What do you mean it's done?" Snyder asked.

"It's done. We'll be back tomorrow morning."

DeMacio and Jongewaard were back in the draft room the next afternoon when the draft started. The rest of baseball may have had some idea who the Braves were going to select with the top pick when the draft started, but they sure didn't know Jones had already signed the contract. Even though it was somewhat anti-climatic, the day was still special at the Jones' house.

"I knew what was going to happen, obviously," says Chipper. "The Braves told me they would call me around 12:00 or 12:15 and let me know and make it official. We were all sitting by the phone. Obviously no one can be picked until I get picked. I figured I would be getting a call pretty quick. Sure enough right on time the call came."

"Chipper we just made you the first pick in the draft," Paul Snyder said. "You're going to be an Atlanta Brave. As soon as your hand gets out of the cast you're going to be playing rookie ball in Bradenton, Florida."

"Yes sir," Jones responded. "Let's get it on."

Being the first overall pick in the draft was important to Jones. It wasn't an ego thing, although there's no doubt his ego had been stroked by being the top pick. It was more about the respect that he had for the responsibility he believed he was going to be required to live up to in that role.

"So much attention is made about the number one pick being the best player in the draft," he says. "I by no means at that particular time thought I was the best player in the draft. It was just a matter of a certain team that had the first pick having a certain need and I filled that need. I was just fortunate that Todd Van Poppel's scenario worked out the way it did and I just kind of moved in right behind him and was able to go number one. But once I went number one, I was dead set on making sure that by the time everybody's careers were over, everyone would know who the best player in the draft was."

As for Van Poppel, after telling every team that scouted him that he was still dead set on going to college, he didn't expect to be drafted at all. Most people believed he just didn't want to play for the Braves, who in 1990 were thought of as a joke in professional baseball. There were rumors he was telling everybody he wouldn't sign so he would scare off every team but his hometown Texas Rangers. But Van Poppel swears the conspiracy theories were not true; he just wanted to play college baseball.

"It wouldn't have mattered who would have drafted me," Van Poppel pleads. "If I had had my mind set on playing pro ball it wouldn't have mattered who it was. My total focus was on going to college. I really expected not to be drafted at all early. I expected somebody down the road may take a chance. I told everybody no and not knowing how things work out I thought, 'Well, I told everybody no and that I'm going to school.' I expected everyone would believe that and move on."

But the Oakland A's didn't believe it. They had seven picks in the first two rounds of the 1990 draft and felt they could take a chance and gamble that Van Poppel might change his mind. So with the fourteenth pick in the first round, the A's took Van Poppel.

"I told every team, 'No, I'm not going to sign,'" Van Poppel states.

But fourteen days after the A's drafted him, Van Poppel allowed Oakland General Manager Sandy Alderson and two of his assistants to meet with him in Texas as a courtesy. At that point the A's were the defending World Champions and were not a financially troubled organization. They were not afraid of the rumors of Van Poppel wanting $500,000 to sign. The Braves weren't either, reportedly offering $900,000 to Van Poppel in their final pitch before the draft. But when Oakland talked with Van Poppel, something clicked.

"They came in and made me realize that my number one goal was to play major league baseball," Van Poppel admits, "and I had to figure out which was my best route to get there. It took a long time for me to really think about, "what is your number one goal?' Even after Oakland came in and talked to me, it didn't even cross my mind for another month before I said, 'hey, maybe I should investigate this a little bit.'"

When he investigated it, Van Poppel also found out the A's were offering a fortune for a draft pick. The deal included a $500,000 signing bonus, along with a $100,000 salary for the rest of the 1990 season, $200,000 for 1991, and $400,000 for 1992. It was a record amount for an amateur draft pick. But even though the money was staggering, and probably would have caused any sane person to re-consider their options, Van Poppel says it was not what changed his mind.

"People think I signed because of the contract I was given and everything," Van Poppel claims, "but realistically I know in my heart that my total goal was to go to school. It's just something that I really felt strongly about. The thing was Oakland came in and made me realize my best route was to sign at that time. You know I didn't even know what I was going to get until after I signed."

Chipper Jones took off for the minor leagues after he got the cast off his broken hand. It didn't take him long to realize there was a lot of pressure being a number one pick.

"Everything you do is under a microscope," Jones says. "I went down to rookie ball and made 18 errors in like 42 or 43 games. I just played terrible. I was having trouble recovering from my broken hand. My bat speed wasn't what it should have been. I just had a miserable rookie-ball season. I heard everything that was said. I read the newspaper clippings. Everybody was dogging me pretty bad, but that just motivated me to go home for that offseason and get strong, get healthy, and be ready for Spring Training because I knew that next year was going to be my breakout year."

And that's exactly what happened. Jones's first full-season in the minor leagues was spent with the Macon Braves of the South Atlantic League. He hit .326 with 15 home runs and drove in 98 runs. Jones also had 56 errors in 136 games. There's no doubt that's a horrible stat, but error totals in the Sally League were often exaggerated by the poor playing fields in that circuit. Brian Snitker was one of Jones's coaches that season, and despite the error total there was little doubt that Chipper was a special player.

"He had all those errors, but I don't remember those errors losing a game for us," Snitker says. "At crunch time, he made the play. I don't think we had a Gold Glove first baseman there to help out either. At that level, somebody that's a little stiff and not good and catching at first can lead to a lot of errors for his other infielders. I never remember thinking that his defense was going to be that big a detriment to him. He's so athletic; you know that if he couldn't play short he'd play somewhere else."

Snitker was amazed to see that even with that high error total,

Jones never seemed to get down on himself. He saw a nineteen-year-old kid that carried himself like he was already in the major leagues, even though he was still four years away. He had that "thing" that every team looks for in a prospect.

He had 'it.'

Jones in Macon in 1991, his first full minor league season.

"Chipper was a big leaguer from the get go," Snitker says. "You knew that guy was going to hit. The numbers he put up that year were unbelievable. He had a great, great year. But he had this inner-confidence along with his God-given ability. Chipper could just hit."

Hit he could– and very well. Jones was in AA by the end of his second full season in the minors and finished 1992 with 13 home runs and 73 RBI. Then in AAA in 1993 he hit 13 home runs and drove in 89, which for a twenty-one-year old is exceptional.

The Braves believed he was ready and brought him up to Atlanta for a cup of coffee at the end of the 1993 season. Jones was still at shortstop until the following spring. Ron Gant, Atlanta's left fielder for the previous four years, had injured his leg in a motorbike accident. The Braves needed a replacement and believed Jones was athletic enough to make the switch to the outfield, particularly since Jeff Blauser was coming off an All-Star season in 1993 and there was no room at shortstop.

Unfortunately, Jones never got his chance to play left field, at least not then. Late in Spring Training before the 1994 season Jones tore the ACL in his knee and missed the entire year's campaign. Then, fully recovered the next spring, Jones made a move again, this time to third base. He finished second in the Rookie of the Year voting in 1995 after hitting .265 with 23 homers and 86 RBI.

And the rest is history.

Jones finished the 2004 season, his tenth in the big leagues, with a career .304 batting average, 1,705 hits, 310 home runs, and

1,039 runs batted in.

"Not a bad draft pick," says Paul Snyder.

As for Van Poppel, the trip to the major leagues was a bit rockier. His phenom status didn't change. At every game he pitched in the minor leagues, it was an event. Fans wanted to see a heralded pitcher who was still being labeled a "can't miss." The A's had him in AA in 1991, his first full season, and in the big leagues for one game at the end of that year. Van Poppel spent much of the 1992 season on the shelf with arm trouble, but finally made it back up to the big leagues after spending half of 1993 in AAA. Van Poppel battled arm and control troubles in the big leagues. He walked 89 batters in 116.2 innings in his first full big league season in 1994 with the A's. Two years later, Van Poppel was claimed off waivers by the Tigers and then became a journeyman pitcher. He would go on to pitch in six more organizations over the next nine years. His career record following the 2004 season: 40 wins and 52 losses in 359 games (98 starts) with a 5.58 ERA.

"Is it the dominating career that everybody expected when I came out of high school?" Van Poppel asks rhetorically. "No. But I'm very satisfied with what I've done and I still feel like I've got a lot more to do and be a little bit better. A lot of guys don't ever get to play but one or two years, and I'm working on nine years now."

While it is certainly an accomplishment for Van Poppel to have stuck in the big leagues for that long, it's also natural to wonder what might have been. If the Braves, a pitching-oriented organization, had gone ahead and drafted and signed him, would he have had a better career? The Braves believe their financial offer was good enough to get him but that he just didn't want to play for a team in rebuilding mode.

"We wanted Todd Van Poppel and he didn't want us," says Jongewaard. "I think if he would have okayed us we would have taken him. He was that impressive. You'd rather take a high school player than a high school pitcher (with the first pick), but he was a very impressive high school pitcher."

"The Braves were very classy," Van Poppel says. "They were very nice to me. It was an honor even to be mentioned in terms of possibly being the first pick. If I had been with a different team who stressed pitching a little bit different or if I had more of a chance to stay in the minor leagues to develop more, then yeah, I may have been more polished. I might have been more ready and wouldn't have had to learn as much as I had to learn at the big league level. But I'll tell you one thing; I've had a tremendous amount of fun. As much as I've been through, I've had fun through it all. A lot of people in the draft that year and years after, they're not playing and I'm still in the big leagues and I've enjoyed it. Could it have been different? Yeah, it could have been. But I wouldn't trade anything in the world right now."

Neither would the Braves or Chipper Jones, who has never spoken to Van Poppel, but will be forever linked with the pitcher. If Van Poppel had gone on to become the superstar pitcher as originally projected, the Braves might have been second-guessed no matter what. But Jones almost feels a debt of gratitude to Van Poppel considering how it's all played out.

"Van Poppel was probably the diamond of our bunch (of draftees)," Jones admits. "Coming out of high school, being able to throw a ball a hundred miles an hour, with a big six-foot-five frame, you would have foreseen him being very successful in the big leagues. But again, (famed agent) Scott Boras strikes again. He basically uttered to Todd what he uttered to me during my senior year when I met him, and that was, 'We'll have you on the steps of the University of Miami with books in hand before you sign a contract for less than X amount.' I didn't really agree with that. Obviously, Todd did. When he told the Braves he wouldn't sign, he made the Braves' decision a lot easier. You know, I guess I have Todd Van Poppel to thank because I was the number one pick in the draft. That's a very high honor, one that I don't take lightly. It's an honor that motivated me throughout my struggles in the minor league system because I didn't want to be a bust. I wanted to go out and work as hard as the fifty-first pick and make it to the big leagues as quickly as possible so I could start gaining my respect at baseball's highest level."

Chipper has gained that respect. But it wasn't because of his high-school RBI's or his on-base-percentage or any other statistic or physical ability- it was because the scouts and the front office were able to take a peek at his makeup and competitive instinct and decide that this was a guy they could win with. If not for that one-punch fight he had late in his senior year, the Braves easily might have gone the other way. Who knows how their history would have differed had Jones not thrown that punch.

"Thank god he punched the guy," says Cronin. "We ought to send the kid who got hit a bonus."

12

THE NEW MAN IN CHARGE

With Chipper Jones in the fold as a huge part of the Braves future, there was more work to do in the summer of 1990 at the highest level of the organization. Bobby Cox had replaced Russ Nixon as Atlanta's manager on June 22nd with the team struggling at 25-40. The expectation had been that the team would at least get closer to the .500 mark, but injuries to first baseman Nick Esasky, starting pitcher Pete Smith, and potential closer Mike Stanton had the team in trouble again. Now it was General Manager Cox's duty to come in and be in charge of the team he had created.

Cox would have both roles as Manager and General Manager for the rest of that season, but Stan Kasten told Cox that would only be temporary. "I've had and continue to have a firm philosophy against coaches or managers being the GM," Kasten says. "So I told him it will be most likely one or the other, but it will not be both."

Kasten planned to take the summer of 1990 to search for a new GM. He knew Cox would probably fall in love with managing again, so it was more logical to look for a front office executive. A month after the managerial change, on July 18th, Kasten was in New York for a meeting of the Player Personnel Development Committee that the late Baseball Commissioner, Bart Giamatti, had asked him to chair. There were a couple of interesting people on that committee, including former Texas Rangers General Partner George W. Bush, and the General Manager of the Kansas City Royals, John Schuerholz.

"It was a morning meeting," Kasten (left) remembers, "and I was going right home. I had practically grown up in Yankees Stadium, but I hadn't been there since I left New York in 1976, which was mind-boggling. There was an afternoon game at Yankee Stadium with the Royals playing the Yankees. John and I were talking and I said, 'You know, I haven't been to Yankee Stadium in years.' He said, 'I've got a car. Why don't you come with me? We'll watch the game.' I said, 'Great idea.'

So Kasten accompanied Schuerholz to Yankee Stadium. The two sat behind the third base dugout and watched the game, but also talked at length about what Kasten was doing.

"He knew our plan," Kasten says. "He said he had been telling people in his own organization that of all the cities in the country that were sleeping giants, Atlanta certainly was one. He was talking from an outsider's perspective. He's not even in my league, but he talked about how many pieces of that plan had been put in place and how impressed he was. So I asked him to think about names for a potential GM, and he said he would do that for me."

One of Kasten's other tasks was to try and fix the horrible field at Atlanta-Fulton County Stadium. It was the worst in baseball and did nothing to help the young pitchers that had been groomed to lead the team into the future. The problem with the field gave Kasten another reason to talk with Schuerholz, who employed the best groundskeeper in the game in George Toma. But whenever the two would talk about the problems with the Braves' field, they would also talk about the situation with the team.

"Along the way he told me two things," Kasten remembers. "One was all the pieces (player-wise) that we had been putting in place were impressive. And the other thing he told me privately was his own personal belief that he always thought the best manager in baseball was sitting in the front office in Atlanta. He just thought that (bringing Cox back in as Manager) was a really strong move and that we were very, very close."

Kasten and Schuerholz continued to talk sporadically, and then in the first week of September, Kasten noticed that the tone of Schuerholz's questions changed.

"How's it going with your search?" Schuerholz called and asked Kasten, who thought it was an odd line of questioning.

Kasten was almost scared to ask the next question, wondering if it was realistic.

"John, is this something you're thinking about?" he asked.

"I don't know," Schuerholz replied. "Maybe."

That was all Stan Kasten needed to hear. He admits he had thought about Schuerholz coming to Atlanta, but he really didn't think it was realistic. Schuerholz had been with the Royals since their inception in 1969 and had been their General Manager for nine years. He had been successful, leading the Royals to the World Series title in 1985. So to think a successful GM would leave a place where he had been for almost twenty-three years and take over a team that was, at the time, the worst in the game, was beyond a pipedream.

Kasten was talking with others as well. Jack McKeon was ending his tenure as GM of the San Diego Padres. Known as "Trader Jack" for his frequent deals, McKeon had an interest in the Atlanta job. Kasten also spoke with Larry Himes, just fired as the General Manager of the Chicago White Sox, Sandy Johnson, the Assistant GM of the Texas Rangers, and even with Pat Gillick, the GM in Toronto, who had been offered the Braves GM job after the death of Bill Lucas in 1979. Former Pirates' GM Syd Thrift, Seattle Scouting and Player Development Director Roger Jongewaard, and even Braves broadcaster Don Sutton reportedly applied for the job. Even during his discussions with Schuerholz Kasten made sure to continue his talks with other candidates just in case his number one choice looked inside his heart and remained in Kansas City.

No one knew Kasten was talking with Schuerholz. He kept it very quiet. "I was fixated on not letting it out," Kasten admits. "I didn't want the circus." He also knew that if the Kansas City media found out that Schuerholz was thinking about leaving, the attention might make it more difficult for him to leave.

The day after the 1990 season ended, Kasten knew he needed to find out if Schuerholz was interested in becoming the Braves' new GM. So he made the call.

"Okay John, the season is over," Kasten said to Schuerholz. "Will you come?"

"Let me talk with you tomorrow," Schuerholz responded.

Kasten believed he had his man, until the next morning, Friday, October 5th, when Schuerholz called him back.

"Stan, I just can't do it," Schuerholz said. "I can't leave. I can't do it."

Kasten was crushed. He thought he had his perfect candidate. That night he visited Manager Bobby Cox in the hospital, who was having surgery on both knees.

"I had a bad day," Kasten told Cox. "You don't know how close we came to getting John Schuerholz."

"Get out of here," Cox responded, unaware that Kasten had even talked with Schuerholz about the job. "Oh Stan, that would have been great."

"We'll be okay," Kasten replied. "But I'm really down. I think if we had gotten him that would have been pretty special."

Meanwhile John Schuerholz was also struggling with his decision. His son Jonathan, now an infielder in the Braves' farm system, remembers the time when his dad was trying to make his decision.

"When he told me he was up for the job, I think I cried like a baby," Jonathan Schuerholz admits. "I was ten years old. He brought up the idea to the family so we could think about it. We talked about it and laid it all out at the dinner table one night. I was upset about it. I came downstairs and finally said, 'Okay, let's vote on it. Let's vote.' It came to a vote and it was 4-0 to go to Atlanta."

While Schuerholz was second-guessing his choice, Kasten was still bummed out. He decided to take the weekend off before going in on Monday and telling Turner Sports Executive Terry McGuirk whom he was going to hire from the remaining candidates. Early Sunday morning he had gone to work-out, but when he got home he received some good news from his wife.

"Stan, John Schuerholz just called," Helen Kasten told her husband.

"He did?" Stan replied, wondering if Schuerholz had a change of heart. "What did he say?"

"We just talked for a while," Helen said. "He asked if you had filled the job yet. I told him I didn't think so and that you had been down all weekend. I told him how disappointed you were that he wasn't coming. So he said, 'would you have him call me?'"

Kasten turned and immediately called Schuerholz.

"You know Stan, I made a mistake," Schuerholz said.

"Yes John, I do know you made a mistake," Kasten said.

"If it's still open, I'd like to do it," Schuerholz admitted.

"If you want it, it's yours," Kasten replied.

When Kasten went into the office on Monday, he told McGuirk and Braves Chairman of the Board Bill Bartholomay that he knew he had the perfect choice.

"I told them, 'I feel 100% sure that this is what I should do,'" Kasten remembers. "Terry said, 'Stan, nothing is ever 100%.' I said, 'Terry, I know that this is 100%.' I remember feeling so strongly about that for what we needed: the credibility boost that John would give us, the experience boost, the atmosphere boost, and for the technical knowledge. This was the perfect solution for what we needed. We had put a terrific minor league operation together. I really felt we had a terrific manager on the field, and I just felt we needed the final piece of the puzzle – a General Manager to make all the pieces work. There are very few times in your life you can say that you were 100% sure about something, but that's how I felt about hiring John."

Schuerholz's departure from Kansas City, a stable franchise with (at that time) one owner in its history, was a shock to most everyone. But a closer look may explain his reasons for leaving.

After winning the World Series in 1985, the Royals had become a very mediocre team, averaging 82 wins from 1986 through 1990. It was a little easier for mid-market teams like the Royals to compete in the 80's, but that was soon to change, as the money in baseball became more of a factor in fielding competitive teams.

"The beginnings of the economic turmoil of the 90's were starting and were starting to manifest," Kasten says. "It was clear that Kansas City was going to be behind whatever economic wave was coming. John saw that. John would have worked there for the rest of his life or make one more move. Do you do this for the rest of your life or do you examine what's out there and take your last big shot? That's why he entertained it. He turned it down and decided to stay in Kansas City, but then it was just eating him up."

Herk Robinson had worked with Schuerholz for twenty-one years before replacing him as the Royals General Manager in October of 1990. He believes there was a little more personal ambition involved in Schuerholz making the move to Atlanta.

"I think some people maybe still looked at John with the same eyes they did when he was twenty-seven-years old," Robinson says. "But John had grown and matured. When he went into a new organization, he came in with a title under his belt, to a club that had not had a great deal of success. He immediately started out in a position of being held in high esteem there that maybe he wasn't in Kansas City. I don't think John was getting the credit he deserved when he was here."

Robinson, still close to Schuerholz today, saw his friend struggle with the decision to leave the Royals. He calls Schuerholz "a loyal soldier." But he thinks Schuerholz almost had to prove to himself that he could take a losing team and make it a winner.

"I think John was at the point where he needed to conduct his own orchestra," Robinson says. "He had been there so long. When you grow up in an organization, I don't think you're ever recognized as much as you should be for your true leadership ability within that organization as when you go somewhere else and you do well. It's almost like starting your own company. He was ready. It gave him a chance to show people that he singularly was in charge and capable of doing this, where in Kansas City there may have been a level of cloudiness in the water."

Robinson had to take over a franchise that quickly fell into disarray. Ewing Kauffman, the only owner in Royals' history, was ill and not expected to live long. He had already sold 49% of the team to Avron Fogelman, who was supposed to buy the rest of the team before Kauffman died. But then Kauffman had to buy Fogelman out, and the franchise would remain in turmoil even after Kauffman died in 1993.

"There was uncertainty here," Robinson says. "After a while we had a Board of Directors running the club, so looking back I think John certainly did the right thing."

Schuerholz also saw a Braves team that had a solid nucleus. Tom Glavine, John Smoltz, Pete Smith, Kent Mercker, and Steve Avery were five pitchers twenty-five-years old or younger with great talent. Plus there were also young position players like Ron Gant,

David Justice, Jeff Blauser, and Mark Lemke.

"He thought we needed to shore up our defense and get some leadership in here," Kasten says.

Schuerholz's first offseason with the Braves was indicative of the type of players he'd bring in over the next fourteen winters. His goal was to add quality players who were also quality people. He wanted to bring winners to the Atlanta Braves. The first signee was third baseman Terry Pendleton, a member of two World Series teams with the Cardinals in 1985 and 1987.

"Bobby and I had talked about Terry Pendleton, but we didn't know Terry Pendleton would be a batting champion and win an MVP," Kasten says. "We had hired Chuck Lamar and gotten a huge testimonial from him about Sid Bream and about Rafael Belliard. John was sure about those moves. Sometimes things have to work out."

Credit is certainly due Kasten for knowing there had to be a long-term plan, and to Cox and Snyder for finding young talent and creating a nucleus that most teams envied, but Schuerholz brought an extra element.

"He taught us how to win," Snyder admits.

Schuerholz looks like a corporate executive, sometimes resplendent in suspenders. Washington Nationals GM Jim Bowden even describes Schuerholz as "presidential." The Braves had many pieces in place in 1990, but he was the final piece of the puzzle. In many ways, his philosophies mirrored those of Cox and Snyder, particularly in stressing pitching, defense, and most importantly, developing and nurturing your own talent.

Dean Taylor worked for Schuerholz with the Royals and in 1991 joined him as his Assistant General Manager in Atlanta.

"He certainly has a plan in place," Taylor says. "I think he's a master at taking the cards that are dealt him – whether it's Kansas City or Atlanta in a higher payroll situation, or now with Atlanta in a little bit of a lower payroll situation – and crafting a roster. I think that John has been very successful because he surrounds himself with good people. His philosophy has always been, and I've heard him make this comment several times, 'The General Manager is the conductor of the orchestra. He's not playing every instrument in the band. He's merely the conductor. The people in the band are the most important pieces of the puzzle – the scouts, the player development people that are out there doing all the work.'"

"One of his great strengths is hiring the right people, putting the proper evaluation system in place, which is very important, so they are out there doing the proper type of player analysis and player evaluation," Taylor continues. "Talking the same language. That's step two. And step three is really listening to those people and relying on their judgments. If you have the right people, have the right evaluation system in place, and you listen to your people, all three of those things click, you're going to make a lot of good decisions."

Among the other "right people" that Schuerholz surrounded himself with in Atlanta was Bill Lajoie, the General Manager of the Detroit Tigers from 1983-90. He helped build the Tigers team that won the World Series in 1984. Lajoie says that even though Schuerholz is very professional, he's also very personal.

"I found John to be very conscience of his employees," says Lajoie, now a Special Assistant in Boston. "He takes great interest in the people that work with him, just like it's a family. There is no problem too big or too small to approach him about. It can be of a personal nature or anything. I found him to be as honest and truthful as anyone I've met in baseball."

"The people that work for him are important to him," says Al Kubski, a longtime scout with the Royals who followed Schuerholz to Atlanta in 1996. "John handles people well. We would have meetings in Kansas City and he'd tell us, 'Look, you guys are the most important part of the organization. Without you guys getting all the players, we'd be in trouble.'"

Guy Hansen was a Royals' draft pick in 1969. He spent four seasons in their minor league system as a pitcher before becoming a college pitching coach. In 1979, Hansen had moved on to become a scout for the Major League Scouting Bureau. He was attending the Scouting Bureau's convention in Scottsdale, when he ran into Schuerholz. The two knew each other, but not well. Schuerholz was a featured speaker at the convention and made a huge impression on Hansen.

"He talked about a prospect being like a piece of rock clay," Hansen remembers. "The scout uses his imagination and his instincts to see how this piece of quality clay could be molded by a sculptor into being a fine work of art. He said, 'That's your job here in the Scouting Bureau.' He really pumped everybody up that their job was extremely important, and at that time it was. He was very inspiring.

He always has been."

Hansen had played college baseball at UCLA in the late 60's. He was in a fraternity that was located right next to Pauly Pavilion. Occasionally, Hansen would sneak into the gym and listen to legendary basketball coach John Wooden.

"When I heard John (Schuerholz) talk, it just brought back memories of Wooden," Hansen says. "He was just very inspiring about how important we were to baseball, how important our jobs were. It was just a talk that got everybody pumped up. Everybody felt better. At the time the scouts that were with individual clubs looked upon the Scouting Bureau kind of negatively. They were almost thought of a little bit as scabs because guys were losing jobs and here were these people coming in. So he made us feel good about our jobs. He talked about how important qualifying players is, how important it is to get in and meet the family, and understanding the makeup of the player."

Hansen approached Schuerholz after hearing the inspiring speech. He told Schuerholz he'd love to get back with the Royals as a scout. A year later, Schuerholz hired Hansen as an area scout in California. With the exception of two years in the mid-80's, Hansen worked with the Royals, first as a scout and then as a pitching coach. He stayed with the Royals until 1998, when he joined Schuerholz with the Braves.

"He's all about hiring people that have talent and letting them go about their business," says Hansen, who left the Braves after the 2004 season to return to the Royals as their major league pitching coach. "John is an expert evaluator of people and can break it down. He knows which scouts have high evaluations, put high numbers on guys, and which ones are conservative. He reads through all that stuff. He takes it upon himself to know the scouts and know his staff. He wants people to be themselves."

Schuerholz's respect for others in the organization is most evident in his relationship with Cox, whom he replaced as GM. From the day Schuerholz arrived, he applauded Cox's ability as a manager. As the years progressed and the winning continued, their relationship became stronger. In today's environment of GM's and Managers battling for power, authority, and praise, the relationship has been founded on mutual admiration, and that extends to the man who created the combination.

"The three of us all saw things the same," Kasten says. "The more we talked the more comfortable we became with each other so that's why it's worked as well as it has. The three of us had a lot of respect for the job, not just the people. We loved each other as people, but we understood what our jobs were and we afforded each other lots of latitude in doing them. That was a very useful combination. It didn't mean we didn't disagree. We disagreed everyday. But there was never a clash. It was never personal. It was a great relationship."

Other executives around the league envy the relationship between Schuerholz and Cox.

"They are on the same page," says Dan Evans, the Dodgers GM in 2002 and 2003 and now Special Assistant to the Executive VP for Player Personel in Seattle. "I think the most important thing is that you never hear any whispers out of the Atlanta organization that, 'Boy, I wish we could have done this' or 'Boy, I wish we could have done that.' You don't hear that. I think you don't hear that because there is a trust and there is a respect for the scouts, and a respect for the way things are going to be done. Quite frankly, when I became a General Manager and looked at other organizations I looked at the Braves as one of the model organizations simply because what they have done for an elongated period is stick to a game plan. The game plan has worked. It's been very successful. I think it's successful because it's not flawed in its theory. It just makes too much sense to do it the way they've been doing it."

Pat Gillick is also now a Special Consultant to the Exectuve VP and GM in Seattle after leading three teams as the GM. "I think John has confidence in his manager and he has confidence in himself. They're headed in the right direction and they won't be swayed from that direction. But I think they're also of the mindset that, 'hey, change in our circumstances, change in economics, and we might have to change part of our game plan, but our overall philosophy is going to remain pretty much the same.'"

Since the Braves have been winners for the last fourteen seasons, Schuerholz has been able to keep his philosophy in place, so that stability, that game plan, has remained the same. Herk Robinson found out after Schuerholz left the Royals that changing a game plan can be catastrophic to a baseball organization.

"Changing directions is the worst thing you can do," Robinson says. "We did it here in the 90's when I was General Manager. There were reasons for it, mainly the situation with ownership. We were more in a reactionary mode than really trying to build something.

We were just trying to keep the ship on course. We wanted to keep the club competitive enough to try to sell it. We couldn't get the payroll too high because the team (dollar) losses would be too big. We couldn't have the payroll too low because the team losses would be too high. So it was a very delicate balance. Every time you change, you're not only starting from scratch, but I think you're starting below scratch. You go back below zero."

The Royals have finished over .500 only three times in the fourteen years since Schuerholz left. Yes, the team is a small market club, but Robinson says the biggest problem was the continual switch in organizational philosophy during his tenure as General Manager.

"If you've got two people in a boat rowing the same way, they're going to row right by ten people where five are going one direction and five are going the other direction," Robinson says. "There's so much panic in baseball. There's so much pressure to win. Everybody just goes crazy and so many of them self-destruct. We had a lot of changes. It was very unstable and unsettled. Even the fans wondered, 'What's going to happen tomorrow?'"

In recent history Braves fans have never had to ask that question. While not necessarily predictable, Schuerholz is as dependable as anything in baseball. Every offseason fans have depended on him to create a winning roster, and he's delivered. And considering the people he learned the game from, it should really be no surprise.

Kasten and Schuerholz enjoying the fruit of their labors.

13
THE ROYAL INFLUENCE

Before the name "Schuerholz" was widely known in baseball circles, it was a name synonymous with high school sports in the city of Baltimore. John Schuerholz's father, also John, is still thought of as one of the best basketball players in the history of Maryland athletics. He had massive 'Popeye' forearms and unbelievable athleticism.

"He was like Bob Cousy," says Al Kubski, comparing the older Schuerholz to the Basketball Hall of Fame point guard. "He could really play. I played basketball with him and against him in baseball. He was a shortstop. The big organizations, the steel corporations, had baseball teams. We worked the steel mills, and then we always got off and we'd play basketball three or four times a week. The whole family was athletic."

The younger John Schuerholz was more of a soccer player, a sport big in the Baltimore area. He also played baseball. When he was in high school he made the baseball All-City team, and he'd go on to play both sports at Towson University, just north of Baltimore. In 1962, Schuerholz was Towson's Athlete of the Year after making the All-Conference team in baseball.

After graduating, Schuerholz became a junior high school

teacher. He was a substitute, or utility teacher, with English composition, spelling, geography, and current events typically on his schedule. But sports would remain a part of John's life.

He had watched his dad play since he could remember, and then as a kid he would play whatever sport was in season. Schuerholz knew his days as an athlete were over, so at twenty-six he decided he would take a stab at working in a baseball front office.

"I had a free period and typed a letter to the Orioles' owner, Jerry Hoffberger," Schuerholz told ESPN several years ago. "He passed it along to Frank Cashen, who passed it along to Harry Dalton, who passed it along to Lou Gorman in the Farm Department. I became his assistant."

For a man who would later be known as a great decision-maker, this was certainly one of his greatest.

"I was so impressed with him," says Lou Gorman. "I was impressed with his enthusiasm, his feeling for the game, his personality, and his desire to get into the game."

"He was a young fellow outside of baseball who really wanted to get into it," Harry Dalton remembers. "You knew he was bright after talking with him for a couple of minutes. You could see how deep his desire was to get into our game. Since Gorman got in like that and I got in like that, we were sort of sympathetic to his position."

Like Schuerholz, neither Dalton nor Gorman were major leaguers who moved upstairs to run a team. Instead, they both had stints in the military and some time working in minor league baseball.

In 1966, Harry Dalton was in his first year as the Orioles General Manager, but thirteen years earlier he was in the same shoes Schuerholz, sitting in an office wanting a job.

Dalton had at least worked in baseball, spending his winter and summer breaks from Amherst College in the late 1940's working for a Cubs farm team in Springfield, Massachusetts. After graduating in 1950, Dalton spent thirty-seven months as a combat press officer in Japan and Korea for the Air Force, earning a bronze star.

Dalton had set his sights on journalism as a career. He had done a little writing for the *Springfield* (MA) *Daily News* when he was in high school and college. But when he returned from Korea in 1953, he went back to Maryland to live with his parents. Then he read an advertisement in the newspaper. The new major league franchise in the area, the Baltimore Orioles, was looking for help. He first interviewed with Herb Armstrong, a longtime baseball man who was the business manager. But Armstrong knew Dalton wanted to be in baseball operations, so he called in Jim McLaughlin, the Farm and Scouting Director.

"I told him I wanted to get into any level," Dalton says. "Two days before Christmas (in 1953) they offered me the job. McLaughlin hired me as Assistant Farm Director. It was wonderful."

Dalton describes McLaughlin as a "dynamo." He had been with the Browns in St. Louis and was the only front office executive to accompany the franchise when it moved to Baltimore to start the 1954 season. The Browns had been a penny-pinching franchise in St. Louis, but a year after the Orioles started play in Baltimore, McLaughlin got a new boss, former White Sox Manager Paul Richards, who would later run the Braves in the late 60's and early 70's.

Richards quickly changed the financial structure of the Orioles, making them just as aggressive with amateur prospects as the Yankees and Red Sox, who even back then had more money than other teams.

"Paul was very quiet," Dalton says. "He was a little bit mysterious in the things he talked about. Paul was pretty much a loner. He had a few close associates. Luman Harris (who would later surface as Richards' manager in Atlanta) was his right-hand man. Paul would have a conversation with only two or three scouts."

Richards had an unorthodox style of running an organization. He was a loose cannon, often signing players to exorbitant bonuses. He often clashed with McLaughlin, and even ignored some of McLaughlin's scouts. But Dalton was able to see several interesting aspects of Richards' style. Since he was both the Orioles GM and field Manager, Richards wanted the entire farm system to be run like the major league team, so he brought minor league managers to major league camp to learn his way, the Orioles' way. He also stressed pitching and defense, and that became a staple of every Baltimore team.

Even though Richards and McLaughlin didn't get along, the Orioles still built a tremendous organization. McLaughlin was an innovator himself, developing the first crosschecker scout, someone to come in after the area scout to offer a second opinion on a player.

"He believed in double-checking on a player," Dalton says. "He would get a territorial man to go see him and have a second look. Many clubs didn't do that then. Many clubs didn't have an expanded scouting staff."

And Dalton was also able to learn from McLaughlin the most important part of determining a player's potential.

"To dig into the mind of a ballplayer," says Dalton. "He stressed the makeup. He would bring the crosscheckers in. He wanted to get into the families."

McLaughlin created a system used by all the Orioles scouts. It was called "the complete circle." It tried to develop "the whole ballplayer." Dalton learned how players had to be judged on more than just on-field ability, and McLaughlin was a pioneer in stressing the makeup of a ballplayer.

The system McLaughlin created, and Dalton helped implement, would lead to a tremendous run of talent in the late 50's and early 60's. Five years after signing a third baseman named Brooks Robinson out of Arkansas, the Orioles' scouts signed first baseman Boog Powell and pitcher Dean Chance in 1959; then pitcher Dave McNally in 1960; pitchers Darold Knowles and Eddie Watt along with catcher Andy Etchebarren in 1961; infielders Davey Johnson and Mark Belanger in 1962; and pitcher Jim Palmer in 1963.

Along the way McLaughlin also assembled a fantastic scouting staff, mainly responsible for signing the great prospects. Jim Russo and Freddie Hofmann were two of the best. Dalton saw how McLaughlin listened to his scouts and trusted their opinion.

"Trusting the scouts was perfectly correct," Dalton says. "Jim had a chance to spread it out. I helped him. Freddie Hofmann helped him. We were all eager-beavers. We loved it. We absolutely loved it."

Lee MacPhail, an Assistant GM with the Yankees, replaced Richards as Orioles GM after the 1958 season. Richards stayed on as Baltimore's manager, but two years later the feud between Richards and McLaughlin reached a boiling point. MacPhail fired McLaughlin and made Dalton the new Farm Director, and then Richards left a year later in 1961 to run the new franchise in Houston.

But Dalton had already learned much of what would create his own philosophy. Now he just needed to form his own inner-circle to get the Orioles to the next level.

Lou Gorman was a Navy man. He spent nine years on active duty and retired as a Navy Captain in the Reserves. He had played in the minors a bit after high school, but was released and went into the service. When he got out, he decided baseball would be his profession.

"I went to the baseball convention and hustled myself a job," Gorman says.

In 1961, the Giants hired Gorman to run their farm team in Lakeland, Florida. The next year he moved to Kinston, North Carolina, to run a farm team for the Pirates. In the fall of 1963, he heard the Orioles were interviewing for assistants.

"I drove up from Kinston to Baltimore and was interviewed by Dalton and MacPhail," Gorman says. "They hired me on the spot."

Gorman became Dalton's chief assistant in Scouting and Player Development. He knew baseball, but since Dalton had been in a major league front office for ten years, Gorman thought it prudent to watch and learn. During his observations he found a man who trusted the people around him, something Dalton had learned from his years working as an assistant to McLaughlin.

"Harry was a terrific executive," Gorman says. "He had a tremendous talent for surrounding himself with very qualified, capable people and being able to distill their knowledge and use it. Harry was a guy that had a great feel for people. I wouldn't say that he was a great judge of talent in the sense of players, but he was a great judge of talent in the sense of people. He was able to take those people, surround them with good people, and then make his sound decisions. That rubbed off on me a lot."

What also rubbed off on Gorman were Dalton's theories of scouting.

"I had a feel for the game and thought I could judge talent," he says. "But it's something you have to learn and work at. Experience is the only good teacher at it." Gorman soon learned about the complete circle, the philosophy Dalton kept around even after McLaughlin left the Orioles.

"We took a round circle and cut it in the middle," Gorman says. "We listed above the things that can be seen with the eye. For example, for a pitcher we looked at arm strength, fastball, curve ball, slider, other pitch, and control. Then for an infielder or outfielder we looked at arm strength, use of arm, speed, quickness, agility, hands, fielding, range, hitting, and power. And for a catcher, arm strength, use of arm, receiving, hands, hitting, power, and speed. Then for all players we look at stamina, speed, quickness, agility, hands, hustle, reflexes, size, coordination, poise, instinct, base running, and eyesight."

"Then below were the things that couldn't be seen with the eye: attitude, desire, drive, willingness, hunger, ambition, aggressiveness, mental intelligence, baseball sense, teachability, coachability, knowledge of the game, personality, improvement, consistency, maturity, adjustment, stability, temperament, disposition, background, family, habits, is he a winner, does he have stomach, does he have heart, does he have pride, is he a competitor, and does he have confidence."

Gorman learned first-hand how the lower half of the circle could define a great ballplayer. One day he was in the Orioles' dugout watching third baseman Brooks Robinson take infield practice. Robinson was in the early years of his string of sixteen consecutive Gold Glove awards. He was one of the best fielders in the history of the game, but on this day he was taking ground ball after ground ball. As Gorman watched Robinson closely, he noticed he didn't have a great arm or the great agility that he assumed a great fielder would have.

"So I was curious and I went back into the office and looked through the files to find the scouting report on him," Gorman admits. "The one thing that stood out in the reports was that nobody graded him exceptional on his physical skills, but they all graded him very high on makeup, and pride, and heart, and confidence, ambition, desire, and competitiveness. Here's a guy who made himself a great player. He never had great speed. He never had a great arm. He made himself a great hitter. Every play at first base was bang-bang, but he got rid of the ball so quick and had great first-step quickness. He was great at releasing the ball, but not great arm strength. He had that great makeup and intensity to make himself a Hall of Fame player."

Lou Gorman learned about the makeup of a ballplayer. Jim McLaughlin taught it to Harry Dalton, who in turn taught Gorman. A few years after coming on as Dalton's assistant, Gorman would have the chance to impart his knowledge on another young, eager front office wannabe.

1966 was a big year in the history of the Baltimore Orioles. Joseph Iglehart, who had a sizable amount of CBS stock, had owned the team. When CBS bought the Yankees before the 1965 season, Iglehart had to either sell his CBS stock or sell the Orioles. He wound up selling the Orioles to Jerry Hoffberger, a limited partner in the Orioles who also owned the National Brewing Company. Several years earlier, Hoffberger had met Frank Cashen, a newspaper writer and columnist for the *Baltimore News-American*. Hoffberger hired Cashen to run his racetrack in upstate New York and then brought him into the National Brewery as his Executive Assistant. When Hoffberger bought the Orioles, he inserted Cashen as the Executive Vice President. Cashen in turn promoted Dalton to the position of Director of Baseball Operations (GM) and Gorman was promoted to Farm and Scouting Director.

"Frank Cashen is a wonderful, outstanding person," Gorman says. "He was the kind of guy who would get you whatever you needed to get the job done and have total confidence in your ability to do the job and never question it. He'd give you the authority, give you the responsibility, and the go ahead to do it."

The first year the Hoffberger, Cashen, Dalton, and Gorman team was in charge of the Orioles, the team won its first American League pennant and then went on to sweep the Los Angeles Dodgers in the 1966 World Series. The players that had been brought into the organization by McLaughlin and Dalton's great scouts, players like Robinson, Powell, Johnson, Etchebarren, Palmer, and McNally, were some of the leaders of the team, along with Frank Robinson, who had been acquired by Dalton in a deal from Cincinnati. Dalton also had brought back McLaughlin in 1966 to be one of his chief scouts, not to mention hiring a young kid who had, in many ways, mirrored the way he and Gorman got into the game.

Even though he was low on the totem pole and making a mere $6,500, John Schuerholz was in major league baseball. He became Gorman's assistant. Some might call him an "office boy" or even a "gopher," but while his duties were not terribly important early on, Schuerholz was able to watch several people form somewhat of a dynasty.

The Orioles would go on to win four American League

Pennants and two World Series titles within a six-year period, and it all started in 1966, Schuerholz's first year with the team.

"Lou and I bonded quickly after he came with us," Dalton says. "Then John came in and we liked him. He was one of us, so to speak. I thought we were a good team. We patted each other on the back. We were enjoying ourselves tremendously. We had a lot of fun in Baltimore. I think the success they've had over the years comes from the roots we planted long ago about getting close to the players, and having a good working relationship with your field people as well as your front office people. If we did all that and did all our homework, we should be prepared to make the right decisions. We had the dedication."

Dalton also hired someone else in 1966 that would later become a major persona in John Schuerholz's life. Al Kubski was a longtime minor league manager in the Pirates and Cardinals organizations, along with some years in the Independent Leagues. He had managed all over the country, but felt a scouting job would keep him closer to home and his young family.

"I had met Dalton at an All-Star game at Bloomfield in the rookie league," Kubski remembers. "Later that year the Winter Meetings were in San Diego and I lived about 100 miles from there. I had heard that a scout they had in the area, Jim Wilson, had quit. So I called Dalton and said, 'I'm looking for a scouting job. I'm giving up managing. I know Jim Wilson's leaving, so how about me applying for that job?'

"He said, 'Well that sounds good. I'm coming up to L.A. in two days. Why don't you meet me for breakfast at the Biltmore Hotel?' I said, 'Shit yeah, I'll be there.'"

When Kubski showed up for the breakfast meeting, Dalton had one of his top scouts, Jim Russo, with him. Dalton asked Kubski for a little background info and then decided to test his baseball intellect.

"Who do you like on that Bluefield club?" Dalton asked Kubski.

"Your shortstop is going to play in the big leagues," Kubski shot back.

The shortstop was a tall skinny guy who could run, throw, and field. The big question was his bat, but there was no doubt the kid could catch the ball.

"Well, you picked the right one," Dalton responded. "That

means you know talent."

The player was Mark Belanger, an eight-time Gold Glove shortstop who would spend all but one of his eighteen years in the big leagues with the Orioles.

In his first year as a scout for the Orioles, Kubski went to Baltimore, his hometown. He saw the name "Schuerholz" in the office and thought he recognized the name. He decided to approach the new kid on the block.

"Is your dad's name John Schuerholz?" Kubski asked.

"Yeah," said the younger Schuerholz.

Kubski asked what he was doing in the office and if he had played sports.

"I played soccer and baseball," Schuerholz said, who then went on to tell Kubski he had played at Towson.

Kubski saw that as an opportunity to give the young executive a hard time.

"Hey, I know that Towson club," Kubski said. "They couldn't beat a high school team in California. They didn't have any ability on that club."

Kubski knew he had the younger Schuerholz flustered.

"See my little finger," Kubski said as he continued toying with Schuerholz. "Your old man's got more athletic ability in this little finger than you've got in your whole body."

Kubski laughs as he remembers his first encounter with a young John Schuerholz. Fact is he respected the hell out of Schuerholz's dad, and he was glad the young man was getting a chance with the Orioles. Kubski would become one of the Orioles and Dalton's better scouts. He would scout and sign Enos Cabell and Bobby Grich, to name two. In the late 70's, Kubski would join Schuerholz in Kansas City as one of his chief scouts. He became a very trusted advisor to the kid he had chided way back in 1966.

"I've only worked for two guys," Kubski says. "Harry Dalton and Johnnie Schuerholz. I wouldn't work for George Steinbrenner if you gave me a million dollars."

For two seasons Schuerholz watched as Cashen allowed Dalton to run the team. He watched Dalton and Gorman as they went after a certain type of player, focusing on makeup and believing in the subjectivity of the scouts. He was there as the Orioles won with pitching and defense.

"We grew up basically in the Orioles' tradition," Gorman

says. "Then when we went to Kansas City we established our own traditions."

Gorman left the Orioles in 1968 and was hired as the Vice President of Baseball Operations for the new expansion Kansas City Royals, who would begin play in 1969. He took Schuerholz with him to help build a team up from scratch. Dalton hated to lose two important pieces of his front office.

"It was not that I expected them to stay," Dalton says, "but I wished we had a structure in place to operate and keep one or both of them with us."

Dalton would leave the Orioles himself after the 1971 season, when Baltimore lost to the Pirates in the World Series. He was hired as GM in California to run the Angels, and then in 1978 was hired by Bud Selig as the GM of the Milwaukee Brewers. Dalton molded both franchises in the image of the Orioles' teams of the 60's, stressing the farm system. The Brewers won the 1982 American League pennant with many of the players Dalton acquired, including a famous trade that had Ted Simmons, Pete Vuckovich, and Rollie Fingers go to Milwaukee in one of the best deals in baseball history.

"The Dalton Gang" was the title given to Harry's group of scouts that produced so many players through the years. Kubski was a prime member in that group, along with guys like Walter Shannon, Dee Fondy, Ray Poitevint, Bruce Manno, Walter Youse, and later guys like Sal Bando and Dan Duquette. But his most famous protégés would take the knowledge they learned and shape a new roster in Kansas City.

The team in Kansas City was coming together. Pharmaceutical magnate and Royals owner Ewing Kauffman hired Gorman and Schuerholz from the Orioles, and as their boss he brought in Cedric Tallis, a former executive with the Angels.

Tallis had overseen the construction of Anaheim Stadium in 1965, and Kauffman knew his franchise was getting a new stadium in 1973. So Tallis was hired as GM, even though the only club he had ran was Vancouver in the early 60's.

The Royals started play in 1969 and went 69-93. After that first season, Gorman hired another assistant, Herk Robinson, who had been the Assistant Farm and Scouting Director in Cincinnati.

Together, the quartet of Tallis, Gorman, Schuerholz, and Robinson would form the team that would make the Kansas City Royals the best expansion franchise in baseball history.

Gorman immediately brought the "complete circle" concept to the Royals. As an expansion team, they would be able to be patient with players, even though Kauffman wanted to win as soon as possible. But it didn't take Gorman & Company long to develop a "Royals' type" of player, and it all centered on makeup.

"So many times over the years players would have ability but wouldn't have that drive or the toughness or the ambition to become what they should be," Gorman says. "Even some of the players that got there never became the players they should have been because they didn't have that lower half of the complete circle in them. I've always believed that I would rather have a team that had twenty-five players with that kind of tough makeup, with average or a little above average skills, than twenty-five guys with superior skills that didn't have the makeup to do it, because makeup drives great players. If you look at all the great players in the history of the game, even if they had the skill, they had tremendous toughness and tremendous drive and tremendous ambition, work habits, tremendous knowledge of the game, and tremendous ability to play 110% every time they walk out on the field."

So they used this criteria to search for players, both in the draft and on other team's rosters.

"We were able to make some trades that I don't think you could make today," Robinson says. "There were guys backed up in other systems, like a John Mayberry, an Amos Otis, and a Hal McRae. I had signed Hal in Cincinnati. We were able to do some things that made that franchise. Those were three pillars that we were able to acquire for almost nothing. We had some low draft choices that came through for us. We gave players a chance."

But Robinson says the biggest help in the early days of the Royals was that the management team had a plan in place and stuck with it.

"I think that was a huge part of it," Robinson believes. "We finished in second place in our third year. You had the depth from the Expansion Draft. Lou and John did a tremendous job from the minor league level bringing guys up and having the right guys for development."

In 1973 Gorman was given another responsibility that further cemented the Royals as an organization committed to developing young talent. Ewing Kauffman had an idea. He was always very creative and innovative, and he decided to run a thought by Gorman.

"There have got to be people that don't play baseball who are good athletes but who could play baseball if we trained them," Kauffman said.

"That's probably true Mr. Kauffman," Gorman responded. "I'm sure there are some football players, basketball players, or track stars that could become baseball players. But how do you find them and how do you develop them?"

"Well, suppose we build something like a baseball academy?" Kauffman asked.

"What do you mean by that?" Gorman asked.

"Well, why don't we buy some property and build this complex with housing and fields and we take these kids and house them and feed them," Kauffman said. "We pay them and put them through junior college and teach them baseball. They're down there 340 days a year. Could we do that?"

"Yes sir," Gorman said, "but what I recommend, if we're going to do that, is to take our best young prospects in our system and put them in that program and accelerate their development. Get people that we know are prospects and put them in there."

I don't want to do that," Kauffman shot back. "So you're opposed to the idea?"

"I'm not opposed to the idea," Gorman said. "But I think it would be better if we take the kids that we know are prospects and subject them to that type of training. They'd be in the big leagues quicker."

Kauffman remained adamant.

"No, I don't want to do that," Kauffman said. "I want you to do the conventional method, your regular development program. I want to take people who don't play baseball and put them in this program."

"Ok, how do we find those people?" Gorman asked, knowing full well the response.

"That's your problem," Kauffman said. "I want you to run tryout camps."

Gorman spoke with Tallis about his version of the idea, and despite similar pleas from Tallis, Kauffman was convinced the Baseball Academy for the non-baseballers would work. So he sent

Gorman to Florida to start he new project. Gorman bought 110 acres of land and constructed a huge new complex, complete with housing for 100 players, classrooms, recreational rooms, offices, an Olympic-size swimming pool, a handball court, a nine hole golf course, and five baseball fields with same dimensions as the new stadium being built at the time in Kansas City.

Syd Thrift, later a GM with the Pirates, Yankees, and Orioles, was a scout for Gorman and was named as the Director of the Academy. But despite Kauffman's desire to find athletes from other sports, the tryout camps run by Gorman produced more baseball players who had slipped through the cracks than track stars or football players.

"The main criteria was speed," Gorman says. "You had to run a 6.4 sixty-yard dash at the least. Frank White ran a 6.39. He was playing amateur baseball in Kansas City, a Pepsi Cola team in the Van Johnson league. He was a center fielder but we made him a second baseman."

White was the first graduate of the Academy. He played in parts of three seasons in Kansas City before becoming the Royals' starting second baseman in 1976. White would go on to win eight Gold Gloves, appear in five All Star games, and was inducted into the Royals' Hall of Fame in 1995. His double player partner for five years in Kansas City, U.L. Washington, also came from the academy.

"I put U.L. in the Academy over everyone's objections," Gorman says. "He had trouble catching the ball and throwing the ball, but I was so impressed with his makeup, his eyesight, and his speed. He played for the Royals for about eight years."

The Academy produced a handful of players that made it to the major leagues, but after five years money became an issue with the Royals. But since it did produce players that made the big leagues, the experiment was a success.

"The one thing about it is the kids that were down there learned how to play the game very well, " Gorman says. "The training was great. The instruction was great. But there were a lot of kids who didn't have a great deal of ability."

One thing the project demonstrated was the Royals' commitment to develop its own talent. They made good draft picks in the club's first seven years of existence and created a solid player base. Paul Splittorff was a twenty-fifth rounder in 1968; Doug Bird was a third rounder and Al Cowens a seventy-fifth rounder in 1969; 1971 saw John Wathan (first round in January phase), Steve Busby (second round in January), George Brett (second round in June), and Mark Littell (twelfth round) come on board; Dennis Leonard was a second round pick in 1972; and the Royals hit a home run with their first pick in 1974, signing speedster Willie Wilson.

But perhaps the best combination of people was not the players on the field, but the foursome leading the team from the front office. Tallis, Gorman, Robinson, and Schuerholz got along very well. It was not a huge operation in the 1970's, so even though the four had defined and specific roles, all were involved in the entire baseball operation.

"We formed a good team," Robinson believes. "John had a development background and my background was in scouting. Lou was consumed with trying to put the best baseball teams on the field. Even though in theory we were the minor league people, Cedric didn't do anything by himself. Cedric never did anything without involving all of us. We were affecting the major leagues as much as we were the minor leagues. We all had our strengths and complimented one another. We all got along. The four of us worked extremely well."

Robinson says that Gorman was a great people-person, which made going to work a joy.

"Lou is a great character," Robinson says. "We just had a ball. Talking about having fun at work...we did. We worked long hours. Lou is a delightful person and a good baseball man. He loved it dearly. He was so caring. Nobody can say they didn't like Lou Gorman or doesn't think he's a delightful human being. He was the funniest guy in the world. We just had some delightful times."

"The best part of our relationship was it was like a family with the three of us, with Herk, John, and I," Gorman admits. "We were close together. We went to lunch together. We'd talk all day together. We shared ideas, shared theories, and shared philosophies. Those were great times. Some of the great days in my baseball career were in Kansas City with John and with Herk."

For many years, Robinson worked side-by-side with Schuerholz in a 10x10 office. So he was able to watch a young man grow into a terrific baseball executive, and an even better friend.

"I love John," Robinson admits. "I just think the world of him. I think John is as good as they come. He's very, very smart.

He's very thorough. He's a tremendous competitor. He doesn't like to lose."

About the only thing Schuerholz and the Royals lost in the mid-70's was Gorman himself. Danny Kaye, the entertainer perhaps best known for his co-starring role in "White Christmas," bought the American League expansion franchise in Seattle and hired Gorman to be the Mariners' first General Manager when the team started play in 1977. Schuerholz was in turn promoted to the Royals Farm Director, and for the first time in his career, the protégé would now get his own protégé. Schuerholz would be able to hire his own assistant.

Dick Balderson was a pitcher in the Royals' farm system from 1968 through 1975. He was playing in Jacksonville in AA when the Royals released him. Newly married to a young nurse, Balderson decided to stay in Jacksonville and get into the insurance business. But then in April of 1976, he took a phone call from his old boss with the Royals.

"John called out of the clear blue," Balderson remembers. "I had known John for a number of years. As a player, he was my contact to the front office. He asked me if I wanted to be his Assistant, so I flew out there and took the job. My wife and I packed our first suitcases and headed for Kansas City."

Balderson had expressed an interest to Schuerholz to stay in the game after he finished playing. When he was a player, he used to write Schuerholz during the offseason asking for a raise. "I don't know if he liked my letters or the time that I took to do it or what," Balderson admits. "But I always got along with him and was obviously flattered that he called me and asked me if I wanted to join him."

Schuerholz in KC, 1976

It did not take Schuerholz long to imprint the same philosophies on Balderson that he had learned from Gorman and Dalton. Balderson quickly learned that Schuerholz was looking for a certain type of player, a "Royals' type of player."

"Growing up in the Royals' system, I knew makeup was the

determining factor in whether or not they would be interested in your abilities and your services," Balderson says. "We've had many a good player who had plenty of ability but had poor makeup. When you talk about makeup, it's not about getting guys who say 'yes sir' or 'no sir,' but guys who prioritize, know what their goals are, are willing to work, and follow the guidelines of the program and of the organization."

Balderson spent five years as Schuerholz's assistant, and when Schuerholz became the Royals GM in 1981, became the Director of Scouting and Player Development.

"He stepped back and really let me run it," Balderson says. "But he also knew I was limited in experience, and based on that he was kind of there for me to lean on, and I did so. I followed his theory and Lou's theory, which was all about scouting. We always felt, and to this day feel, that scouting was the essential aspect of a successful organization. You have to have good scouts, and you have to listen to them. John didn't pretend to be a scout and didn't pretend to have the best judgment in the world, but he had good judgment in finding people who did have good judgment, which is a theory I embraced, and still do to this day. You've got to surround yourself with people who are better than you in certain areas and trust them. He did."

As Balderson continued to work for Schuerholz in the early 80's, he also learned that his boss was imbued with tremendous patience. The Royals lost the 1980 World Series to the Phillies, but they never lost sight of the big picture. The goal was still to win a title.

"We had an established core of young players ready, and we knew we were in it for the long haul," Balderson says. "We were very oriented on high school players. You just can't rush that age bracket. We didn't push the envelope every year to get guys to the big leagues."

Balderson was in charge of the Royals' draft when they selected Mark Gubicza (second round) and David Cone (third round) in 1981, along with Danny Jackson (first round) and Bret Saberhagen (nineteenth round) in 1982. That was the foundation for a Royals pitching staff that beat the Cardinals in the 1985 World Series.

"Patience was just an established trait in Kansas City," Balderson says, "and when you grow up in an environment like that you take over that particular belief. The things I learned with John in Kansas City were in my formidable years as an executive. You saw how it worked and you saw what it took to do that. That was just the way we operated. John has always been a very good communicator. He delegates and I think that's why people enjoy working for him. They are hired to do a job and he lets them do it. If you don't, he tells you, which is the way it ought to be."

Meanwhile, as Balderson settled into the Royals' front office in 1976, Gorman was tasked with building another organization, but this time around he faced differed pressures. His new boss was anxious as to how long it would take to build a winner. They had done it in three years in Kansas City.

"Lou, how long will it take to build this team into a competitive club?" Danny Kaye asked Gorman.

"Well Danny, the average for a major league expansion club generally takes nine, maybe ten years before they're reasonably competitive," Gorman said. "Some, like the Royals, have done it quicker, but it's always going to be eight or nine years."

"Fine," Kaye responded. "Don't tell the rest of the people that. Let's tell them it will take ten years."

So Gorman and Kaye sold patience to the fans. They wanted to build the Mariners for the long-term, not a quick winner that might only last for a year or two. But then in 1980 Kaye and his investors sold the Mariners to George Argyros, who quickly took a different approach.

"Patience is for losers," Argyros told Gorman. "We're going to win the pennant in three years."

Gorman left the Mariners not long after Argyros took over the club.

Ironically, six years after Gorman left the Mariners, Argyros hired like-thinking Dick Balderson away from the Royals to be Seattle's GM, but that marriage lasted only a few years as a result.

"Argyros was an astute business guy, but patience was not part of his vocabulary," Balderson says. "I think it proved to be very fatal in the development of his players. They had outstanding young players (Ivan Calderon, Phil Bradley, Danny Tartabull, Harold Reynolds, Alvin Davis, Spike Owen, Mike Moore, and Mark Langston). I just grew up in a different environment where patience proved to be an attribute. Argyros was preaching that patience was not an attribute. Rush, rush, rush, and do this and that. I had grown up in an organization where ownership didn't get involved but requested answers and needed answers and respectfully got answers. But George was on the phone everyday. After a while, it wears you out."

Argyros grew impatient with the losing, but couldn't see the big picture that Balderson was trying to build a consistent winner. With his hands-on approach, Argyros didn't let Balderson build his kind of team, with the philosophies he had learned in Kansas City.

"They couldn't be implemented in the Seattle environment with George Argyros as the owner because the atmosphere wouldn't allow it," Balderson says. "The demands and needs of that particular franchise would not allow that type of patience."

Unfortunately, Balderson never had another chance to be a General Manager. He returned to player development with the Cubs and Rockies before joining his old boss again in Atlanta in 1997. He is currently one of Schuerholz's point-men on potential trades.

Meanwhile, Argyros finally sold the Mariners in 1989 after nine straight losing seasons under his ownership.

"It took the Mariners seventeen years to win their first division title," Gorman reflects.

After Gorman left the Mariners, he was called to New York, where his former boss in Baltimore, Frank Cashen, had taken over as General Manager of the New York Mets. Gorman became Cashen's Vice President of Baseball Operations.

"When I was there with him, it was like family," Gorman says. "With Frank, if you made a recommendation he would accept it. I made the Sid Fernandez trade. It was my recommendation to him. And the Ron Darling deal was my recommendation to him. Frank was just excellent to work for. I hate people that deal in minutia, that question this and question that and change this and change that. It drives you nuts. There's an old Navy term, 'when you run your own ship, you make your own orders, and you serve your own cause.' I believe that. If you put someone in charge of something, give them the authority and the responsibility and let them go do it. If they can't do it, replace them. Frank recognized right away he had good people."

Cashen and Gorman assembled another strong team of scouts and administrators. Joe McIlvaine became the Director of Scouting. He would later come back as the Mets GM in the early 90's and is now an Assistant in Minnesota. McIlvaine was a great judge of high school talent. They also had Terry Ryan, the Twins GM and McIlvaine's current boss, and Jack Zduriencik, the current Scouting Director of the Milwaukee Brewers. Both Ryan and Zduriencik now stress high school players for their organizations. The Mets scouted and drafted a tremendous group of young players in the early 80's: Darryl Strawberry, Doc Gooden, Lenny Dykstra, Randy Myers, Roger McDowell, Kevin Tapani, Rick Aguilera, Calvin Schiraldi, and Wally Bachman. When Gorman left the Mets to run the Red Sox in 1984, he would have to face many of the young Mets players when they beat his Boston team in the 1986 World Series.

Gorman would spend a total of ten years as the Red Sox GM, and the team won the American League East three times including the pennant-winning season in 1986. He became Boston's Executive VP of Baseball Operations after the 1993 season and was replaced by another disciple of Harry Dalton, Dan Duquette. Now Gorman serves as an Executive Consultant for the Red Sox.

Perhaps his favorite accomplishment is helping mold John Schuerholz into the executive he is today.

"I'd like to think a little bit of my influence helped him along the way," Gorman says. "He had a lot of natural ability and a great feel for the game. We ended up building a club that was probably the most successful expansion club in baseball history at the time. Most of the young talent that was there that he and I were responsible for developing was the nucleus of their World Championship club in 1985. George Brett, Willie Wilson, and Frank White were all kids that we actually helped draft and sign through conventional scouting methods."

Gorman is not surprised one bit at Schuerholz's success. He knew Schuerholz had tremendous intellect when he entered his office for the job interview back in 1966.

"He was intelligent," Gorman says. "He was just perfect for the job. He had the ability to be an outstanding executive. John had the ability to handle people, good management skills. He utilized people very well. So that was a great experience working with him and being so close to him and at the time being his boss. But we were kind of like a team really. It wasn't so much that I was his boss. We worked together so closely and shared our input and shared our ideas together."

The philosophies that were first formed in Baltimore in the

mid-50's stretched out into other organizations. Pat Gillick, a player in the Orioles' system back then, followed Paul Richards when he went to Houston, which was at about the same time Gorman came in to assist Harry Dalton.

"I think really if you want to say the foundation from where all this came from – even though one group split off and went to Kansas City and the other group split off and went to Houston at the time, the philosophy and the style would go back right to Baltimore," Gillick says. "A lot of credit would have to go to Harry."

Dalton would go on to impact the California Angels and Milwaukee Brewers. Gorman would be involved with the Royals, Seattle Mariners, New York Mets, and the Boston Red Sox. Gillick would implement many of the same philosophies at the tremendously successful Blue Jays franchise in Toronto, then back in Baltimore as their GM, and in Seattle most recently.

But the most successful protégé of the philosophy is John Schuerholz, whose success is unrivaled. That's why Gorman says that while the philosophy is important, it's the people that make the difference.

"I've always believed that organizations don't win because of policies," Gorman says. "They win because of people. People make the policies. Anything you do it's not so much the policy you establish, but the people that implement those policies and the way you're able to deal with them and motivate them. John was very good at that. I think we worked together that way."

There's a common thread to the current purveyors of scout's honor, instinct and preparation. Frank Cashen, Harry Dalton, Lou Gorman, Herk Robinson, and John Schuerholz never played pro baseball. Yet they all learned and came to believe in the same qualities for building a big league roster. Patience, trust in scouts, a preference for high school talent, and the reliance on the makeup of a ballplayer were all part of a royal blueprint. It started in Baltimore, then developed the Kansas City Royals into a model franchise, and was also seen in Milwaukee, Seattle, Boston, Toronto, and in New York with the Mets. But the final and most successful result was when Schuerholz took the game plan to Atlanta.

14
TRADING PITCHING PROSPECTS

Over the last fourteen years, John Schuerholz has been able to continually remake the Atlanta Braves roster. Since the Braves are traditionally associated with having a high payroll, there's been the perception that they've simply "bought" their players. A closer examination however, reveals that the payroll is traditionally high because the Braves have had to pay their own homegrown players big money when they become eligible for arbitration, and then later when they approach free agency.

Since Schuerholz arrived on the scene in Atlanta, free agency has certainly been one way for him to add players, but it has not been a major avenue for acquisitions. When he took over in the winter of 1990, Schuerholz signed six free agents, but only two can be considered major signings (Sid Bream and Terry Pendleton).

Then two years later, he added a huge piece with pitcher Greg Maddux, who spent eleven years with the Braves on his way to 300-plus victories and the Hall of Fame. But it wasn't until five years later that Schuerholz signed his next two big free agents, Andres Galarraga and Walt Weiss. Then the next year Brian Jordan was signed to a five-year contract. Vinny Castilla signed on to replace Chipper Jones at third base before 2002, and then the next winter Paul Byrd signed a two-year contract. But only five (Bream, Pendleton, Maddux, Jordan, and Galarraga) can be considered major free agent signings, in the span of 14 years.

The farm system has been the major source of replacement value for the Braves organization. "Replacement Value" is a frequently used term to describe the ability of a franchise to replace players on the roster. There are three main ways to make changes: sign free agents, make trades, and utilize the farm system.

However, another misconception is that if an organization's farm system cannot directly provide a replacement, it is not doing its job. In fact, a farm system's function is two-pronged: first, to provide direct help to the major league team by placing a player on the big league roster, and second, to use the talent in the farm system to acquire players from other organizations that can directly be placed on the twenty-five-man major league roster.

"First and foremost, we want to sign guys that are going to help us win championships at the major league level," says Roy Clark. "But the farm system is also for John to use to acquire players to help us win championships at the major league level."

Schuerholz arrived in Atlanta with a huge advantage in 1990. Paul Snyder and Bobby Cox had built up the Braves farm system so that it was one of the best in the game. It had tremendous depth. After he signed his six free agents to plug some holes, Schuerholz created even more depth by allowing some minor leaguers to get additional time on the farm.

The success of the Braves' homegrown talent at the big league level also allowed additional players to develop fully and then be used in deals. For example, with Chipper Jones fully entrenched at third base in the late 90's, Schuerholz was able to use Wes Helms in a deal with the Brewers and a former first round pick, Troy Cameron, in a deal with the Indians. Since Javy Lopez spent ten seasons (1994-2003) as the Braves' starting catcher, Schuerholz was able to use minor league catchers Tyler Houston and Fernando Lunar in deals to strengthen the organization.

But the biggest source of trade material has come from one position: pitching. All you have to do is look at major league rosters in 2004 and see how many former Braves have pitched for other organizations to know how successful the Braves have been at using pitchers in deals. There were forty-three pitchers on other teams in 2004 that were at one time in the Braves' organization, with 47%

of those forty-three pitchers either drafted or signed originally by the Braves. Of those twenty pitchers, nine were starting pitchers for other teams in 2004. The list shows the Braves have an impressive alumni association:

PITCHER	TEAM	2004 RECORD
Jason Schmidt	San Francisco	18-7
Jason Marquis	St. Louis	15-7
Tom Glavine	New York Mets	11-14
Kevin Millwood	Philadelphia	9-6
Darrell May	Kansas City	9-19
Rob Bell	Tampa Bay	8-8
Odalis Perez	Los Angeles	7-6
Bruce Chen	Baltimore	2-1
Jung Bong	Cincinnati	1-1

In contrast, there were only nineteen former Braves' position players on other team's rosters in 2004, with only nine of those homegrown.

So, a closer look at John Schuerholz's trades over the last fourteen years will find a lot of names with the letter "P" to the right.

Schuerholz has involved forty-one pitchers in thirty-one trades since he came to Atlanta, and he's made a deal including a pitcher in every year except 1994. Of those forty-one pitchers, twenty-four were drafted by the Braves, eight were international signees, four were traded to the Braves and spent time in the farm system before being traded again, and the remaining four were undrafted free agents.

Another luxury for Schuerholz was the fact that there was consistency in the big league rotation, which allowed him to use up-and-coming pitchers in deals to strengthen other areas. From 1991 through 2002, there were three groups of three pitchers who were in the Atlanta rotation for at least six years together. Tom Glavine, John Smoltz, and Steve Avery were together from 1991-1996. Glavine, Smoltz, and Greg Maddux were together for seven years from 1993-1999. And Glavine, Maddux, and Kevin Millwood were together from 1997-2002.

Most teams have some type of revolving door in their starting rotations, but the consistency and dependability in the

Atlanta starters and relievers provided Schuerholz with tradable commodities.

Without question, the top name on the list of former Braves now doing well for another team is San Francisco right-hander Jason Schmidt, who has arguably become one of the best pitchers in the game. Schmidt was 35-12 with a 2.79 ERA and 459 strikeouts in 2003 and 2004. He's averaged 15.25 wins and 6.75 losses from 2001-2004.

Schmidt, an eighth round pick by Atlanta in the 1991 draft, first joined the Braves in their championship season of 1995. But the next season, at the age of twenty-three, he made the Atlanta rotation out of spring training. Schmidt struggled a bit, going 3-4 in 11 starts with a 6.75 ERA. When the Braves sent him down to AAA, he did much better going 3-0 in 7 AAA starts with a 2.56 ERA.

The Braves had a tremendous rotation in 1996, as Smoltz (24-8 and the Cy Young Award Winner), Glavine (15-10), and Maddux (15-11) all had fantastic seasons. Steve Avery struggled a bit with injuries and went 7-10 with a 4.47 ERA. Avery's contract was up at the end of the 1996 season, and the Braves knew they were not going to re-sign him.

In Pittsburgh, the Pirates had a twenty-eight-year-old lefthander who was soon to be a free agent himself. Denny Neagle had become the solid lefty the Braves had hoped Avery would develop into. He had gone 27-14 for a very bad team from Opening Day 1995 into the late summer of 1996 (those 27 wins were almost a quarter of the Pirates victories), while Avery had slipped to 14-23 and a 4.58 ERA during the same time. Avery was no longer the talented pitcher who dominated the Pirates in the 1991 NLCS, and the Braves looked at Neagle to take his place.

The Braves were not really in a pennant race in 1996. They were eleven games ahead of the second place Montreal Expos by late August. But in Neagle they saw a pitcher who could help them in the postseason that year and be apart of their great rotation if he signed a contract extension.

With Schmidt in AAA, the Pirates saw their chance to get a young arm that had yet to fulfill his potential. On August 28th the trade was made, Neagle to Atlanta for Schmidt, minor league first baseman Ron Wright (a solid prospect but blocked from moving up by Atlanta veteran first-bagger Fred McGriff), and minor league outfielder Corey Pointer.

Neagle did well in the playoffs for Atlanta in 1996, pitching in four games (two starts) with an ERA of 2.65. He signed a contract extension and then went 36-16 in the next two seasons with the Braves. Schmidt took a little more time to develop. The Pirates were not a very good team in the late 90's, and Schmidt was able to take his bumps in the major leagues without having to worry about being in a pennant race, unlike his situation in Atlanta. Five years after the Braves traded him for a veteran pitcher, Schmidt was the veteran moved in a trade deadline deal for younger talent. His career took off when he got to San Francisco, going 7-1 in 11 starts after the trade from Pittsburgh in 2001. Schmidt is 55-21 since joining the Giants.

Even though Schmidt developed into a good pitcher, the trade didn't hurt the Braves. Neagle did what the Braves needed him to do, and there was another young pitcher behind Schmidt in the Atlanta system that basically took his place. Kevin Millwood joined the Braves' rotation in 1997, replacing Schmidt as the next young Braves pitcher.

"The thing is you have to be able to put a timetable on the player you're giving up," says Bill Lajoie, Schuerholz's point man on the Neagle deal. "Jason Schmidt was not a real contributor until a few years ago. When he went over to Pittsburgh he was not that successful and they subsequently moved him. But for us, there was no immediate impact by Schmidt leaving. So, by the time he got pretty good, we had had a few years to re-supply. It's like when I traded Smoltz to the Braves. He was successful a couple of years after we moved him from Detroit. Let's say he went over there and won sixteen games the following year. Now that would not have been a very wise decision."

A few years later the Braves developed perhaps their biggest surplus of pitching since the early 90's. They won 106 games in 1998 (most regular season wins in their 14-year run) and had a remarkable starting rotation. Glavine (20-6), Maddux (18-9), Smoltz (17-3), Millwood (17-8), and Neagle (16-11) combined for an 88-37 record in 153 starts. Plus the Braves also had a group of young pitching prospects that rivaled "the Young Guns" from the late 80's. Odalis Perez (twenty years old at the time) and Bruce Chen (twenty-one years old) both made their big league debuts late in 1998. The Braves knew they were close. Then in High-A the Braves had twenty-one-year-old Rob Bell and twenty-year old Jason Marquis.

After watching his Braves lose in the NLCS to the San Diego Padres, Schuerholz knew his team needed more offense, and specifically at second base. A year after allowing Mark Lemke to leave as a free agent, the Braves had a two-headed monster at second base. Keith Lockhart (97 games) and Tony Graffanino (93 games) split time at second and combined for a .237 average with 14 home runs with 59 runs batted in.

Schuerholz looked to Cincinnati, where the Reds had an All-Star second baseman in thirty-year old Bret Boone, coming off a season where he hit 24 home runs and drove in 95. Teams that have a player with that type of production at second base usually don't give him up very easily, and Reds GM Jim Bowden was hesitant to make a deal.

"You've got to remember that his father Bob was an employee of ours (Assistant to Bowden and later the Reds Manager)," Bowden says. "Bret was one of my first trades as a GM acquiring him (from Seattle in 1994). He was one of my favorite people in the clubhouse. He was one of the best defensive second baseman in the league. He had power. I loved him as a player."

But as a lower market franchise, the Reds had trouble acquiring top level pitching. They couldn't go out on the free agent market and compete with larger market clubs for top-of-the-rotation starting pitchers. So when they had an attractive commodity like Boone, it was a chance to get a solid arm.

"I did not want to trade Bret Boone," Bowden admits. "But John needed a second baseman. He felt he needed, in his words, 'more energy and enthusiasm.' And he had that surplus of starting pitching, which we all know is abnormal."

There was no way Schuerholz was going to trade Maddux, Glavine or Smoltz, and since Millwood was still only twenty-four-years-old and relatively inexpensive, he was off limits as well. So Neagle became the automatic candidate to be traded. He would immediately be an upgrade for the Reds, who had been led by Brett Tomko (13-12) and Pete Harnisch (14-7) in 1998. The Braves would send Neagle and left-handed hitting right fielder Michael Tucker (who was expendable with the free agent signing of Brian Jordan) for Boone and left-hander Mike Remlinger, who had started twenty-eight games for the Reds in 1998. It could have been a straight two-for-two trade, a position player and a pitcher for a position player and a pitcher, but Bowden wanted more.

"One of the big arguments that I had there was since Boone had three years left on his contract and Neagle had two years left under control, there was a control difference," Bowden explains.

"My feeling in the time of our negotiations was, 'If Denny Neagle can walk in two years, then you'll still have Bret Boone. I need to have a young pitcher coming up to make up the difference.'"

Bowden's logic made sense, but he was dealing with someone who didn't like to give up young pitchers easily. The Reds GM knew he was going to have to work a bit to get the deal done.

"In the negotiations we wanted Odalis Perez," Bowden says. "That's the pitcher we wanted. We wanted Perez first, Bell second, and then Chen. We held out for Perez for a while. He didn't want to give up Bell because his makeup made you believe in him. But I think John knew very clearly that we weren't going to give up Bret Boone without getting an additional pitcher back. It just wasn't going to happen."

So Schuerholz relented and gave up Bell, who had gone 7-9 with a 3.28 ERA in High-A in 1998. Bell was the perfect Braves' prospect. He had been drafted in the third round of the 1995 draft out of a high school in New York. At six-foot-five, 225 pounds, the hard-throwing right-hander simply looked like a Braves pitcher with his good stuff and his All-American looks. But to get the Boone deal done, Bell had to go to Cincinnati.

"Atlanta had so much pitching," Bowden says. "They still had Perez and Marquis and Chen. Now, what I didn't know back then was whether they were concerned about Rob Bell being upside down with his delivery. I don't know. We had some concern about it, but his makeup was so good and he had a great curveball. He had size and he had velocity. John didn't want to give him up. I mean it took many conversations before it got to the point where he knew the deal wasn't going to be made unless he put one of them in there."

Boone played only one season in Atlanta before Schuerholz traded him to the San Diego Padres the next winter. Remlinger had a great career with the Braves, pitching in 291 games (all in relief) over a four-year span with an ERA of 2.65 before signing a three-year deal with the Chicago Cubs before the 2003 season. Neagle battled shoulder trouble with the Reds and went 9-5 with a 4.27 ERA in 19 starts in 1999. After starting the 2000 season 8-2, the

Reds traded him to the Yankees in a six-player deal. Neagle then signed a free agent contract with the Rockies, but has battled elbow trouble the last few years. In his six years since leaving the Braves, Neagle has gone a mediocre 43-37.

"I think the one thing that you know when you're dealing with the Atlanta Braves is that John Schuerholz and Bobby Cox don't make many mistakes on players," Bowden says. "They know their makeup, they know their character, and they a lot of times have vision of when a player's value is about to go down. Like a stock, they have a pretty good idea of when to sell that stock before the value drops. They have a long history of that."

As for Bell, he joined the Cincinnati starting rotation in 2000 as a twenty-three-year-old. He went 7-8 with an ERA of 5.00. He struggled early in 2001 and Bowden traded him to the Texas Rangers for outfielder Ruben Mateo and third baseman Edwin Encarnacion, who is the Reds' top position player prospect. Bell spent parts of two seasons with the Rangers, and has been a member of the Tampa Bay Devil Rays' rotation in 2003 and 2004 (8-8 in 2004). Overall, in five seasons as a big leaguer, Bell is 29-33 with an ERA of 5.58.

The summer after the big trade with the Reds, Schuerholz was looking for a late season deal to strengthen his club for the stretch drive. The Braves were 63-43 on July 31st, the first trade deadline day, and they had a half game lead on the New York Mets. Schuerholz made a five-player trade with the Chicago Cubs, acquiring left-handed pitcher Terry Mulholland and infielder Jose Hernandez for three young minor league pitchers: left-handers Micah Bowie and Joey Nation and right-hander Ruben Quevedo.

Both Mulholland and Hernandez immediately became important players for the Braves. Odalis Perez, the Braves' number five starter in 1999, was injured on July 22nd, just over a week before the deadline. Perez went down with Tommy John surgery on his elbow, and Mulholland stepped right into his spot in the rotation. Mulholland was 4-2 in 16 games (8 starts) with an ERA of 2.98 for the rest of the way. Hernandez replaced the struggling Walt Weiss (hitting only .226) as Atlanta's starting shortstop, and had 4 home runs and 19 RBI in 45 starts at short for the remainder of the season.

The two acquisitions helped the Braves tremendously, as the team went 40-16 after the trade to win the National League East by six and a half games. Atlanta won the National League Pennant but got swept by the Yankees in four games in the World Series.

The price for the two veteran players was not cheap. Nation, Bowie, and Quevedo were all decent pitching prospects, but with Chen and Marquis rated ahead of them, all three were somewhat expendable.

"I can tell you that when we had the discussions about whether we wanted to give these guys up, the answer was, 'yeah, it's going to be difficult to give these guys up,'" says Dean Taylor, the Braves Assistant GM at the time. "We didn't want to, but we're fortunate that we had enough depth in the system that we could afford to do it."

Joey Nation was the highest rated prospect of the three traded players. Nation was a second round pick in the 1997 draft out of a high school in Oklahoma.

"He did things real easy and had a great changeup," says John Flannery, one of the Braves' scouts that saw Nation in high school. "I thought he was going to be a big leaguer for a long time. I thought he had a chance to be a Glavine type guy."

It was common for Braves' scouts to look at many young lefties and picture another Tom Glavine. He had been the cornerstone of the franchise for many years, and it was natural for scouts to look for another one. Nation was a bit bigger than Glavine, at six-foot-two and 205 pounds, but he had similar stuff.

The year Nation was traded to the Cubs, he had gone 6-5 with a 4.05 ERA in 23 starts between the two Braves' A clubs in Macon and Myrtle Beach. Nation walked only 46 hitters and struck out 118 in 124.1 innings of work. The Cubs gave him a couple of starts in the big leagues in 2000. He lost both decisions and had a 6.94 ERA. Those were Nation's only two big league appearances. A heart condition forced him to retire shortly thereafter at the age of twenty-two.

Bowie was a bit older than Nation at the time of the trade, twenty-four years old and six years from being drafted in the eighth round in 1993. Bowie spent most of 1999 in AAA Richmond, going 4-4 with an ERA of 2.96 in 13 games started. He also had a cup of coffee with the Braves, allowing six earned runs in three games. After the deal to Chicago, the Cubs gave Bowie a chance to start. He started eleven games with Chicago and went 2-6 with an ERA of 9.96 in 54 innings. The Cubs released him after the 2000 season and he then went to the A's, where he spent parts of the 2002-2003 season in Oakland. Bowie is 4-8 in 33 games in the major leagues with a 7.70 ERA.

Quevedo had the most success of the three young pitchers involved in the trade. The portly right-hander started fifteen games for the Cubs in 2000 and went 3-10 with a 7.47 ERA. Chicago traded him to the Brewers, where he started forty-three games in parts of the next three seasons and went 11-20 with a 5.68 ERA.

None of the three pitchers dealt to the Cubs was successful. For the Cubs, the three went 5-18 in 34 games (28 starts) with an 8.23 ERA. Overall, after they were traded, the trio of Nation, Bowie, and Quevedo went 18-39 with an ERA of 6.51 in 98 games (71 starts).

There's one more item to consider when grading this trade. While Mulholland stayed and pitched with the Braves in 2000, Hernandez filed for free agency and signed with the Brewers. Milwaukee had to give the Braves two draft picks as compensation, and the Braves took Kelly Johnson and Bubba Nelson with those two picks.

So, the Braves traded three second-tier pitching prospects for two veterans who helped them win their division and make it to the World Series. Then the players whom they traded struggled as big leaguers, and one of the veterans they acquired in the deal resulted in two draft picks, one that is currently a top prospect and one that was subsequently used in another deal to strengthen the major league roster.

Not much to complain about there.

"I remember John used to have a philosophy in Kansas City that for every five young pitchers that are thought to be quality prospects in Class A, only one or two of those pitchers is going to end up pitching successfully for your club at the major league level," Taylor says. "The other three or four are going to be injured, or traded, may fizzle out, or lose their prospect status from a lack of performance. Again, it speaks to the need for depth, especially with regards to pitching; young pitching is an uncertain commodity when you try to evaluate it at the lower league levels. There is safety in numbers."

Numbers, and more specifically depth, can also help complete trades. In the winter of 2001, the Dodgers were shopping right fielder Gary Sheffield. He was unhappy playing in Los Angeles, and had said as much as possible to force the Dodgers to trade him. Despite having a shaky reputation, and not necessarily being the poster child for players with good makeup, Sheffield didn't scare off John Schuerholz, who knew his presence in the Atlanta lineup could make the Braves much better.

"I inherited a situation where he wasn't happy from the previous year," says Dan Evans, whose first offseason as Dodgers GM was 2001. "We had a player who didn't want to be there anymore. That happens in our game. What I was trying to do was then take a player that I respected as a real good offensive player that had some value and perhaps start the Dodgers on their way back. One of the ways to do it I thought, was to see if we could get some pitching for him."

The Dodgers pitching staff was undergoing a huge change that winter. Evans traded Luke Prokopec (8-7 in 22 starts in 2001) to the Blue Jays in a deal for Cesar Izturis and Paul Quantrill, and then three of their free agent pitchers signed elsewhere: Chan Ho Park (15-11 in 35 starts) with Texas, Terry Adams (12-8 with 22 starts) with Philadelphia, and James Baldwin (3-6 in 12 starts) with Seattle. L.A.'s Evans saw a Sheffield trade as a way to add to a pitching staff that had a few holes.

"John had an interest in Sheffield, and the good thing was he also had some players that we liked," Evans says. "Odalis Perez, because of the depth of the Braves' rotation and the depth of the Braves' pitching staff, was a player that they could talk about. He made a lot of sense for us for a couple of reasons. He was young, left-handed, and another thing was a critical element for me was the fact that he had very little in the way of service time. So as a result, he was a player the Dodgers could keep under control for a three or four-year period, which was an immediate need for us because we didn't have to worry about him being a transient player. He was going to remain with the Dodgers for an extended period."

The conversations between Evans and Schuerholz started at the winter meetings in December. But then talks heated up after Sheffield triggered a trade. "Some things happened around the first of the year where Gary said some things publicly about our organization and about some things that had gone on in our organization and as a result we had to move forward."

Evans knew the Dodgers were going to have to take back Brian Jordan in the deal. After all, the Braves other two outfielders, Chipper Jones and Andruw Jones, were not going anywhere. Even though there were rumors that Evans and Schuerholz threw around more names like Kevin Millwood and Eric Gagne (unproven yet as a closer and coming off a season where he was a spot starter in 2001), the main part of the deal was Sheffield for Jordan and Perez. But Evans wanted more.

"I realized that I was getting in Brian Jordan a terrific presence," Evans says. "He's a guy that I really enjoyed having, a real pro with a great way about him, but he wasn't Gary Sheffield. In Perez, it was kind of an unproven entity, so we felt we needed a third player that was a prospect that could go into our system and really add to our talent base. We hadn't had any production from our first round picks for about a four or five-years period. We really needed somebody else."

After going back and forth with Schuerholz on a couple of minor league pitchers, Evans settled for six-foot-six right-hander Andrew Brown, who was only twenty years old at the time of the trade. Brown, who missed all of the 2000 season after having Tommy John surgery, was 3-4 with a 3.92 in 23 starts for the Braves rookie league team in Jamestown, New York in 2001. Brown had a reputation as being a solid strikeout pitcher, and with his great size, was only going to get better.

"One of our scouts really liked Andrew as an amateur," Evans says. "The third player might have been a sticking point and for some clubs it could have been a deal-breaker. But I think John understood what we were trying to do. I was very upfront with him saying we weren't going to make the deal without a third guy. Brown turned out to be a guy who moved right into our system and had a lot of success."

Brown went 10-10 in High-A Vero Beach in 2002 before missing most of 2003 with additional elbow trouble. The Dodgers used him in a trade to acquire Indians outfielder Milton Bradley early in 2004. He is one of Cleveland's top pitching prospects after posting 125 strikeouts in 117.2 innings between the Dodgers and Indians AA affiliates.

Jordan played out the remaining two years on his contract with the Dodgers and had a solid 2002 season (18 homers and 80

RBI) before playing in only 66 games for L.A. in 2003. He then signed a free agent deal with the Texas Rangers, but continued to struggle with injuries in 2004, playing in only 61 games. Perez finally lived up to his promise and became a solid middle-of-the-rotation starting pitcher for the Dodgers, going 34-28 with a 3.55 ERA in 93 starts between 2002-2004.

Sheffield hit an other-worldly .319 with 64 home runs and 216 RBI in his two seasons with the Braves before signing a big money contract with the New York Yankees.

"Luckily it was one of those things where both organizations had a common feel for what they were trying to accomplish," Evans says. "That's really what a trade is all about when it comes right down to it. It's not necessarily that you have what they want, but that both sides have something the other guy wants. We got down to it and it was a trade that ended up helping both ball clubs. Our focus was on pitching and on seeing if we could not only help the Dodgers short-term but long-term as well. Odalis went out and made the All-Star Team his first year, and Andrew turned out to be a terrific prospect."

In four of the last five seasons, John Schuerholz has made a late season or trade-deadline-day deal to help the Braves down the stretch. In all four trades, the Braves have given up a young arm. Right-hander Luis Rivera was part of the package to acquire B.J. Surhoff from the Baltimore Orioles on deadline day (July 31st) in 2000. Righty Brad Voyles was one of two prospects given to Kansas City on deadline day in 2001 for shortstop Rey Sanchez. Matt Belisle, another right-hander and a former first round pick for the Braves, was traded to the Reds for left-handed reliever Kent Mercker. And then on deadline day in 2004, the Braves acquired lefty reliever Tom Martin from the Dodgers for left-handed prospect Matt Merricks.

Not one of the four pitchers traded was considered a top prospect in the Braves system at the time of their deals. Belisle was arguably the best prospect of the four, but he spent 2004 in AAA for the Reds. Rivera and Voyles have battled injuries, and the interesting thing about Merricks is that he was not even one of the Braves top fifteen pitching prospects at the time of his deal to the Dodgers. But he was able to be the price for acquiring a solid lefty reliever for the stretch drive in 2004.

Even if these four pitchers had gone on to do well in the

major leagues for the teams they were traded to, the Braves depth would have compensated for their absence. There is an assembly line of talent in place within the Braves farm system, and as soon as one pitcher gets traded, another one simply steps forward to take their place. This is the plan: allow the accumulation of young arms to create the depth that will supply talent to the big league club either directly or to supply material for potential trades.

"Good farm systems don't necessarily mean that everybody in the system has to play for your club," says Dick Balderson, a major league scout for Schuerholz who set up the Tom Martin trade and the Braves Farm Director from 1999-2002. "I think so many people don't believe in that. If you have quality guys, then you can either funnel them through your system or funnel them to somebody else and get the guys you need. I think John has done an excellent job of that."

As has been well documented, most of the Braves' prospects, including the ones that have been traded away, have been high schoolers. Dan Meyer however, was a college pitcher who quickly rose to prominence in the Braves' system. The Braves actually do draft college kids once in a while, but you can bet that when they do, they have a very good reason to.

"He's a different bird," says J.J. Picollo, the scout who first found Meyer and subsequently signed him. "He's a left-hander all the way. He's funny. His physical ability is what we need for a guy to be a highly successful major league player, but his mental makeup, his drive, and his cockiness is something you need in a player."

Picollo first saw Meyer in high school, when J.J. was a college coach at George Mason and Meyer was a prospect in New Jersey. At that point, Meyer didn't throw very hard and wasn't very big. But he was good enough to continue his baseball career, and Meyer chose James Madison University in Virginia.

"When I first got there I wasn't much of a pitcher," Meyer explains. "I was at 80-83 miles an hour, a real tall, skinny left-hander with not much meat on me. I had to work for it. My freshman year I maybe got ten innings. I think I was just raw. I wasn't developed yet. Up in the north it's so cold, and we don't get to play year round. We play two or three, maybe four months a year while the guys down south get to play all year or deep into the fall before it gets cold. I wasn't able to do that."

So Meyer had to accumulate experience before he had a true idea of whether or not he could pitch. He worked out a little more, got bigger, and then got more innings as a sophomore. And then, as he was heading into his junior season, Meyer made the decision to go to the Cape Cod League, a premiere summer league where many rising college juniors get more innings and try to make an impression. Meyer did just that, catching the eye of Picollo, who had left George Mason and was in his second year as a Braves' scout.

"He had a great summer up there," Picollo says. "He was becoming a prospect."

Meyer became even stronger as he entered his junior season, knowing he had to repeat his strong performance from the Cape Cod League in order to have a chance at playing pro ball. All of a sudden he had ten, fifteen, maybe even twenty scouts showing up at his games. The word was getting out that there was a lefty at James Madison with pitchability and the potential to get even better.

"I felt myself getting better," Meyer says. "I had gained ten to twelve miles an hour since my freshman year on my fastball. I felt myself getting bigger and stronger."

"As an organization we did a tremendous job scouting him because early in his draft year he didn't pitch very well," Picollo says. "We had Paul Snyder, Roy Clark, (East Coast Supervisor) Paul Faulk, and myself all see him in his first start. It was raining and it wasn't a great environment. He didn't pitch well. His velocity wasn't there. His breaking stuff wasn't there. But as the season went on, we stayed on top of him. Tim Conroy (National Crosschecker) saw him with about three weeks left in the season and said we needed to get back on him."

"One of his best attributes is his gamesmanship, his presence on the mound," says Crosschecker Conroy, a former first round pick of the Oakland A's in 1978. "Dan's a battler, a gamer. You know when he's on the mound he's enjoying himself. I don't think you can put a number on that. He's a guy who enjoys the battle and enjoys the game. With pitchers, it's all about presence. It's a team concept, but it's you against the hitter. So it's all about the presence. The more you see that in a young pitcher, whether he's in high school or college, you keep an eye on that kid."

"Tim saw him pitch real well, and then we all went back in there for Dan's last regular season game and he was outstanding," Picollo says. "He touched 94 mph and pitched at 91, 92. He was throwing a changeup that was devastating. He had people swinging and missing all night long and had outstanding command with it. His changeup was so good that we knew we had a guy with a plus fastball and a plus changeup. We're working with two plus pitches on a physical kid. He was five-foot-eleven in high school and now he was a solid six-foot-three, 200 pounds."

The Braves also had another reason for looking at Meyer. Early in the 2002 season, they had made a minor league trade with the Texas Rangers, swapping left-handed pitching prospects. The Braves got Andy Pratt and traded Ben Kozlowski to the Rangers. Both pitchers were marginal prospects, but when Pratt first came over and pitched in AA Greenville, he was horrible, while Kozlowski pitched well in the Rangers' system. The Braves thought they might have made a mistake, so they decided they had to try to replace Kozlowski with a draft pick a few weeks after the trade had been made. So they targeted a college lefty that could step in and accelerate through the system faster than a high school pitcher would have.

"There were a few other left-handers out there in the country that I think were high on our board that weren't in my area, but I knew Dan had kind of gotten into the mix with his last three outings," Picollo says. "The last regular season game, an NCAA regional, he performed really well. He made those jumps to get ahead of the other guys around the country. I think we zeroed in on him late. Those important games show the makeup of the player. He pitched well when his team needed him, and that's the thing we like to see. As a college player, he's got to have at least two pitches, two above average pitches, and he did."

So the Braves surprised Meyer and picked him in the Sandwich Round, thirty-fourth overall. He knew the Braves didn't draft many college pitchers that high, so he felt special the Braves had faith in him to take him with such an important pick.

"To me it was kind of an honor," Meyer says. "Maybe they saw something in me that they don't see maybe in 95% of the college pitchers. It was kind of nice. I thought, 'Maybe I've got something here that they really like and they think I can excel in the big leagues.' I signed the next day. I was ready to go. They came in with a great offer, and I was ready to get to work."

Meyer made a quick impression after putting on the Braves' uniform. He had a 2.74 ERA in thirteen starts for Danville in the Rookie Appalachian League with 77 strikeouts and only 18 walks in 65.2 innings pitched. Then in 2003 he split the season between Rome and Myrtle Beach, the Braves' two Single-A affiliates. Meyer went 7-10, but had an ERA of 2.87 and 158 strikeouts in 160 innings pitched. The Braves bumped the twenty-three year old up to AA in 2004, and he went 6-3 with a 2.22 ERA, 50 hits in 65 innings pitched, 12 walks, and 86 strikeouts. Meyer then got the call to AAA late in the season and didn't disappoint. He went 3-3, a 2.79 ERA, and 60 strikeouts in 61.1 innings of work. The Braves felt so confident in his ability and his confidence that he actually got the call to Atlanta for the final two weeks of the regular season. Meyer continued to impress, pitching two scoreless innings for the big league club. That's quite a quick trip from a junior pitcher at James Madison to the Atlanta Braves in a little over two years.

"Meyer is fearless," says his AA Manager Brian Snitker. "He expects to get hitters out. He loads it up and turns it loose. He's very confident. If you talk to him, you know he's a big leaguer."

The Braves envisioned Meyer going to Spring Training in 2005 to battle for a spot on the big league roster. However, sometimes when teams get involved in trade talks, those penciled in plans can change in a hurry. In November of 2004, the Braves started discussions with the Oakland A's about one of their starting pitchers. The A's had "the big three" of Tim Hudson, Mark Mulder, and Barry Zito, three of the best young pitchers in the game. The trio had been mainly responsible for the A's success in the first half of the new Millennium, but with the inevitable big payday on the horizon for all three, they suddenly became available on the open market.

Rumors had the Braves initially interested in Zito, with the A's wanting second baseman Marcus Giles and Dan Meyer. Then in late November, the buzz was that John Schuerholz was interested in Mulder. But the most logical choice was Hudson, a native Georgian who grew up across the Chattahoochee River in Phenix City, Alabama and was an avid Braves fan as a kid. Using the same strategy he used the year before when he acquired J.D. Drew, Schuerholz believed if Hudson came "home" to play for his favorite team, he would be more willing to sign a long-term extension the following season.

As the 2004 Winter Meetings approached, rumors started heating up that the A's and Braves were going to talk more about a potential deal. The first night of the meetings in Anaheim, California, 'celebrity GM's' Schuerholz and the A's Billy Beane met to talk trade. Beane continued his demand for Giles and Meyer, but Schuerholz would not budge from his desire to keep his All-Star second baseman. The two executives ended the meeting with no deal. Schuerholz was not going to trade Giles, not even for Tim Hudson.

With that deal seemingly dead, Schuerholz moved on to find a top-of-the-rotation starting pitcher, but he did it in a roundabout way. John Smoltz had been practically begging the Braves to move him back into the starting rotation, and since it looked like Hudson was not coming to Atlanta, Schuerholz granted Smoltz's wish by acquiring Milwaukee Brewers closer Danny Kolb for right-handers Jose Capellan and Alec Zumwalt, two of Atlanta's better pitching prospects.

But Billy Beane called Schuerholz back. He wanted to meet again to talk more about a possible deal. Beane realized Giles was off limits, but that hadn't been his main target anyway. Beane wanted Dan Meyer – badly.

"It's funny because in many baseball minds these are the two best GM's in baseball...Schuerholz and Billy Beane," Meyer says. "The fact that one of them was trying to hold on to me and the other one was going after me was a compliment."

Beane believed Meyer could step into the Oakland rotation and be the number four starting pitcher in 2005. And it really wasn't a big shock that he wanted Meyer since Dan's prominence came about while he was a college pitcher, and as detailed extensively in the book about Beane and the A's titled *Moneyball*, those are Beane's preference.

The A's scouted Meyer heavily at James Madison. But the young lefty was like every other pitching prospect drafted by the Braves. He wanted dearly to pitch for Atlanta and be the next lefty to step into that heralded rotation. So the rumors were troubling to him.

"It was all over the media," Meyer says. "It was tough to stay away from. It's just something you can't think about too much. It was my first time going through it. You can't think about it. Names are always going to pop up and stuff like that. But I tried to stay away from most of it for as much as possible."

Meyer spent the week after the Winter Meetings with his girlfriend, getting some shopping done for Christmas. He knew there was a chance his cell phone could ring with some news, and on December 16th it did just that.

"Dan, it's Dayton Moore," Meyer heard as he answered his phone, with Braves Director of Player Personnel on the other end.

"As soon as he called me, I knew," Meyer says. "So right there I started preparing myself. He told me that he loved me and that they had me with the Braves for the future but it was something they had to do in order to get Hudson. I can't be bitter about it. It's Tim Hudson! The guy is amazing. He's an established All-Star."

There is little doubt that the Braves did acquire a terrific pitcher in Tim Hudson. He was 92-39, an unbelievable 53 games over .500, in his first six seasons in the big leagues. Once again, when the Braves needed to improve their major league roster, they turned to their strong farm system to make a move. Meyer may go on to become a tremendous pitcher for the Oakland A's, but the Braves wanted an established starting pitcher to help get them into the playoffs for the fourteenth straight season. It's interesting to note that to replace one of their farm-raised gems Oakland had to turn to a pitching factory in Atlanta where there has always been a veritable smorgasbord of homegrown hurlers.

15
STRIKING GOLD
IN THE FIFTY-THIRD ROUND

The Atlanta Braves second baseman for most of the 1980's was the five-seven, 170 lb. Glenn Hubbard. He was drafted in the twentieth round of the 1975 draft, debuted in Atlanta in 1978, took over as a starter the next season, and spent the next nine years as the Braves' primary second sacker. His best season was 1983 when he hit .263 with 12 home runs, drove in 70, and made his only All Star appearance.

The next decade saw five-nine 170 lb. Mark Lemke as the starter at second base. Lemke was a twenty-fifth round draft pick in the 1983 draft and made it up to Atlanta in 1988. Lemke was part of the magical season in 1991 when the Braves went from worst to first. It was his first year as the starter at second, and he held the job through the 1997 season. Lemke was very similar to Hubbard: good, solid defense, a tough competitor, and not a very big man.

So it was only apropos when another diminutive second baseman made his way to Atlanta at the start of the current decade. Marcus Giles stands five-foot-eight, 180 pounds. In many ways he's a carbon copy of both Hubbard and Lemke, and not only in size. He's perhaps the toughest player on the Braves' team, a tough out, and now, a player with a very good glove.

There are a few differences, but none more important than the journey taken by Giles to get to Atlanta. While Hubbard was drafted in the twentieth round and Lemke the twenty-fifth, Marcus Giles was drafted in the *fifty-third* round of the 1996 draft. Now a late pick is a late pick, and all three players were certainly that. But when you consider that they don't even have the fifty-third round in the amateur draft anymore, you know Marcus Giles was one late pick.

For many years Marcus was known as Brian's little brother. Brian Giles is with the San Diego Padres, but he was drafted by the Cleveland Indians in the seventeenth round of the 1989 draft. Brian would become a star player when he was traded to Pittsburgh before the 1999 season, and then the Pirates traded him home to San Diego in 2003. That's where it all started for the Giles' brothers.

Ed Olsen is the Head Baseball Coach at Grossmont College, the junior college in Giles' hometown of El Cajon, California. In 1989 Olsen recruited Brian Giles, but he also took notice of a very energetic eleven-year-old kid named Marcus. "I went over there to talk with Brian to see what his thoughts were for coming to Grossmont College, and there was this little guy, a stocky kid," Olsen explains. "He had a bunch of baseball cards he wanted to show me. He was a likeable kid. You couldn't help like him. He was always smiling. He was in the eighth grade then."

A few years later Olsen would see Marcus Giles again, but this time on a high school baseball field.

"He was in the outfield and he played a little second base," Olsen says. "He was a scrappy little ballplayer. He was a line drive hitter. He didn't hit that many long balls."

Olsen happened to be close to Al Kubski, one of John Schuerholz's most trusted veteran scouts. Kubski was also at Granite Hills High School scouting Giles.

"You see, he played right field," Kubski says. "He was a better hitter than Brian. Brian had a good hitting stroke, where the younger boy had more power to me. When he hit a ball he would put a charge into it. I told John Ramey (the Braves' area scout at the time), 'He can swing the bat. We ought to make him a second baseman.'"

Giles played right field for most of his high school career, but started playing second base in his senior season.

"Boy was that tough," Giles says. "I had no confidence, almost to the point where I didn't want the ball hit to me."

When the draft rolled around, Giles believed he would be a first-day draft pick.

"I thought at least top fifteen rounds,' he says. "I thought anywhere from ten to twenty maybe – at least the first day. Then I didn't even get a call the second day. On the third day I got a call."

Giles was the Braves' fifty-third round draft pick. He was disappointed and downright shocked.

"I was debating whether I wanted to play the game at all," Giles admits.

"It was kind of frustrating to see people that I played against that I thought were not as good as I was go in the sixth and seventh round. There were always scouts at our games, but you don't know if they're looking at you or at somebody else. You can't worry about that, but it's hard not to as a seventeen-year-old kid. Most of the scouts just didn't see me getting much better from high school. They saw me staying the same."

It was obvious that Giles' size (or lack of it) and his defensive shortcomings were the reason he slipped so far down. But Al Kubski knew Giles could hit. After the draft, he and Ramey took off for Marcus's house for the normal post-draft meeting. They did not meet a happy camper.

"Man, you don't think I can play," Giles told the two Braves scouts. "You drafted me in the fifty-third round?!" It was as if Marcus couldn't believe it himself.

"Let me tell you something about you," Kubski said. "You're a good hitter. You're better than you're brother. We'd like to bring you in and play you at second base. If you come and play second base, you could hit 10 or 15 home runs. That's super. We've got Lemke right now and he hasn't hit 15 home runs in his life."

"Where will I go to play second base?" Giles asked.

Kubski told him about a semi-pro team that was coached by an associate scout of his that was playing that summer in Wichita. He wanted Giles to go play there in the summer and then go to Grossmont and play for Ed Olsen.

To his credit, Giles became the MVP of the semi-pro team that summer, and then took off for Grossmont. Olsen promised Kubski he'd play Giles at second base full-time.

"Marcus came out and worked at second base," Olsen said. "He worked diligently. He spent hours at second base. Time never bothered him. He just loved being at the ballpark. He was getting two hundred ground balls a day at second base."

Giles doesn't believe he really improved his defense that much while at Grossmont, but there's no doubt that his offensive performance showed he was a baseball player. He led all junior college players in the state of California with a beefy .481 batting average, 20 home runs, and 79 RBI in 44 games.

"He was really strong," Olsen says. "I think he really developed the power here at Grossmont. He was a smart hitter. He learned here what to look for in counts and then swing for the fences. He put the ball in play. He'd hit the ball to right-center and left field. He ended up hitting the most home runs ever hit here."

Even though the Braves had drafted him, Giles believed the fifty-third round was an insult. He decided he was going to have to go out and prove that he could play baseball, and that he was more than just "Brian's little brother."

"I think it was motivation," Giles admits. "That's what the main thing was: motivation. In junior college I hit 20 home runs. In high school I hit like 9 and 12 in my junior and senior seasons."

"He tore up that league," Kubski says.

"He was a little sore at the beginning that he wasn't drafted higher," Olsen says. "But he came here and devoted his whole time to baseball and didn't think about anything else. He just wanted to prove himself."

"Marcus had a chip on his shoulder," says Roy Clark, who saw him as a National Crosschecker that year. "I went to see him one time in batting practice and saw him get a couple of at bats. The way that ball came off his bat you knew he deserved a chance. He was one of those guys you watched and just said, 'Sign him.'"

The Braves still had to do just that, sign Giles as a draft-and-follow player before the draft in 1997. Other scouts started to show up at Grossmont just in case the Braves didn't sign him. If he went back in the draft, he was sure to be higher than a fifty-third round pick, and the Braves didn't want to lose him. Kubski and Ramey had to go back into the house to convince Giles to sign. Kubski decided to tell him a story. He was good at that.

"There was a kid I saw play in high school who was a pretty good player," Kubski told Giles. "He played at about 155,

160 pounds. He was a left-handed hitter. He thought he was Ted Williams, but he never hit a home run. One day his dad spoke to me and asked, 'Al, do you think my son has a chance to play pro ball?' I said, 'To be a pro player, you're supposed to have a plus arm, be a pro runner, plus fielder, and plus power. You're son is not even average at anything.' He had to get stronger and he had to improve. So this kid went to college up in Irvine, California. He was in his junior year and I saw his college coach and asked, 'How's this kid doing?' The coach said, 'Al, he's a pretty good player. He's gotten bigger and stronger. He hits, throws, and fields all right.' Well, the Red Sox took him in the tenth round and signed him for $12,000. They sent him to the Florida State League and he hit .320 and stole 40 or 50 bases. In two years, they brought him up to the Red Sox. His dad sent him to a track coach in L.A., to a strength coach, and bought him a batting cage. He went from 160 to 190 pounds. He went from a 7.2 runner to a 6.6 runner with that track coach. What this kid did from high school to pro ball was unbelievable."

The kid's name was Brady Anderson.

"He hit 50-something home runs one year," Kubski says. "I wouldn't have bet he could have hit 50 home runs if he had played 50 years. I saw Anderson play for three years in high school. Nobody drafted him and nobody even thought about drafting him. It's all about the makeup. I told that 'Brady Anderson story' all the time. If you want to be a ballplayer so bad, it helps. But you still have to have the ability. I can train a jackass for five years, but he's never going to be a thoroughbred no matter what the hell he does. I had kids I loved that wanted to be ballplayers, but the Lord just didn't give them enough ability. Marcus had the ability, but he had to work hard."

Along with the Anderson story, Kubski also told Giles about Glenn Hubbard. The former Braves' second baseman was going to be sent to Macon that next year to work almost exclusively with Giles.

"They said, 'We're going to send you to Macon,'" Giles remembers. "That was their main plan. Al had that planned from the beginning. He said, "We're going to send you with Hubbard and this is going to be the guy that turns you around (defensively).' So I just told my dad, 'Let me get my foot in the door. Let me the ball be in my court for once. Let me prove myself wrong. Don't let them prove me wrong. I'm not going to let them tell me I can't do it. I need to prove it to myself before I really believe it.'"

So Giles signed for $40,000. He spent his first season of pro ball in the Appalachian League with the Danville Braves and hit .348 with 8 home runs and 45 RBI in 207 at bats. Then the Braves sent him to the Instructional League in Florida after the season. It was there he met Glenn Hubbard.

"So you're the guy that's going to make me a Gold Glover," Giles said to 'Hubby.'

"No, I can't do it, but you can," Hubbard barked back.

The next April Giles was sent to Macon, where Hubbard was the coach and Brian Snitker managed the team. "Well, he looked like somebody that had never played second base before, trying to play second base," Snitker says.

"He knew he could hit," Hubbard says. "God gave him the ability to hit a baseball. The one chink in his armor was defense. So he was willing to work at it."

Giles would often show up to Luther Williams Field in Macon even before Hubbard. When his coach arrived, they would go out on the hard surface of the park and work continually on his defense. Hubbard wasn't just there to hit him fungos, but to work on specific mechanics that would make him a better fielder.

"He had to work on double plays," Hubbard says. "We worked on high choppers, because he was so awkward with the high choppers. He'd throw across his body instead of catching it and facing the bag. To me, it doesn't do any good to go out there and just take ground balls. I think you have to work on specific things. Extra work and early work is for specific things."

"We worked our butts off," Giles admits. "We were out there in that heat down there. I went through a lot of cramps, a lot of sweat, and lost lots of weight."

"It was incredible," Snitker says. "It wasn't that it was an accident either. I get there about 1:30 for a night game, but they would have already been on the field for an hour by the time I got there. They got there early everyday. It was hot as hell that year too. They would be out there with nobody around and Hubby would hit him ground ball after ground ball and show him how to catch it. They'd work on fielding and then the next thing I'd know they'd be in the cage hitting. I'm not talking a couple of days a week, but everyday. It was non-stop."

But after the first half of the season, Giles had 20 errors. He was improving, but still making mistakes. So at the All-Star Break, Hubbard gave Giles a new goal. "Listen, we can't cut them out, so let's just cut them in half."

At that time Hubbard was also working on Giles' confidence. "Well yeah, because he didn't like to make errors," Hubbard explains. "But I just said, 'Hey, keep working. We're going to get there.' In the minors, there's a lot of that. You can't hammer the kid and say, 'Let's go, damn it.' You've got to say, 'you'll get better. Let's keep going. We're going to get better.'"

Giles and Hubbard continued their hard work. Whether they were at home or on the road, they spent extra time working in the field. The second half of the 1998 season was much better. Giles made only five errors the rest of the way.

"He just looked smoother," Hubbard says.

"I saw it," Snitker says with pride. "I was there with him. It's the damndest thing I've ever seen. It was total dedication – day and night. It went from the glove not fitting his hand to becoming a second baseman. Catching a pop up, ground ball, everything was tough for him. I told Hubby that he (Hubbard) might have been one of the most improved players because I thought his play at the end of the year was a lot better too. He kind of worked himself back into playing shape by doing that. He'd get somebody else on the end of the fungo and he'd get out there with Marcus. That was the greatest thing. Hubby could show him how to do it. He wasn't that far removed from playing, so he could still do it himself. He could get out there and show a guy how to do it and how to do it right at full speed. His feet were still lightning. He could still do everything."

Giles saw someone his own size do great things in the field. He also was able to have long talks with Hubbard about how tough it can be for a little guy to make it to the big leagues.

"That helped a lot," Giles says. "He could relate to me and share what he had to go through and the same obstacles he had to climb."

Snitker believes Giles' success on the offensive side gave him hope that he would get better defensively. "This kid had some inner confidence," Snitker says. "He knew he could hit. There was a part of the game he could compete at, and if he let in two, he'd drive in three. He'd always end up on the plus board at the end of the day because of his offense."

Surprisingly, even after his 1998 season when he hit .329, 37 home runs, and drove in 108 runs to win the South Atlantic League MVP award and make drastic improvements in the field, some in the Braves front office still wanted to move him back to the outfield.

"I told somebody, 'you put him in the outfield and I quit,'" Hubbard recalls. "I said, 'All the work we did…you have to see how much better he is now.' To have a guy hit like that and play second was pretty special. He had become a good second baseman."

The work ethic and dedication made Marcus Giles better. That's the type of player the Braves are looking for when they draft a player, but it's not often found in a player picked in the fifty-third round.

"When you sign a kid, they're all hungry to get to the big leagues," Hubbard believes. "So they're willing to work. But it was surprising that he was basically the only guy that would show up like that. He'd show up and we'd do our ground balls and defense first, then I'd flip him some curve balls to hit. We did offense second. He was there everyday."

The next season Giles went to Myrtle Beach in the Carolina League and was joined by Snitker as his manager. Hubbard was sent up to Atlanta to be the first base coach with the big league team. But even though Giles' mentor was no longer around, the work they had done the year before in Macon still carried over. He continued to show he was a hitter, putting up a .329 batting average with 13 home runs and 73 RBI, but he also cut his error total down from 25 to 8.

"The work you do with a kid in the minor leagues one year pays off the next year," Hubbard says. "Snit (Snitker's nickname) would call me and say, 'You wouldn't believe how well he's playing.' People that had seen him struggle the year before would come up and say, 'Golly, he's just totally different.'"

"He won the league MVP that next year in Myrtle Beach too," Snitker says. "I told him then, 'you know Marcus, this was a defensive MVP as much as it was offensive.'"

"My proudest moment in Myrtle Beach was winning that MVP because of my defense," Giles says. "The year before when I won it in the South Atlantic League it was mainly because of my offense. I was pretty bad defensively. But I think a lot of it in Myrtle Beach had to do with the defense."

Giles spent the 2000 season in AA Greenville and hit .290 with 17 home runs and 62 RBI in 458 at bats. He made 18 errors that season. Then in 2001, he started at AAA and bounced back and forth from Richmond to Atlanta until July 31st, when the Braves released Quilvio Veras and made Marcus the starter. He finished with a .262 average in his rookie season with 9 home runs, 31 RBI and 6 errors in 62 games. Then in 2002 he started with Atlanta but then severely sprained his ankle in late May. Giles would miss six weeks, and after a month long stint in AAA, finally got back to the big leagues in mid-August. He finished with a poor batting average (.230), 8 home runs, and 23 RBI in 213 at bats. His defense was still okay, as he committed 6 errors in 52 games. The Braves even played him at third base in 8 games, but he committed 2 errors in 21 chances.

As late as the winter of 2002-2003 there were still questions about whether or not Giles could be a starter in the big leagues. Rumors even had John Schuerholz talking to the Padres about sending Giles home to San Diego in exchange for pitcher Brett Tomko. But the Braves decided to hold onto Giles, and he rewarded them for their decision.

"I think in 2003 in spring training he took it to another level," says Hubbard, now Giles' first base and fielding coach in Atlanta. "Then during the regular season he just made play after play after play. You'd watch him and go, 'Son of a gun, there's no way he should make that play.' He makes diving plays now that he never would have dreamed of diving for in Macon. But the confidence makes you better too. He's more confident. He knows he can pick it. He knows he can play. He had a chance to win a Gold Glove in '03."

Giles made only 14 errors in 139 games at second base in 2003 and led the National League with 471 assists and 763 total chances. He also had the highest batting average ever by an Atlanta second baseman with a .316 mark, to go along with his Braves' modern franchise record of 49 doubles. Giles also hit 21 home runs and drove in 69.

"My defensive skills picked up with Hubbard," Giles believes. "Hitting was always okay for me. My dad always had a pretty good idea on how to hit and he threw great batting practice too, so he was always out there throwing to me and my brother."

"I was talking to Hubby last year about Marcus," Snitker

says, "and he said, 'Snit, you know that confidence that he has now in his game has transcended him to another level – where you get to know that you can play the game and you can get over that hump.' It's like realizing, 'hey, I can play here.' You allow the skills and everything to go to the next level because you know you can play here."

The 2004 season was somewhat frustrating for Giles. He was enjoying another great year, hitting .339 in his first 118 at bats, when he broke his collarbone going back on a ball in short center field in Milwaukee on May 15th. He finished the season hitting .311 with 8 home runs and 48 RBI, but there's no doubt the injury slowed him down.

But Giles has become an integral part of the Atlanta Braves and his story is a true indication of how a kid's makeup, no matter how low they may be drafted, can still get them to the big leagues. It's a story often used by the Braves' coaches in the minor leagues.

"You know Marcus was a lot like Mark Lemke in that they both had that same inner desire to get better," Snitker says. "Work ethic. They weren't naturals at what they did. There are not a whole lot of Andruw Jones's out there who are just naturally blessed and it just happens. You've got to work to get to that next level. I think Marcus had to work hard to get better."

"Marcus was not going to be denied," says Roy Clark. "We want our guys to go out there and have a chip on their shoulder and show everybody they are the best. Marcus did that."

"I had a lot of motivation," Giles says. "It was like, 'All right, I want to prove you wrong.' I think there's no better satisfaction than showing somebody that you can do something that they think there's absolutely no way you can do. And if it weren't for Glenn Hubbard coming into my career, I wouldn't be here today."

16
"THIS IS ADAM LAROCHE -
HE'S OUR STARTING FIRST BASEMAN"

Patty LaRoche was making breakfast early one morning when she heard her five-year-old son Adam coming down the stairs. The sound was louder than normal, accompanied by the banging of a baseball bat dangling from the youngster's one hand, while the glove in the other hand clipped along the staircase slats. He had his uniform on, all decked out like he was headed for Game Seven of the World Series.

"Adam, where are you going?" Patty asked.

"I'm going to work," Adam responded.

Twenty years later, not much has changed. He's a bit bigger now, but he's just as serious about his approach to the game he loves. Occasionally people describe ballplayers as having baseball in their blood. For Adam LaRoche, nothing could be more accurate.

Adam's dad, Dave LaRoche, was a left-handed major league pitcher for fourteen years. He was what you could call a journeyman, pitching for the Angels, Twins, Cubs, Indians, and Yankees, in his big league career. LaRoche was pretty good. He saved 126 games, though he's surely more famous for his trick "eephus" pitch, the one with the trajectory of a rainbow, called "La Lob." LaRoche pitched to thousands of batters in his big league career, but his most important pitching may have come in his own backyard. That was where Adam and his two brothers learned how to hit a big leaguer. "He was constantly throwing to us in the cage," Adam says.

But Dave wasn't just throwing to his boys, he was stressing the important things he had seen hitters do over the years to become successful in the big leagues. He told Adam during the practices that if he hit one ball to his left, if he pulled one ball, he'd walk out. Dave forced Adam to learn how to hit the other way with a bit of tough love. He had to learn how to hit the right way or their batting practice session would be over.

"I heard scouts talk and they always talked about what they were looking for was whether a player could hit the other way and drive the ball the other way. If they did, they felt then the guy can hit," Dave LaRoche says. "Anybody can pull the ball. Guys can show power down the line. Don Mattingly was my big example. I watched Mattingly in the minor leagues. He got a lot of doubles, but very few home runs. He used the whole field. He knew how to hit. When he got to the big leagues and learned the league, they taught him how to pull pitches and look for pitches. He got a little smarter. Pitchers are taught to pitch down and away a big majority of the time, so if you can hit that pitch and drive it the other way, then you're going to be able to hit."

LaRoche also knew a bit about hitting since he had swung the bat part of his minor league career. The Angels drafted him as an outfielder in the fifth round back in 1967, signed by Rosey Gilhousen, who later went on to scout for John Schuerholz in Kansas City. During his second year in the minors, Dave was sitting on the bench taking a day off, when his manager came up to him and made him do something that would eventually change his life.

"LaRoche, go get loose," the manager said. "You're in the next inning."

"OK," Dave replied. "Where am I at? Left field? Right? Center?"

"No, you're on that hump out there in the middle of the infield."

Dave had pitched in high school and then a bit of batting practice in the minors; everybody had back to back then, so the coaches knew he had a good arm. For the rest of that season, he split time between the outfield and the mound. Then at the end of that year, the Angels told LaRoche they wanted him to concentrate on pitching.

But his time as a hitter made him a better pitcher, and it also helped make his son a better hitter, especially when ten-year-old Adam was struggling at the plate.

"When I was still an outfielder, Chuck Tanner (later the manager in Atlanta) had me try something in spring training," Dave says. "I was intense and trying to hit the ball before it came out of the pitcher's hand – typical young kid. He was just trying to relax me, so he suggested I not open up as much in my stance and pretty much just stand there. When Adam was real young and the pitchers started getting a little better, he started getting a little antsy so I stood him up. It was just a temporary thing, but he liked it. He was closing off. So I said, 'Now open up so you can see the pitcher and then have a nice soft stride toward the pitcher.' He took off with it and loved it."

Environment was something else Dave was able to provide his son. When LaRoche finished up his playing career with the Yankees, he became a minor league pitching coach in their system. Then five years later he became the major league coach for the White Sox for three years, followed by two seasons as the Mets' pitching coach. Through those years, Adam was in uniform as a batboy for many games. He was able to see exactly what it took for kids to become major league players.

"When dad got to the big leagues (as a coach), I got to see first-hand what that was like and how different it was from A ball and AA that we had been in," Adam says. "It was cool. That's the first time I realized those guys were the same as everybody else. Those guys were just like the AA players. Yeah, they wear nicer clothes and drive better cars, but baseball's not that different."

"I would take either or both Jeff (Adam's brother) or Adam on the road trips," Dave says. "They would be a batboy or shag flies in the outfield. The players were great to them. They'd play catch with them. They would ride the bus. The players would take them back and he'd watch the card games. They knew the lifestyle. They knew going to the ballpark everyday was a job. Then when I got to coach in the big leagues, it really helped because being in a big league clubhouse, being on a big league field, and seeing all the big leaguers, it's not intimidating 'cause he's been around them a thousand times."

You would think growing up around a big league pitcher would have made Adam want to follow in his dad's footsteps. But there was something more important to Adam: he wanted to be a hitter. For as long as he can remember, hitting was always the most important thing in his baseball life.

"I can never remember wanting to be a pitcher in the big leagues," Adam says. "I can never remember seeing a big league pitcher and thinking how cool that would be. I'd always be looking at the hitter thinking how cool that would be. I loved pitching – maybe even a little more when I was little. But I wanted to hit in the big leagues."

Adam LaRoche at bat with his dad pitching
and brother catching.

When Adam got to high school, he was good enough to do both. But he first had to get serious about baseball. He loved the game and played it well, but he was a normal teenager, getting into innocent trouble here or there – nothing serious just the usual partying with his friends and being eighteen. His high school coach was his uncle, his mother's brother David Regan, and he got Adam on the right track to concentrate on the game a little more.

"He's probably one of the toughest guys I've ever met," LaRoche says. "I can't even explain what he would teach you about life, about respect toward adults, about the way you talk to women, the way you talk to your parents, the way you treat your teammates, the way you fight with each other. If anything happens to your teammate, you back them up whether it's their fault or not. He would make speeches on that. I calmed down because of the morals that he put in everybody. I really needed him to put it in me that I had to be serious. You can still have fun, but remember why you're out here and what it is to win."

LaRoche got serious his senior year and hit .667, best in the nation for a high school player. But he also had an ERA on the mound under 1.00, so scouts looked at that more than his offensive potential. If he had hit .667 in Texas, he probably would have received more attention. But he was in Kansas, and a lefty pitcher is going to get attention anywhere he has an ERA under 1.00. And plus, he was the son of a former big league pitcher, and teams thought he would simply be like his dad. But LaRoche was adamant about his desire to be a hitter.

"Scouts would tempt him by saying, 'You won't even pitch for $2 million dollars?'" Dave LaRoche says. "They would kind of hint that he could be a first or second rounder (as a pitcher). He said, 'No, not even for $2 million. I'm going to hit. So don't bother drafting me unless you're going to give me a chance to hit.'"

The Marlins did draft him in the thirteenth round of the 1998 draft. They told him they were going to let him do both, but Adam and his dad had their doubts.

"I think they saw me with more potential as a pitcher than as a hitter," Adam says. "My dad was saying it would be a lot easier to sign as a first baseman and play a few years and then if something happens to go back to pitching rather than pitch and go back to first. So that was my thought process. It would have been very easy for me to sign and for them to say, 'Well, we just want you to pitch.' There would have been nothing I could have done about it then."

"They said they were going to give him a chance to hit," says Dave. "But just the way they talked you knew the chance might be slim. After a month if he wasn't hitting, you knew what they would do."

So after turning down $80,000 to sign with the Marlins, Adam decided to stay at home and play for his dad, who had taken over as the head coach of the local junior college there in Fort Scott, Kansas. But he had one requirement to play at Fort Scott. Adam wanted to go against the norm and hit with a wooden bat instead of the aluminum bat. His dad had no objections.

"I encouraged it," Dave says. "He wanted to be a big leaguer. Being old-fashioned like I am, old school, I didn't hit with aluminum. I knew if you could hit with wood you could hit with anything. Just because you can hit with aluminum doesn't mean anything. We talked about it. He wanted to do it and I was in his corner."

"I don't know if I'd do it again because I don't like being cocky," says Adam. "I don't like people thinking I'm better than they are. It may have come across like that. My teammates were awesome about it because I explained it to all of them that the reason I was staying there was to use a wooden bat. If I'm hurting the team, I'll use metal. But I was thinking in my mind that I was going to be in the big leagues soon. I wanted to get used to a wood bat. I knew that the biggest obstacle when I signed was going to be getting used to it, so I wanted to go ahead and start early."

LaRoche didn't hurt his teammates one bit, who had no objections after watching him hit .350 with 10 home runs. But after his freshman season was over, Adam felt he needed to get away from home a little. Fort Scott is a small town, and he was just ready to go off and have the college experience. So he transferred to Seminole Junior College in Oklahoma, where he would be coached by Lloyd Simmons, the winningest coach in college baseball history, and a very disciplined man, much like his uncle David.

"It was tough," Adam remembers. "It was really tough. We ran so much there. We did so many weights at five o'clock in the morning. He didn't care who you were. It's win, win, win. We'd lose and we'd be out there running until midnight. He'd have the lights on and we'd be out there running if we lost. And we didn't ever lose. We lost like a handful of games the whole year. We'd crush people."

Once again LaRoche played first and pitched. With the Marlins now out of the picture, teams started scouting LaRoche heavily again to draft him after his sophomore season. He hit well, though Simmons forced him to hit with the aluminum bat, but the more he pitched, the more scouts got wide-eyed at the chance to take him as a pitcher. He was just good on the mound, but it didn't deter him one bit. He still wanted to be a hitter.

"I had our coach talk to the scouts," Adam says. "I told him to tell every scout there was no chance I was going to sign as a pitcher. Just forget I even pitch. I did it there because I wanted to win. I think that really upset a lot of scouts."

But one scout wasn't upset at all. Brian Kohlscheen was the Braves' area scout for Oklahoma. About the only thing he had heard about LaRoche before he saw him was that he had a good arm, of course. So when he went to see him play, Kohlscheen expected to scout Adam as a pitcher. But then, things changed when he saw

LaRoche come to the plate.

"I first saw him down in a tournament," Kohlscheen says. "I had some interaction with his coach and he said, 'you know this guy's got a great arm but he can hit too. You need to look at his bat. He really likes to hit.' So I said, 'Okay, that's fair.' So I started watching him. I liked the way he swung the bat."

Kohlscheen heard other scouts behind home plate ridicule LaRoche's desire to hit.

"This guy's really not going to hit, especially with his set-up," they'd say.

But Kohlscheen didn't agree. He knew the approach was different. LaRoche still had the stance his dad had taught him when he was ten years old. He stood upright until the pitch was delivered, then he'd swing through the zone. The swing itself was not only normal, but also extremely smooth. Kohlscheen could tell LaRoche was serious about hitting.

"We felt he could hit," Kohlscheen admits. "I liked the way he went about it, the way he made adjustments, the way he used the whole field, and the way he worked the count when he needed to. He was a very confident person when he got in that box. A lot of people said, 'Well, he starts open and then he's got a lot of movement and all that stuff.' All I know is that he seemed to arrive on time. He was strong and he could drive the ball and he competed very well. Plus, he was an excellent first baseman. After talking with Lloyd Simmons, I never brought anybody in to see him pitch because if we were going to have any chance to get him in our system it was as a hitter and I thought he could hit."

LaRoche hit .430 and was second in the nation with 23 home runs. But not many scouts were talking to him. Simmons had told them, in his abrupt manner, that Adam was in no way going to pitch. Kohlscheen even saw scouts go away saying there was no use scouting him anymore if he was that determined to hit. So when the draft rolled around, LaRoche only knew it would be a confirmation that he would be continuing his college career the next year at the University of Arkansas. But then, on the morning of the second day of the 2000 draft, Kohlscheen called.

"We're thinking about taking you," Kohlscheen told LaRoche. "Do you want to sign just to play first?"

"That's all I needed to hear," LaRoche says.

"Yes," was his response.

The Braves drafted LaRoche in the twenty-ninth round, the 880th overall pick. Kohlscheen had a feeling he had a steal.

"The worst thing you always had to fall back on as a scout, worst-case scenario, was that if he can't hit he was going to be able to pitch," Kohlscheen says. "It was a whole lot easier to like him as a pitcher because of his attributes. They were special. I'm not trying to sound like a genius here because I've made a ton of mistakes, but there were very few people that were on him as a hitter. I think we had him projected anywhere from the third round to the sixth round. I think he's got a great feel for pitching, but just even more of a feel for hitting. He's got a great feel for both sides of the game. One thing that might have turned off Adam a bit with other people was the fact that he wasn't a big rah-rah guy. He did things easy, and sometimes when you do things easy, scouts say, 'Oh, this guy is too cocky.' But in reality, it was just the way this kid grew up."

That's the other thing that convinced Kohlscheen that LaRoche would be a solid prospect. He believed being the son of an ex-major league would give him an advantage over other kids in the minor leagues.

"I think bloodline makes a big difference," Kohlscheen explains. "I think it makes a difference in the makeup of the person because they're comfortable. They're not awed. They realize when you go into a big league clubhouse they're still just people. And they know that because they've been there already."

After Kohlscheen had spoken to him a few times on the phone, LaRoche was confident the Braves were serious about letting him be a hitter. Then Kohlscheen made the first offer to try to sign him; $20,000. LaRoche wasn't too hung up about the money; he was ready to play. But he wanted to get himself a little spending money, knowing that it's not easy in the minor leagues if you're not a high round draft choice. Plus, his dad's former agents, the Hendricks Brothers in Houston, were telling him to hold out a few more days to get the Braves to increase their offer. A week later, the Braves increased the bonus figure to $30,000, while LaRoche was asking for $40,000. Finally, after sitting around anxious to get his minor league career started, LaRoche took things into his own hands to get the deal done.

"I was ready to play," he says. "I called my agent and said, 'Listen, this has gone on long enough. You guys did everything you could do. Let me call him. Let me call Kohlscheen and see what's going on and I'll negotiate something.' I didn't want to step on anyone's toes so I asked them. They said fine."

LaRoche called Kohlscheen and decided to try to wrap things up quickly.

"Listen, you just bring me a contract and whatever it says, I'll sign," he told the scout. "I just want to play. Whatever you guys give me, whatever you think is fair, I'll sign."

Kohlscheen was a little shocked. He had never had a player ask him to bring over a blank contract. So he decided to go to bat for LaRoche to try to get him the best deal possible. He called Roy Clark in Atlanta to tell him what LaRoche was wanting.

"Hey Roy look, this kid really wants to play," Kohlscheen told his boss. "I think we can get this thing done. But I've got to give this guy more than what we've got on the table. Can you give him just a little bit more?"

"Okay," Clark said. "Try to keep it under forty thou, but if you've got to go to forty, then give him forty."

That was all Kohlscheen needed to hear. He was giving LaRoche the $40,000 he had wanted.

"They could have showed up with thirty or even the twenty, which was cool," LaRoche says. "I would have been happy with that."

"If I could have given the kid $100,000, it wouldn't have been a problem because that's where we had him evaluated," Kohlscheen admits. "He was going to be a good sign no matter what, just because of his attitude and the way he goes about it."

So LaRoche took off for Danville, to play in the Appalachian League with a few other picks from the draft like Adam Wainwright and Chris Waters. But when he got to the minor leagues, there was still more resistance over his swing. He found himself on the bench, as a backup to Garrett Jones, a fourteenth round pick from the 1999 draft that was repeating Danville. His spot on the pine did nothing to deter LaRoche's confidence.

"Even when I wasn't playing, I knew I was going to be fine," he says. "I knew I was still eventually going to make it. It didn't really bother me, except for the sitting everyday. I was sitting on the bench for two weeks. I was beside myself. I had never sat on the bench for an inning in my life."

J.J. Cannon, Danville's manager, Franklin Stubbs, the roving minor league hitting coach, and Jim Beauchamp, another minor league coach, all told him he'd never make it to the big leagues with his unusual approach at the plate. They wanted him to close off from the pitcher and bend his knees. LaRoche agreed to at least give it a try one day in batting practice.

"I can't tell you how bad it felt," he says with a grimace. "It was horrible."

LaRoche was in somewhat of a dicey situation. He didn't want to act like a difficult college player, someone unwilling to take instruction from his new coaches. Yet he knew there was no way he was going to be effective if he changed his stance. So he called his dad and asked for advice. Dave LaRoche came up with an idea for him to take to his manager the next day at the ballpark.

"Give me a week or two with my stance, and if you don't like it and it's not working, we'll change it," Adam promised Cannon.

Cannon agreed to the proposal. LaRoche got hot, finished with a .308 batting average, and never heard another negative word about his swing that season.

The next spring, LaRoche would make such a good impression that he convinced the Braves he could handle a jump over Macon, in the South Atlantic League, and go all the way up to Myrtle Beach in the Carolina League, which is High-A. The Braves started to see that his swing was special, and that his defense was exceptional. You started to hear comparisons that spring to Mark Grace, which just happened to be one of LaRoche's favorite players.

"We used to watch the Cubs on WGN all the time," he says. "He was just a little first baseman. He wasn't a big first baseman. He was pretty smooth over there at first base. He got some Gold Gloves. But I liked the fact that he was a small first baseman and he didn't have to hit forty home runs."

When LaRoche got to Myrtle Beach, he encountered his first true test as a professional player. The Carolina League is known as a pitcher's league, not to mention the fact that the park in Myrtle Beach is a pitcher's paradise. So LaRoche struggled, hitting only .251 with 7 home runs and 45 runs batted in.

"That was the first time I really learned how to play baseball," LaRoche admits. "Brian Snitker was my manager. That was baseball. Danville was like college baseball. It was like a wood-bat summer league. Myrtle Beach is rough. I could have sworn everybody was throwing 120 mph. Everybody's curveballs were just hammers."

"That was a big jump for him, going to Myrtle Beach," says

Brian Snitker. "That's a pretty fast league for anyone. I don't care who you are. That's a pretty tough league. He had never played April to September. If you've never done that, you don't know how to do it. That was just a big year for him right there, just to get it over with – just to play."

Even though LaRoche had vehemently resisted pitching when he was breaking into pro ball, after he established himself as a hitter, he started pressing Snitker to come in and pitch in extra inning games and blowouts. He didn't want to make a permanent change, but he still had a small pitching itch inside him. So finally, in an extra inning game, Snitker called for his first baseman to come in and pitch. Not surprisingly, he did very well, allowing only a hit and striking out a hitter in one inning of work. His fastball was clocked at 95 miles an hour.

"He looked great," Snitker admits. "It's amazing how a guy can just step over from first base and be as good as any other left-handed reliever in the league. That's how gifted and talented he is. He's a natural."

"There was some sentiment of moving him to the mound when he was struggling at Myrtle Beach," Kohlscheen says. "He got on the mound that time and he did what he did, and it was like, 'Geez, we've got a problem. What are we going to do?' He was that good both ways. I remember Paul Snyder saying, 'Man, it would have been something to see him on the mound.'"

But the Braves knew three things. First, they believed he was good enough to be a productive major league hitter. Second, they believed he was an exceptional defensive first baseman. And lastly, there was no doubt in their minds that LaRoche had the makeup to be a major league player.

"Adam's got great inner confidence," Snitker says. "He's just a gifted player. I don't know if he knows how much talent he has. He had an unorthodox swing with his setup and everything, but it works. You don't screw with it. It's not something you probably teach, but what are you going to do with it? If you start tinkering with his swing, you'll screw him up. Defensively, he could take ground balls all day long and never miss one. He's got a chance at being a Gold Glove first baseman. He's got a strong and accurate arm that he's got confidence in, and he's got great hands."

The Braves sent LaRoche back to Myrtle Beach to start the 2002 season. They often do that with players who struggle at that level in their first year. The hope is they'll go back, make the adjustment to the league and play well, and then get out of there by midseason. And that's exactly what LaRoche did. He hit .336 with 9 home runs and 53 RBI in only 250 at bats.

"It was a totally different league," he says of his return. "It was like I had been in the league for ten years. I was comfortable. I felt like a veteran."

After missing almost a month with a jammed finger, LaRoche was promoted to AA Greenville. He finished up the season by hitting .289 with 4 home runs and 19 RBI in 173 at bats. His combined stats: .317, 13 home runs, and 72 RBI - very Mark Grace-like. The Braves' coaches helped him improve offensively, but they knew better than to tinker with that swing.

"The only thing they mentioned was with two strikes maybe shortening up a bit," LaRoche says. "Stubby (Franklin Stubbs) and I got along great and he's helped me a lot. A lot of the stuff they would tell me I would feel was stuff I already knew. It was stuff I knew I was doing but it was good to hear it from somebody else seeing it."

The one question everybody had with LaRoche was whether or not he would develop more power. The thirteen homers he hit in 2002 had been his highest in the farm system, although he had twenty-three back at Seminole. But he started to answer the power question in 2003 when he started off the season back in Greenville and hit 12 homers in 219 at bats. Then after his promotion to AAA Richmond, he hit 8 home runs in 264 at bats. The power, along with the 33 doubles, often an indication of developing power, quieted those questions. Overall in 2003, he had a .290 average in 483 at bats and once again drove in 72. With the impressive season, rumors started to spread that with Robert Fick not being a long-term solution at first base in Atlanta, LaRoche could take over in 2004.

"I knew they liked me just from the way Dayton (Moore) would talk and when rovers would come in they wouldn't mess with me a lot," LaRoche says. "I knew they were confident. I didn't know when or what their date was going to be for me to come up there. I was just counting down the days. Dayton said, 'You've got a great shot.' He never said when. He always said, 'Keep doing what you're doing. Your day will come.' That's all I could think about."

LaRoche believed he might get his chance in September of 2003 to at least show the Braves he was ready for the big leagues.

But they didn't call him up; they didn't have to. They knew he was ready for a chance to start in the majors.

After the 2003 season, Fick was allowed to leave via free agency. Even though there were rumors in the media the Braves were thinking about trading for Minnesota first baseman Doug Mientkiewicz, a player very similar to LaRoche, they had already made up their mind who their first baseman was going to be in 2004. LaRoche was finally convinced when he spoke to Moore on the phone during the winter.

"He was saying it was my job to lose," LaRoche says. "Every time I talked with him, all he would say is, 'It's your job to lose.'"

The Braves didn't bring in another first baseman, only re-signing the ageless Julio Franco to split time with LaRoche as the right-handed part of a platoon. Rookies don't normally start everyday for Bobby Cox. Usually they have to start off by platooning a bit, especially if they hit left-handed. The lack of a move was the most obvious sign that the organization had full confidence in LaRoche's ability to come in and make an impact as a rookie in the big leagues.

"There were two things with Adam," says Assistant GM Frank Wren. "From the first time I saw him in Myrtle Beach, in all of my written reports to John (Schuerholz), the guy he reminded me of was John Olerud. He's just a quiet and confident player, great swing, and very good defensively. It's just a quiet confidence, and part of that I think is just the major league exposure he had as a kid as a batboy and being around his dad. I don't think he was in awe of the big leagues. So that gives you a confidence that the big leagues are not going to scare him. The second thing is we all felt it was just his history. If you watch Adam play at every level he always struggles in the first half. And then once he figures it out, once he gets his feet on the ground at every level, he excels. We knew once he got his feet on the ground, he'd be fine. But we knew he wasn't going to be in awe."

When LaRoche arrived at spring training he was a little surprised to be thrown right in with the regulars in batting practice. There he was, hitting in the same group with Chipper Jones, Andruw Jones, and J.D. Drew. But to look at him, you would have thought LaRoche was just as experienced as the other three.

"I was pretty comfortable," he admits. "But I was nervous. You'd probably never know when I'm nervous. I've got a pretty good poker face. I got to know them last year (2003). I felt like they liked me, accepted me as one of their teammates. So that wasn't it. I was just more nervous about having a good spring, doing what people thought I could do and proving people wrong, the people who didn't think I could do it."

But one person who did think he could do it was his platoon partner, Julio Franco.

The Braves made it pretty clear that they were handing the first base job to LaRoche, even though Franco was going to get plenty of action. But at forty-six years old, twenty-one years older than LaRoche, Franco was not in Spring Training "competing" with the rookie for playing time. It was pretty much a certainty that the two would platoon at first base.

LaRoche never felt threatened by Franco, and he could not have been given a greater vote of confidence from the veteran than an encounter midway through Spring Training. LaRoche was dining with his wife, Jenn, and their two kids at the Kobe Steak House, just miles from the Braves training complex in Orlando. Franco came in with his son, who was on spring break. When Julio introduced Adam, LaRoche was surprised at how he was described by his teammate.

"This is Adam LaRoche," Franco told his son. "He's our starting first baseman."

The comment may have shocked LaRoche's wife even more than Adam, but there was no doubt it gave them both a tremendous feeling. Here was a player who made his major league debut when Adam was only two years old (April 23, 1982) affirming the belief that LaRoche was, in fact, going to be the Braves' starting first baseman.

"It was awesome," LaRoche admits. "It was really comforting to hear him say it, just the way he said it. Like he was excited about it or like he was an outfielder or something. Not like he was a first baseman at all. I think it made me feel more comfortable in talking to him about first base. Before that, and I still don't even now, I didn't want to act like I was the starter and he was the backup. I was kind of afraid to say something that he might think, 'Who is this kid thinking he's going to come in here and start?' But for him to say it...I think he's happy for me. I think deep down he really wants me to do well. It's not like he's saying he wants me to do well, but he really wants me to go out there and struggle so he can play. He's not worried about his at bats at all. He wants to win. What a great guy to have over there."

LaRoche had a good Spring Training, making Franco's words somewhat prophetic. The rookie hit .290 with 3 home runs and 12 RBI in 62 at bats. The Braves felt good about the kid's chances to make an impact in 2004.

"Adam has a great gift of patience and relaxation," says Dayton Moore. "He has the ability to slow the game down. He has a great day-to-day approach. It's an even-keel approach to the game. It has allowed him to adjust quicker than others have due to that approach. We talk a lot about being able to distinguish one at bat from the other, and not let a negative at bat affect the next at bat, and 'Rochy' has the ability to do that. He has the naturalness and consistency in his swing and in his approach and he trusts his approach. That's going to allow him to be successful."

Braves Manager Bobby Cox didn't say anything special to Adam to let him know that he was on the team or even the starter at first base. Adam knew he was in good shape when the trainers informed him he was making the trip to Atlanta for the season opener. LaRoche didn't play on Opening Night, since the Braves faced a left-hander, allowing Franco to get the start. But the next night was something LaRoche will never forget.

"I wasn't nervous the whole day," LaRoche admits, "and then "DeRo" (Mark DeRosa) and "Gilly" (Marcus Giles) and a bunch of the guys were coming up basically telling me that I was nervous. I'm trying to tell them, 'Listen, I'm not nervous.' They said, 'Yes you are. Don't try to act tough. You're nervous just like we all were.' And I really wasn't. Then when I got on the field and started stretching and throwing, I kind of looked up to see how many people were there, and then it hit me that I was about to go out in front of all these people. It was something I had never felt before because none of that had ever bothered me. But I think when it's something you think about everyday, you don't understand it until you go through it."

With his mom and dad in the stands, LaRoche made history in the fourth inning. He singled early in the inning for his first big league hit, and as the Braves batted around, he came up later in the inning and got another base hit, this time a double that scored both Chipper Jones and Andruw Jones. LaRoche became the first National League rookie and just the fourth in major league history to get his first two career hits in the same inning during his major league debut.

"I didn't even know afterwards that I did it," LaRoche says. "I think that's just the state of mind you're in at the time. It never crossed my mind until Marcus ran by me going to second at the top of the next inning and said, "Man, I don't know if anybody's ever done that before.' He started talking about it and I started thinking about it. You're just not right your first game. There are a few screws loose, some butterflies. They went back and checked it out after the game. That was neat."

After his record-setting debut, LaRoche then proved Frank Wren's theory that he was a slow starter. He hit only .214 in April with 1 home run and 8 RBI in 56 at bats. Then in May, he hit .264 with a homer and 4 RBI. On May 28th in Philadelphia, LaRoche was running to home plate and collided with Phillies catcher Mike Lieberthal. LaRoche flipped in the air and came down awkwardly on his left shoulder. LaRoche didn't think anything was wrong until he was back in the dugout and made a throwing motion. Then he felt a pop. He had separated his left shoulder. The Braves had to place him on the fifteen-day disabled list and expected him to miss four to six weeks.

LaRoche may be patient at the plate when he's hitting, but he wasn't very patient while rehabbing his injury. He knew that before his injury there were questions about whether or not he could play in the big leagues, and they would only ferment as he sat on the DL.

"I had just started to get that feeling when you know you're going to hit the ball hard and that's the best thing you can have as a hitter," he says. "You go to the field and you know it doesn't matter what you do. It doesn't matter what kind of batting practice you take; when the lights come on that you're going to be totally locked in and going to crush the ball. I was just starting to get that, and then the injury. I knew that after I got back from the injury, I was going to have to start over, almost like a new spring training. It was frustrating."

On July 2nd, LaRoche was activated from the disabled list after missing thirty-one games with his shoulder injury. Cox put him right back into the platoon with Franco, even though the veteran had played very well as the primary starter in LaRoche's absence. Adam still struggled a bit for the rest of July, hitting only .250 with 2 homers and 7 RBI. But then, in the month of August, LaRoche lit up like the Georgia sun. He hit .298 with 4 home runs and 10 RBI in 57 at bats. He continued that fine play into September, hitting .347 with 5 home runs and 16 RBI. After returning from injury the rookie batted .301 with 11 home runs and 33 RBI in 196 at bats.

With his strong second half, LaRoche had found the comfort level that had been so elusive in the first half of his season.

"I started to learn how, even when the comfort level's not there, to make it be there, to kind of falsify it, psyching myself into thinking I felt it," LaRoche says. "This is so important in hitting everyday. I don't care if you're in high school or the big leagues. When you're not seeing the ball well, you've almost got to make yourself think that you're fine, that you are seeing it good. It's crazy how much can happen if you do that."

Overall on the season, Adam finished with a .278 average, 13 home runs, 45 RBI, and 27 doubles in 324 at bats. He also played solid defense, committing only 5 errors in 98 games at first base. As soon as he got his feet on the ground, LaRoche's rookie season was a smashing success.

"I am happy with the comeback I made and the way I handled myself," he says. "I think I possibly gained some respect from the guys just from the way I was in the clubhouse, on the field, and off the field. Plus, I'm proud of the fact I beat Chipper in the bet that I had. I had to hit .275 or better. So now I get to go shoot deer on his farm. I get a free dinner from him whenever I want it. For hitting .278!"

It looked like Chipper Jones might have a hunting buddy for a while, as Adam LaRoche became entrenched as the Braves' first baseman. A possible platoon situation is still likely with Julio Franco at first base, but that would be more about the Braves' affection for Franco than any doubts about LaRoche's ability. He's made it. He now heads to work every day with a bat in one hand and a glove in the other.

Just like he did many years ago.

17

THE NEXT DALE MURPHY?

Millions of kids all over the world play baseball. Most who love the game are able to play for their high school team. Some are lucky enough to go on to play in college, while others are talented enough to play pro ball.

And some kids are just special.

David Francoeur knew his son Jeff was special. The first word young Jeff said was not "mom" or "dad," but "ball." It made perfect sense considering Jeff was always playing some kind of "ball."

"Anything, football, baseball," says David Francoeur. "Any kind of ball, he would just lie down in front of the TV and play catch with himself. Always had a ball in his hand. He would sit in front of the TV and just toss the ball up in the air."

Jeff Francoeur was much like many young kids. He would hang around when older brother David had his friends over to play pick-up games.

"Instead of playing ball with kids his own age, he was basically playing ball with kids that were about four years older than him," says his dad.

Actually, Jeff's first association with sports was golf.

"I was like three and my dad got me a set of clubs," Jeff says.

But it didn't take long to know that football and baseball would be his favorite two sports. He started playing baseball at four and football at six. His dad knew he was a bit different from the other kids when Jeff was playing T-ball very early on.

"He had a competitive spirit that I didn't see in other kids," David Francoeur says. "His concept of the game, his knowledge, his awareness was just better."

Jeff's dad might have helped nurture that early talent by teaching the intricacies of the game of baseball. There was a bonus room in their house that was big enough to set up a small baseball diamond.

"I would have him stand on a base, and I'd say, 'Okay, if a ball is hit here then what do you do?'" David Francoeur says. "I was teaching him about force plays and everything else. We'd go over him thinking ahead like, 'If the ball is hit to me, what do I do with it?' He'd say, 'Okay, give me some more examples.' You couldn't give him enough. Others would say they couldn't be bothered with it. He always wanted to have some of those scenarios so he could figure out what to do with the ball when he got it. I think a lot of that is when I started to realize that at that age a lot of kids didn't want that and he did. I knew most five-year-old kids aren't thinking about those kinds of things. He was."

Jeff remembers one specific incident in T-ball where he believes his parents knew baseball was going to be important to him.

"We were like 17-0 in T-ball my second year," Francoeur explains. "I was six. We were in a championship game and I had already hit three home runs. So I was 3-for-3 and I came up and we were down 25-24 in the last inning with the bases loaded and two outs. I popped up to lose us the game. After the game, I was crying. Everybody else was going to the juice box or something. That's when my mom and dad said they pretty much knew that I was going to be a baseball player."

Jeff's love for baseball was also aided by the fact that his dad took him to see the hometown big leaguers. The Francoeurs lived in Lilburn, Georgia, a suburb north of Atlanta. Even though the Braves weren't very good in the mid-late 80's, it was baseball, and the Francoeurs wanted to go and watch.

"The first one I remember I was like three years old," Jeff says. "That's when Bob Horner hit four home runs in a game."

"We would probably go to ten to fifteen games a season," says David Francoeur. "We've been Braves fans ever since we've been in Atlanta."

David says he and his two sons would get to Atlanta Fulton-County Stadium as soon as the gates opened. Watching batting practice was important, but Jeff wanted to get there early for another reason.

"He couldn't wait to get down there and get in the autograph lines," David says. "Craig McMurtry gave him an autograph on two or three occasions. He would always take the time and stop."

"I loved Andres Thomas," says Jeff, referring to the Braves' starting shortstop from 1987-1990. "I loved how he hit. I just thought he had the most unique style of hitting."

And then there was Dale Murphy.

"I loved the way he played the game," Francoeur says. "He always played hard. He was stuck on a horse crap team, but he always came out and played his hardest. He couldn't do anything about it, but he just made his team better by just being there."

When he was ten years old, Jeff started playing baseball on a traveling team for the East Cobb baseball program, one of the best amateur programs in the country. The traveling baseball was more of a challenge for Jeff, who really overmatched everyone in T-ball. He played in about a hundred games a year, mostly during the summer. But then when he was twelve, Francoeur got burned out. He decided to take a step back from baseball, at least for a while.

"My dad never pushed me," he says. "I always wanted to play. Finally, I had just had enough and I quit that summer and played golf. All summer I played in the Atlanta Junior Association and I went to the grand championships down in Jekyll Island (on the South Georgia coast). I loved playing golf but I missed the whole aspect of a team sport. So I almost had to get away from baseball to realize how much I missed it."

When he got back playing with an East Cobb team, Francoeur started to realize that he was pretty good at the game.

"When I would play in those tournaments across the country, I'd do well," he says. "When I started getting closer to high school in sixth, seventh, and eighth grades I felt like I wanted to play in the big leagues one day."

Throughout his early teenage years, Francoeur continued to play team sports. He gave up basketball when he got to the ninth grade, and he started to concentrate a little more on baseball. He could tell he was going to have a chance to do more than just play in high school.

"When I was a freshman some of the guys who were seniors were getting drafted," Francoeur explains. "I saw them doing that and thought, 'Well, I could do that.' I could kind of match up with what they did. I starting thinking, 'Yeah, that would be cool. I want to get drafted and do that.'"

But then in Francoeur's tenth grade season, something happened to put a halt on his immediate thoughts of a baseball career. He had continued to play football simply because high school football was a way of life, not only in Georgia, but also at Parkview High School. Francoeur was a defensive back, and a good one. All of a sudden, he was becoming a two-sport star in high school.

"I always tell people the most fun I had in high school was playing in football games on Friday night," Francoeur says, "even better than baseball. It's just so big. I just loved the aspect of the game. I loved being out there and hitting people and scoring touchdowns. It was so much fun."

The fun of football forced Francoeur to split his time between the two sports. He stopped playing as much summer baseball, since it started to cut into his time of football practice late in July. His name was already known in the Atlanta area, but with football being so big in the state of Georgia, Jeff was becoming a popular high school sports figure in the entire state.

"In the south, football is just so big," says David Francoeur. "It has been and always will be. Baseball just doesn't get the notoriety that football does down here. When you're at Parkview and you're nationally ranked all the time in football and you're always in the playoffs, that's where the notoriety was. When you're playing youth football here, everything is geared to being a Parkview High football player."

Jeff believes the commitment he made to both sports made him a better athlete, a better teammate, and a better competitor.

"I always said that for me football made me a better baseball player and baseball made me a better football player," he says. "With baseball you've got to be calm at times. In football you get carried away at times but you've got to come back a little bit. At the same time, in baseball I can get riled up and I think that comes from my football mentality. I don't think, especially when you're really young, you should put everything into one sport and say, 'This is all I'm going to do.' Whether it's baseball and basketball or basketball and football, whatever combination it is, I don't think you need to limit yourself."

Francoeur helped his Parkview football team win the state championship in his junior season. That prompted college coaches to start eagerly recruiting him to play football. Even though his first love was baseball, Francoeur admits he got caught up a bit when several big name coaches wanted him for their team.

"I had my dad and Coach Buck (Parkview Baseball Coach Hugh Buchanan) sit me down and bring me back a little bit," Francoeur admits. "They knew in my heart that baseball was what I always wanted to do. Sometimes it was easy to get carried away like in May of my junior year when I was getting calls from Lou Holtz and Bobby Bowden. It's pretty overwhelming since you're not used to that. It definitely got me thinking that I might want to play college football."

Francoeur was maturing into a tremendous athlete. By his junior season he was six-foot-three and 190 pounds. He was getting better as a football player, and after leading Parkview to a state football title, he got his Panthers baseball team to the state finals. That same weekend, the Braves were preparing for the upcoming draft. But Roy Clark had heard about this star junior baseball player in North Atlanta. So he, Paul Snyder, and two of their scouts, John Flannery and Tim Conroy, left their draft room and decided to go watch Francoeur play.

"He was playing a two out of three game series against Stephen Drew and Lowndes County," Clark says. "Of course it didn't get to a third game since Jeff hit a home run in game one to win the game and in the second game he hit two more home runs. That's the kind of player he is. He thrives under those situations."

"He just carried the team," Conroy says. "We knew very early on how good of a player he was and how interested we were in him. We couldn't wait for the opportunity to draft him."

While baseball teams like the Braves were showing interest, the publicity Francoeur was getting as one of the top upcoming seniors in high school football had put baseball on a backburner, at least temporarily.

"In October of my senior year, I took my first official recruiting visit," Francoeur says. "I went up to Notre Dame. I was like, 'Oh my God.' I got a chance to be in the locker room, be on the field during the game, and then talked and went to dinner with (Notre Dame Football Coach) Bob Davie. Wow. Forget baseball. I'll come play baseball, but I want to play football too."

The recruiting process was intense. Along with Notre Dame, Francoeur received offers from Florida State, Georgia Tech, Vanderbilt, Ole Miss, and Clemson. He was intent on playing both football and baseball, but NCAA rules forced Francoeur to sign a football scholarship, even if baseball was equally important.

"Clemson was the best fit," Francoeur says. "It was only two hours away from home, which I liked. It was enough to get me away, but not totally far away from home. Coach Tommy Bowden (Clemson's football coach) and Coach Jack Leggett (Clemson's baseball coach) talked with me. They told me while I was playing baseball the other one wouldn't bother me, and while I was doing football the other one wouldn't bother me. So it was very good."

Francoeur made it very clear to Coach Bowden that baseball was still very important to him. But Bowden had a convincing story for Francoeur. Bowden's dad, legendary coach Bobby Bowden, coached Deion Sanders when he was a two-sport star at Florida State. While coaches at other schools were a bit hesitant in agreeing that Jeff could play both sports, Bowden had no problem.

"He said, 'if you can help the University, I don't see why not,'" Francoeur says. "That gave me great respect for Tommy."

So with a football and baseball commitment to Clemson, Francoeur still had to play his senior season of baseball. Pro teams still believed there was a chance Francoeur would pick baseball, so they showed up in droves to watch him play. Coach Buchanan had prepared Jeff for the rush of scouts, but there was nothing quite like the first day Francoeur saw the unbelievable number of scouts there to watch him play.

"It was nuts," he says. "I figured there would be some scouts, but I pulled into the parking lot at 3:30 that first day, our game was at 6:00 and we were going to hit in the cages at 4:00. I remember looking down where our cages are in the right field line and seeing eighty grown men down there with stopwatches. I remember thinking to myself, 'Here it goes. It's beginning.' So I was nervous."

Parkview started off the 2002 season slowly, and so did Francoeur. He hit only .250 for the first month, while the team lost two games early in the season. Francoeur could tell all the attention he was personally getting was affecting his team, so he decided to take matters into his own hands. He called a team meeting, with no coaches present, and told his teammates that they had to go back to having fun and playing the game. The attention was going to be there, but they couldn't let it affect the team.

"We lost three games that whole year and we lost two games at the LaGrange tournament early in the year," Francoeur says. "I think it was because it was a little uncomfortable for the whole team, not just myself. The whole team was pulling for me and they were trying to do stuff to make me look good. When we were in the cages, they were trying to throw balls right down the plate. It was just very uncomfortable. Usually our team in the cages before a game, we were always joking around, talking about each other's sisters or whatever. Just being guys. And then all of a sudden, it was dead silence and everybody was being serious. So after about five or six times of that, I had a meeting with the whole team and said, 'Look this is how we're going to do things. I don't care if there are a hundred scouts and a bunch of GM's, we're going to go back to being ourselves, joke around, and cut up. If they don't like it, that's their fault. They can leave.' After that, things got really easy. It was fun after that."

Francoeur and the rest of his team bounced back. He showed why he was such a great baseball prospect with a tremendous season. But many of the pro teams started to bow out of the hunt. The talk was out there: Francoeur was going to play football, and unless a team paid him big money, he was going to school.

The Braves, however, were undeterred. Even though they had the twenty-third pick in the first round, and despite Francoeur being a top five talent, the Braves had a feeling they could get him. They knew he had grown up a Braves fan, and they knew he really wanted to play baseball. They knew Francoeur was someone they had to get.

"We all knew," Clark admits. "We all knew that day when we went back to the draft room that he was a special talent. He interacted with the crowd. He was the guy. He's a special player with leadership qualities. As the next year evolved, and football came into it, and the signability made him a question mark."

Al Goetz was in his first season as the Braves' area scout for the state of Georgia. He first saw Francoeur at the age of twelve, when Jeff came into Goetz's baseball facility to work out. In 2000, when Francoeur was a sophomore, Goetz saw Francoeur again.

"At that point, you could tell he was going to be something special – more from that mental side of the approach to the game," Goetz says. "His confidence wasn't cocky, but you knew that he knew he was going to get it done. I'm sure that the guys that he played against all thought that he was cocky, but he's anything but that. He's a solid kid. He loved the game. He loved to play. He loved to compete."

Then when Goetz joined the Braves, Clark put him on a Francoeur watch. Goetz did what all Braves scouts do when they follow a player: he got to know the family and the player as much as possible. The Braves wanted to make sure Francoeur was their guy, and having the area scout get to know him gave Clark confidence the team could get him.

"Al did a fantastic job," Clark says. "We knew Jeff and the family."

"When I talked with the family, I felt that he knew baseball was his future," Goetz says. "I don't think he ever had aspirations of being a NFL player. I think he could have been, but I think his first love was baseball. When I talked to the family, that was kind of what they indicated."

A week before the draft, and a few days before Francoeur's senior season would end with the state finals, the Braves sent in Goetz, Snyder, and Dayton Moore to have an in-home visit with Francoeur. The rumors were pretty heavy that he wanted to play football at Clemson, and the signability issues had already scared off some teams. When the three scouts arrived at the Francoeur home, Jeff asked his mom and dad to leave the room. He wanted to talk with the Braves himself.

"He wanted to handle it," Snyder says. "Then he talked to us. We didn't say anything for a while. He just told us what he thought he was capable of and what he could do to make us better."

"Jeff handled himself well in the meeting we had with him," Moore says. "He was honest and up front. There are just a lot of character traits there that you would want in your own son."

"He basically came out and said, 'If you guys draft me, I'm going to get there,'" Goetz recalls. "He said, 'I'm going to be a major league baseball player.' The biggest thing was how he did it. He took control of the entire situation like he takes control of baseball games. He got his parents out of the room. They jumped up and left and he sat there and talked to us like a grown man."

"I just wanted to show them too that I could talk without my mom and dad being there," Francoeur explains. "I don't need them there. I'm a big boy too."

But Francoeur had more to prove to the Braves' three than just being able to speak without parental supervision. He wanted them to know that he wanted to play baseball and he wanted to play for the Braves.

"They were asking why I felt they should take me," Francoeur remembers. "They wanted to know what I thought I brought to the table as far as being a first rounder and possibly playing for fifteen years in Atlanta. I just told them my baseball skills, but that there was more than that. Just being a leader in the clubhouse, being someone guys could talk to. I just told them I thought I'd be a good addition. I just wanted to let them know that I wanted to play baseball. I wanted to be upfront with them and tell them that I wanted to play baseball more than anything and if the price and everything feels right, then I felt that I would be a good fit for the organization."

But there was more to the meeting than just finding out if both the Braves and Francoeur wanted each other. Again, with the Braves holding a late first round pick, it was going to be a gamble to assume Francoeur would slide all the way to twenty-three. So the Braves had to come up with a strategy.

"We said, 'Only you can make this thing happen,'" Snyder admits. "We couldn't make it happen, but he could."

To slide to the twenty-third pick, Francoeur was going to have to tell other teams picking in front of the Braves that he only wanted to be a Brave, and that if they drafted him, he was going to Clemson. Since he did want to be a Brave and he had that leverage of holding a college scholarship over the heads of other teams, Francoeur was holding all the cards. The talk was already out there that he was going to cost above "slot money," a term used to define the Commissioner's Office pre-arranged bonus figure for every single drafted player. Francoeur was going to have to ward off other teams if he was going to fall to his favorite.

So after the Braves and Francoeur strategized, the three scouts left feeling confident. They were convinced that baseball was his first love, and that he wanted to be a Brave.

"When Dayton and I walked out of that house I said, 'Dayton, we just interviewed the next Dale Murphy,'" Snyder says. "The way that kid handled himself reminded me of Dale so much. I didn't realize how much he loved this game of baseball. I didn't know if he could lay that other one down. I didn't know that until I went in the house that night. He wanted to be a baseball player. He had a little something about him with the body language. I always say just follow the player. They can tell you something without saying a word."

"He wanted to be a Brave," Goetz says. "We knew that when we left his house."

"That's kind of what I wanted to have happen," Francoeur admits. "To be honest with you, we had some teams call, like Seattle and Boston and a few other teams that were willing to pay a little more if I could get there. But the more I thought about it and the more I talked to mom and dad, the more I realized that I love Atlanta. I've grown up here, I'm a Braves fan, and I've always imagined myself walking into Atlanta-Fulton County Stadium and then when that got torn down I imagined walking into the Ted (Turner Field). So, when I got the chance to do that, I thought to myself, 'This is what I want to do.' Those were the guys that were the decision-makers, and I just wanted to let them know that I was mature and ready to play professional baseball. That's what I wanted to do. I felt like that was the best way to show them that I wanted to play and that I could play."

Francoeur still had one obstacle. He had to make sure the other twenty-two teams picking before the Braves passed on him. So he wrote them letters saying he was going to need a sizable payday or that he was going to Clemson. He felt that he had to scare the other teams off, and that's exactly what he did. He was just being honest with them. They were either going to have to pay him a fortune, which was unlikely, or he was going to Clemson. It was a serious threat. Both Jeff's mom and dad are educators, and they had no trouble with their son going to Clemson if that's what it came down to.

"We knew that the figure had to be enough that would have caused us to give up the opportunity to go to Clemson," David Francoeur says. "We told Jeff during the entire baseball scenario, 'If the money ain't right, if it's not there, you go to Clemson and you don't even think twice about it. We'll think about this draft three years down the road.' We were prepared to do that. No way was I going to jeopardize Jeffrey's opportunity to go to Clemson. No way. We knew the Braves liked high school guys. They had a track record with that. They had that kind of history, unlike Oakland where we knew they didn't."

Both sides were simply a perfect match. The Braves felt they had found themselves another Dale Murphy, though this one was from the Atlanta area. Francoeur carried himself like Murphy. He was an outfielder with power, and he had the charisma of a leader. While Francoeur saw a chance to be a hometown hero, he also liked the fact that all of the Braves' farm teams were close by, so he could be near his family and friends as he was developing in the minor leagues.

"The last thing I wanted to do was go far away…like when the Blue Jays came to my house and said they were going to send me to Medicine Hat in Canada," Jeff says. "I was like, 'I don't want to be up there.' Heck, I didn't even know where that is. Family has always been important for me, and I knew it would be great for them to watch me."

But Francoeur still had more baseball to play with the state finals the weekend before the draft. Goetz went to the Lassiter High School to watch the youngster one last time and stood alongside the Parkview dugout, almost hidden away in a corner.

"He was up in the top of the sixth inning," Goetz remembers. "He knew I was there. He had waved at me a couple of times. The bases were loaded and they had just changed pitchers. He looked at me and before he went up to hit he just winked at me. And then he hit the longest ball I've ever seen a high school kid hit. It was over the trees and into a yard. It was almost like he said with his wink, 'This one's for you buddy.' I had never seen a kid do that much – who knew he was going to do something special. And he did it."

Francoeur helped lead Parkview to its second straight State title, with six hits, four homers and seven RBI in seven at bats, of course that's not to mention he was the winning pitcher in both games. He ended his high school career with a .443 average, 55 home runs, and 164 RBI.

Three days later came the draft. Seattle General Manager Pat Gillick had seen Francoeur play in the weekend tournament, but his Mariners picked twenty-eighth, five picks after Atlanta. The Indians, picking twenty-first, were a worry. They expressed heavy interest in Francoeur, and even though he told them not to draft him, they said they were going to. Teams were forced to do some serious soul-searching: draft Francoeur without giving him money above slot and possibly lose him to the football scholarship or take a gamble that they could convince him to sign after they drafted him. It was a huge gamble, and some teams tried to hedge all the way up until the time of the draft.

"The White Sox (pick eighteen) called that morning," says David Francoeur. "So did the Twins (pick twenty) and Dodgers (pick nineteen). Several teams called. Again we just kept saying that Jeff wouldn't be signing for slot money."

"I was nervous," Francoeur admits. "It was nerve-racking when a couple of them called that morning like the Reds (pick three) and the Royals (pick six). They picked before the Braves. But I felt pretty confident when I got off the phone that I was either going to the Braves, Seattle (pick twenty-eight), or Boston (pick fifty-seven)."

But the Braves weren't going to let him get past the twenty-third pick. So, as Francoeur was listening on the Internet just before the twenty-third pick, the phone rang.

"It was John Schuerholz," Francoeur says. "He congratulated me for being picked by the Braves and then put on Roy. They just said they'd be in touch in a couple of days, have fun, and congratulations."

Francoeur (below) was ecstatic, but not as happy as the scouts in the Braves' draft war room. They knew they had pulled one off. A top five talent in the draft had fallen all the way to their pick at twenty-three.

A Braves fan from the beginning.

"Roy was the main guy to orchestrate getting Francoeur," Dayton Moore says. "Roy Clark believed we were going to get Jeff Francoeur when a lot of us were saying, 'this guy's not going to get to us. Why are we going through this process?' Roy believed 100% that we were going to be able to get this guy. It was just Roy's vision of Jeff Francoeur."

"We knew that he was a special player," Clark says. "We knew we'd love to have him in the organization, but a lot of things had to fall just right. Guys like him don't come around that often. We were fortunate when he was available that we could get him."

The Francoeurs had planned a family vacation for right after the draft, so they took off for a week to Destin, Florida. The trip gave the entire family time to consider the options at hand. Jeff wanted to play baseball, but the lure of getting a college education was still very strong. It was more than just leverage; he wanted to go to school. The trip gave Jeff and his dad a chance to talk about the future.

"We'd talk about it everyday for a little while and then just go and forget about it," David Francoeur says. "We didn't want to just talk baseball, baseball, baseball. We needed to get away from it. We would talk about it for probably about a half hour a day. Then we were out in the ocean there together and Jeff said, 'Dad, if it's right I think I do want to sign.' So when we came back from vacation, we pretty much were saying that if it was right, we were going to sign."

The negotiations dragged on for a few weeks after Jeff returned from his trip. The Braves were going to pay him above the slotted money set aside for that spot in the draft (around $1.4 million), but coming to an agreement took time. For a few weeks, the Braves had $2 million on the table, while Jeff was asking for $2.4 million.

"We had never given a kid over $1.75 million," Goetz says. "We were at our max, and I didn't think that was going to get it done. Then we invited him down to the stadium."

The Braves used a trick that many teams use when trying to sign a draft pick. They invited Francoeur to Turner Field to take batting practice with the big league team before a game with the Montreal Expos. The team had set up a locker for him with his name on a uniform. It was a chance for him to make an impression, to make the Braves know they needed to sign him, and a chance for the Braves to let Francoeur hit in the stadium he had dreamed of playing in for many years. Francoeur had not hit in several weeks, so he wasn't sure how he was going to do.

"It was a little bit overwhelming," Francoeur admits. "I knew they were trying to get me down there to schmooze me a little bit. That's what you do."

Francoeur stepped into the batting cage with all eyes in the stadium on him. Instead of placing him with the pitchers in the BP lineup, the Braves threw him right into the fire, right between Chipper Jones and Gary Sheffield. Stan Kasten, John Schuerholz, and Bobby Cox were all watching. The first three pitches Francoeur popped straight up right into the cage. Not a good first impression.

"I was swinging hard," Francoeur admits.

"I thought we could forget about that extra couple hundred thousand that we needed to get to," Goetz jokes.

Then Francoeur showed the Braves why he was so important to sign. After fouling off the first three pitches, he hit eight straight balls out of Turner Field.

"It was neat," Francoeur says, understating the obvious. "It was fun to be out there with Gary Sheffield and some of those guys. It definitely made me see where I wanted to be someday."

Goetz knew an impression had been made when Expos catcher Michael Barrett, himself an Atlanta resident and a friend of the scout, came over and asked him to go hear what the Expos relievers were asking.

"Michael said to those pitchers, 'Tell Al what you just told me,'" Goetz remembers. "They go, 'Well, we're just trying to figure out how to pitch to this Francoeur guy tonight.' I went over and told Roy and John and Stan, who said, 'Well, I guess we can give him a couple of hundred thousand more.'"

But the biggest impression on the Braves may have been made afterwards when Francoeur joined the Braves in their clubhouse.

"It didn't faze him one bit," Goetz says. "He walked in the clubhouse and Greg Maddux said, 'Hey, I hope you don't sign. I want them to re-sign me and we'll use that money.' I walked around and introduced him, then minutes later he was in there playing cards with Chipper and everybody else. He was an eighteen-year-old high school kid. Everybody else that age would have been hiding in the corner."

"After taking batting practice, we met with Al and Roy and all of them and got talking," Francoeur says. "We could tell that we were getting closer. Then they said, 'We're going to go up a little bit. We'll talk to you in the next couple of days.' At that point, I knew things were going to get done and that I was going to sign. It was just a matter of time."

Just a few days later, the Braves signed Francoeur to a contract with a $2.2 million dollar bonus. For the scouts that had stayed on top of Francoeur, there was no doubt that he was worth every dime.

"He was a player with a lot of options," says Dayton Moore. "He made a commitment to sign with us. So obviously he respects what we do and had a trust level with us that would allow him to be part of it. The makeup of Jeff Francoeur is what sets him apart."

"With his gifted abilities to play this game and with his special talents makeup-wise, he's got tremendous leadership qualities," says Roy Clark. "I'd love to get a guy just like him every year. He's what we're looking for."

Francoeur went to Danville in the Appalachian League to start his pro career. He hit .327 with 8 home runs and 31 RBI in 147 at bats. Then in 2003, the Braves sent him to Low-A Rome in the South Atlantic League. Rome, Georgia, is just about an hour from Francoeur's home in Lilburn. Once again, Francoeur had a solid season, hitting .281 with 14 home runs and 68 RBI in 524 at bats. The Rome Braves finished first in the Southern Division during the second half of the season, advancing to the Sally League playoffs. Once again, Francoeur was apart of a winning team, and once again he shined in the playoffs.

The Braves were playing the Hickory Crawdads in the first round. With the series tied at one and with Rome down 1-0 in the seventh inning of the deciding Game Three, Francoeur was due up second in the order behind third baseman Wes Timmons. As the two were on deck waiting for the inning to begin, Francoeur shocked Timmons with his comment.

"Hey Wes, if you get on with a hit, be ready 'cause the first pitch I'm going to lay one down," Francoeur said.

Timmons looked at Francoeur like he was nuts.

"Well, just be ready," Francoeur said again.

The team home run leader was suggesting that he was going to bunt with runners on, needing two runs to win.

"To be honest with you, when I'm feeling good I'd be trying for a bomb," Francoeur admits. "But at that point I had been playing really well toward the end of the season and played really well in the first game against Hickory, but then in the second game I struggled a little bit. We only had like one hit that whole game in Game three. So I knew I had to get something going. I saw the third baseman back. I figured the way this pitcher was throwing, coming inside a little bit, that I could put one down there."

Also going through Francoeur's mind was the possible end of his season. Hickory had had their way with Rome all year, and he didn't like the potential of the Crawdads ending his season. The pitcher for Hickory was weaving a gem, so Francoeur believed he had to do something to jumpstart his team.

"Usually, 99% of the time I make something happen by hitting the ball," Francoeur says. "But that time I thought, 'Well, what if the the third baseman doesn't throw it? Then we've got first and second and nobody out.' As a third hole hitter, I needed to make something happen."

Timmons did his part by getting a leadoff base hit to left field. Then with the whole stadium expecting Francoeur to swing for the fences, he laid a perfect bunt down the third base line. The third baseman was in shock and his throw was late. Then the first baseman threw to third, but Timmons was safe and Francoeur advanced to second base. In the third base coaching box was a flabbergasted Rome Manager, Rocket Wheeler.

"I had no clue what was going on when he did it," Wheeler admits. "He did that bunt on his own. I was like, 'No,' but it turned out good. He knew he wasn't swinging good so he laid down a bunt. He's not selfish. He's a team player. It shows what kind of winner he is. The worst possible scenario was that he gets Wes over, we get him in, and he ties the game. The best scenario is he ended up on second base on an error and then wound up scoring the go-ahead run."

And that's exactly what happened. Two batters later, Rome outfielder Ardley Jansen singled up the middle, scoring Timmons and Francoeur. Rome hung on to win the game 2-1 to advance to the Sally League Championship Series.

"It all kind of worked out beautifully," Francoeur says.

One week later, Rome would defeat the Lake County Captains to win the South Atlantic League Championship.

"It was amazing," Francoeur says. "It got to the point that we knew we were going to win. It was such a special team, such a good group of guys."

The 2004 season was expected to be a challenge for Francoeur, as he advanced to the Braves High-A team in Myrtle Beach, South Carolina. The park in Myrtle Beach is about one mile from the ocean, and the high winds are a good test for power hitters. Francoeur did well, hitting .293 with 15 home runs and 52 RBI. There was even talk about Francoeur knocking on the door of the big leagues in another year. But then, two days before he was slated to be promoted to AA Greenville, Francoeur was struck down with a horrible injury. Facing the Delmarva Shorebirds in the Carolina League, Francoeur got a pitch inside – too inside. He was hit in the face with a 90 mph fastball.

"I was trying to lay one (bunt) down," Francoeur says. "At the same time I just put my bat up in front of my face to try to get out of the way. That team had been throwing at me a lot inside. I understand that. That's part of the game. It just nipped my bat. You couldn't even tell, so it just went flush into my cheek. Right away, I thought I was blind. I couldn't see for a day and a half out of my right eye. The eye was swollen shut."

After the swelling went down, Francoeur had to have surgery on a facial bone near his right eye. Before his injury, Francoeur was on the fast track to the big leagues, but the surgery slowed him down.

"I'm lucky," he says. "Anytime you're dealing with the face or the eye, you're thinking it could cost you the sport that you love. Another fourth of an inch up and I would have never been able to play again. I think it definitely taught me a little humility and patience."

Francoeur returned after missing almost a month of action. He finally got the promotion to AA, but struggled the rest of the season hitting only .197. But the Braves were not discouraged one bit about Francoeur's potential. They believe he will be a tremendous everyday player for many years to come.

"I just love watching him play," Roy Clark says. "He can be as good as he wants to be. As long as he stays healthy and plays with the same passion, then the only limitations are the limitations that Jeff puts on himself. He is everything that we thought he was going to be – and better. We're looking for him to hopefully spend a long career with the Atlanta Braves and win a lot of championship rings. There's just something special about him when he walks on the field. You just know it."

That's the same thing they said about Dale Murphy when he arrived in Atlanta. Murphy struggled at times in the minors, but once he got to the big leagues, there was no stopping him. Jeff Francoeur is the same size as Dale Murphy, plays the same position, and has those same All-American good looks. The similarities are ironic, and Francoeur knows the comparisons are a lot to live up to.

"I first heard the Dale Murphy comparisons when Paul Snyder walked out of my house," Francoeur says. "He had talked to me and my family and saw what we were like. I just remember thinking how cool that was. For me character has always been a big issue. I think character is the most important thing you can have as a person. A person remembers you by your character. So when I heard that, it was the biggest compliment I've ever gotten. He believed I played like Murph on the field, but was like him off the field too. That's something I've prided myself in...that my dad installed in me. You know, after the game signing autographs for kids after you've gone 0-4. You know anybody can sign if they've gone 3-3 with a double. But I think it takes a real person with character, a real man to sign after a game when he's gone 0-4. That shows character. So Paul's comment was a big compliment."

Francoeur knows that as he gets closer to the big leagues, the Murphy comparisons will only get louder. But it's going to be extra special for him when he makes it to his hometown Atlanta Braves.

"I think there will definitely be some pressure, but it's something I look forward to," he says. "Dale never grew up here. So you're talking about a kid in me that did grow up in the area. That's why I maybe feel a little extra pressure cause I'm the hometown kid. I've lived here for twenty years. The whole Atlanta area and my community is what made me and molded me into the person that I am. I don't think anyone should ever not look forward to a chance to give back to kids and the community like that. The impact that you can have on a community and on kids like that is amazing. It's a good thing."

"I'll tell you...we thought Chipper and Murph hit the Atlanta market," says Snyder, "if Francoeur ever hits it there's no end in sight. There's no end in sight. He's got so much charisma about him. He likes everybody. He's going to make so much money away from baseball. He's just so charismatic. You may vote for him for President one day."

"There's just one thing about Mr. Francoeur," says Roy Clark. "He's a winner. That's all he's about."

And that's all the Braves were ever looking for.

18

THE GEORGIA BOYS

The priority placed on the scouting and eventual signing of local sensation Jeff Francoeur was all part of a grand scheme developed during the Roy Clark era in Atlanta. Clark and his staff never set out to pursue high school kids from the state of Georgia so feverishly. It just worked out that way. In fact, the philosophy actually started out as kind of a fluke. It just so happened that Clark's first draft produced four Georgia kids in the first thirty rounds, and that was all it took to create a philosophy.

"I did not even consider going heavily after Georgia kids," Clark admits. "As a matter of fact, when I scouted the Carolinas, Georgia was one of those states where no one wanted to go because it was so big and the players were not that good."

That was the 1980's, when Georgia was known mainly for producing solid football prospects. But things changed in the 1990's for several reasons.

First, after years of not having a winning pro team, Georgians had a winner in the Braves. The interest in baseball carried over to kids who wanted to play the game. They watched Tom Glavine pitch and David Justice hit, and they wanted to do it too.

"All their life, or at least the last fourteen years, they've turned on the tube and seen Bobby Cox and John Schuerholz and the teams that Paul Snyder has put out there, win," Clark says. "And everybody wants to be with a winner. In Anchorage, Alaska, you can't say the same thing. But in the southeast, it's kind of evolved that way."

Secondly, it was helped by the improvement of the feeder systems, amateur baseball leagues that allow kids to play baseball beyond their ten to fifteen games at the YMCA or rec leagues. The best system in Georgia is also perhaps the best in the country, East Cobb Baseball in Marietta, just north of Atlanta. They take kids starting at the age of eight and teach them the specifics of baseball, and then the kids play teams all over the country. In the mid-80's and before, traveling baseball was non-existent. Kids were lucky if they picked up a few summer league games after rec league or the high school season. But now, kids can play a hundred games in a calendar year. East Cobb's success has produced better talent that has bled into the high school ranks, making that level of ball better as well. And most of the kids in Georgia high schools have grown up not only watching the Braves, but watching the Braves win.

"The one thing about the entire southeast that's different now than other parts of the country, is that everybody wants to be a part of a winning organization," Clark says. "They want to be a part of all this. For example, we've got guys who have signed college scholarships with Florida State or Georgia or Alabama, good baseball schools, but they want us. They say, 'Look, you draft me, and I'll sign with you. But I'm not going to sign with anybody else.' So with signability such a big issue these days, you see more teams drafting regionally."

Clark's very first draft pick set the tone for these theories. The Braves loved Adam Wainwright as a pitcher, but they also recognized his huge desire to be a Brave. They knew the story of the picture his mom had of Adam dressed in a Dale Murphy uniform when he was three years old. They knew Adam and his brother Trey watched the Braves every night at 7:35. He was their type of pitcher, their type of person, but he also had a strong desire to put on a Braves' uniform.

"I just considered myself a Braves guy," Wainwright says.

"Adam Wainwright was a special talent," Clark says. "He was the guy we were hoping would be there. We realized Adam wanted us as much as we wanted him. So it was a good fit."

The Braves paid Wainwright $1.25 million dollars, so it's not as if he took a hometown discount to play for the Braves. But the team realized something the day of the 2000 draft: Georgia kids were going to feel special about playing for the Braves, and that, in turn, would push them even harder to get to the big leagues to play for their hometown team.

"We knew that Georgia was strong that year," Clark says.

Early on in the 2000 draft Clark found two more pitchers, right-handers Bryan Digby and Blaine Boyer. The latter let the Braves know when they invited him to a pre-draft workout that he wanted to play for his favorite team. Boyer grew up a Braves fan, going to games with his dad beginning when he was four years old. And it just so happened that Boyer was in the same third grade class as Skyler Cox, Bobby Cox's daughter.

"We grew up together," Boyer says. "I asked her if she could get me a David Justice autographed baseball. She came back two days later and Bobby had gotten it for me. It said, 'To Blaine: God Bless. David Justice.' From then on man, I was hooked. I was hooked on David Justice and everything about him. I loved him."

Now that Boyer is one of the Braves' top pitching prospects, he has tremendous respect for the possibility of one day following potential Hall of Famers like John Smoltz in an Atlanta uniform. It's a point of pride that he feels is pushing him not only to get to the big leagues, but to get to the big leagues as a Brave.

"I've got a history with the Braves, even before I played baseball," Boyer says. "Imagine being a Braves fan all your life, and then being drafted by them. You almost question yourself, 'Why do I deserve this?'"

The success that Wainwright, Digby, and Boyer all had in their first season after being drafted gave the Braves even more reason to look closer to home for talent. So as the 2001 draft approached, Clark made Georgia a high priority. Once again, there was a good high school pitcher in South Georgia, but this one was shaped a bit different than the lanky six-foot-six Adam Wainwright.

Macay McBride is 5'11" and was around 185 pounds when he was the Braves' first pick in the 2001 draft. He grew up in Sylvania, Georgia, a small town right on the Georgia – South Carolina border and about two hundred miles from Atlanta. McBride saw dozens of games at the old Atlanta-Fulton County Stadium when he was a kid, and he gave up a scholarship to the University of Georgia to sign with his favorite team.

"I knew two weeks before the draft that I was going to be taken by the Braves at some point early," McBride admits. "Teams that were interested early fell off, and the teams that weren't started coming on. The Braves had stayed there the whole time."

The left-handed McBride had success from the moment he put on a Braves' uniform. He went 4-4 with a 3.76 ERA in 11 starts in the Gulf Coast League in 2001 with 67 strikeouts in 55 innings pitched. Then in 2002 in Macon, he was named the South Atlantic League's Most Valuable Pitcher after going 12-8 with a 2.12 ERA in 25 starts. McBride also had 138 strikeouts in 157.1 innings pitched and allowed only 119 hits. He followed up that season with more impressive numbers, going 9-8 in Myrtle Beach with a 2.95 ERA in 27 starts.

Since the day McBride was drafted, he's been compared to Billy Wagner, the accomplished closer with the Philadelphia Phillies. Both are left-handed, both are the same height, and both throw very hard. The comparison made even more sense in 2004 when the Braves moved McBride to the bullpen. They felt he still might be a starter one day, but with their abundance of starting prospects, McBride might get to the big leagues quicker as a reliever.

He struggled in 12 early starts at AA in 2004, so the Braves made the move. McBride's bullpen numbers give the Braves every reason to believe they made the right decision. After giving up five earned runs in an inning and a third in his first relief appearance, McBride settled down and was outstanding as a reliever. He went 1-0 with a 1.93 ERA in 25 games, 38 hits allowed in 42 innings, 18 walks, and 42 strikeouts.

"I feel like I've come a long way," McBride admits. "I've never been so relaxed as a player as I have been as a reliever. Usually I'm very intense when I get out there on the mound. But you can't be too intense for seven innings and then go into the eighth and go in and pitch an inning. It's a little different ballgame."

Whether McBride pitches out of the pen or as a starter, his only preference is that he does it in a Braves' uniform. McBride is determined to show the Braves' brass that he's good enough to pitch in the big leagues, and good enough to fit in with Atlanta.

"If I had my way I'd be a Brave for the rest of my life," McBride says. "I think if it comes down to arbitration one day or a deal, if it means staying in Atlanta, I would definitely probably consider taking less money just cause it's closer to home. You can't pay for comfort. You could be across the country and making tons of money but be unhappy. For some people like myself, there's more pride when you put on this uniform."

Five picks later in the first round of the 2001 draft, the Braves took another Georgia kid, Josh Burrus, from Wheeler High School in Marietta. Burrus was a hotshot pitcher and shortstop that was compared to a young Gary Sheffield when the Braves drafted him. But another attraction to the Braves was Burrus' love for their team. He grew up watching the Braves, but the turning point of becoming a die-hard fan came in 1993, when he the opportunity to go on the field at Atlanta-Fulton County Stadium.

"When I was ten years old I went to this thing called 'Opportunity Through Baseball,'" Burrus says. "It was some kids from Georgia that went to a camp in Colorado. Before we went out there we went to a Braves game and we went down to the field. David Justice asked me to go pick up his glove, and I went and picked it up and I gave it to him. He gave me his bat. Ever since then…"

That next year Burrus started playing serious baseball when he joined East Cobb and started traveling.

"Even when I was twelve years old, we played all summer and played in almost a hundred games," Burrus says. "You get used to playing everyday and going on the road and places."

Burrus was unlike Jeff Francoeur in that he only played baseball when he was growing up. Along with traveling with his East Cobb team, he also played in several summer showcases beginning when he was sixteen years old. By the time he was in the eleventh grade, Burrus started making a name for himself as a big-time prospect.

"I got looks and everything, but not really until the end of my junior year," he says. "I had a good junior year. We went to a showcase, the Perfect Games, down in Florida. I played outstanding down there. That got me noticed a little bit."

Burrus committed to play baseball at Clemson, so many of the pro teams backed off just a bit. The Cubs, Reds, and Mariners were interested in him, but none more than the Braves, who saw a chance to add another hometown kid to their farm system. And Burrus was more than willing to forego Clemson to be a Brave.

"I was definitely excited to be able to play at home," Burrus says.

Burrus is a tremendous athlete, with great instincts and very good speed. The Braves saw a young Sheffield in Burrus, someone who could eventually develop power and be a five-tool player. But just like Sheffield in his early days with the Brewers, Burrus was moved from shortstop to third base. He played third in 2002 in Danville, but his struggles in the field carried over to his offense. Burrus made 16 errors in 68 games that season, and also hit a meager .236. Then in 2003, the Braves decided to move Burrus to the outfield, which is exactly where Sheffield eventually wound up. The Braves gave Burrus an entire season to learn his newest position, hoping he'd also be able to slowly improve with the bat as well.

"People had said, 'The outfield is more relaxing, so you can work on your hitting more,'" Burrus says. "It was fine. I had no problems with it. I really love chasing down balls, making diving catches, and throwing people out. I love the infield. I'll probably always love the infield. There's just a lot of action playing there. But I put a lot of pressure on myself in the infield. I'm more relaxed out there in the outfield and playing better."

Burrus showed in 2004 that the move to the outfield was a good one. His offense improved tremendously, as he hit .272 (up from his .225 career average coming into 2004) with 11 home runs, 30 doubles, and 30 stolen bases. And he also became a very solid defensive outfielder.

"He made some spectacular catches," says Rocket Wheeler, Burrus' manager in Rome. "He scored a bunch of runs and stole 30 bases as a leadoff hitter. He's probably got one of the quickest bats in the organization."

The speedy outfielder still has a lot of work to do. Burrus has been mandated to cut down his strikeouts (he had 123 in 503 at bats), and to continue to develop his power. But the Braves believe they could have another top outfield prospect in a few years. And Burrus hopes that by then he'll be sharing a Braves uniform with more Atlanta kids.

"That would be amazing," Burrus says. "And it wouldn't just be kids from Georgia, but it would be a lot of us that played together since we were like ten years old."

Four rounds later in the 2001 draft, the Braves would draft a kid that played with Burrus since both were ten years old.

Kyle Davies lived south of Atlanta, in Stockbridge, but he was also an East Cobb kid. Unlike Blaine Boyer, who didn't become a pitcher until the region playoffs of his senior season, Davies has always been a pitcher – a good pitcher. In fact, he was so good as a young pitcher that he was even recognized by a national publication. *Baseball America* has an annual report called "Baseball For The Ages." In the report they list the player whom they think is the best prospect at every age between twelve and twenty-five. Davies won the award when he was both a thirteen year old and a fourteen year old.

"It was fun," Davies says. "My dad showed it to me. It was pretty neat to see that stuff written about you."

Davies showcasing his abundant talent at an early age.

For Davies, the exposure he received from the article was priceless. Scouting Directors may say they don't read those reviews, but they do. Davies continued pitching summer ball and by the time he was a junior in high school, he had one of the best young arms in the country. He committed to play college ball at Georgia Tech, so he had that as leverage. But when the Braves started showing interest, Davies started thinking more about pro ball.

"I talked to Roy Clark a lot," Davies says. "Paul Snyder was at a bunch of my games. I played extremely well my junior year of high school. People started talking to me and getting a read on what you can do with the mental exams. But then I didn't pitch particularly well my senior year."

Davies' struggles caused him to slip in the eyes of many scouting directors, but not Clark, who knew he had another homegrown kid who loved the Braves and had a tremendous makeup. Davies had a reputation as a bulldog on the mound, at that's exactly what enticed the Braves to draft him in the fourth round.

"Leading up to it, I knew I should have done a lot better in high school," Davies says. "I had a chance to go to school at Georgia Tech. I figured if someone was going to give me a chance it had to be early 'cause I was planning on going to school. It happened to be a close-to-home team, so that kind of helped me out. I decided to try this thing out."

Davies was thrilled the Braves drafted him. His family had Braves season tickets for years, and his dad, Hiram Davies, grew up five miles from the old stadium in Atlanta. "It sure made the decision (to sign) a lot easier being the Atlanta Braves," he says.

The Braves brought Davies along slowly, mainly since he was only seventeen years old when he graduated from high school. But their patience was rewarded in 2003 when the youngster became the ace of the Rome Braves team that won the Sally League Title. He went 8-8 with a 2.89 ERA in 27 starts, but even more important is that he pitched and won all three games when the Rome team had a chance to clinch in the playoffs.

"He's going to get it done no matter what it takes,' says Kent Willis, Davies' pitching coach in Rome in 2003. "His preparation is superb. He's his biggest critic. For himself, he's going out there not to be embarrassed but to give you everything he's got because he's prepared himself. He trusts his stuff. When you've got that type of makeup and that type of mindset, you're going to have to run him off the mound."

Davies' success continued in 2004 when he made three minor league stops. He started off the season in Myrtle Beach and went 9-2 with a 2.63 ERA in 14 starts. He allowed only 55 hits in 75.1 innings of work, along with 32 walks and 95 strikeouts. Then he went to AA Greenville, and his numbers were even better. He was 4-0 with a 2.32 ERA, 40 hits in 62 innings, 22 walks, and 73 strikeouts. The Braves were so confident in his ability that they sent then nineteen-year old Davies to AAA Richmond, where he actually clinched another postseason game. Davies allowed only one run on two hits over 5.1 innings to beat Columbus giving Richmond the series victory.

"He's got poise beyond his years," says former Richmond pitching coach Guy Hansen.

Davies is armed with an outstanding changeup, one that Braves' coaches compared to Tom Glavine's devastating change.

He's also in possession of a fastball that tops out at 95 mph, and also a very good curveball.

Overall in 2004, Davies was 13-3 with a 2.72 ERA, 100 hits allowed in 142.1 innings, 57 walks, and 173 strikeouts. Having turned twenty-one in September of 2004, Davies is now being mentioned as a possibility for Atlanta's rotation sometime in 2005.

"Kyle Davies sets himself apart," says Greenville Manager Brian Snitker. "Kyle Davies wins."

After having so much success in Clark's first two drafts, it was essential to keep finding talented players in Georgia. However, 2002 would bring a big change as the area scout for Georgia, Rob English, left to take a similar job with the Boston Red Sox. Clark turned to a man who had a great network of contacts.

Al Goetz knew all about baseball in Georgia. Several years after pitching in the Detroit Tigers minor league system, he opened his own baseball facility in Duluth, a northern Atlanta suburb. Goetz saw many young players in the East Cobb program and other amateur programs train at his complex, and then he became an associate scout for English. He was also a pitching coach for Duluth High School and spent one year at DeKalb College, a junior college in North Atlanta. So Goetz was able to watch as talent in the state of Georgia improved dramatically.

"I knew to be a Braves' scout in the state of Georgia was a real positive," Goetz says. "Back when Rob was scouting there were very few major league teams that would come in here consistently. Now you are battling everybody. It's not as easy to get Georgia kids now as it used to be."

Goetz might have trouble living up to the success he and the Braves had in the state in his first year on the job. The 2002 draft will probably always be known for being able to "pull off" getting Jeff Francoeur with the twenty-third pick, but there were a few other players from Georgia that helped make it a special draft. The second best player in Georgia in 2002 was Brian McCann, a catcher from Duluth High School, just north of Atlanta, and his relationship with Goetz went back a ways.

McCann's dad, Howie McCann, was the head baseball coach at Marshall University in West Virginia and a former assistant coach at the University of Georgia. Goetz hired McCann to come work at his baseball facility in Atlanta, and while his wife stayed in West Virginia to sell their house, Howie and Brian lived in Goetz's office for a couple of weeks. Brian was only twelve years old, and at that point, Goetz had no idea the younger McCann was going to be a baseball player.

"If you had ever told me that Brian McCann at twelve would be a major league baseball player, I would have laughed at you," Goetz says. "He was slow, short, and chubby. But he could always hit. He was a third baseman and that summer he converted to catcher. I think they saw the handwriting on the wall as far as his mobility. They knew he was going to have to be a catcher."

But short and chubby little Brian started to grow up, and more importantly, work out. By the time he was in high school, McCann was six-foot-two and 200 pounds. He hit in the cages constantly at Goetz's facility, and it didn't hurt that his dad was a hitting coach.

"Brian lives and sleeps and walks baseball twenty-four/seven," Goetz says.

The Braves saw that, and they also knew that McCann grew up as a Braves fan. Before Howie McCann left to go to Marshall, he frequently took his sons (Brian's older brother Brad is in the Marlins' system) to Fulton-County Stadium. Howie was close friends with Jim Guadagno, Baseball System Operator for the Braves in the 90's.

"Jim was a big family friend to us," Brian McCann says. "He took care of me and my brother when we were little. So we had kind of a Braves tie there. I remember getting a bunch of free stuff. When you're little, everything's great. We got to meet a lot of the Braves' guys and got to go in the clubhouse. I met Dale Murphy, so it was a great experience."

The Braves wanted McCann badly. They had not had to develop a young catcher for years since Javy Lopez had been the catcher for a decade, but his era was coming to an end and it was a perfect time to find an eventual replacement. McCann had a good throwing arm, good receiving skills, and a very solid left-handed bat.

"Obviously at that time Jeff was our main guy, but Brian was a not-too-distant second," Goetz says. "Jeff possessed all five tools where we thought Brian was going to have to work defensively to get himself major league caliber. I actually thought that as far as a pure hitter, Brian was better prepared professionally at that time. Jeff hadn't developed a trigger and was a little bit anxious where Brian just had that left-handed strike that I thought would propel him pretty quickly."

Another factor that added to the Braves' attraction to McCann was the fact that he and Francoeur were best friends. They had played baseball together since the age of twelve, and even though they played at separate high schools, they became great buddies.

"I looked at those two like two twin brothers," Goetz says. "I think they feed off each other. I think Brian feeds off Jeff and his competitiveness and going hard all the time. I think Jeff sees Brian's dedication to the game and feeds off of him. They just get along so well. They just abuse each other all the time like two brothers."

The Braves liked the thought of two best friends, two Braves fans, potentially being part of their future. So after taking Dan Meyer out of James Madison with the thirty-fourth overall pick, the Braves gambled that McCann would still be available when they drafted next at sixty-four.

"After we took Dan I said, 'We're not going to get Brian,'" Goetz admits. "I knew there were a couple of other clubs that liked him and that were picking ahead of us in the second round. But when everybody passed on him and we picked him, my son and daughter and I ran around the room screaming."

But then Goetz really had to go to work. He still had to sign McCann, and while you'd think that would have been easy considering his relationship with Brian and his dad, it got a little rocky when Sherry McCann, Brian's mom, got involved.

"I knew Brian was going to sign, but then Brian ended up being almost as difficult as Jeff," Goetz says. "I didn't talk to Howie or Brian until the day he signed. His mother would not let me talk to those two 'cause she knew if I did they'd be done. You can call Scott Boras or any of them out there and talk about how tough they can be, but nobody's tougher than Sherry McCann. She's hung up on me more than a couple of times during the course of the negotiations. We signed Brian the day before we signed Jeff. It was probably the most agonizing month in my professional life."

But well worth the agony, since Brian has developed into one of the top catching prospects in the game. He hit .290 with 12 home runs and 71 RBI in 2003 with the Rome Braves, and caught a pitching staff that was dominant down the stretch. Then in 2004, McCann hit .277 with 15 home runs and 65 RBI at Myrtle Beach. Some have even compared him to a young Jason Varitek-type player, one who is a tremendous leader on the field. It's not easy to find legit left-handed hitting catchers, but the Braves may have one in McCann. Despite all the hoopla, he's trying not to think about when he could be starting in Turner Field.

"It's overwhelming to think about," McCann says. "Every time I go into the clubhouse or go down there for anything I look around and think I'm dreaming. I don't even think it's real. It's getting closer and hopefully it becomes a reality one day. But you've got to go one step at a time and if you start thinking about it you might not get as good as you can get."

The thought of playing with his best friend in Atlanta one day is also a dream for McCann. He's played with Francoeur in Rome and Myrtle Beach, but McCann knows it would be very special playing together in the big leagues.

"We're about as close as you can possibly get as friends," McCann (at left, with Francoeur on left) says. "The fact that we come out here and play baseball everyday is a plus. We're very competitive in everything we do. He wants to outdo me and I want to outdo him. At the same time, we both know our main goal is to get to the big leagues."

McCann, Francoeur, Boyer, and Davies were all apart of a very special team in Rome in 2003 that won the South Atlantic League title. It's difficult to find a team in Low-A that has great camaraderie, mainly since the kids usually haven't known each other long and don't stay together for very long. But the Rome team had five kids from the state of Georgia, and that rapport was evident. They knew one another, had played against and with each other through the years, and those relationships carried over to the other players who were not from Georgia. The result was a very close team that rallied together and won a league title.

The fifth member of the Georgia boys on that Rome team was Jonathan Schuerholz, son of the Braves General Manager. Not surprisingly, Jonathan was much like his dad in high school and college. Both were middle infielders, hit well but not much power, and played very hard.

But Jonathan had an advantage over his dad in that he was able to play in the East Cobb program. The extra baseball made Jonathan a better player, and as he would probably tell you, maybe even better than his dad was in his day.

"You play everyday, day in and day out," the younger Schuerholz says. "It was unbelievable. For guys who love to play like myself, you can't get anything better. It's like pro ball. You're out there playing baseball for a living. They really teach the fundamentals of how to be a good baseball player and just the basics all the way up to the advanced parts of the game."

By the time Schuerholz got to his senior season, he was hitting .400. He helped Lovett High School win a state title that season, and got the attention of a few scouts. Both the Braves and Indians scouted him, even though he knew he really needed to go to college. Furman offered him a scholarship, but his heart was in Alabama.

"I wanted to go to Auburn even since my sophomore year," Schuerholz says. "I played a showcase with East Cobb down at Auburn. As soon as I walked in there I knew that was where I wanted to go."

But then the Braves tried to derail his college plans when they drafted Schuerholz in the thirty-seventh round of the 1999 draft. They offered him $25,000 to bypass Auburn and join the team his father had made a champion. But a talk with his dad helped him make up his mind.

"Dad approached it from the business side of being my father rather than being the General Manager," Jonathan says. "He said, 'The best choice for you would be to go to college and get three or four years of education and if it works out after that, it works out.' I think the Braves knew there was a shot at me going to play pro ball, but I wasn't ready yet. I knew I wasn't ready yet."

So Schuerholz went to Auburn. It didn't take long for him to get a reputation as a tough player who was solid defensively and needed improvement on offense. He hit .305 his freshman season, and then struggled his sophomore year. But his defense was just getting better. The Auburn coaches decided to move Schuerholz from second base to shortstop, and he played tremendously in the field. But then Auburn brought in some top freshman recruits in Schuerholz's junior year, and he found himself on the bench to start the season. He played sparingly, even getting time in right field. But with the third baseman struggling, the coaches decided to insert Jonathan at that corner. He again showed he knew what to do with the leather.

"I played good defense," he says. "Third base in the SEC was life-threatening. You've got grown men hitting with a lightning bolt in their hand ninety feet away. I remember one time I'm playing third base and I was at double play depth. A guy from Florida was up and I remember thinking, 'This guy is going to kill me.' He hit a ball so hard, and I jumped for it, by the time I came down and looked back at the left fielder he was already throwing it back in. After that, I knew I didn't want to play third base."

But he had proven that he could play the field and that he was a hard-nosed player, which is important if you're not a power hitter in college. Five teams scouted him heavily his junior year at Auburn: Texas, Cleveland, Philadelphia, Baltimore, and Atlanta. The scouts told Jonathan he might go somewhere in the top fifteen rounds of the draft, but he wasn't certain where he'd go. When the draft rolled around and the Braves took him in the eighth round, Schuerholz was thrilled.

"Growing up, the ultimate dream was to be on the other side of the fence at Turner Field," he says. "You want to be between the lines at Turner Field and have people cheering for you instead of you cheering them on."

Almost immediately, the Braves were criticized for drafting the son of the General Manager. Critics called it a blatant case of nepotism. But John Schuerholz had nothing to do with the drafting of his son, and there's little reason someone like Roy Clark would feel the need to try to impress his boss by drafting Jonathan. The Braves simply believed Jonathan had a chance to improve and become a major leaguer.

"He had nothing to do with it," Jonathan says. "Roy told him, 'Hey we're thinking about taking Jonathan in the next round.' He was like, 'Roy, this is your deal. Whatever you want to do. If you think he's the next best player on that board, take him.'"

The one thing the Braves were not worried about was the expected pressure Jonathan would be under playing in the Atlanta farm system. It wouldn't be easy being the son of such a high profiled person as he was bound to get people questioning why he was wearing a Braves uniform. But Jonathan has taken the pressure in stride.

"You could look at it both ways," he admits. "It's going to be a good thing if I got picked by the Braves since I obviously knew everybody inside the organization. On the flip side, it would also be good to be picked up by another organization so there wouldn't be much pressure. But you know what? There is no pressure. I've lived with the pressure of having my dad hang over me my whole life. There's zero pressure at all. I'm used to it. If people want to think I'm here because of who my dad is, well they can just think that. The Braves have put together an organization that is truly respectable and they're not going to take somebody in the eighth round who they don't think could be a good player. They're professional. You're going to get the daddy's boy comment and you've just got to laugh. I'm going to hear it, no matter what. If I make it to the big leagues, I'll hear it ten times worse I'm sure."

Since Schuerholz grew up around the Braves' clubhouse, he'd like nothing more than to make it to Atlanta as a Brave. While the other Georgia kids grew up Braves fans, Schuerholz grew up with his dad putting the team together every year, so it might be just a tad more special for him. And he knows it would be very special for his dad.

"Setting aside the fact that he is the General Manager of the Braves, I think he'd be just as proud of me as any other father would be of their son if they make it to the big leagues," Jonathan says. "Obviously, those times when we hit the wiffle ball in the backyard and he pitched me BP and we played catch are times where he would look back if I ever made the big leagues and say, 'Man, he's made it.' I'm his only son, so I think he'd be very proud."

The Braves took one more college player from Alabama in the 2002 draft that was originally from Georgia; left-handed pitcher Chuck James from Chattahoochee Valley Junior College in Phenix City. James was not drafted out of high school, mainly because he was also an outfielder for Pebblebrook High School in Mableton, just west of Atlanta.

"I played center field in high school, but I wasn't a starting pitcher," James says. "They'd bring me in to close it out."

James' high school team wasn't very good, and he wasn't like many of the other Georgia kids in that he didn't play with East Cobb, didn't play much summer ball, and he wasn't even drafted. So his only chance at continuing his baseball career past high school was to play at Chattahoochee Valley.

"I went to a couple of schools to try out," James says. "They pretty much told me that they just wanted me to pitch, so I ended up going to Chattahoochee Valley because they said they would let me play the outfield too. I loved playing the outfield."

Chuck James was like many young pitchers who are torn between pitching and playing everyday. He was simply used to playing everyday with his buddies, and hated the thought of having down time and having to watch games when he wasn't pitching. His first year at Chattahoochee had him on the bench a lot, since they already had a set starting outfield. He pitched every now and then, but not much. Then in his second season, he started in right field more often and pitched against conference opponents.

"That's when more scouts started showing up for my games, so I started pitching a lot more then," James says. "That's when I kind of figured that I wasn't going anywhere as an outfielder. I just couldn't hit enough, but I could throw hard."

James reached 94 miles an hour on the radar gun, and the only other pitch he threw was an occasional changeup. It doesn't take long for scouts to hear there's a left-handed pitcher throwing 94 miles an hour, even if he's at a small community college. Twelve scouts came to see James throw, and they knew he was a very raw product, still needing good instruction to advance as a pitcher.

"I saw him throw a one-hitter in Alabama with a fastball and a changeup," says Al Goetz. "But he has command and pitchability. He was impressive, but unpolished."

The Braves were all set to draft James pretty high, possibly even in the third round. But then, right before the draft, James suffered a horrible injury. He was out swimming with some of his friends, when someone made a bad suggestion.

"We didn't have dorms in college, so we all lived in an apartment," James says. "So we were there at the swimming pool and there was like a bathroom right there next to the pool. Somebody had the bright idea to jump off the bathroom roof and into the pool. My name came up first. The first time I actually made it. It wasn't an incredible jump. Then the other guy got up there and his jump looked better than mine. So my pride was hurt and I got back up there. I hit a rotten spot in the roof and my foot went through the roof, so I didn't get a good push. So I actually bounced off the pavement and into the pool. I broke both my wrists. It was pretty tough. I was supposed to pitch our last game of the season. I ended up going to the field with the casts on my arm. When I got there, I think I counted thirteen scouts in the stands. They all looked at me and just walked off. They didn't say one word to me."

But the Braves still believed James had talent, so they took him in the twentieth round of the draft. They wanted to monitor his progress after his wrists healed to see if he could still pitch. As a twentieth rounder, James wasn't much of a gamble. If he got back and became a prospect, then it was worth the risk. If he didn't, it was a twentieth round pick, and twentieth rounders often don't make it anyway.

The Braves have brought James along slowly, and again they've been rewarded with their patience. James stayed in Extended Spring Training in 2003 getting his wrists completely healed. The Braves slowly increased his workload, and in mid-June sent James to Danville in the Appalachian League. To say he dominated the league would be an understatement. With a 1.25 ERA in 11 starts, he allowed only 26 hits in 50.1 innings, along with only 19 walks and 68 strikeouts. Then in 2004, his numbers were even more impressive at Low-A Rome. James went 10-5 with an ERA of 2.25, 92 hits allowed in 132 innings, 48 walks, and 156 strikeouts.

Two years after breaking his wrists and not knowing if he'd ever pitch again, Chuck James has become one of the Braves' most promising prospects. But the scary part is he's still learning. James had only two pitches in college, and his breaking ball wasn't even very good. He's had considerable success mainly as a one-pitch pitcher.

"In Danville, I threw mostly fastballs," James says. "I threw a few changeups, but not many at all. I threw a lot of fastballs. That was the pitcher I was for my whole life. I just threw fastballs. Then I was working on my slider, but I don't think I threw it once in a game in Danville. They got on me a lot that I needed that third pitch."

So when James got to Rome he started to work with pitching coach Kent Willis, who immediately started working with him on his changeup and slider.

"We worked all year on his breaking ball," Willis says. "We wanted to get his slider to be a competitive pitch and to get a feel for that pitch. We got it to where it was very effective against left-handers. He learned how to pitch. He learned how to repeat pitches. He learned about his delivery. Once you learn those things, you're on your way. He's a bulldog. He's a competitor."

"If he ever develops that breaking ball, he's going to be somebody's second or third starter," Goetz says. "He's a (Mike) Hampton type of pitcher. He has absolutely no fear. I think he's got a legitimate shot to get there."

James knows he's getting better. In his mind he's still a center fielder learning how to pitch. But the extra incentive he has to make it is the thought of putting on that Atlanta uniform.

"A bunch of guys I played baseball with in high school...we always used to go eat at Taco Bell," James says. "We used to sit there and laugh and say we'd sign for a burrito to play with the Braves. It was never even a thought in my mind about pro ball. Of course it's every kid's dream to play it, but I just went out there and played. And now, I know I can pitch with a fastball and a changeup. I'm hoping when I get that slider going, I'll be dominating."

Before his March 2005 trade, Nick Green was the first of this group to make it to Atlanta. But Green's story is a bit different. Even though he grew up in Duluth, Georgia, he didn't grow up a huge Braves fan. While he watched them on TV occasionally, he really didn't go down to the stadium to see them play. Mainly he was just a normal kid. He played high school baseball and had other interests. He wanted to continue playing baseball past high school, but he didn't really have a huge desire or think he'd play for the Braves.

When the Braves drafted Green in the thirty-second round in 1998, they treated him as a 'draft and follow' player. Green was going to go to Georgia Perimeter College, and after his freshman season the Braves would still own his rights and be able to sign him if they thought he was more prepared to play pro ball.

"I just wanted to play professionally," Green says. "I played good in college and I didn't feel like I needed to be there any longer."

With that in mind, Green signed with the Braves in the spring of 1999. Over the next several seasons, Green would become a decent prospect, but nothing spectacular. He never hit over 15 home runs, only hit over .270 once, but his biggest attributes were his steady defense and his versatility. He played shortstop in high school, second base in college, and then both positions throughout his time in the Braves' farm system. He was also able to play a little third base when called upon. Green was a solid player, but never thought of as someone who could push Marcus Giles out of a starting job at second base, or even knock Mark DeRosa off as the top reserve on the Atlanta roster.

"There are really no spots to open up," Green says. "You can't worry about that stuff. You have to go out and play just like you were when you were a kid. When I was a kid and had success, I never thought what I was doing. I didn't know better."

Green also didn't know whether he'd even have a spot in the Braves' organization in 2004. He went to Spring Training with a minimal chance at a roster spot, and with a couple of veteran minor leaguers brought in, he also had to fight for a spot in AAA. Green won the second base job in Richmond, and proceeded to have the best period of baseball in his life. He hit .377 in his first twenty-two games to lead the International League in hitting. Green knew he simply needed to prove that if called upon, he was ready. All he was waiting for was his chance.

"I was talking with someone who was a lifelong Braves fan," Green says. "He was talking about a guy who used to be in the organization who was a pretty good player and just never got a chance to show what he could do up here. I realize that not many people get the chance."

Green's chance came on May 15, 2004. Atlanta's reserve infielder, Jesse Garcia, had a death in the family and was placed on the Bereavement List for three days. The Braves called up Green to finish the weekend series in Milwaukee. But in the bottom of the first inning, Marcus Giles went back on a Texas League pop into short center field. He collided with center fielder Andruw Jones and spun twice in the air until he went down in horrific pain. After the game he was diagnosed with a fractured right clavicle.

Nick Green came into the game to replace Giles and got his first major league hit and RBI off Brewers reliever Brooks Kieschnick in the fifth inning. He also made several solid plays in the field at second base.

"I didn't have time to think about anything," Green

remembers. "I wasn't expecting anything but getting to pinch hit that whole series. Then he gets hurt and I wasn't even ready to go in there 'cause I've seen him fall down and do all kinds of stuff and not get injured. So I just thought he was going to get back up and play. They threw me out there, which was the best thing for me. I think if I had time to think about what was going on I probably would have struggled."

Then the next day Green got a single off Ben Sheets, who only gave up three and struck out eighteen Braves for the game. The loss of Giles was a tremendous blow to the team, as he arguably had been their MVP for the first five weeks of the season. But Green's play in the first two games gave everyone hope that Giles' absence might not be felt as much as if, say, Jesse Garcia, a very weak hitter, had stayed in the lineup.

"When we got back in town and Marcus went on the DL, the media was all over me the whole time because I'm from here," Green says. "I didn't really have time to sit down and think about what was going on. I just wanted to get to this level just to prove to myself that I could play here."

Green proved that to himself and to everyone else as well. When Garcia returned, Bobby Cox kept Green in the starting lineup. He rewarded Cox's confidence with a seven game hitting streak that started on May 21st. Green hit his first career home run on May 31st off Livan Hernandez, and his best performance came on July 2nd when he had a game-tying sacrifice fly in the bottom of the tenth inning against Boston and then won the game with a three-run home run in the bottom of the twelfth. Green held down the fort at second base until Giles returned by hitting .283 with 3 home runs and 25 RBI.

"I know I can play here," Green says. "I think I got out there, got the opportunity, played hard, made a good impression, and I'm still here. If I had made a bad impression, then I'm sure I would have been sent down and they would have sent somebody else up."

But the Braves stuck with Green, even though he entered the 2004 season with a career minor league average of .256, which would have had him released in many other organizations.

"I was fortunate enough to be at the right spot at the right time as far as being on the roster for a few years," Green says. "You know everybody expects a first rounder to get here, but those people like me and Marcus are not expected to get here. A lot of times people can take this game for granted. If you're here for some years, you can take it for granted and not hustle and run out a ball and not give 110% when you're out there. I'm going to give it my best every time I'm out there and I'm not going to let something stupid like not running out a pop fly or not running a ground ball out affect my future. That's what I think I can bring: the drive to stay here and be a big league player."

When Green, a hometown kid, made it to Atlanta in 2004, the Braves hoped it would inspire their other Georgia kids to push themselves. Even though Green wasn't as much of a Braves fan growing up as the others, he knew how special it was to play in his own backyard.

"It's really neat," Green says. "I think people are realizing the Braves are going for local guys. There's a lot of talent in the area. I think more kids are more excited about getting drafted by their hometown team. I guess I was just kind of out of the loop when it happened to me. Now looking back on it I can see how kids get excited. You get to play in front of your family and friends and you're right at home. It's really fun once I've gotten here and gotten to do it."

That's exactly what the Braves are counting on. They see the pride building in the players they've already drafted from Georgia. In Clark's five years as Scouting Director, the Braves have taken thirty-four kids from high schools or colleges in Georgia, at the end of the 2004 season fourteen were still in the system. That's not to mention a greater emphasis on drafting players from the Carolinas, Alabama, and Florida. The emphasis on Georgia kids is one of the reasons the Braves have one of the best farm systems in baseball. Goetz believes that as long as the talent is there, Georgia will continue to be the first option for scouting.

"Every year seems to be getting a little better," Goetz says. "I think it's always going to be in the top four or five states just because of the amount of baseball the kids play. I don't think we've suddenly developed better athletes. I just think we've developed better baseball. Roy Clark is always saying, 'we don't want to get beat in our own backyard.' I agree. I don't remember a kid in my four years from Georgia, Alabama, or North Florida that wouldn't have rather played for the Braves. All things being equal, if two kids are on the board and one's from Georgia and one's from somewhere else, we'll usually go with the one from Georgia." A position that certainly runs contrary to those teams that believe in numbers and math above all else.

And the players that Goetz has drafted hope that in a few

years a large percentage of the Atlanta roster will consist of hometown players. The Braves have developed a winning tradition that would make someone from the North Pole proud to put on the Atlanta uniform, but they could never have more pride than the kids who grew up dreaming of being a Brave.

"If we do all make it up there, myself, Macay, Francoeur, Davies, Burrus, and McCann, people in Atlanta and people in Georgia and the southeast are going to absolutely love it," says Boyer.

"It would be unbelievable to play in your hometown, where you grew up," says McCann. "You know a lot of people are going to come to see people from the area. You could be just another guy, not even a superstar, and they're going to want to come out and see you."

Georgia Boys: (l. to r.) C.J. Bressoud, Clint Sammons, Jonathan Schuerholz, Blaine Boyer, Jeff Francoeur, Braves' GA Scout Al Goetz, Jon Mark Owings, Bryan Digby, Kyle Davies, Brian McCann, Josh Burrus, Johnnie Wiggins

"It's special," says Davies. "I think it would be great to have a hometown team of Atlanta kids. How often does that happen? Never. I think it would be awesome."

"I think it could be something special, much like the group in 1991," says Jeff Francoeur. "We're just a bunch of guys that have been close together coming up. It's a new generation. I don't think I could even put into words what it would mean to me to wear that uniform."

These kids simply have the Braves in their blood, but as one Georgia kid found out, when dreams unravel, it can certainly compound the pain.

19

TRADING ADAM AND BUBBA

They were born a week apart and even drafted a round apart, but besides being top Braves' pitching prospects, Adam Wainwright and Bubba Nelson don't have a lot in common. Wainwright is an outdoorsman, born in South Georgia with a love of hunting, fishing, and golf, while Nelson is more of a free spirit whose life revolves around baseball. Wainwright is more serious while Nelson considers himself somewhat of a comedian, always telling people that they can call him Bubba, but "the ladies call me Kenny."

"Bubba and I aren't the same kind of guy," Wainwright says. "We have a lot of differences, but we're both very serious competitors. I think we brought out the best in each other, not that we wanted to one-up the other guy, but it was almost like, 'Hey, if you can do that, I can do this.'"

It didn't take long for Wainwright and Nelson to become a good tandem in the Braves' farm system. In their first full season of minor league baseball, they combined for 22 wins in Single-A Macon. Then in 2002 in Myrtle Beach, Wainwright led the Carolina League with 167 strikeouts, while Nelson led the league and all of minor league baseball with a 1.72 ERA.

After the 2002 season Wainwright and Nelson were ranked

1-2 as pitching prospects in the Braves' system. Fans were starting to talk about "Adam and Bubba" being the centerpiece of the Braves' future rotation.

"Everybody did that," says Bubba's dad John Nelson. That's something that's gone on since Macon. *Baseball America* did it. It was always Adam and Bubba, Adam and Bubba."

The attention put the spotlight clearly on the pair, and it also created a little friendly rivalry between the two right-handers.

"We definitely pushed each other more than any other pair because we were constantly fighting for that top prospect spot," Bubba Nelson says. "People always doubted me and people always doubted him. They would say Adam was better than me and some would say I was better than Adam. But it pushed us both. Every day we were trying to out do each other."

It was the same type of competitiveness that pushed Glavine, Maddux, and Smoltz in Atlanta for so many years. They were pulling for each other, but if Adam watched Bubba throw a shutout, he'd want to throw a shutout. If Bubba saw Adam throw a three-hitter, he'd want to throw a two-hitter. The Braves liked having two pitchers with similar talent develop that competitive spirit in the minor leagues.

The 2003 season was important for both twenty-one year olds. They say if you can pitch in AA, you can pitch in the big leagues, so both Wainwright and Nelson wanted to do well to hopefully get on the Braves' radar screen for a possible late-season audition in the big leagues.

Wainwright started off sinfully slow. He lost five games in a row to start the season, but two of those games he lost 2-1. It wasn't that he was necessarily pitching poorly, but mainly he was just not getting any run support. Then after the All-Star Break, Wainwright turned it up a notch and started showing exactly why he was the Braves' top pitching prospect. He went 5-1 in his last 10 starts with a 2.40 ERA. His last start in Birmingham he pitched 6 shutout innings allowing only 2 hits with 7 strikeouts. Wainwright was no longer just a hard thrower. He was developing into a pitcher.

"I went in there thinking I had everything figured out, but I quickly found out that I had a lot to learn," Wainwright admits. "I learned more when I was in AA than I learned in my whole career. Mike Alvarez (Greenville's pitching coach) helped me out with a lot of things – on and off the field. Growing as a pitcher, from the beginning of that season to the end, I would say I was 100% different. I was a different guy on the mound. I had more confidence. I thought I could have pitched against anybody at that time, just the way I was going about things and the way things were clicking. I had learned a lot and was happy with the way it ended."

Nelson also had a solid season. He went 8-10 with a 3.18 ERA in 20 starts for Greenville, and then the Braves' front office presented Bubba with a challenge. They wanted to see if he could pitch out of the bullpen. Again, not all of these Braves' pitching prospects can be starting pitchers, so they had to think of some who could make the transition to the bullpen. Nelson went up to AAA Richmond and relieved in 11 games and posted a 1.88 ERA. There was even talk Nelson might get a September call to Atlanta, but the Braves decided he wasn't quite ready. However, Nelson proved he could do whatever the Braves wanted him to do, pitch out of the rotation or the bullpen.

"It kind of lit an extra little fire under me that I could possibly have made the big leagues that year, whether it was as a starter or a reliever," Nelson says. "I always want to start, but whatever can squeak you into the big leagues, that's what you do. I actually had a lot of fun pitching out of the bullpen."

Once again after the 2003 season Wainwright and Nelson were named the Braves' top two pitching prospects by every publication. For Wainwright, he thoroughly enjoyed being thought of as the Braves' top prospect. He thought of himself as a Brave, an All-American kid with great stuff and great makeup. He was a Georgia boy, full of love for the team whose uniform he wore every game. If you had put the qualifications for a Braves pitcher into a computer, Wainwright would spit right out. It was his job, many believed, to lead the Braves' pitching staff into a new generation.

"I always assumed that I would be that guy," Wainwright admits. "I didn't feel any extra pressure from anybody else. The only pressure I felt was from myself, and I wasn't putting any pressure on me. I just felt like I was going to be the next one to jump in line with John Smoltz and Greg Maddux."

The Braves were facing their most precarious offseason in John Schuerholz's tenure as GM. For the first time, the payroll was going down. Time Warner had delivered an edict that the team payroll would decrease almost 20%. This would make Schuerholz's job difficult since there were several important players facing free agency. Greg Maddux, Javy Lopez, and Gary Sheffield all wanted to return, but they also all wanted to return with a pay raise. With the new orders in place, re-signing them would be impossible.

Sheffield was determined to cash in on his tremendous 2003 season when he hit .330 with 39 home runs and 132 RBI. Even in October, there were rumors that Yankees owner George Steinbrenner was prepared to offer Sheffield a huge contract. Both were residents of Tampa, and Sheffield's uncle, former Mets and Yankees pitcher Dwight Gooden, was an advisor to Steinbrenner. When Schuerholz and Assistant GM Frank Wren visited Sheffield in Tampa in November, they were convinced there would be no way to meet his contract demands. Therefore, they were going to have to look for a new right fielder with modest salary demands.

When Schuerholz and his inner circle met to map out their game plan for the offseason, they went over numerous possibilities for Sheffield's replacement. The free agent list did not have many attractive alternatives, so they then searched for a potential trade. One name kept popping up, no matter how many times they went through every team's roster: J.D. Drew of the St. Louis Cardinals.

Drew was a player that had never reached his potential. He was a tremendous college player at Florida State and was then drafted second by the Phillies in the 1997 draft. His agent, Scott Boras, could never work a deal with the Phillies and instead Drew signed to play with the St. Paul Saints of the Independent Northern League. Then in 1998 the Cardinals drafted him with the fifth overall pick, but they were able to sign him. Over the next several seasons Drew developed a reputation as a brittle player, never playing in more than 135 games and averaging only 120 games in his first four full seasons in the big leagues. The talent was there, with a sweet left-handed swing that was compared to Mickey Mantle, and tremendous athleticism that made him a great baserunner and a great outfielder. But with a number of injuries, he was never able to fully reach his potential.

The Braves believed Drew would thrive in their environment, and the main enticement would be that Drew would be playing close to home. He grew up in Hahira, Georgia, just twenty miles north of the Florida border in South Georgia. The drive from Atlanta to Hahira is about three and a half hours by interstate, definitely doable on off days. The Braves hoped that maybe, just maybe, Drew would finally live up to his potential by playing closer to home, a philosophy they had already developed with other draft picks.

So in early November John Schuerholz called Cardinals General Manager Walt Jocketty to express an interest in Drew.

"He knew we were looking for pitching," Jocketty says. "John was very aggressive. He really wanted Drew. He told me he would do whatever he had to do to get Drew. He had offered me a couple of players, and we kind of backed off a bit."

Jocketty admits there is both good and bad in dealing with Schuerholz, whose track record in trades sets him apart from others in the profession. He knew once Schuerholz called there would be more discussions.

"John is shrewd," says Jocketty. "He's one of my idols. I've watched how he's operated over the years, and no General Manager has had the success that he's had. So you've got to be a little cautious going into a deal with him because you know that he's had so many great deals. The thing I like about him is that he's right up front. A lot of guys talk and try to do different things, but I prefer to deal straight, right up front. That's the way John operates."

The two spoke again at the General Manager's Meetings in mid-November. Then as the Winter Meetings approached in December, talks started to heat up. Jocketty told Schuerholz that he was not only going to have to give the Cardinals some of the Braves' pitchers, but the Braves also had to take back Cardinals outfielder Eli Marrero in the deal, who was scheduled to make $3 million in 2004. The Cardinals wanted that extra payroll flexibility to get a veteran pitcher and an outfielder to replace Drew. Schuerholz didn't have much trouble in taking on Marrero, seeing him as a versatile player that his manager, Bobby Cox, would love to have on the 25-man roster. But the hang up was in the pitchers Jocketty was wanting in the deal: starting pitcher Jason Marquis, reliever Ray King, and Adam Wainwright.

"We thought Ray King was a guy who was going to be very serviceable for us," Jocketty says. "We thought he'd do a great job and pitch a lot. Marquis was a guy we liked a lot, but there was some uncertainty as to where he was going to be. We felt good about him, though. But the key was to try to get one more guy, a guy we could build on for the future. That's what Wainwright represented to us."

Schuerholz didn't have much trouble with the request for Marquis and King. The right-handed Marquis had somewhat run his course with the Braves, never fulfilling his potential, bouncing back and forth between the Atlanta rotation and bullpen and AAA. King was a solid pitcher who the Braves liked, but they knew they were going to have to give up talent for talent. But Wainwright was the Braves' top pitching prospect, and it's not easy for Schuerholz to give up top pitching prospects.

"We felt we needed a top pitching prospect back in the deal," Jocketty says. "He was very reluctant to give him up obviously. Their system is very deep, and there were a lot of guys we were interested in. But we shot to the moon and Wainwright was the number one guy we had on our list. Our reports indicated that he had three or four quality pitches. It was a matter of experience before he'd be ready to pitch in the big leagues, and once he got there he had a chance to be a number one or two starter. He throws hard and has a good curveball, good changeup. He's a guy that has a very, very high ceiling."

Obviously Schuerholz knew that. He had several one-on-one discussions with Jocketty at the Winter Meetings, and he continued to resist including Wainwright in the deal. Jocketty was straight with Schuerholz when he told him that the Dodgers, Giants, Red Sox, and Rangers were also calling him about Drew. Then it became somewhat of a chess match, which is normal in trade discussions. Jocketty knew that Schuerholz really wanted Drew, that Drew was Schuerholz's first choice to replace Sheffield. Schuerholz knew that there were other teams calling for Drew, but that Jocketty really wanted some of his pitchers. The two had cocktails on the Friday night during the Winter Meetings and Jocketty was adamant with Schuerholz on what he was going to have to have to get the deal done.

"We're going to have to have Wainwright," Jocketty said.

"Let's meet in the morning," Schuerholz asked.

"No problem," Jocketty replied.

Jocketty knew it was going to be tough to pry Wainwright away from Schuerholz, so he assembled his inner circle and headed to Schuerholz's suite at the Winter Meetings hotel.

"I swear to God when we went up there I knew what the dynamics of the room were going to be," Jocketty says. "It was going to be John and Frank (Wren, Schuerholz's Assistant GM), Bobby (Cox), and I knew Jim Fregosi (Schuerholz's point man on trades) was going to be in there. So I took my assistant, my manager Tony LaRussa, and Bob Gephart, who is my Vice President/Special Assistant kind of like Fregosi."

Jocketty felt that he had his even playing field. After some general discussion about the meetings, Jocketty made the first move.

"John look, we can't make this deal unless Wainwright is in there," Jocketty said.

"Geez, you know, you want for us to take on all this money and you want for us to give you our best pitching prospect?" Schuerholz asked.

"That's right," Jocketty replied.

Schuerholz tried to float a few more counter-proposals Jocketty's way. Again, there was no problem including Marquis and King in the proposal, but instead of Wainwright, Schuerholz included minor league left-hander Andy Pratt's name along with a minor league infielder. Jocketty wouldn't budge. It had to be Wainwright, or he was going to talk with the other teams that wanted Drew.

"Well, let us have a little meeting outside," Schuerholz said.

So Schuerholz, Wren, Cox, and Fregosi went to another room in the suite to discuss the deal. A few minutes later, with Jocketty and his group awaiting the answer, Schuerholz walked back in.

"Alright, we'll make the deal," Schuerholz said.

Jocketty was a little surprised. The men shook hands and the trade was done. J.D. Drew and Eli Marrero for Jason Marquis, Ray King, and Adam Wainwright. The Braves were thrilled to get Drew and Marrero, but it was at a high price.

"I think what it comes down to is a principle that Stan (Kasten) believed in, and I know John believes in it, but Stan really drilled it into my head when I first got here," says Frank Wren. "The team is above all – more than any one individual. Putting a team on the field is more important that having any individual. When you go into a negotiation or when you go into a trade, you're looking at putting the very best team out on the field. You hate to lose guys. We had depth with our pitching. Was it a no-brainer to trade Wainwright? No. We had to give it a lot of thought. At the end of the day, when we analyzed all parts of it, we thought it was the best thing to do."

Roy Clark was downstairs in the lobby of the hotel. He was afraid that his first draft pick as Scouting Director might be traded away. Clark admits when he heard Wainwright was gone, it was like someone had kicked him right in the stomach.

"Nobody in that room wanted to trade Adam Wainwright," Clark says. "But if you want to win championships and you're going to bring in quality, championship type players, sometimes you have to give up quality in return. The Cardinals people said if we didn't include Wainwright, they would not have made the deal."

Dayton Moore was with Clark when the word came down about the trade. As Farm Director, he was the one that was going to have to place the call to Wainwright.

"The hard thing about what we do from our standpoint is that we develop close relationships with the players," Moore says. "It's really about relationships. The better relationships you have, the better you communicate, and the more production and the quicker a player is going to reach his ceiling. The dreams and the expectations of these players when they join our organization are the same that we have in scouting and player development. So we all share in those expectations."

But Moore knew telling Wainwright that he was no longer a Brave would be tough. While it certainly is a function of the minor league system to supply talent for trades, this was a kid who had dreamed all his life of being a Brave. Most prospects don't have that dream; they just want to make the big leagues. But Wainwright wanted to play for one team. He wanted to be a Brave.

Moore immediately tried to call Wainwright, but got no answer on his cell phone. It just so happened that December 13, 2003, was a big day in Adam Wainwright's life for an entirely different reason. Wainwright had dated Jenny Curry since high school, and on this day he was at her parent's home in Gainesville, Georgia, asking her dad for Jenny's hand in marriage.

"It was in the middle of the conversation," Wainwright says. "I was asking him for permission to marry his daughter. Then all of a sudden my cell phone started ringing off the hook. Of all times, I'm like, 'What in the world?' So I turned it off. Then the phone at their house rang. He answered the phone call. I was like, 'No, don't get up and answer the phone. Let's talk about this.' He was probably glad to get away from that conversation a little bit. He was giving his little girl away. So I was like, 'What's going on here?' My mom was on the phone and she was crying. The first thing I thought of was that somebody was hurt. I thought maybe my dog had died or my brother was in trouble. I was thinking the worst."

Adam's mother finally got through her tears to tell her son what was the matter.

"Adam, you've been traded," said Nancy Wainwright.

"Is that it?" said a relieved Adam.

"Yeah, they traded you," replied his mother.

"Who did they trade me to?" Adam asked.

"The Cardinals."

"Okay well, I've got something more important going on right now. I've got to go."

As soon as the phone call was over, Adam sat back down with Jenny's dad and continued the conversation. He was taken aback by what he had just heard on the phone, but he was pre-occupied with what he was doing in the Curry's dining room.

"Being traded was weird and something I was definitely shocked about," says Wainwright, "but considering what I was doing at the time, it came second. I had to deal with other stuff. He gave us his blessing. We went into the weight room and the first thing I see on television was on the bottom line on ESPN: 'Cardinals trade outfielder J.D. Drew and Eli Marrero to the Braves for Jason Marquis, Ray King, and a minor leaguer to be named later.' I knew that was me. By the time we left the gym, my name was on the bottom line. So a lot of thoughts were going through my head at that time."

Then Dayton Moore finally got through on Adam's cell phone.

"We had a good ride while it lasted," Moore told Wainwright. "We needed an outfielder and you were what the Cardinals wanted."

Wainwright felt a little better knowing the Cardinals wanted him, but then when all of his Braves' teammates started to call wanting to know if he was really the one involved in the deal, it all started to sink in.

"That's when it really hit me," he says. "It was about two hours later. Everybody was calling and I was having to tell everybody yes. Then eventually I had to just turn my phone off. It was getting crazy. A lot of thoughts were going through my head. I was disappointed that I wouldn't be able to play with Atlanta, but at the same time excited about being able to start new and go somewhere and maybe have a good opportunity to make the big league team."

The next day, Wainwright would leave to go on a cruise with his girlfriend, who became his fiancée five days later when she accepted his marriage proposal. The trip was also a chance for him to get away from the stir that had been caused by his trade. He was the Braves' number one prospect, then all of a sudden, he was gone.

"A trade was not what I was expecting," Wainwright says. "I felt when I was traded that they were just going to go with Bubba. I thought that they had decided to make him their guy."

With the trade of Adam Wainwright, Bubba Nelson assumed the position as the Braves' best pitching prospect. He went to Spring Training with an outside chance at being Atlanta's fifth starter and perhaps a slightly better shot at winning a bullpen position.

"I definitely went into spring training with a mindset that I was going to make the team," Nelson says. "I had a lot of confidence in that. I thought I had a good opportunity with a lot of spots open, regardless of whether I was going to be starting or be coming out of the bullpen. I stepped it up a little bit with my offseason workout routine and I did a lot of work on the side with my pitching mechanics to try to get ready for spring training. I thought I was a highly rated prospect."

As spring training progressed, two things became obvious. First, the Braves really wanted Nelson to go back to AAA. He pitched only sparingly in big league games during March. Also, the Braves were having trouble with their bullpen. Schuerholz had signed former Cubs right-hander Antonio Alfonseca and former Marlins left-hander Armando Almanza over the winter to join their bullpen. But Almanza was battling a nagging injury and Alfonseca struggled. He had an ERA of 7.36 in nine games, allowed 18 hits in 11 innings and walked six. Kevin Gryboski, one of the most trusted relievers in Bobby Cox's bullpen the last several years, had some questions with his shoulder. Finally, Trey Hodges, who pitched in 51 games out of the Atlanta bullpen in 2003, struggled with his control by walking 12 batters in 13 innings.

So Schuerholz set his sights on a handful of relievers for a potential trade. The main objects of his desire were Cubs right-hander Juan Cruz, a flamethrower often compared to Pedro Martinez, and Reds righty Chris Reitsma, who possesses one of the best changeups in the game.

When Schuerholz called the Reds, there was instant interest in having discussions. Dan O'Brien had been brought in over the winter as General Manager to help turn the Reds franchise around. He had extensive scouting and player development experience with the Rangers, Astros, and Mariners, and his father, Dan O'Brien, Sr. was a longtime baseball executive with the Rangers, Mariners, Indians, and Angels. O'Brien knew some of the philosophies he wanted to install with the Reds were some of the same beliefs of Schuerholz and the Braves, most notably to accumulate as much young pitching as possible. He got his chance to start the process when Schuerholz called.

"Organizationally, coming in here and being a newcomer, we had a definite need to develop some starting pitching from within our organization," says O'Brien. "It had been a deficiency, an acknowledged one. There are very few organizations that would have any sufficient depth in pitching to provide us with two starting pitchers. There's no doubt that the Braves do an excellent job of not only identifying but developing pitchers from within their organization. The trick is to select the right ones."

O'Brien and Schuerholz spoke for about a week. As the discussions evolved, a potential deal took a variety of shapes and sizes. The Braves keyed in on Reitsma, while the Reds had two main targets: left-hander Jung Bong, who had spent most of the 2003 season as a reliever in Atlanta, and Bubba Nelson.

"We were not necessarily predisposed to trade Chris Reitsma," says O'Brien. "But they had a need in their bullpen to set up Smoltz. We were very forthright in saying that there had to be multiple starting pitchers coming back our way in order to make it work. So we went from that premise. You have prospects classified into different categories based on their future potential. Basically you try to position yourself to be able to acquire as many of the desirable prospects as possible in any given transaction. We had those two individuals in the upper end of their system. Obviously Jung Bong had spent much of the year in 2003 with Atlanta and Bubba Nelson – both of whom we view as starters. We knew they would not be of immediate help to our ball club, but we knew that down the line this was a trade that we needed to make."

Schuerholz made the deal for Juan Cruz on Thursday, March 25th. Atlanta sent lefty Andy Pratt and AA second baseman Richard Lewis to the Cubs in exchange for the twenty-five year old right-hander. The Braves saw Cruz as a pitcher who could either start or relieve, but with a solid rotation, his immediate need would be in the bullpen. Lewis was considered a very solid prospect, but with Marcus Giles entrenched in Atlanta, his road to the majors was blocked. Pratt was simply lost in a numbers game in the Braves bullpen.

Nelson was one of many of the Braves minor leaguers who went to an Orlando restaurant that night to wish Pratt and Lewis well. It was an eerie scene, as the kids were saying goodbye to teammates they had been around for several years. It made many of the prospects wonder who would be next, considering they had lost Wainwright, Pratt, Lewis, and late in the 2003 season, right-handed prospect Matt Belisle in a trade with the Reds. The Braves were using their farm system to improve the big league club, and no one felt safe.

"I felt I could be traded," Nelson admits, "but at the same time, I wasn't going to let it bother me because I just had to go out and do what I had to do. I knew anything was up in the air."

The next morning, Friday the 26th, Nelson reported to minor league camp. He had pitched well in big league camp, but the Braves felt he needed more time in AAA. Chino Cadahia is the Braves Field Coordinator, essentially in charge of spring training on the minor league side. Chino moves from field to field on a golf cart, organizing the training and monitoring the progress of the players. But on this morning he had another duty. Nelson was on Field 3 stretching with some of his teammates when he saw Chino calling him over to get in the golf cart.

"He didn't say anything to me really," Nelson says. "I kind of knew something was up. I could tell on his face. He's always got that bright look on his face and he's always saying good things to me, and I didn't hear anything out of him. Normally, he'd be talking, but he was just silent. I know Chino better than that. So I knew something was going on."

Nelson and Cadahia arrived at the Braves minor league clubhouse at the Disney Complex. Cadahia led Nelson to a back conference room where the coaches usually meet before and after practice. Waiting for him was the Braves Farm Director, Dayton Moore.

"When I walked in the room Dayton's eyes were red," Nelson explains. "I could just feel the air was tense as soon as I walked in the room."

"You've been traded to the Cincinnati Reds," Dayton told Nelson.

Bubba knew it was not easy for Moore to give him the news. Moore didn't have small talk; he just kind of spit it out. Nelson sat down to digest what he had just heard.

"I didn't really know what to think," Nelson admits. "I've never really seen a grown man in tears before. He was really upset. I was kind of upset too. I could tell it was tough for him because he was talking about how we grow with the system, and he kind of grows with us too. We have this bond with each other through the system because all the coordinators and all the scouts and all those guys are involved in everything we do. They always come up to us and are talking to us, wondering how we're doing, how our family is doing. They're always interested in everything. They're your best friend too. They're always willing to help you. He was saying that he hated to see me go and that it's been tough since Adam was gone and then the two guys the day before."

Unlike Schuerholz, who as Wren described has to treat any deal with the club in mind first, Moore gets extremely close to the prospects. He scouted many of them, including Nelson, in high school, and he's been there from their first days in the Gulf Coast League to their first days of big league camp. It's his job to get to know the players as people, so the Braves will know exactly what they're getting with every player. He's also genuinely concerned about every player reaching their potential, so when he has to tell them they're leaving, it's perhaps the hardest part of his job.

"It's difficult," Moore says. "Every time you make a decision about another person, you try to put yourself in that person's shoes the best you can. How will they react? What will they think is the best for them? It makes it difficult. I know there's disappointment in some of these kids. Adam, and Bubba Nelson, and Richard Lewis, Jung Bong and Andy Pratt. All those guys with the exception of Andy, we raised. I've been here with them since they became part of the organization and watched them develop from a very young age. I know what we went through to sign them. It's tough to let them go. But the good thing is that somebody wants them. Nobody wants a bad player. Everybody wants good players. They were wanted. We in the minor leagues are here to support our major league team. We did our job. Our job is to sign and develop major league caliber players and to help our team continue to win championships. Those are two pretty good arms for guys that have limited major league time. Our organization, in the eyes of our boss John Schuerholz, who is ultimately who we trust and who we follow, thought it was a good day."

But that didn't make it any easier for the guys who got traded. Nelson called his dad, who was in Orlando spending the month watching his son battle for a job in the big leagues. John Nelson was in the shower, so Bubba left a memorable message on his dad's cell phone.

"Dad, I'm over at the field," Bubba said. "You might want to come over. Chino took me into Dayton's office. Chino and Dayton sat me down and Dayton told me that I've been traded to the Cincinnati Reds. I'm packing my stuff up now."

John Nelson could tell by his son's tone it wasn't a joke, so he went right to the Braves' complex. He had wanted his son to be a Brave, maybe even a little more than Bubba himself. He knew the importance of a young pitcher playing in Atlanta. Plus, over the years he had also developed friendships with other players and their families. He and his son were part of a family, and all of a sudden, they were gone.

"He wanted to be a Brave," John Nelson says. "I wanted him to be a Brave. He didn't want to be a Red. But he knew that's the way it is. I had a feeling that something like this might be happening when he was only pitching a little bit here and there. I felt like something was going on. We know now what was going on. They needed some help. They didn't know if they could count on some of the guys they had. They needed some help right away. That's why they went out and got Reitsma."

When John Nelson arrived at the complex, Bubba was back in a golf cart. He had cleaned out his locker in the Braves clubhouse and was on the phone with Reds Assistant GM Dean Taylor. Then Nelson had to make the longest walk of his life. He had to walk back out to the fields to say goodbye to his now former teammates.

"That's got to be the worst thing I've had to do in baseball,"

Nelson says. "I'm used to saying goodbye to those guys at the end of the season and going home. But this time it was for good. I wasn't really ready to do all of that yet. Those guys were some of my best friends. We never left each other's side during the season and even during the offseason too. They were closer to me than any of my friends in high school. I had spent so much time with them and their families, especially Chris (Waters), his wife (Krissy) and kids, and Krissy's parents (Scott and Toni Alvarez). They have a wonderful family, and I felt apart of that."

"It was an emotional day," says Waters. "It was basically my best buddy gone – just like that. It kind of breaks you down to reality that it could happen to me at any minute."

Nelson threw his stuff in the back of his Chevy Tahoe and headed down I-4 to Sarasota. His dad also walked around the Braves' complex saying his goodbyes and thank you to the coaches that had helped his son get close to the big leagues. When he ran into Dayton Moore, he had a different message.

"Dayton, thank you for helping my son become a man," Nelson told Moore.

In a span of seven months, the Braves traded seven pitchers (Matt Belisle, Adam Wainwright, Ray King, Jason Marquis, Jung Bong, Bubba Nelson, and Andy Pratt) in four separate trades, with Wainwright and Nelson being the Braves' two best pitching prospects. It was clearly an example of how the Braves use their farm system to help the major league roster. In a year when the payroll was going down, the flexibility to simply add big name free agents or expensive players was not there. Instead, the Braves had to offer quality minor league players for talented major leaguers that had decent contracts. Not many organizations have the depth or the talent to pull off that many deals with that much young talent.

"We've got a lot of quality young pitchers and quality position players that have bright major league futures," Moore says. "The truth of the matter is that some of those guys will play for us and some will play elsewhere. We all take pride in the fact that we have more major league players who were drafted and signed and developed by the Atlanta Braves than any other organization in baseball. I know that our players understand that, and they realize that they're probably not going to play here. But I think they're here, and they're committed and trust the process we have to develop players."

J.D. Drew did exactly what the Braves hoped he would do. He stayed healthy, playing in a career high 145 games, and he put up the unbelievable numbers that most baseball observers believed he was capable of if he stayed healthy. Drew hit .305 with career highs in home runs (31), RBI (93), hits (158), runs scored (118), and walks (118). He also played tremendous defense and was an outstanding baserunner. While Drew didn't exactly duplicate the numbers Sheffield had put up the season before, he gave the Braves the production they needed to keep the lineup as one of the best in the league.

Eli Marrero proved to be a very valuable member of the 2004 Braves team. After missing part of the first quarter of the season, Marrero eased into a platoon in left field with Charles Thomas. He hit .320 with 10 home runs and 40 RBI in 250 at bats. Marrero and Drew combined to make $6.2 million in 2004, relatively half of Sheffield's salary with the New York Yankees.

The Braves used Reitsma and Cruz as two very important parts of their bullpen, and they turned in their best years as a pro. Reitsma was John Smoltz's primary set-up man, pitching in a Braves' record 84 games, winning six, and saving two. Cruz was the main long-man in the bullpen, going 6-2 with a 2.75 ERA in fifty games, 59 hits allowed in 72 innings pitched, with 30 walks and 70 strikeouts. Even though Alfonseca and Gryboski both turned in solid seasons, the additions of Reitsma and Cruz solidified the Atlanta bullpen, which was one of the best in the National League.

The success of the players the Braves acquired in the winter and spring trades was a huge reason the club won their thirteenth straight division title in 2004. If they had not had the minor league talent to acquire players to adequately replace Gary Sheffield, and if they had not had the minor league talent to acquire the pitchers needed to stabilize the bullpen, there is no way the Braves would have made it back to the playoffs. So even though it was tough to give up the promising talent, especially the top two pitching prospects, the trades were well worth it.

"The strength of our system gave us so much more flexibility than a lot of other clubs," says Frank Wren. "We were able to make some deals. We were able to get Reitsma for two players that had value in the market. In J.D. Drew's case, without him and Marrero, we don't win this year. Pitching is the number one commodity. If you have pitching, you can make deals and keep your team going. Our scouts have done a great job in finding pitchers. We've done a real good job in developing them. That gives us the ability to have the currency that's necessary to make deals. We traded Wainwright and Nelson and Bong and we still felt like we had plenty of depth to be able to do that."

That could be the most amazing aspect of all. Even with all of the young pitchers traded, the Braves had other young arms step up and become top prospects in 2004. Kyle Davies is arguably one of the top arms in baseball. Zach Miner and Macay McBride had impressive showings in the Arizona Fall League in 2004 and became possibilities for 2005. Anthony Lerew, Blaine Boyer, and Matt Wright are three players headed to AA that have value for the future. And in Single-A, guys like Chuck James, Jake Stevens, Bryan Digby, Charlie Morton, Sean White, Chris Vines, Luis Atilano, and Matt Harrison are all considered legitimate arms for the future. The Braves have never been deeper in young pitching, and that goes right to Roy Clark and Dayton Moore's philosophy of continually stocking the farm system with solid, projectable arms, and as importantly, solid personalities.

"You've got to have pitching," Moore says. "Pitching has got to be the foundation in the organization. Everybody wants a good pitcher. The more pitchers we have, the more strength we have in our organization. Paul Snyder always said, 'You got to have about twenty pitchers to get two in the big leagues.' We have strong depth, but we've got to continue to build."

Meanwhile Adam Wainwright and Bubba Nelson carried on with their pro careers. Both found the road a bit rockier out of a Braves' uniform.

Nelson struggled to fit into the Reds' system. Jung Bong, who was traded with Nelson to the Reds, was there with him, and Matt Belisle was a former top Braves' pick that was in his first spring training with the Reds. Nelson knew everybody with the Braves, but now he was starting over.

"It was weird to put on a Reds jersey," Nelson admits. "It wasn't as inviting as I thought it was going to be. It was tough walking in that locker room not knowing anybody. That's the toughest thing. It's like going to a new school when you're in elementary school. You don't know anybody and you're uncomfortable."

Nelson was uncomfortable from the time the Reds started him off in AAA. After a 1-10 start the Reds moved him back down to AA in midseason where he pitched much better. Overall, Nelson went 2-12 with an ERA of 5.67 in 21 starts, 135 hits in 112.2 innings, 38 walks, and 80 strikeouts. The Reds know that it takes many young players traded out of their original organization time to adjust to their new home.

"Well, I think the overall organizational perspective on Bubba hasn't changed," says Dan O'Brien. "We think very highly of him. I think perhaps we may have pushed him a little bit being at such a young age at AAA. I think in hindsight the reality is that he probably wasn't quite ready for such a jump. But he regrouped, as we knew he would and he pitched very well at AA. We have no doubt that he has a bright future."

"It was definitely a transition year for me, but you can never have an excuse in baseball or you'll just stay behind all the time," Nelson says. "I didn't see myself staggering as much as I did. As hard as I worked to get to this point in my career, to see it fall apart in one season was a shocker for me. I wasn't comfortable. My confidence wasn't like it used to be. But it's the beast of the game. I wanted to be a Brave so bad. Bar none, they are the best organization in all of baseball. Who wouldn't want to be on a playoff team every year and get a ring? And to play with guys like Smoltz, and Rafael Furcal, Andruw Jones, and Chipper Jones, who wouldn't want to play with those guys, you know? But now over here I have a chance to play with Ken Griffey, (Austin) Kearns, and Adam Dunn."

While he hated to be away from his friends and the Braves, Wainwright was happy to be with a great organization like the Cardinals. But like Nelson, he also struggled in AAA, going 4-4 with a 5.37 ERA in 12 starts. Adam's biggest problem was an old high school injury that crept up on him again. He partially tore the ligament in his right elbow ending his season in late June. The injury put a huge damper on his first year with the Cardinals.

"I didn't pitch well, but I had some lights-out games and some very mediocre games," Wainwright says. "I gave up like four home runs in my last two games and I was throwing a lot slower and couldn't control anything. My arm was just killing me."

But just like four years earlier, Wainwright didn't require surgery. The ligament was not completely torn so he was able to avoid the dreaded Tommy John surgery. Wainwright rested until appearing in a handful of games in the Arizona Fall League.

The injury, however, did nothing to help him get over his trade from the Braves. He had a lot of time to just sit and think. After believing for almost four years that he was going to wear an Atlanta uniform, Wainwright still has trouble accepting the trade that made him a Cardinal.

"I still don't think it's hit me all the way," he admits. "I could have never bet on being traded. I just thought I would be a Brave forever. The hardest part about it by far was being away from guys like Adam (LaRoche), Blaine (Boyer), and Kelly Johnson. There are so many guys in that organization that I feel like I was close to. It'll be hard for me to have as much fun with somebody else as I had with those guys. But the trade shows you what kind of business it is. If the big team needs something, you're not always protected. You're always on the market if there's a better deal out there. Look what J.D. did for the Braves. You can't really argue about the trade. Some people might say, even with as well as Marquis and Ray King pitched for the Cardinals, that the Braves came away pretty well in the deal. But I consider the Cardinals one of the top organizations in baseball from top to bottom. I was very fortunate to go where I did go."

For almost three full years, Wainwright and Nelson, Adam and Bubba, were thought of as the future of the Atlanta Braves rotation. But they got caught up in the primary function of the farm system, and the opportunity of being teammates at Turner Field went away in one quick offseason.

"That was the plan," Wainwright says. "We had a lot of conversations. We thought that's what the plan was."

"I had grown up with Adam and played with him on every team, every year," Nelson says. "It was easy to think we were going to be there. But I will always be a Brave, and I think Adam will too. When I turn on the TV and watch the Braves, they're still in my heart. It's like I'm still with them. Someday who knows? I might wear one of those uniforms again."

For two very different players, Adam and Bubba turned out to have one sizable commonality in the end: they were both traded by the Atlanta Braves. It wasn't the similarity they had in mind.

20
SEARCHING FOR ANOTHER LEFTY

The loss of Tom Glavine via free agency to the New York Mets after the 2002 season was a tremendous blow for the Atlanta Braves. Not only did they lose the franchise's most successful left-handed pitcher since Warren Spahn, but in many ways they also lost the face of the Braves' turnaround. Glavine was the first of the minor league kids to make it in Atlanta and help stop the bleeding of the 80's, so his departure was a sign that a new era of Braves baseball was forthcoming.

It's unfair to say that anyone can replace a pitcher like Tom Glavine or Greg Maddux; pitchers that enjoyed tremendous success in a Braves' uniform. Never would anyone want to put that type of pressure on a young pitcher. But perhaps the biggest challenge for the Braves' brass is to continue the pitching dominance it enjoyed so much in the 90's, even when Glavine and Maddux, and eventually Smoltz, are long gone.

Finding a lefty to step into Glavine's shoes was a task almost too daunting to ponder. Glavine was so identified as a Brave that replacing him would not only mean picking up thirty-five starts a season, but also assuming the role as a team leader. When the Braves arrived at spring training in 2003 and were without #47, they were forced to look elsewhere, and it was no surprise that the first place they would look was internally.

Horacio Ramirez was no Glavine or Steve Avery; he didn't receive much press in the minor leagues that would have shone a spotlight on him coming up. Instead, he was somewhat of a no-name when he got to Orlando and was given the opportunity at winning a spot in the rotation. Ramirez's name was familiar to the Braves, but it had lost some of its luster after he missed almost a season and a half after Tommy John surgery in 2001.

Ramirez grew up in a basketball neighborhood in Inglewood, California, just south of Los Angeles. But ever since he can remember, he was a baseball player. His dad told him stories of how he picked up a plastic bat when he was a year old and "swung it like a pro." When he was eight, Ramirez started pitching, and by the time he was a teenager he was pitching in the Beer Leagues of Los Angeles. The Beer Leagues are mainly Sunday baseball where grown men in their twenties, thirties, and even forties suit up and play. Ramirez would throw nine innings against grown men when he was just fourteen years old.

"It was fun," Ramirez says. "I loved the competition. I loved going out there and having people say, 'Watch this kid pitch. He's pretty good.' You know I enjoyed that even though I never really believed it."

But he started to believe he was pretty good when he pitched in the Babe Ruth World Series when he was sixteen. He broke a record for strikeouts in a game when he fanned nineteen in a seven-inning game. Then he came back in a second game and struck out seventeen.

"That's when scouts started to notice me a little bit," Ramirez says.

Doug Deutsch, the Astros' scout for the West Coast, invited Horacio to a tryout in Los Angeles when he was a junior. Ramirez went, but never heard back from Deutsch. Neither did he hear from his hometown Dodgers, whom he grew up loving as a kid.

"I don't think I even received a letter from the Dodgers," Ramirez says. "There was one day where my high school coach lined up the scouts to come in. The Dodgers' scout got there and he didn't seem interested at all. To me I was a little hurt since I grew up in L.A. He didn't seem interested at all."

But there was one scout who was very interested. John Ramey, who first found Marcus Giles for the Braves down in San Diego, was very intrigued by Ramirez. Ramey saw Ramirez pitch once and then brought in Paul Snyder and Bob Wadsworth to crosscheck the lefty.

"That day I think I pitched nine innings, struck out sixteen and walked nine," Ramirez says. "I threw about 180 pitches. The whole game I think I was 89-91 mph."

Ramirez had no idea the Braves were that interested in him. He thought they might draft him, but the Rockies also showed some interest. When his coach told him the Braves grabbed him in the fifth round, he was a little oblivious to the entire process.

"I knew this was a real good organization," he says. "I knew about the pitching. I knew they were real good at breeding their pitchers. But Ramey only saw me pitch two times. There were scouts that saw me pitch five or six times. Ramey said the first time he saw me he knew that something was there."

The Braves coaches found out Ramey was right. Ramirez was impressive from the first day he put on a Braves' uniform, but it wasn't until 2000 that he really burst onto the scene as a legit prospect. Ramirez went 15-8 with a 3.22 ERA in 26 starts for Myrtle Beach with only 42 walks and 125 strikeouts in 148.1 innings of work. He then opened Bobby Cox's eyes with a sterling performance in a big league spring training game in 2001.

"It was against the Dodgers," Ramirez remembers. "I threw seven pitches – all fastballs. I think they saw I don't give in. I don't throw 94 or 95 (mph) but I throw 88-91. I don't get easily intimidated. I remember the first pitch was a foul ball, second pitch was a broken bat, and the third pitch the guy hit a double. The catcher put down change up, curve, and slider – every pitch except the heater. I shook him off until I got the fastball. I threw a fastball, and then another one, and I got out of the inning and came in. I was so nervous, but I was telling myself, 'Act like you've been here, act like you've been here," as I was walking off the mound calm and collected. I remember Leo (Mazzone) said, 'Good job. That-a-boy kid.'"

A good first impression usually means a lot in Cox and Mazzone's eyes, and Ramirez definitely did just that. He took off for AA Greenville with the hope of putting together one more solid season before maybe getting a chance in Atlanta. But then, a pitcher's nightmare came calling for Ramirez.

"I was in Greenville facing the Dodgers' team from Jacksonville," Ramirez says. "I threw a pitch and felt a little tweak in there. I threw two more pitches and I think I struck the guy out. I walked around the mound and I kind of glanced out at the bullpen. I remembered Winston Abreu (former Braves farmhand) had Tommy John a couple of years before that. I told myself, 'I don't want that.' But in my heart I felt like something was wrong. When I would throw a ball or make little movements I wouldn't really feel it. So I thought I was being paranoid. But the next day there was some swelling there and it was hard for me to open the fridge or turn a doorknob- a tell-tell sign for a guy who needs Tommy John."

Ramirez required the surgery and immediately started rehab. For some unknown reason, the Braves had a run on Tommy John injuries in 2001. Derrick Lewis, a decent right-handed prospect who was already in AAA, had the surgery in June. Ramirez was able to go to Orlando at the Braves' Training complex and work out with Lewis and Matt Belisle, who at the time was perhaps the Braves' best pitching prospect, but had injured his back in spring training. Together the three pitchers worked out diligently, pushing each other to get back to where they were before each got hurt.

"I was lucky to be around those guys," Ramirez says. "There were days when it was real hard. It helped a lot to have them there. Derrick Lewis, who is as much of a warrior as anybody, Matt, and myself. I'd come in some days kind of down, not feeling like doing much of anything, and I'd see them working out and I'd say, 'Ok, they're getting better, now I've got to get better.' For the whole year basically to go out there and work your butt off every single day is tough."

But Ramirez never got too discouraged mentally. He knew from day one that he would get back. His philosophy was simple: the injury happened, now rehab and get right back in step as a top prospect for the Braves.

"Swallow it," he says. "Just go ahead. That's what God has planned for you, so go ahead and do it. And that's something that got me through it: faith. Always believing that I'd be able to bounce back. I never had one doubt. To me it was like, 'this is what's given to you, now go ahead and get through this and proceed with your career.'"

Ramirez did just that in late May of 2002 when he started his comeback in Low-A Macon. He pitched two games before being bumped up to AA Greenville. Ramirez did pretty well, going 9-5 with a 3.03 ERA in 16 starts. His numbers were solid across the board, but it still took some time for him to feel like he was back.

"I pitched those 92 innings in Greenville off my curveball," Ramirez says. "I just pitched. Sometimes I'd go out there and my fastball would be 82, 83. I just had to find a way."

At the end of that season in Greenville, Ramirez wanted to know how he had done in the Braves' eyes. So he approached his pitching coach in AA, former big leaguer Bill Champion, and asked a simple question.

"Champ, what do I need to do to make it to the big leagues?"

"Just show up for spring training," Champion told his lefty pitcher. "Look, a lot of kids treat the Arizona Fall League like a vacation, but you need to go out and get everybody who comes up to that plate out. Starters only pitch around three innings, so you need to make an impression. There are tons of scouts at those games, so good reports out of Arizona will carry over to Spring Training."

Ramirez was a bit startled. He knew he had done relatively well since he returned from his rehab, but he wasn't sure he was that close. But then he started to believe what Champion had told him when he went to the Arizona Fall League and pitched lights out. He got his velocity back and felt better about his immediate future.

"One thing I've always been is realistic with myself," Ramirez says. "I could have been in Myrtle Beach and I could have thrown seven or eight scoreless innings, and at the end of the day I would ask myself, 'Was I good enough to pitch in the big leagues?' And if I didn't throw enough changeups or two-seamers or sliders I'd be mad. It would be hard for me to sleep. Next time out I'd make sure I did those things. But I always believed I was going to make it. In the conversation with Champ, he just said come back healthy. That AFL season I got my fastball back, but my control wasn't there. I was so happy to get my velocity back and my movement back on my two-seamer, and that's all I threw. But I was erratic. I wasn't happy with the way I pitched, but for Tommy John it's something you have to go through."

Even though he wasn't totally satisfied with his performance in the AFL, the Braves were. They immediately started thinking he might be ready to challenge for a spot in the Atlanta rotation. The one thing they did know was that Ramirez would have the confidence to compete for the job.

"The injuries that Horacio had to battle and overcome were tremendous challenges," says Braves Farm Director Dayton Moore. "He faced those challenges and he overcame the things he had to overcome to be major league pitcher. The people that understand the circumstances that they face are simply tools that allow them to learn, are the ones that are going to be successful. The circumstances that you face day in and day out, you look at those as opportunities instead of setbacks. Horacio's makeup is the thing that has allowed him to persevere."

Ramirez went to Orlando and had an outstanding spring training. He went 4-0 with a 1.90 ERA in 6 starts and won a job in the Atlanta rotation.

"I wasn't surprised," Ramirez says. "I think if you ever surprise yourself, you're selling yourself short. I believe I can do just about anything on the field, on that mound."

That's exactly what Ramirez proved in his rookie season. He went 12-4 with an ERA of 4.00 in 29 starts. Even though it wasn't talked about too much, Ramirez did pretty well in "replacing" an Atlanta legend in Tom Glavine. But it was another legend that made a big difference in his career from the first day he stepped onto a big league field.

"Greg Maddux, I can't even tell you how much he helped me out," Ramirez says. "I soaked in as much as I possibly could."

Ramirez used that newfound knowledge as he pitched in his sophomore season in 2004, and it was obvious he had learned well from Maddux and the other veterans. He started out the season with a 2.28 ERA in 9 starts, despite a 2-4 record from low run support. Then in Montreal in late May, Ramirez had to come out of the game with shoulder pain.

"It was tendonitis," he says. "It was rotator cuff tendonitis. It's like somebody stabbing you in the shoulder. Any little movement hurts. You can't do much. I got a cortisone shot and that took a lot of the pain away, but not all of it."

Ramirez's pain would never go away. Doctors couldn't find any structural damage, so he continued to rehab in an attempt to return before the end of the 2004 season. But in his only appearance, in late September against the Marlins, his shoulder was still bothering him. So after the season, doctors went in to "clean up" some damage. The procedure was a success, and he's once again a vital member of

Atlanta's rotation.

"I've had two surgeries and I'm going to stick with it until they take this jersey off my back," Ramirez says. "I'm not going anywhere until God says, 'It's time for you to find another job.' Until then, I'm staying here."

That's exactly where the Braves expect him to be – right in their rotation. After struggling for so many years to find that productive left-handed starter, the Braves developed one of the best of the last fifty years in Tom Glavine. They just hope that, with a little luck and some tender-loving-care, lightning has struck twice.

21

WHO THE HELL IS CHARLES THOMAS?

Donnie Poplin first saw Charles Thomas in the fall of 1997. He was a scout for the Seattle Mariners, while Thomas was a freshman outfielder for Western Carolina. It was "Scout's Day," a chance for scouts to see the talent the college had to offer.

"He just kind of stood out," Poplin says. "He ran well. He threw well. He had all the raw tools. I'm not so sure that the industry knew who he was as a high school senior. I can't speak for all thirty teams, but the majority of people that I knew at the time had never seen him play in high school. So he shows up as a freshman at Western Carolina coming from the same state and all of a sudden, 'How did we not see this guy?'"

Charles W. Thomas was born in Northern California the day after Christmas, 1978. Eleven years later, after his parents divorced, he moved with his mom to Asheville, North Carolina, to be near her mom and dad. Charles always loved playing ball, telling his teachers that when he grew up he was going to be a big league ballplayer.

"They said I had to have a backup plan if that didn't work

out," Thomas says. "I always said, 'No, I'm going to be a baseball player.'"

By the tenth grade Thomas started getting playing time on the varsity baseball team at Asheville High School. The team was not very good and the competition even shakier, but Thomas became one of the best players on the team. He had a solid senior season, but as a speedy outfielder on a mediocre high school team playing in the mountains of North Carolina, he didn't get any looks from pro scouts or even the college baseball recruiters for that matter.

"In fact, I got recruited by the soccer coach at UNC-Asheville, which is the university right there in town," Thomas remembers. "But they never said anything about baseball."

Luckily, he'd attended a baseball camp at Western Carolina the summer before his senior year of high school.

"I stood out like a sore thumb," Thomas says. "Everyone else there was like thirteen, and there I was seventeen years old." But the coaches at WCU followed Thomas after that $85 camp and offered him a baseball scholarship.

"My freshman year I started out on the bench," Thomas says. "But then the second game of the year we were down at Stetson and I got to pinch hit and got a hit up the middle. The next day I pinch-hit in the sixth inning and it went to like twelve innings. I was 3-for-3. So the next game was a tournament in Charleston, South Carolina, and I got to start. I started after that. The guy starting was struggling to start out and he continued to struggle. I got an opportunity."

He led the Catamounts in hitting in his freshman season (.364), but Thomas' sophomore season was when he really made a name for himself. He was a first team All-Southern Conference pick in 1999 after leading the league with a .406 batting average.

"They had several other guys that year who were getting scouted heavily because they were draft-eligible, so you were having to see Western Carolina play quite often because of those two guys," Poplin says. "Charles was not draft-eligible, but he had a very good year that year. He always played very well for me when I would go in and see the other prospects. He kind of got on the radar screen for me that year, and I had him down as a guy that I wanted to spend some time with the following year, when he would be draft-eligible."

Thomas, always a slow starter, got off to a terrible start his junior season. The Catamounts lost several important players in their lineup, so Charles was moved from leadoff to the number three spot. He had been a slap hitter, one that would get on base and then be driven in, but when his role changed he struggled, sending most of the scouts away. But Poplin, who by the fall of 1999 had left the Mariners and joined the Braves, still stayed on him.

"I felt like Charles was trying to carry the whole team on his shoulders," Poplin says. "The team wasn't quite as good. He struggled a little with the bat, so I kind of referred back to his sophomore year. If he did it one time, he ought to be able to do it again. I'm not going to say it didn't affect his draft status. It did. I think the other scouts tended to be a little less aggressive because of what his performance was at that time."

Thomas finished his three years at WCU with a .374 average (fifth in school history), 5 homers, 101 RBI, 39 doubles, and 38 stolen bases. Solid numbers, but certainly not great. But the stats were not what turned Poplin on to Thomas's ability.

"The thing that really put me over the edge with Chares was I really felt he had tremendous baseball instincts," Poplin says. "Defensively, he played center field in college, and when a ball was hit in the air, he was always standing where he needed to be. He was always standing at the right spot. That's a sign of good instincts. He could run. His arm was playable. I always believed in Charles' instincts."

Thomas decided that if he were drafted in the top ten rounds of the 2000 draft, he would sign. If it was somewhere between the tenth and fifteenth rounds, he'd still consider it. But if he went past the fifteenth round, he was probably going to return to school for his senior season. As draft day progressed, it looked like he was going back for one more college season.

"The Indians scout called in the eleventh round and asked if I'd sign," Thomas remembers. "I said, 'Yeah, I think so.' So he said, 'Well alright, let me call them and I'll call you back.' But he never called back. So I'm watching movies and stuff and the time was going by and in the fifteenth round the Padres called."

"We've got you next on our list, but we haven't talked to you," the scout said. "We know we haven't talked to you so we were wondering how much you want?".

"Honestly, I just want whatever's fair for whatever round I'm drafted in," Thomas replied.

"Well, this is what we can do," the scout said. "We can probably give you $10,000 and two semesters of school. Would you sign for that?"

"No," Thomas said. "I appreciate the interest."

The scout thanked Charles for being honest with him, and then Thomas called his buddies to tell them he was probably heading back for his senior season. Meanwhile, Poplin, in his first year with the Braves, was urging Roy Clark to draft Thomas. "I just kind of stuck to my guns and tried to convince Roy that we needed to take a shot at him somewhere."

Clark knew that Poplin had a gut feeling about the speedy outfielder. So when the nineteenth round rolled around, he drafted Thomas. Poplin called his prospect with the news.

"Charles, congratulations," Poplin said. "We just drafted you."

"Oh thanks," Thomas replied with tempered enthusiasm.

Not unlike most kids who believe they're better than their draft position might indicate, Thomas was a little disappointed that he lasted until the nineteenth round. But it did help that it was the Braves, whom he had watched through the years growing up. About a week later, Thomas signed with the Braves for $20,000, with the team paying for his last year of college.

"My projection was that Charles Thomas could be a solid fourth outfielder at the big league level," Poplin says. "I felt that he had enough instincts and defensive ability to have value and probably hit enough to where he could at least be an extra outfielder at the major league level. When you walk into the park and see a Charles Thomas you see a five-foot-eleven type build who is not going to overwhelm you with his body. He's not going to overwhelm you in batting practice with his power. His speed is obviously somewhat attractive, but at the time it wasn't world-class speed. So he doesn't blow you away. Charles is one of those guys that as a scout the more I watched him the more I learned to appreciate him as a player and appreciate what his abilities allowed him to do. The little things start showing up the more you watch him, whether it was running the bases, the jumps he gets on balls, or the routes he took in the outfield, just those little things. He really didn't have that one big tool that you could hang your hat on."

But Poplin had seen enough of Thomas to know he did have ability and as importantly, his makeup. He talked extensively with the college coach and others to crosscheck his instincts.

"I felt pretty good about what I was seeing with his ability, but I wanted to make sure that this was the kind of character that was going to fit into the Braves' organization," Poplin admits. "He was not a guy you needed to spend a lot of time on since he's a class person."

Thomas is pure and simply a good kid. He's quiet and unassuming. In a world full of cocky ballplayers, Charles Thomas is a breath of fresh air. It didn't take long for the Braves' minor league coaches to discover this. When Charles got to his first stop in the minors, Jamestown in the New York/Penn League, he started out on the bench. But he didn't complain or pout. He simply waited for his chance, just like he did in college.

"Jean-ses Langlois, who has played there the year before, had started out in right field and started out like 2-for-30 or something," Thomas remembers. "So Big Jim (Saul, the Jamestown Manager) put me out there and I started out well so I got to stay."

Jamestown was the first place Jim Beauchamp saw Thomas. He's the Braves' minor league outfield instructor. "You just had to watch him everyday to see how he did things and went about things," Beauchamp says. "To get to know him, with his makeup and his work ethic and his personality, he was a manager's dream. You wish all of them were like Charles."

Thomas finished his first minor league season with a .303 average, 1 home run, 25 RBI, and 10 stolen bases. The next spring the Braves sent Thomas to Myrtle Beach, the High-A team in the Carolina League. College players often skip over the Low-A team in Macon, just as Adam LaRoche did that same year. But Thomas struggled early on, hitting only .159 in the first twelve games of the season. The Braves sent him down to Macon to get on track, but his struggles continued. He split time in right field with Alec Zumwalt, but his averaged hovered around the .200 mark the first half of the season.

"Randy (Ingle, Macon's Manager) kept putting me out there and giving me the opportunity," Thomas remembers. "At the time I appreciated it so much because I was horse crap."

But Thomas never stopped working, even when he was struggling. He bounced back in the second half of the 2001 season to finish with a .250 average, 11 home runs, and 59 RBI. It was a pretty solid comeback considering how poorly he played earlier in the season, and the recovery was all due to his hard work.

"It felt good to finish strong," Thomas admits. "In that first half I'm wondering if the year before was a fluke and if I could really do this. There were all kinds of things going on in my head. I was struggling. I really was. The coaching staff was awesome. They worked with me every day. Bobby Moore (Macon's hitting coach) was out there with me every day early. In the hot Macon sun, it was tough. But we were able to get it turned around."

"He was always the first one to the park and the last one to leave," says Ingle, himself a former Braves' minor leaguer in the 80's. "One night I asked him if he was paying rent in the clubhouse. I asked him if he was going to spend the night. He was always the last one to leave. He worked extremely hard. He'd be in there lifting weights, sitting in the ice tub, or cleaning his shoes. He took a lot of pride in the game. As far as hustling, you never had to worry if he was going to run a ball out or wonder if he was going to pull up on you. Everything he hit, whether it was a pop up, fly ball, ground ball, or a base hit, he gave you 100% on every one of them."

Three days before the end of spring training in 2002, when Thomas was scheduled to leave to go to Myrtle Beach, he tore a ligament in his elbow. The injury forced him to remain in Orlando to rehab through late May. Two weeks after he got to Myrtle Beach, the Braves needed him to go to AA Greenville after Ryan Langerhans was injured. He wasn't ready for AA, but the Braves needed him there anyway.

"It would have been tough even if I had gone there right out of spring training," Thomas says, "but to come from Extended Spring Training, playing those games and go to AA was tough. I was hitting about .180 with two or three weeks left. Finally, I started getting it and making the adjustments. Mel Roberts (Greenville's coach) and Snit (Greenville Manager Brian Snitker) were great. So I ended up at .231."

A .231 hitter in AA is not going to get on the top of any top-prospect lists. Neither is it going to guarantee a player a promising financial future. Charles Thomas spent his offseasons working, first at Arby's and then as a host in the dining room of the Grove Park Inn, a mountain resort in Asheville. While other players were playing winter ball, he had to make extra money to pay the bills.

"I had been working since I was fourteen years old," Thomas says. "I had worked summers when all the other kids were going to camps. It wasn't anything new. Generally, I tried to work in the mornings and then get to my workouts in the afternoon. It's a little different when you come home, even when you're in the minors. Everyone thinks you're rich and all that. So to be working in a fast food restaurant...that was different."

But despite the poor batting average and working a "regular" job during the offseason, Thomas was never deterred from his dream. His determination and work ethic had all of the minor league coaches pulling for him to make it.

"He would come up and tell you, 'I'm going to play in the big leagues,'" remembers Jim Beauchamp. "And you'd say, 'Well Charles, I sure hope you do. Nobody deserves it more than you do.' You'd walk away and say, 'Golly, I hope he plays in the big leagues.' He was just such a good kid."

Beauchamp took a special liking to Thomas. Himself a former big leaguer, "Beach" knew Thomas didn't have off the charts talent, but he saw the kid push himself every day to become better. Thomas's work ethic gave Beauchamp and the other coaches even more motivation to try to help him improve as a player, but it wasn't always easy.

"Charles's biggest problem in the minor leagues was he put too much pressure on himself," Beauchamp says. "He'd tinker too much with his swing. He almost would overdo things. He'd be the kind of kid that if he didn't get a hit, the next day he'd be trying something different in the cage. But you still loved him for it. He's the kind that would go in after a ballgame and if he was 0-for-4, he's liable to turn the lights on in the cage at ten o'clock at night and be down there hitting on a tee with stance number 432."

When Spring Training rolled around in 2003, Thomas again found himself battling for his job. Several other outfield prospects started to make progress, so at the end of the spring, the Braves called Thomas in to talk about his future.

"It was Chino (Cadahia, Field Coordinator), Dayton (Moore), Beach, and Roy Clark," Thomas remembers. "Dayton did the talking. He just said it was a situation where they felt a lot of guys had jumped ahead of me. I was a person they wanted in the organization character-wise and all of that, but there weren't any spots. They said, 'You can go there (back to Myrtle Beach as a reserve) or we could give you your release if that's what you want.' The coolest thing was they asked me how I felt about going down there. Most of the time they just do what they do and you live with it. I was ready to go back to Greenville and prove I could play there. So when they asked me how I felt about going to Myrtle Beach, that was a shock."

But earlier that same day, Adam Stern, an outfield prospect who was scheduled to start the season in Greenville, was injured. The Braves' brass told Thomas that if Stern was out for a while, it might open up a spot. Once again fate stepped in and gave Thomas a hand, as Stern was seriously injured and it opened up a starting role in Myrtle Beach.

"I started out hitting like .400 and then just started slipping, slipping, and slipping," Thomas recalls. "I was hitting .242 and I had been changing everything. I was wearing myself out. I was switching bats everyday and stances and this and that. I was just thinking too much. Then somebody got hurt in Richmond, and I go up to Greenville but I don't play. I pinch hit. I think I got nineteen at bats in two weeks."

Thomas was becoming a utility outfielder, simply going wherever the Braves needed a body. He was showing progress, but not enough to stick in one place. After a game in Carolina, Greenville Manager Brian Snitker waved Thomas over for a talk outside the shed that acts as the visiting team's clubhouse.

"Charlie," Snitker said as he puts his hands on Thomas' shoulders.

Thomas' heart skips a beat as he thinks he's getting ready to be released.

"You're going back to Myrtle Beach," Snitker continued.

A relieved Thomas then heard some encouraging words from Snitker. His manager believed he was making progress, getting better as a player.

Snitker says now, "The only thing I could tell him was, 'Charlie, you're getting better. You're improving as a player.' You hate to send a player down. I never wanted to send him down. He did well and I liked having him around. That's the way it works out sometimes. As a manager, you just do what you're told. But I remember telling him, 'the best compliment I can give you is that you're getting better. You are proving you are a better player.'"

The talk fired Thomas up to go back to Myrtle Beach and prove to the Braves what he and Snitker already knew: he was better than a Single-A ballplayer. But he again found himself on the bench. With sporadic pinch-hitting appearances, his average dipped from .242 to .200. Thomas then read something that triggered his mind. He got a note from Jack Maloof, the hitting coach at Myrtle Beach: "Relax and beat the pitcher. Focus on the pitcher and not yourself. Too much thinking and not enough doing."

"It finally got to the point where I was like, 'he's completely right," Thomas remembers. "And not saying that the pitchers never got me out, but I knew I was doing it to myself. I wasn't playing the game anymore. There was just so much going on in my head. So finally I said to myself, 'I'm sticking with this stance and I'm sticking with this bat.' I stayed out of the bat room. It really worked. I got right back up to .242 again. I was feeling great."

"It was hard getting him in there," says Ingle, "but every time I could I'd get him in the lineup because that's the kind of guy that just gave it everything he had. He played hard and worked his tail off. He was getting to play a regular bit because of injuries. He was making solid contact. I wanted Charles to succeed because of what he put into it."

Another injury in AA gave Thomas yet another chance to prove himself at the higher level. Snitker inserted him right into the lineup, and this time Thomas showed he belonged. He sparked the Greenville lineup in early August, hitting safely in his first eighteen games back, going 31 for 76 (.408) with 11 runs scored and 12 RBI.

"He ignited our team," Snitker believes. "It's outstanding when you're able to see a guy step up and get the results he's looking for and compete and do well, especially when they've been beat down a bit. It was great to see Charlie come back and do so well. You know everybody gets beat down a little bit in this game. The ones that survive are the ones that make it."

Thomas finished the 2003 season in Greenville with a .324 average. It pumped up his career minor league average to .263 – not great, but the late season performance gave Thomas reason to believe he was getting closer to his goal. When he got to Spring Training in 2004 Thomas "felt like I could breathe a little bit," he says. "I felt like I could relax a little bit. Coming into this Spring Training, I wasn't thinking I'd get released."

But again there was good competition with some solid players vying for the team. They had brought in Russ Branyan, a former big leaguer with the Reds and Indians, along with three other players who'd had cups of coffee in the big leagues in DeWayne Wise,

Damon Hollins, and Ryan Jackson. Ryan Langerhans was slated for AAA, Kelly Johnson was moving to the outfield in Greenville, and Adam Stern and Billy McCarthy were headed back to AA after injury-plagued 2003 seasons. So despite his solid finish in Greenville the previous summer, Thomas was not guaranteed of a spot on any roster. Toward the end of Spring Training, Thomas asked Dayton Moore where he was headed.

"Well, we don't know what we're really going to do right now," Moore admitted. "It's Greenville or Richmond."

Thomas was at least relieved there was little chance he was going to be offered the option of being released. The Braves wanted him, but they just had to find room.

"At one point when we were talking in Spring Training it didn't look like there was going to be a spot on the (Richmond) 24-man roster for him," admits Richmond Manager Pat Kelly. "We would have taken him north with us, but he probably wouldn't have been active. He might have been on the Disabled List just so you could carry him."

Thomas had played for Richmond for most of Spring Training, so Kelly got a chance to see first-hand why Brian Snitker wanted him back in Greenville.

"Charlie's the kind of guy you are rooting for just because of the way he plays the game and goes about his business," Kelly says. "But unfortunately in this game that's the type of guy who ends up being the odd man out a lot of times."

But once again, fate stepped in. Eli Marrero, Atlanta's fourth outfielder, started the season on the Disabled List allowing Mike Hessman to make the Opening Day big league roster. That opened up a spot for Thomas on the Richmond roster as the fourth outfielder.

"I don't think you watch Charlie (as closely) unless "Beach" (Beauchamp) would constantly be saying, 'Now watch this guy,'" Kelly admits. "The more you see him the more he grows on you. That's kind of the way Spring Training was and we were able to take him with us."

"Pat Kelly pulled me aside before the first game in Richmond and talked to me," Thomas remembers. "He said that I wasn't going to be playing very much, especially in the first month. They were going to try to get Branyan going. So I needed to just be ready and not be disappointed, but to work hard. I appreciated him talking to me and telling me that."

Thomas started the 2004 season on the Richmond bench, but again opportunity knocked. Ryan Jackson was sold to a team in Korea, Branyan then was traded to Milwaukee, and Damon Hollins got called up to Atlanta. Thomas got his chance to play everyday in Triple-A.

"Once we got him in the lineup everyday, there was no taking him out," Kelly says.

The success Thomas enjoyed at the end of the 2003 season in Greenville simply carried over into 2004 – once he got a chance to play regularly. Thomas hit .374 in May with 3 home runs and 18 RBI. Then in June, Thomas started to take the International League by storm. He hit .392 in June and by the 23rd of the month led the league in hitting with a .358 batting average.

"By the time he was leading the league, I was a believer," Kelly says. "Earlier in the year when he was hitting well and producing in our lineup I said, 'You know, second time through the league they're going to figure some things out and we'll see what happens. We'll see if he can make some adjustments.' But he just kept getting better. They kept pitching him differently and trying different things and he just kept getting more hits. His hustle – the word spread around the league and you could see infielders panicking. He'd hit a two-hopper to shortstop and the guy would just try to get rid of it as soon as he could. They'd throw the ball away and make mistakes just because they knew he was going to run every ball out."

Thomas' fine play became contagious on the Richmond roster. And another no-name player, Pete Orr, himself a career backup, got a chance to play everyday and did so with the same energy and enthusiasm. The other players had already seen Nick Green, the starting second baseman for Richmond at the beginning of the year, lead the league in hitting (.377) and go up to Atlanta to replace the injured Marcus Giles. Having three unheralded players perform well jumpstarted the Richmond team.

"All of a sudden everybody on our club is running balls out," Kelly says. "They saw Peter Orr do it and they saw Charlie do it. It was just a pleasure to see. At this level that's one of the hardest things to get guys to do- play hard every night. When you have two young guys like that showing the way, it was great. Charlie's a special person. He's always got a smile on his face. He's always got energy. He's always bouncing around. Those kinds of guys are special. It's very refreshing to see in this game. I think a lot of times because we're in pro ball, players think, "We're cool. We can't run full speed. We can't use all our energy. We've got to save it 'cause we play every day.' Here's a guy who just goes all out every day and doesn't worry about what's going to happen tomorrow."

"I was having fun," Thomas says. "It was a lot less pressure on me. I wanted to put together a whole year. I was hoping that maybe I'd get on the 40-man roster that next winter or maybe even get an invite to Spring Training (in 2005)."

The Richmond Braves were two games over .500 and a game out of first place on their off day of June 23rd. They had bused into Pawtucket to start a four game series the next day with the Red Sox AAA affiliate. Thomas, his roommate Buddy Hernandez, Orr, and Richmond catcher Bryce Terveen had planned to use their off day to drive from Pawtucket to Boston where the Red Sox were playing the Twins that night. They were excited to see Fenway Park for the first time.

The team got to the hotel at 6:00 a.m. after their all-night trip from Scranton, Pennsylvania. Around 10:30 that morning there was a knock on the door of Thomas' hotel room. Hernandez, in the bed closest the door, got up to see who it was. It was Pat Kelly.

"Where's Charles?" Kelly asked.

"He's sleeping," Hernandez answered.

"Well, I've got to talk with him," Kelly said.

The manager then walked over and sat down on the end of Thomas' bed. Charles had heard Kelly's voice at the door, and when he came in Thomas thought the worst had happened: he had either been traded or released.

"Wise got hurt last night and you're going up," Kelly said.

Thomas sat up in bed and just looked at Kelly. He was still half asleep, so he wasn't sure he had heard his skipper correctly.

"Get your stuff together," Kelly said. "Jay (Williams, Richmond's trainer) will be calling you with the flight details."

Thomas was in shock. He had never even been on the 40-man roster. He had never been in big league camp during spring training, except when they borrowed him two years prior to play in a road game. He thought sure Ryan Langerhans, who was on the 40-man, or even Damon Hollins, who had been up earlier in the season with Atlanta, would get the call.

"The genesis of the whole promotion was DeWayne Wise

got hurt," says Assistant GM Frank Wren. "His elbow got so bad he couldn't throw. We started talking internally, and we wondered who was the guy that was most polished in all areas, whether it was defensively or offensively, preferably a left-handed hitter. That eliminated Damon Hollins, who had been up earlier and done a real good job, and it eliminated a guy like Billy McCarthy, who was similar in that he had never been to a big league camp. But when we talked to Dayton Moore, he said, 'this guy has such great makeup. He does all the things that you want him to do, and he's leading the International League in hitting.' Bobby (Cox) had never heard his name before."

"I don't think he believed me when I told him," Kelly says. "Buddy finally told him, 'you've got to get a shower. You've got to get ready.' The hardest thing was not to cry while I was telling him. It just doesn't happen that often. When you can give that word to a guy like that, it's just unbelievable."

"I just really couldn't believe it," Thomas admits. "Pat said, 'Congratulations, you really deserve it. You worked hard. I just couldn't be happier for you.' He leaves and my mind is going 1000 miles an hour. I remember I just kept rubbing my head. I didn't know what to do. It was unbelievable. I really couldn't believe it."

Hernandez finally convinced Thomas that he was not dreaming. He had to get out of the bed, take a shower and get to the airport to catch a flight to Miami, where the Braves were playing game two of a three game series with the Marlins. He tried to call his mom, an accountant in Asheville, on his way to the airport, but she was at lunch. Then he called his sister. No answer. Then he tried his grandparents. No answer. Charles was finally able to tell a friend that he was headed to the big leagues. On the plane trip down to Miami, he tried to get some sleep since he had only slept four hours before Kelly knocked on his door, but he could only think about what he was getting ready to do. Finally, on the cab ride from the airport to Pro Player Stadium, he got his mom on a cell phone.

"Mom, are you sitting down?" he asked.

"Yeah," she answered.

"We made it," Charles said with a smile on his face.

Thomas explained to his mom exactly what was happening. He was a big leaguer, on his way to his first major league game.

"She was excited," he recalls. "That was real cool because

being a single mom and all the sacrifices she made for my sister and I really made it possible. It was like 'we' had made it. She always had confidence in me, even when I didn't."

The game started at 7:05, but Thomas' plane didn't land until 6:00. When he pulled into the stadium parking lot, the game was starting. As soon as he stepped out of his cab, he realized he wasn't in Richmond anymore.

"I get there and they wouldn't even let me walk my bags in there," Thomas says. "I had to wait for a golf cart. This was when I was like, 'you've got to be kidding me.' Obviously I was in a whole new world. So they're driving me up there and the Marlins cheerleaders are walking by the tunnel and I was like, 'Gee.' It was a grand thing. I just thought it was larger than life. It was just so big to me. Eli (Marrero) and (Mark) DeRosa were walking out of the tunnel when I was walking in. Eli was like, 'what, you couldn't get here in time? You didn't want to play tonight?'"

Thomas knew Marrero was just messing with him, but what he didn't realize was that Braves Manager Bobby Cox had planned on starting him that night. Cox is known for throwing his rookies right into the fire, and if not for Thomas' plane being late, he would have gone from being asleep in a hotel room in Pawtucket to playing left field for the Atlanta Braves in a little less than nine hours.

The game was already underway when Charles arrived and he found himself in an empty clubhouse. The first thing he saw was his locker with his Atlanta Braves jersey waiting for him. "That was a thing in itself – putting on a major league jersey," he says. Then he made the walk down the tunnel to the dugout and walked right up to his new manager.

"I'm Charles Thomas," he said as he extended his hand to Bobby Cox.

"Of course, I know who you are," Cox said, stretching the truth just a bit. "We had you in there tonight."

"Yeah, I'm sorry," Charles said. "The plane was late."

"No problem," Cox responded. "But be ready to pinch hit. And be ready day after tomorrow to start."

"Yes sir."

Thomas introduced himself to pitching coach Leo Mazzone and then went to find a spot on the bench. "I was scared to sit down," he admits. "I was afraid I was in somebody's seat. I asked someone, 'Can I sit here?' I didn't know what to do. I was meeting some guys as they were coming off the field. Some I didn't want to bother. Some I met in the shower after the game. It was crazy."

The new Braves outfielder knew only four players on the team: Nick Green, Adam LaRoche, Horacio Ramirez, and Travis Smith. Most of the players, and even his manager, had never heard of him. But then in the fifth inning they all had the opportunity to see Charles Thomas in action.

"I went to the (indoor batting) cage and hit with Rochy (Adam LaRoche) and all of a sudden Glenn Hubbard walks up and tells me I'm hitting third in the fifth inning," Thomas says. "So I'm looking for a helmet and I'm thinking it's the minor leagues and there are a bunch of helmets. But in the bigs everybody has their own helmet. So I'm looking for one I can use and I finally get Horacio's. It's too big. But I get on deck and I never look up. Eli pops up and I'm in. Then it was just like another game. That's what I was thinking of it as so I wouldn't be in awe of the whole thing. Here it is (Marlins starter) Brad Penny and he's throwing cheese. I fouled some pitches off and I felt I didn't embarrass myself."

Thomas struck out, but Penny struck out seven that night in his six scoreless innings of work. The next night, Thomas would get his first big league hit off Marlins righty Ben Howard. It was a slow dribbler to shortstop, but the speedy Thomas beat it out by running as hard as he had in Richmond. Then he was off to Baltimore.

"It was unbelievable," Thomas says. "Being in a stadium, especially like that, Camden Yards, with the history there, it was even better."

But Thomas' first big league start was representative of the Braves' night. He was 0-for-3 and the team was shutout 5-0. The loss was the seventh in the last ten games, and the Braves fell to six games under .500 and five and a half games out of first place. The next morning, June 26th, there were rumors GM John Schuerholz might trade pitcher Russ Ortiz and maybe even outfielder Andruw Jones to the Chicago White Sox. But then things turned around with Charles Thomas right in the middle of everything. He started on that Saturday, getting two hits. But his biggest contribution was made in the field.

It was the fourth inning. The Braves were up 2-0. Oriole Miguel Tejada had singled and was on first base. Then Rafael Palmiero doubled to right field. The throw to third base by J.D.

Drew got away from Chipper Jones, but Thomas was right behind the bag to back up the play. He caught the ball and the runners were unable to advance. Russ Ortiz was able to get out of the inning, and the Braves went on to shutout the Orioles 5-0.

"Beauchamp had taught me that in the minor leagues," Thomas says. "He taught us to back up bases and be where we were supposed to be. That was the first time I think that I had backed up a base and a ball had actually gotten by somebody. It made a difference."

Jim Beauchamp was watching the game on TV.

"You don't see that in the big leagues anymore," Beauchamp says. "We teach it in the minor leagues and it's what we call an 'absolute.' If you want to get on my bad side, don't back up bases or back up infielders. I told Charles one time back in Jamestown about backing up bases and I've never had to mention it again. Charles is that kind of player. He'll do whatever you need him to do to help you win a ballgame."

The play also got the attention of Bobby Cox. The next day on his pre-game radio show, he asked announcer Skip Caray, "Did you see Charles Thomas back up third base?" Thomas had made an impression, which is awfully important in getting playing time with the Atlanta Braves.

Thomas didn't start the next game, the rubber game of the series with the Orioles. He pinch-hit and flied out to left field. But the Sunday game was an important one. The Braves were down 7-0 after the sixth inning, only to rally for one run in the seventh inning and seven runs in the eighth inning to win 8-7. When Thomas arrived four days earlier, the Braves were a lost team. But it all changed that weekend in Baltimore.

"I think early in the year they maybe would have lost that game (on Sunday)," Thomas believes. "I heard guys talking about that. To come back and win gave us a lot of momentum."

The rookie quickly eased into a platoon with Eli Marrero in left field. Over the next two weeks, Thomas hit .348 with 3 home runs and 9 RBI. The Braves finished the first half of the season only a game back of the Phillies. They had made up five and a half games in the eighteen days since Thomas arrived. But he was curious as to whether he was sticking around. DeWayne Wise was healthy, but with Charles playing well it seemed unlikely he'd go back down. So as the team was heading back to Atlanta for the three-day All Star

Break, Thomas decided to ask about his immediate future.

"I had three hits in that game (Sunday against the Phillies) with two home runs," Thomas remembers. "I talked with Fredi (Gonzalez, Atlanta's third base coach). I was trying to figure out if he had any idea if I needed to try to get my stuff or what was going on with that. He went in there to talk with Bobby and he said, 'you don't have to worry about it. You're going to be here.' That was a good day."

The All-Star Break gave Thomas a chance to regroup a bit, but when play started again he was more or less a regular in the lineup. While he was one part of a platoon, since he hits left-handed, he was in there most of the time when right-handers were pitching. Thomas continued to hit, but even more impressive was his defense. He did exactly what Donnie Poplin had seen at Western Carolina: read fly balls well, made diving catches, showed a strong arm, and most importantly showed tremendous baseball instincts. It didn't take long for Braves' fans to fall in love with him, even if they didn't really know who he was. It was fairly natural to ask: Who the hell is Charles Thomas?

"I had never been on the 40-man, never was a top tier prospect," Thomas admits. "So I'm sure I surprised a lot of people. Who is this coming up? I read and heard that a lot, which is completely understandable. I'm sure there were five or ten outfielders that most fans or most people would have thought would have come up before me. Coming from a guy who in Spring Training or before or after games in the minors, the fans allow to walk past without asking for an autograph. You have all those people out there with their baseball cards and all that and they're calling Wilson Betemit's name or Adam Wainwright's name or Kelly Johnson all the time and letting me walk on past. To go from there to have all these different people wanting to interview you and all the kids and parents...the support was amazing. We'd pull up in each park and all of a sudden they'd have your photos from wherever and different things for you to sign...it was nice. I'll never forget that. "

Thomas' success gave the Braves an example to use with other players in their minor league system. You don't have to be a big name to make it to the big leagues. Thomas proved that dedication and hard work does pay off, and now he'll be someone the Braves can point to that will hopefully motivate others to follow in his footsteps.

"It makes it easier for us to coach when we have somebody like that to use as an example," Beauchamp says. "I came from the Dominican Republic and talked with the outfielders down there. They were talking about Charles Thomas."

Roy Clark says, "If you believe in our philosophy and the way we do things, if you believe in makeup, then Charles Thomas is a wonderful example."

The organization was obviously rewarded by its patience. Of course they were a little lucky too. The player took advantage of his playing time and produced – not all players do that. But for a player who was almost released, who was mainly an extra outfielder, Thomas proved the Braves were right in not releasing him when they had their chance. Many other organizations, seeing a career minor league batting average in the .250 range, would have let him go. But Thomas' makeup, his personality, and his work ethic convinced the Braves he was worth keeping around. Once again, for the Braves, the makeup trumped the math.

"I think the patience and understanding that we have in the organization is that if someone feels like a player is a prospect, they wont' be released," Beauchamp says. "That doesn't hold true with a lot of organizations. But Dayton Moore is the type of person, along with Paul Snyder and Roy Clark, that if I think a guy is a prospect, but there's someone who doesn't think he's a prospect, we're not going to release him until we're all unanimous about it. If we've got one or two guys that think he has a chance to make it, we're not releasing that guy in the hope that if he gets the opportunity, he can eventually prove himself. That's exactly what Charles did."

The Braves took control of first place on July 24th and never looked back. They would go on to win the N.L. East by ten games over the Phillies. Their resurgence can be attributed to many things, but it's more than a coincidence that the debut of Charles Thomas and his production was a major factor. Thomas hit .342 in the month of July and by the end of that month had a .347 average. He slumped a bit (comparatively) in August (.265 average) and September (.237 average), but his final numbers were still very impressive: .288 average, 7 homers, 31 RBI in 236 at bats. From a no name in late June to an important part of a division-winning team, Charles Thomas lived out a dream in 2004.

"The way it's all come about and the things that I've gone through and things that I've learned and the adversity I've faced…to be able to experience it for half a season has been tremendous," he says. "If something happens and I'm never able to experience it again, then I certainly lived out a dream. It's been a great ride."

But the dream and the ride took a detour in mid-December 2004. Thomas was playing winter ball in the Dominican Republic when Brayan Pena, a minor league teammate who was also playing winter ball, called to wake him from an afternoon nap.

"Two things Charles," Pena said. "One, Jose Martinez (Special Assistant to John Schuerholz for Player Development) wants to talk to you."

"Ok," Thomas responded.

"And number two," Pena continued, "You just got traded to Oakland."

"What?" Thomas asked.

"Yeah, I think it's for Mark Mulder."

Pena had that wrong. The trade was for Tim Hudson. It was the second time in 2004 someone had woken Charles Thomas with news that would drastically change his life. He immediately turned on his television.

"ESPN News had the 'Breaking News' Logo in the bottom corner," Thomas remembers. "It said, 'Hudson to the Braves.' So then I went to ESPN and on the bottom line...and you see your name. You're like, 'Wow.' Your heart just drops. To wake up and see that was crazy. It was almost like it wasn't real. There had been times before I might have been released and there was always that time in the season where you can get traded. I thought maybe it could happen then. But honestly I didn't think for a second that I could get traded. It was a complete surprise."

Once again the Braves used one of their young players to improve the big league roster. But unlike many of the other kids traded in previous years, Charles Thomas was able to make it to Atlanta and realize a dream. He was never supposed to be there in the first place, but he did. To leave now would be very difficult.

"It's just tough," Thomas admits. "I had been with them my whole career and had followed them prior to that. I had just been through a lot with this organization. Then to make it up there and then just like that...you're gone."

The fans didn't know his name when he arrived in Atlanta, and despite his short tenure in a Braves' uniform, his impact will be felt in the organization for a while to come.

22
THE ATLANTA INFLUENCE

It was the summer of 1981. Dean Taylor had just joined the Kansas City Royals as an administrative assistant. His new boss, the Royals Vice President of Player Personnel John Schuerholz, sent him to California on his first assignment.

"Dean, I want you to go out and spend a week with Rosey in California," Schuerholz told his new protégé.

"Rosey" was Rosey Gilhousen, a legendary scout with the Kansas City Royals who signed more than one hundred players that made it to the big leagues. Schuerholz believed Rosey would be the perfect guy to break Taylor in as a scout. Taylor had been a minor league General Manager before, but scouting was something brand new.

"I'm out there with Rosey and we're talking about players," Taylor explains. "I'm soaking everything in like a sponge and he says, 'Young man, let me tell you something. I've been scouting for thirty-two years and there are a lot of young guys who think they know what's going on. But every day I go to the ballpark I learn something new.'"

Now the Assistant General Manager of the Cincinnati Reds, Taylor has learned a lot over his twenty-plus years in the game. But he knew even on his first day on the job that Rosey's words would be something to live by.

"There's a mentality out there now that some people think they've got all the answers," Taylor says. "But what Rosey said has stayed with me."

Taylor came up in the Kansas City farm system, not as a player, but as an administrator. The year Schuerholz became the General Manager of the Royals he promoted Taylor to Assistant Director of Scouting and Player Development. After the Royals won the World Series in 1985, Taylor became Schuerholz's right-hand man in the front office.

Over the years he would learn from Schuerholz the simple blueprint to Kansas City's success: The only way to be competitive over a long period of time is to sign and develop your own players.

"We always had the philosophy that draft day was the single most important day for the organization," Taylor says. "It's the day that you have the opportunity with some quality draft picks to replenish your organizational pipeline every year. If you don't do it, you're not going to be successful over the long term."

Following the tremendous run in the late 70's, the Royals focused more on pitching in their drafts in the early 80's. Three draft picks in particular would become very important. In 1981 Kansas City drafted Mark Gubicza, a right-handed pitcher out of William Penn Charter High School in Philadelphia, in the second round. Then in 1982 the Royals made two very good selections: Danny Jackson, a left-hander out of the University of Oklahoma in the first round of the January phase, and Bret Saberhagen, a right-handed high school pitcher from California, was taken in the nineteenth round in June.

Gubicza, Jackson, and Saberhagen would develop in the Royals' system and become members of the Kansas City starting rotation in 1984. A year later they combined for 48 wins and helped the Royals win the 1985 World Series.

"Young pitching – we weren't afraid to draft a high school pitcher," Taylor says. "We were fortunate in being able to develop them and nurture then and protect them early in their professional careers in terms of pitch counts and things of that nature."

Taylor also learned that the Royals wanted guys who could play well, but were looking for good makeup as well.

When Schuerholz left for Atlanta in the fall of 1990, he

would call on Taylor to be his top assistant once again. Taylor had left the Royals a year earlier for a job in the Commissioner's Office, but the chance to try and implement the same philosophies in a new environment was an exciting challenge.

"There were significantly more dollars available at the major league level in terms of payroll," Taylor says, "but the blueprint was very similar."

The Braves would go on to have tremendous success during the 90's, and some critics point to a high payroll as the main factor in their championships. But Taylor scoffs at that notion.

"The team that was on the field the night we won the World Championship, the sixth game in 1995, if you go around that particular diamond that night, Javy Lopez was the catcher," Taylor explains. "He was signed and developed by the Braves. Third base was Chipper Jones, signed originally by the Braves. (Mark) Lemke was at second base, signed originally by the Braves. David Justice was in right field and (Ryan) Klesko in left field – both originally signed by the Braves. (Tom) Glavine started the game and pitched eight innings, and then (Mark) Wohlers came in and got the save. They were both original Braves signees."

"First base was (Fred) McGriff, who was obtained in a deal for a package of minor league players that we sent to San Diego. The players that were sent to them in the deal were players that we had signed and developed. So it's a known fact in player development that one reason you develop players is to possibly use them to obtain quality major league players and that's exactly what we did with some of the prospects we used to obtain McGriff. Center field was (Marquis) Grissom. Again, like McGriff, obtained in a deal which we utilized our own players that we had signed and developed."

"The only asterisk in this whole equation is the shortstop position where (Jeff) Blauser was the shortstop all year – he was the Associated Press All-Star shortstop that year – but he was hurt for the series and (Rafael) Belliard was playing. But the original guy that played there all year was signed and developed by the Braves. That club won the World Championship that night and Belliard was the only free agent on the field and he was there only because he was substituting for Blauser. I've always used that as an argument when people said, 'The Braves were big spenders and scouting and player development was not a big deal there.' I think that's a great argument for the importance of a solid scouting and development program even for a large market club."

After being Schuerholz's right-hand man for nine years in Atlanta, it was inevitable that Taylor would be called on to run his own ball club. That call came in October of 1999, when the Milwaukee Brewers selected Taylor to be their new General Manager. It didn't take him long to determine a huge difference in how things were run in Milwaukee.

"What was different was the resources, as far as depth from a player standpoint just not being there," Taylor says. "That was the biggest adjustment for me. I was always used to operating in an environment where you had a number of young players available to talk about in potential deals. So that made it a much more difficult challenge."

When Taylor arrived, most publications rated Milwaukee's farm system as one of the worst in the game. So he had to put the Kansas City/Atlanta blueprint in place as soon as possible, and it all started with the amateur draft. "We were going to take the best player available on the board," Taylor says. "We didn't have enough depth in our farm system to be able to make the kind of deals we needed to make to improve our club. Now that's what the Braves have had over the years – depth in the farm system that allowed them to trade."

So Taylor approached the draft with the concept of accumulating talent that could either play in Milwaukee or be used in trades to strengthen the major league club.

"When all you have is Ben Sheets (Milwaukee's best prospect at the time)," Taylor explains, "you're not going to be able to give him up. If you've got Ben Sheets and five other guys, then it makes it easier. Depth in the farm system is very important. I think people lose sight of the fact that one reason you develop players is to trade them to acquire other major league ready players who can help your club right now."

Taylor and his Scouting Director, Jack Zduriencik, hired by Taylor away from the Dodgers, went to work to find talent. The preference was young high school talent, and during Taylor's three years there that was the focus in the first round.

David Krynzel, an outfielder out of a Nevada high school, was the number one pick in 2000. Mike Jones, a high school pitcher from Arizona, was the top pick in 2001. And finally in 2002, Prince Fielder, son of former American League slugger Cecil Fielder, was selected in the first round.

But Dean Taylor would not last to see the talent he drafted cultivated. He was fired after the 2002 season after the Brewers had their third straight losing season at the big league level.

"I knew it was going to be a huge challenge," he says. But patience is not always a virtue with fans and team owners. Results in the major leagues are more important than any promise or hope down on the farm. Even while the Brewers were 92 games under .500 in Milwaukee while Taylor was in charge, they were developing the best farm system in the game.

"*Baseball America* said early in 2004 that Milwaukee was the most improved organization in baseball over the last several years," Taylor says. "I'm proud of that from the standpoint that we put a blueprint in place that had worked before and it did successfully there. Obviously, Jack Zduriencik and the scouts deserve a lot of credit for that. They've really raised the bar in that organization. There are a number of young quality players there now: Dave Krynzel, Brad Nelson, Corey Hart, Manny Parra, J.J. Hardy, who are sort of on the cusp of being ready for the major leagues. Prince Fielder is another one. Then the year after I left they got Richie Weeks and kept it going."

In fact, in the spring of 2004, *Baseball America* rated Milwaukee as having the most minor league talent in all of baseball. When Taylor arrived in 2000, they were ranked thirtieth – last in the game. The emphasis on more high school players obviously helped. In 1999, the year before Taylor arrived, only thirty percent of Milwaukee's first thirty draft picks were from the high school level. During Taylor's tenure, that percentage increased to 45.5%. Following the Royals/Braves blueprint helped Dean Taylor put his imprint on the Brewers' organization, even if he won't be around to enjoy any future success.

In the fall of 1991, twenty-six year old Derek Ladnier's minor league career with the Kansas City Royals was coming to an end. A shoulder injury had taken its toll, and Ladnier was ready to do something different. After his last game of the season, he got in his car and drove to Atlanta to sign a contract to be an area scout with the Braves.

"I had seen John Schuerholz and Dean Taylor in spring

training that year, and they asked me what I was going to do after my playing career was over," Ladnier recalls. "I told them I had an interest in getting into scouting. One thing led to another, and they had an opening ironically in the same area to which I grew up and went to school. They gave me a job."

Ladnier took over as the Braves' area scout in Alabama, Mississippi, Louisiana, and Arkansas. He didn't really know anything about scouting. To him and other minor leaguers, those were the guys with the stopwatches in the stands during the games. But it was a side of the business Ladnier was interested in. He wanted a career in baseball, and even though he knew he could always get back on the field as a coach or manager if he wanted to, scouting intrigued him.

Ladnier was brought up in the Royals' organization as a player, so he knew the type of players they had in their system. Plus, with Schuerholz and Taylor, two former Royals executives, implementing the same system in Atlanta, Ladnier had an idea of what to look for.

"The Kansas City Royals back at that point in time were very tool-oriented. From a scouting perspective they had been doing very well in drafting and signing good players. And from a fundamental standpoint on the player development side, they were teaching them how to play the game of baseball. It was very fundamental. Fundamental baseball: catch the ball; throw the ball, timely hitting, and those type things. It was a model organization. That philosophy carried over to the Braves."

His new boss in Atlanta was Chuck Lamar, whom Schuerholz had brought over from Pittsburgh to run the scouting and player development departments.

"He was outstanding to work for," Ladnier says. "Chuck was very regimented in his approach to scouting and player development. He stuck with the fundamentals and he obviously liked the athletic-tooled players. That was the philosophy of the organization: young talent. That was basically what we went looking for: young, sometimes raw. They were willing to take a chance on raw talent, but they had to have the physical tools to be an impact type player. Not just bench type players, but impact players."

After the 1995 season, when Atlanta won the World Series, Lamar left to become the General Manager of the expansion Tampa Bay Devil Rays. Ladnier was then promoted to the job of Assistant

Director of Scouting and Player Development. He worked in the front office with Paul Snyder, who got his old job of Director of Scouting and Player Development back when Lamar left for Tampa Bay.

"He's the best listener I've ever been around," Ladnier says of Snyder. "He had tremendous respect for his evaluators. He would really, really listen to all of our guys, not just the crosscheckers or national guys, but he believed in the area scouts. He believed in the job they did. He was very good at not only listening to what they said but what they didn't say."

Ladnier would also learn how the Braves ran their farm system. It was obvious that a key to the success was the faith Snyder and all the scouts had in the development staff.

"If you look at the people they have in player development, you know Bill Fischer was there at the time, who has fifty-plus years in player development. Bill Slack was there. Bruce Dal Canton. Brian Snitker. I mean all of these guys are lifetime Braves. They have very little turnover. And these guys are probably some of the most unselfish instructors I've ever been around in my life. You know, I think everybody's goal is to be a major league coach or a major league manager. But these guys, their goal when they wake up in the morning is to simply make that player better today. They get a tremendous amount of satisfaction out of watching a player go from rookie ball to A-ball, to AA, and then ultimately to the big leagues. And they all know they play a major role in that process," Ladnier explains.

Ladnier quickly learned that the Braves believed development was the key in the minor leagues. "It wasn't about running a guy out there that's going to help you win a hundred games in the minor leagues. They were willing to put a third baseman out there that they knew was going to make fifty errors, but they knew that the upside was that he was going to be a major league player. They were willing to deal with the struggles of a player, just to allow him to develop. A hitter can't develop unless he gets five hundred at bats a year. And a lot of these guys, the priority guys from an evaluation standpoint, were given those five hundred at bats or those 120 innings. Even though the numbers weren't outstanding, they'd stick with these guys and allow them to develop as players."

One player that the Braves stuck with, despite shaky minor league numbers, was Kevin Millwood. He was the big, six-foot-four right-handed pitcher out of North Carolina that Roy Clark had signed after the Braves drafted him in the eleventh round back in 1993. Millwood was just a lumbering country boy, who was as comfortable fishing as he was pitching. He went to the South Atlantic League in Macon in 1994 and struggled, going 0-5 with a 5.79 ERA in 12 games. Then in 1995 in Macon, he struggled again going 5-6 with a 4.63 ERA in 29 games. Millwood was 6-9 in 1996 at Durham with an ERA of 4.28.

"I mean you look at his numbers and go 'Well, this guy's not a prospect," Ladnier recalls. "And then when you look at him on the field and you watch him pitch and you go 'Yeah, this guy's a prospect, and a big-time prospect.' He was just learning how to pitch. I mean you could see all three pitches on any given night, it was just the consistency lacking."

Millwood started the 1997 season at Greenville and went 3-5 with a 4.11 ERA in 11 starts. The Braves promoted him to AAA and Millwood turned it up a notch, going 7-0 with a 1.93 ERA in 9 starts. That convinced the Braves he was ready and they promoted Millwood to Atlanta. Over the next five and a half seasons, Millwood would go 75-46 with an ERA of 3.73 in 168 games (160 starts).

"You know from a scouting perspective, you sit there and the numbers aren't as important as the talent was and they just kept running him out there every fifth day and he kept getting better and better and better," Ladnier says.

Once again, the balance between statistics and player evaluation was crucial as Ladnier learned his craft.

"You could sit there and look at stats all you want to, and then you can sit there and look at a guy who is throwing 94 mph with a plus slider but he doesn't have the best command. Well, that's what development is all about. That's why you give them to the Bruce Dal Cantons and the Bill Fischers and the Guy Hansens. You put that talent in their hands and say, 'Okay, make this guy a pitcher.' That's what they do. They just chip away."

At the end of the 2000 season, after spending a year as a major league scout under John Schuerholz, Ladnier was called home to become the Royals Senior Director of Scouting. His time in Atlanta shaped his philosophy as an evaluator and as an administrator.

"I was fortunate from the standpoint that I was able to do a lot of different things for that organization: area scout, crosschecker, assistant, and all that," Ladnier says. "It really built a foundation for me not only in scouting but in player development, and then the opportunity to work around people like Paul Snyder, Dean Taylor, Chuck Lamar, Mike Arbuckle, Tony DeMacio, and John Schuerholz. You know those people that you learn from, if you're smart enough you'll listen and you'll watch and you'll see how they do business and then try to implement all the knowledge that you're able to acquire from those people into your own particular style. The guys over here (Kansas City) have embraced it."

But as the Scouting Director in Kansas City, Ladnier has to work under different conditions. The Royals are one of the smaller market teams in baseball, and their financial environment is different from what Ladnier worked under in Atlanta.

"If we make a bad decision here, it's monumental," Ladnier says. "It can directly affect the organization for years to come. If you're working with a little bit bigger market club, you can make a mistake and then go sign another player. But we don't have that luxury here."

Ladnier knew, however, that the key to building the Royals into winners again was to stockpile talent with solid drafts. Therefore, a player's upside is essential.

"I've always taken the approach that we're going to take what we feel is the best player – whether it's a high school player or whether it's a college player. If there's a high school player that we feel has a greater upside than a college player, even though understanding it's going to take him four or five years versus three years (of a college draft pick), then in the best interest of this organization we've got to take the high school player. That's the only chance we have to get an impact player at the major league level. I don't think we should settle for a number four starter when we've got a high school kid who we think can be a number one or two starter. We can't go out and acquire those type of guys or go out and buy them."

In the two years prior to Ladnier taking over the Royals' drafts, only 26.7 % of Kansas City's first thirty draft picks (in each year) were high school players. From 2001-2003, the percentage of high school players taken with the first thirty picks increased to 44.4%. Ladnier has had top ten picks in the first round in each of his first three years. He's taken two high school pitchers (Colt Griffin and Zach Greinke) and a high school outfielder (Chris Lubanski). Greinke made his big league debut in 2004 and is one of the best young arms in the American League, while Lubanski remains one of the Royals' top prospects.

"You know if you're picking high in the draft like we've done in the past, we should be able to get an impact player whether it's a Greinke or Lubanski or even a Colt Griffin," Ladnier says. "This jury is still out on Colt. Yeah, his walks are too high (235 in his first 317.2 professional innings), but if you sit behind home plate, like we talked about with Millwood, and watch what's coming out of this kid's hand, you'll say 'Wow. This kid's got a chance to be a good player.' It's in the hands of development to harness that talent and have him get a little bit better command. But we can't go out and acquire that kind of talent. This kid talent-wise is phenomenal."

After averaging almost sixty-nine wins between 1996-2002, the Royals busted out for 83 wins in 2003. The team consisted mainly of homegrown talent from outfielders Carlos Beltran and Michael Tucker, infielders Mike Sweeney, Ken Harvey, and Joe Randa, and pitchers Chris George, Kyle Snyder, Runelyvs Hernandez, and Mike MacDougal. Then toward the end of the season, Royals General Manager Allard Baird was able to reach into his farm system and use four players to acquire veterans Rondell White and Brian Anderson.

"We have to maximize the value of every player," Ladnier explains. "That's what gives Allard the flexibility to go out and acquire a few guys while we're trying to compete for a championship. That's the point where we're finally starting to get to where we've got some talent. If we can go out and acquire a Brian Anderson or something like that with talent, I mean that's the reason a scouting department exists- to make sure number one the major league level has talent and to make sure the minor league system has enough talent that the General Manager has the flexibility to do the things he needs to do at the major league level."

Ladnier has learned that stockpiling talent is a huge function of the minor leagues, and it's his job to place the talent in the hands of the Royals' development staff. But he must trust his area scouts to bring him the talent. He had a great teacher in Paul Snyder, a man who trusted his judgment as a talent evaluator.

"I was an area scout for the Braves and had been there for two years," Ladnier remembers. "We're in the twentieth round of the draft and Paul calls me up on the phone. He says, 'Derek, do you have any players left that you really have a gut for?' I said, 'Yeah

Paul, I've got one guy that I really like. He's a scrawny little kid, but I think he can really hit.' The kid's name was Roosevelt Brown."

Roosevelt Brown was five-foot-eleven, 165 pounds soaking wet. He was from a small high school in Vicksburg, Mississippi. He didn't have a lot of power, but he had convinced Ladnier that he was a hitter. All Ladnier had to do to convince Snyder was to say the word.

"I told him that there was something about this kid that I really liked," Ladnier says. "Sure enough, one more round, we draft Roosevelt Brown, and he made it to the big leagues. But that was a classic example of Paul Snyder listening to an area scout saying 'Yeah, I like this guy.' He never saw him. No one ever saw him because he was down on my list. But I had a good feel for this kid and I liked him."

Brown would become valuable to the Braves two years later, when during the pennant drive they needed an extra bat off the bench. They traded Brown to the Marlins to re-acquire Terry Pendleton.

"There's a classic example of being able to acquire a major league talent for a prospect," Ladnier says. "That's just pure scouting. That's one boss calling an area scout and saying, 'Hey, who do you like?' That to me is what scouting is all about."

When Mike Arbuckle left the Braves in fall of 1992, he wasn't sure what was facing him as the Philadelphia Phillies' new Director of Scouting. The Phillies were a veteran major league team full of players mostly acquired from other organizations. They were a year away from going to the World Series, but the minor league system was a mess.

"When I came to our first spring training here in '93, my first thoughts were kinda, 'Oh my God,'" Arbuckle admits. "They had been drafting polished college players; not very athletic, banking on the bat, a lot of them kinda thick-bodied kids with no projection physically. Any projection was going to be out, not up."

Arbuckle believes the Phillies' concentration on college players in the late 80's was close to eighty percent. Plus the organization had no Latin American program. He knew he had to make drastic changes, and team owner Bill Giles and General

Manager Lee Thomas gave him no resistance.

"Lee was finding it hard to make deals because we didn't have anything people wanted," Arbuckle says. "So I think when I was brought in they wanted that type of change and coming from Atlanta was a huge factor in my getting the job here. They were looking and they knew Atlanta was starting to have success. They were simply hungry for a different approach."

The changes Arbuckle would implement would take time. The coaches in the Phillies' farm system were accustomed to the college player, so Arbuckle had to educate and re-train his development guys to be more patient with their younger players.

"You can't write off a guy after the first summer because he hit .220 in the Gulf Coast League," Arbuckle explains. "You've got to look at the long term and the big picture and continue to be positive and stay with this guy."

At the major league level, the Phillies were a one hit wonder. They were in the World Series in 1993, losing to Toronto, but would not have a winning season again until 2001; yet another organization unable to maintain success at the big league level on a consistent basis. That pointed straight to the weak farm system inherited by Arbuckle.

"Taking eighty to ninety percent college players really limits the pool of players you have to work from," Arbuckle says. "So we had to re-establish a Latin program which took a few years to do, and then getting back into the high school market entailed a lot of things: patience on the development side, a willingness to spend more money in the draft so I could go ahead and take that kid in the eighth or tenth round and still sign him even though he had good scholarship situations. So it took time to establish that here. But I think over time we've been able to do that. The players – the Marlon Byrds, the Jimmy Rollinses, the Scott Rolens; those players pretty much fit the same mold of players that Atlanta would have taken or did take over the same course of time."

Arbuckle learned his craft climbing up the Braves' scouting ladder. He began in 1980 and spent seven years as a Midwest scout. Then he was the Central Regional Crosschecker from 1988-1990, before spending his final two years as a National Crosschecker. The lessons he learned in the Braves' system were as much personal than professional, and no surprise, it all goes back to Paul Snyder.

"Paul Snyder is one of those people that I learned very early on I had tremendous allegiance to because number one, no matter how hard I worked, I couldn't outwork that man," Arbuckle says. "Now having had the opportunity to do what he did, and I realize the hours, and the phone calls, and the time on the road, and all of that. This guy was just a human dynamo."

Arbuckle says all the Braves' scouts during the 1980's had the utmost respect for Snyder, and a main reason was his controlled ego, something unusual in the business of baseball.

"Any credit that did come along his finger would always point to an area scout or a minor league manager or coach," Arbuckle explains. "I think guys come to appreciate that so much because scouts and people in the minor leagues get so little credit. Everyone was so appreciative of the way Paul handled them, gave them responsibility, trusted them, and respected them. Because of the way he treated his people and the total trust and confidence he puts in you, I think it makes you embarrassed if you don't succeed for him."

Arbuckle learned how baseball people could treat baseball people, something sometimes lost in the hustle and bustle of people clamoring for their own personal careers. "I learned a tremendous amount from Paul Snyder," Arbuckle admits. "I think maybe even more the people skills and the way you go about trying to get the most out of people is more important than a philosophy of what types of players you are going to draft. I've learned a tremendous amount from Paul."

But Snyder also passed along his player philosophy to Arbuckle, a preference for young projectable players that you can turn over to your coaches for development.

"I still to this day prefer getting the kid at eighteen if all things are equal," Arbuckle says, "because you get him three years sooner away from the aluminum bat and it doesn't matter if he's a pitcher or a hitter, the pitcher is probably pitching backwards with the aluminum bats and living with the breaking pitch instead of challenging with a fastball. So I just think it's better all around. The sooner we can get these kids in the program doing the things we want the better."

The philosophy also included a penchant for young high school pitchers. Arbuckle was able to draft three pitchers in a four-year period that now make up the future of the Phillies' rotation: right-hander Brett Myers was drafted in the first round in 1999 out of a Jacksonville, Florida high school; right-hander Gavin Floyd was drafted in the first round in 2001 out of a high school in Maryland; and Cole Hamels is a left-handed pitcher drafted in the first round in 2002 from a California high school.

"We have no problem taking high school pitching," Arbuckle says. "We've had good success. And I think that our success is based on the same ingredients that we had in Atlanta and that they still have. Body type, delivery, arm action, and a development staff that's willing to go about developing them in the right way."

Arbuckle was with the Braves in 1985 when Bobby Cox came back to the organization as General Manager. He watched as Cox moved the Braves more toward the Toronto Blue Jays' philosophy of going after the athletic, well-bodied, tooled athletes. Arbuckle believes Cox's time with Toronto as their manager in the early 80's influenced his thinking when he took charge of Atlanta's organization. He watched as Cox and Snyder went after young pitchers and athletic position players.

"It was an overall philosophical approach of being willing to go after the highest ceilings – what our scouts would view as the highest ceiling guys available, period," Arbuckle remembers. "In most cases those were young high school guys. Those turned out to be the Steve Averys and so on. It was the approach of looking at ceiling and to do that with a pitcher you're looking at things like body type, projection of the body, the way the arm works. Is that projectable? Is there arm speed? Is there a clean arm action? All of those types of ingredients that from a pure scouting point you're looking for you need to be able to project."

"I think the end result was we ended up getting a lot of good arms – good, successful, big league pitchers both left and right-handed because we were able to take that approach, identify those high ceiling guys, and that, coupled with a developmental system, was a key part of what Atlanta's done. They've established a development system that was willing to be patient and positive and bring along kids that were less polished than when they came in the door- maybe than those polished college players. And the result of the fact that there was a philosophy in place of taking high ceiling, athletic type guys and handing them off to a department on the development side that was willing to nurture and have the patience to work over and over in a positive manner with those young players. All of that working together resulted in a very successful major league club years down the road."

"When I left in 1992 and came here to set up my own program the thing I looked at well were what were probably the two most successful systems in baseball in the early 90's," Arbuckle says. "I looked at Toronto and Atlanta. I said 'Okay, how did they get there?' Basically they have taken the same avenue from a player procurement standpoint by basically going after the same type of thing. And basically I don't think up until the J.P. Riccardi days, Toronto veered much from it either. You look at Roy Halladay. He fits the same mold as those young Atlanta pitchers: high school pick, good athlete, good delivery, projectable all the way around. Toronto's top young position player is the Puerto Rican kid Alexis Rios, and it's the same thing with him. You break him down as a high school kid and he fits the same identical mold. So I don't think there's any question Bobby had to have been influenced by what Toronto and Pat Gillick were doing."

Now, after more than ten years in Philadelphia, Arbuckle has established his own system. He learned his craft by being around "the Braves' way" and now he's hopeful he's created "the Phillies' way."

"We continually talk about doing things the Phillies' way," Arbuckle says. "The Phillies' way in reality may be the Braves' way or the Toronto way – at least the way it use to be. I think it's the way that produces a winning organization. It goes back to this whole picture of the type of players you draft, the philosophy you have, and how you are going to develop them. All of that is tied to the same thing."

And all of it was tied to Paul Snyder.

One of Arbuckle's protégés is Brian Kohlscheen, mostly known in the Atlanta circles as the scout who believed in Adam LaRoche's swing. Kohlscheen was a coach at a junior college in Nebraska in the late 80's and had worked as an associate scout for Arbuckle. He would mostly act as a sounding board when Arbuckle would call to ask him about whether to scout certain players in that area. Then, when the Braves had an opening for a scout to work the Northeast, they hired Kohlscheen. Ten years later, with Arbuckle running the Phillies scouting department, he lured Kohlscheen to Philadelphia to be his Central Regional Supervisor. Along the way,

Arbuckle and Snyder had the most profound effect on Kohlscheen's development as a scout.

"Basically, Mike is a clone of Paul in a lot of ways," Kohlscheen says. "I was very fortunate enough to be able to be in the same places with Mike and really pick his mind. A lot of the things I learned from Mike were the same things that Paul had passed down to Mike. I was very fortunate that I had gone into the house, listened to the coaches, watching the kid interact, going to practice and watching how the young person interacts with the other people on his team. That's huge. Is he a team guy? Is he a 'me' guy? You've got to have a combination of both a little bit. It's watching how they handle themselves in adversity. Paul told me, 'You know, it's easy to go when a guy goes 4 for 4 and hits a home run, but try to find that guy when he's 0 for 4 or 0 for 5. See how he responds to that. If he responds the right way, then you've got something.'"

It didn't take Kohlscheen long to figure out that the Braves, along with Snyder and Arbuckle, were looking for a certain type of player. But what intrigued him was the discovery that the makeup of the player they were looking for was very similar to the makeup of those two men as individuals.

"I think in scouting if you don't have the right makeup, it's easy to be average," Kohlscheen says. "Paul would always say in meetings, 'which players are going to seek their level? Which scouts are going to seek their level?' In order to seek your level you have to have good makeup. They'll be enough people that will tell you that you aren't good, whether you're a player or a scout. The people that are made right, that are able to overcome that, and to keep that focus on the goal are the ones that put rings on their fingers."

"So many people go into scouting and say what the player can't do," Kohlscheen explains. "Those guys taught me that the players would tell you what they couldn't do, but look for everything that they can do. The positives. It separates you from the industry when you look at that."

Kohlscheen watched as Arbuckle brought the same philosophies both learned in Atlanta from Snyder to the Phillies. The result has been a system that has produced much better talent. In fact, the minor league depth came into play late in the 2004 season when the Phillies made three late season trades to acquire pitchers Cory Lidle, Todd Jones, and Felix Rodriquez. Arbuckle's system gave Phillies GM Ed Wade six players to use on those deals, including pitchers Josh Hancock and Elizardo Ramirez.

"Mike has done a good job of educating the ownership here with the philosophy that he grew up with the Braves and bringing it over to the Phillies," Kohlscheen says. "Look at Ryan Madsen going in the ninth round (in 1998). We gave him a little bit more money, but yet if he didn't have the opportunity to give him that little bit of extra money we don't get him. Taylor Buchholz (traded to the Astros in the Billy Wagner deal in November of 2003) went in the sixth round and we had to give him a little bit more money. With the Wagner deal, to be able to give up three players was all due to our depth. If we weren't able to deal from a position of strength, then we can't make that deal. So Mike's been able to do a lot of the same things that were in place with the Braves."

Like Ladnier, Kohlscheen was also able to learn a great deal from Chuck Lamar. It was somewhat uncomfortable when Lamar replaced Snyder as Braves Scouting Director before the 1991 season. Most everyone in the Braves' organization loved Paul, but John Schuerholz brought in his own man to run the department. But Kohlscheen says that after a while, Lamar was able to bring the scouting department together by including Snyder and making sure there was synergy between the scouting and player development departments.

"He did some things that helped bring us together that were good things," Kohlscheen says. "I remember one year he brought all the scouts and the player development folks together. He had two different T-shirts made up. For the scouts, on the back of the shirt it said, 'When I put them on the plane they could play.' For the player development people, they had on the back of their shirt, 'Who signed this guy?' It broke the ice. We had a softball game and had a lot of fun. Chuck leaned on Paul a lot since he had been over both of them before that. He was able to bring things together. It was a great working relationship."

Whenever a new guy comes in to lead a scouting or player development department, the tendency is to make changes to fit his own personal style. Lamar was a bit different from Snyder in that his strength was more on the administrative end, while Snyder was always better in field scouting. Again, at first the situation was a bit uneasy, but then Lamar quickly learned that the Braves' farm system was in pretty good shape, and it was mostly due to Snyder.

"Chuck could run a meeting with the best of them,"

Kohlscheen says. "He wasn't afraid to get other people involved. He was a great facilitator. He would get other people involved like Paul, Donnie Williams, or he would bring in someone like (former Braves outfielder) Ralph Garr (now a scout with the Braves) to talk about hitting and his experience in the big leagues. As a young scout, that helped me grow and figure out what are the things you want to look for. A handshake does mean something. Eye contact does mean something. Watch for those things. See how they interact with people. See how they interact with their parents. Stuff like that will separate you as a scout if you listen to those people who talk, you can really pick up some things."

"Chuck was an excellent motivator," says Roy Clark. "I learned a lot from Chuck and enjoyed working for him. That first year he was put into a little bit of a tough situation. But all I can tell you is how he treated me and that is with respect. He allowed me to do my thing. He knew I was going to be out there working. He allowed me to sign a lot of players that they didn't necessarily see."

Rod Gilbreath was Snyder's right-hand man when Lamar came in and became the Scouting and Farm Director, but Lamar kept him on as his Assistant Director in Player Development. Gilbreath says that it was difficult at first learning to work with Lamar's more corporate style, in contrast to Snyder's more laid-back approach. But after a while, everyone got on the same page.

"When he came in, we were all so close to Paul, it was just heartbreaking to see someone else come in and take that position," Gilbreath says. "Chuck was not a real good people person at first, but he got better and he really treated me fine. I think after the second or third year he started to realize that this organization was in pretty good shape before he got here."

"I think to Chuck's credit when we had scouting meetings he would have Paul basically sit at his right hand," Kohlscheen says. "He would start a conversation and then he would ask Paul a question. When Paul was asked a question, everything just flowed. I think initially when Chuck came on he wasn't quite sure what shape the scouting department was in and then he discovered that it was in pretty good shape. Chuck figured out that what Paul had going here, the philosophy, was pretty good. I think he just needed to tweak a few things and to his credit I think he did. I think if you would ask Chuck Lamar he learned so much from Paul that it helped in his development as a person. He's been a mentor to so many people it's just silly."

Lamar obviously saw how Snyder, along with Bobby Cox when he was GM in the late 80's, stressed the high school players in the draft.

"He knew we had success with high school guys," Gilbreath says. "They realized after everybody went through our system and saw what we had in our organization that the high school way was the way to go. And then they realized how many players in our system, something like forty-five or forty-eight, who were real prospects. Most of those guys were from high school."

Lamar took what he learned in Atlanta and moved on to become the General Manager of the expansion Tampa Bay Devil Rays in 1995. From the Devil Rays' first draft in 1996, it was obvious they were going to take the same philosophy as the Braves and concentrate on high school talent. The first five players they drafted were high schoolers, and over the next five drafts, all of their top picks were young, high school players. Now the core of the Tampa Bay team is made up of high draft picks taken by Lamar and his staff out of high school: outfielder Carl Crawford (second round in 1999), outfielder Rocco Baldelli (first round in 2001), shortstop B.J. Upton (first round in 2002), and their top prospect Delmon Young (first overall pick in 2003). The only difference in these type players is that they are a bit more "toolsy" than the ones Snyder usually looked for. They had great athleticism, and Lamar believed all would learn how to be better baseball players as their development continued.

"He didn't spend as much time on makeup, but on the ballplayer part," Kohlscheen says. "Paul was much more interested in high-ceiling, athletic baseball players with good makeup. You could cheat a little more on the makeup the higher they were, but really not a lot. Chuck was more, 'we want high ceiling and athletic players and I think we can team them how to play the game a little bit.'"

Kohlscheen learned from Lamar how to look at athletic players, even ones who might primarily play other sports, and project them as baseball players. The Braves did it with George Lombard, an All-American high school football player in Georgia whom they took in the second round of the 1994 draft, along with former LSU football player Jamie Arnold and Andre King, a high school football star in Florida. Lamar's philosophy was just another way for the Braves to search for players and project their ceiling, and he's carried that philosophy to the Devil Rays, who may be ready to finally become a winning franchise with their deep, young talent.

Kohlscheen is a Phillie now, but in his heart he'll always be a Brave. Perhaps one day he'll be able to move up and become a Scouting Director just like Arbuckle was able to do, or maybe even a GM like Lamar. When that eventually happens, you can bet Kohlscheen will have a solid mixture of the philosophies he's learned over the years from Lamar, Arbuckle, and Snyder.

Tony DeMacio was an athletic director, head football coach, and head baseball coach at a small college in Stanton, Virginia. He was happy, but believed he wanted to do something else with his life, something more. He had a number of friends in the scouting business, and knew he could be a baseball scout. But like so many, he simply needed an opportunity. He decided to write every major league club to see if they had any openings.

Only one man decided to check him out.

DeMacio was managing one night in Stanton when Paul Snyder showed up at one of his games. DeMacio believed Snyder had come to see a player, but the veteran Braves scout actually made the trip to come meet him, the man who had written him for a job as a scout.

"We exchanged pleasantries and the whole thing," DeMacio remembers. "Then I ran into him again about a week later in Charlottesville, Virginia at the Virginia High School State All-Star Game. He was sitting by himself, so I went over and sat with him. I re-introduced myself, and we sat together for the whole game. He asked me after the game if there was anybody on the field that I thought could be a prospect."

DeMacio told Snyder that two players impressed him: a first baseman and a pitcher. Later DeMacio would find out the first baseman had just been drafted and the pitcher, while he had not been drafted, would later pitch in the big leagues.

"I got a call from Gene Hassell, the area scout at the time for the Braves, saying that Paul wanted to hire me on a part-time basis to help him in the area," DeMacio recalls. "I said, 'Whatever he wants me to do is fine with me.' I just wanted to get in. So I thought that was what was going to happen, and then one night about 10:30 I got a person-to-person call from Paul offering me a job – a full-time job."

It didn't take long for DeMacio to develop a close relationship with Snyder. As a new scout, he had to learn a lot, and Snyder was there to teach him. But Paul also meant a lot to Tony DeMacio the man, not just the scout.

"He's just a good human being," DeMacio says. "He cares about people. Nothing is superficial with Paul. Everything is well meant. Everything is sincere. He's just a special human being. How many scouting directors will drop everything they have when your father is dying and drive to see him – a man he's never met. He sat at the table together in the kitchen and cried together. Now how many people would do that?"

DeMacio would soon learn what all Braves' area scouts lived by: they would be respected by their boss no matter how much or little experience they had. "He believes in his area people," DeMacio says. "He always has. He knows that a crosschecker can come in one day and the kid might not have a great day. He listens to his area scouts. I think that's why we always loved working for him so much."

After seven successful seasons with the Braves, where he scouted and signed stars such as Tom Glavine and Chipper Jones, DeMacio left in 1991 to join the Cleveland Indians as a National Crosschecker. In 1994, he became the East Coast Scouting Supervisor with the Chicago Cubs. And then in December of 1998, Baltimore General Manager Frank Wren, now John Schuerholz's Assistant GM in Atlanta, hired DeMacio to be the Scouting Director for the Orioles.

"Frank and I talked and we believed in young pitching," DeMacio says. "My philosophy was to try to do it the same way Paul did it – along with some of your own ideas of course: build around young pitching, start with left-handed pitching. This system here was devoid of left-handed pitching. They haven't had a left-handed starter here for years. My first year we had seven (early) picks, and I took three high school left-handed pitchers."

The three left-handed pitchers did not work out – at least not yet. Two of the three had injuries, including Richard Stahl, drafted out of the Atlanta area. The third one was Scott Rice, a 6'6" pitcher out of California, who was only seventeen when he was drafted. DeMacio knew it would take time for both to develop, and they are slowly starting to show some positive signs. Stahl and Rice both rebounded in 2004 from injuries to do well in the minor leagues.

DeMacio soon found out that his situation in Baltimore was not like Atlanta. Wren was fired ten months after he was hired in a dispute with Orioles owner Peter Angelos. DeMacio would then have three more General Managers to deal with over the next five years. Through it all, he tried to maintain his core beliefs.

"Before I got there, some years they'd take high school guys high and some years they'd take college guys high," DeMacio says. "They had tried both ways but they weren't developing anybody. Everybody has their own philosophy on college guys and high school guys. Paul always said, 'You know I want to grow our own.' You figure if you take the high school guy you can groom them the way you want. I believe that as well."

"We were trying to build a foundation for their minor league system that would allow that club to operate like we (the Braves) operate," Wren says. "If you look at Tony's first draft after I hired him in '99, he's got five or six players in the big leagues and a few of them are real good big league players. That's the talent pool that you've got to have. He drafted Willie Harris (twenty-fourth round – now with the White Sox), Larry Bigbie (first round), who was their leftfielder in 2004, and Eric Bedard (sixth round), who is now in their rotation. That's pretty good for his first draft. I thought Tony had great ideas for what we were trying to accomplish, with the kind of players we wanted, and how we were going to get depth. When I was fired after the first year, Tony didn't have free reign to do what he needed to do to get players."

Considering the instability in Baltimore, DeMacio's task as a Scouting Director was very difficult. Angelos, notoriously known as an impatient man, pressed him and all three GM's that followed Wren to take college talent in the draft. So Beau Hale (University of Texas), taken in 2000, left-hander Chris Smith (Cumberland University) and second baseman Mike Fontenot (LSU), taken in 2001, and Nick Markakis (Young Harris Junior College) in 2003 were all college players taken in the first round. Adam Loewen, a left-handed pitcher out of Canada, was the only other high school player taken in the first round by the Orioles during DeMacio's tenure, and he even had to attend a junior college before being signed as a draft-and-follow player in the spring of 2003.

The Orioles have not been able to produce a lot of homegrown talent in the last several years, and much of that comes from DeMacio having to compromise his philosophy in order to please Angelos. The philosophical split came to a head in 2004 when DeMacio wanted to use the Orioles' first round pick in the draft (number eight overall) on Chris Nelson, a hotshot high school shortstop out of Redan High School in Stone Mountain, Georgia, just east of Atlanta. The Braves also loved Nelson, but they knew he would never last until their first pick late in the second round.

Angelos had other ideas, however. He preferred the Orioles draft a college player, one that would agree to a pre-draft deal below even the $2.2 million dollars that the Commissioner's office laid out as the "slot" money for the eighth pick. So instead of Nelson, and against DeMacio's recommendation, the Orioles chose Rice right-hander Wade Townsend. Nelson went to the Colorado Rockies with the very next pick. But Angelos offered Townsend only $1.85 million, and by late summer, with no agreement in place, Townsend returned to Rice for his senior season. The Orioles lost all negotiating rights to him, losing their top draft pick.

After the season, Angelos refused to renew DeMacio's contract as Scouting Director. DeMacio was never able to fully implement his philosophies, the ones he learned under Snyder. Instead, a meddlesome owner who didn't see (or ignored) the big picture, undermined DeMacio.

These aren't the same Orioles John Schuerholz worked for back in the 60's. Angelos bought the team in 1993, and three years later got rid of a solid baseball man in Roland Hemond, a former Milwaukee Braves' executive and a winning GM with the White Sox in the 80's. Then Angelos brought in Pat Gillick, who led the Orioles to the American League Championship Series in 1996 and 1997, only to leave after 1998. When Angelos fired Wren after only one season, he then promoted Syd Thrift, another solid baseball man who as GM built the Pittsburgh teams that got to the NLCS for three years in a row in the early 90's, and helped Lou Gorman start the Royals Baseball Academy back in the 70's. Thrift lasted only three years before Angelos replaced him with a peculiar two-headed GM scenario where Jim Beattie and Mike Flanagan now actually share the duties.

The Orioles' situation is a true example of what many Scouting Directors face in today's baseball climate. Many owners are impatient, wanting an immediate return on their investment. They fail to see the long-term commitment needed to make a franchise a consistent winner. In this case, Tony DeMacio was the victim, but Frank Wren believes others in baseball should learn from the Orioles' mistakes.

"They really had no concept of what we were trying to do," Wren says. "Look at the difference (between the Orioles and the Braves). We have continuity. We don't feel like we have to have a quick-fix draft. We don't feel that we have to rush players though the minor league system to get them to the big leagues. The ones that do just don't work."

And Tony DeMacio, a good baseball man, paid the price for that impatience.

23
THE PHILOSOPHY

Continuity is perhaps the best attribute in describing the Atlanta Braves' hierarchy. Paul Snyder is the dean, having been with the organization since 1957. Bobby Cox's history with the team goes back to 1978, when he first managed the Braves. And John Schuerholz, the longest tenured General Manager in baseball, has been around since the Fall of 1990.

This isn't a franchise where GMs come and go, where Scouting Directors aren't able to establish their philosophies before they get bounced out, or where the Manager leaves a pitcher in too long and gets fired. There is a level of patience and trust in Atlanta, a firm belief that what's been done works, and if it ain't broke, don't fix it.

Just as the Braves develop players, they also develop a pretty good front office executive. Dayton Moore has a good chance to follow in John Schuerholz's shoes one day, and he's the type that might be like Snyder and stick around for fifty years. He's part corporate, part old-time baseball. Put him in the office or in the field, and chances are he'll do pretty well.

Moore's analytical nature started out early. When he was growing up in Kansas, he often watched "Monday Night Baseball" on ABC. He would tape the games and then go back and chart the pitchers and dissect the hitters, and also watch the managers and their strategies. When he played the game in high school, he knew he was doing more than just playing. He was thinking, always thinking, about strategy and why baseball was played and managed the way it was.

"I knew from the time I got into the game of baseball, just as a little kid, that I wanted to make my career out of it, my life out it," Moore says. "It was my passion."

Like most young people with a passion for baseball, Moore loved to play. He was good enough to play baseball at George Mason University in Virginia. Scouts told him there was a chance he'd get drafted, but the call never came. So he played for a while with an independent league team, and then finally realized coaching was what he was supposed to do. His coach at George Mason, Billy Brown, offered him a chance to be a college coach at the ripe young age of twenty-two.

"He took somewhat of a risk," says Moore. "But as a player, I was always a coach on the field anyway. I had to be that type of player, an instinctive, intelligent, hustling, team-oriented player. That's what I had to do to be successful."

Along with being George Mason's third base coach and recruiting coordinator, Moore also managed in the Shenandoah Valley League during the summer. That's where he met Roy Clark, who scouted that area, but had just been made a crosschecker by the Braves Scouting Director at the time, Chuck Lamar.

"Chuck asked me to recommend five people to take my job," Clark says. "I told Chuck that I didn't have five people to recommend, only one. It's sort of like when you meet your wife for the first time. You just know. Your instincts are telling you it's the right person. Once you talked to Dayton, it was over. You just knew that he was special. Chuck was totally sold on Dayton and we hired him."

It didn't take Moore long to make an impression as a scout. He worked the Mid-Atlantic States, and then two years after joining the Braves, Snyder asked him to come into the office to work with him. For a young baseball executive, Moore's time with the veteran of the Braves' organization was invaluable.

"Paul gave me tremendous freedom to grow," Moore says. "He gave me tremendous guidance. He installed confidence in me as a baseball person. Just being able to watch him work and how he processed information and made decisions was invaluable. Paul believes in the people that he works with. He listens to them and evaluates what they say, but then he makes his own decisions. He was outstanding."

Moore also made an impression around baseball. In 1999, when he was thirty-one, the Kansas City Royals wanted Moore to be their Director of Scouting. It was a dream come true for Moore, who grew up a Royals' fan. But just like with Snyder and with Schuerholz, loyalty was important to him, and he decided to stay put.

"I knew I wanted to be in Atlanta and wanted to be with John and Paul and Roy and all the people that I had grown up with in this organization," Moore says. "It was a tough decision, but I wanted to stay with the Braves."

Moore became the Braves Director of International Scouting in 2000 when Clark took over as the Scouting Director. The two developed a very close friendship.

"He's like a brother to me," Clark says. "It just goes with respect. When I interview scouts, I'm looking for somebody that's going to be more organized and outwork me. There's one person that does that and it's Dayton. Besides being a true professional, he's totally prepared. He's as close as I've seen to being another John Schuerholz."

"Roy's a great friend," Moore says. "He's one of the people out there that I know I can speak honestly with and he can speak honestly with me and it doesn't affect the friendship. That's special."

Schuerholz saw how well Moore and Clark worked together. He watched as Moore helped Clark orchestrate three excellent drafts from 2000 through 2002, and he also knew Moore was still a hot commodity in the baseball world. So in July of 2002, Schuerholz promoted Moore to Director of Player Personnel, in charge of the Scouting and Player Development Departments. In effect, he became the boss of the man who originally hired him.

"Technically, I guess you are right," Moore admits. "But I've got as much confidence in Roy Clark as I have in myself and probably even more. We're very close. If Roy says we need to do something and feels strongly about it, why would I go against that? If I felt 100% strongly in the other direction, we'd sit down and talk about it and I guarantee you we'd come up with a happy medium. Chances are we're going to be right because of the give and take of our relationship and the strong convictions that we both have. Roy has a proven history of being successful. But John is the only boss."

That is Moore and Clark's primary responsibility: to implement the philosophies John Schuerholz has had in place for many years. They are fully aware of the type of players Schuerholz needs to complete his roster and the type that Bobby Cox wants in his dugout. Even though Moore is above him on the depth chart, Clark still pretty much runs the draft, while Moore oversees the minor league system. They have developed a well-oiled machine that is completely fulfilling the functions of a farm system.

"There's only one boss and that's John Schuerholz," Moore says. "We've just got to make it work. Every decision I make I say, 'What's best for the Atlanta Braves?' That's how I start processing any decision. 'What's best for the Atlanta Braves?'"

Moore's work in his latest position has continued to get him recognition as one of baseball's rising young executives. In 2003, *Baseball America* named him the number one candidate to become a General Manager. He'll be one eventually, maybe in Atlanta, but for now the job is to work with Clark to keep the tradition alive.

The blueprint is simple. It's the same thing Schuerholz learned in Baltimore from Harry Dalton and Lou Gorman, and the same one Snyder learned from Paul Richards and Eddie Robinson, and then implemented with Bill Lucas. It is the philosophy, and it is the reason the Braves have won for so long:

1. MAKEUP

This is the most important word used in Braves Nation. Whether it's the scouting of an amateur player, of a minor leaguer that might be promoted, or of a potential addition from another team, it's all about makeup. To the powers that be in the Braves' organization, makeup is just as important as on-base percentage.

"You have to be able to apply moral principles in your life no matter what you do," Moore says. "If you have intelligence and you have a passion for doing something, but you don't have integrity, then it's not going to work. If you have the passion for something and you have integrity but you don't have the intelligence, which is the ability to make good decisions about what your passion is, then you're going to have problems. If you are intelligent and have integrity but you lose your passion, then it's not going to work. So all three of those things have to happen to be successful in any aspect of life, not only baseball."

That's not something you expect to hear from a baseball guy. In some ways Moore breaks the mold of a "traditional scout." He is one, make no mistake, but he also applies simple principles for finding talent in baseball as if he were hiring a new employee for a Fortune 500 company. He not only wants to find players who can play, but players who can win.

"Many players don't make it to the major leagues because of who they associate with or what they do off the field, or the way they respond to negative things that happen to them on the field," Moore says. "Let's face it, most of us perceive ourselves based on the success or lack of success we have in the things that we love the most. You've got to be able to apply moral principles in your life to be successful, and you've got to be able to have that balance on and off the field. The same character traits that make a baseball player successful are the same character traits that make a schoolteacher or a President of a company successful. It's the same character traits."

"Makeup is not something you can put a grade on," says Tim Conroy, a former pitcher with the Oakland A's and now an Assistant to Schuerholz. "It's not something you can look at and put a number in a box. To see how fast a guy is you can put a run time down or put a gun out there to check the velocity. We really need our area scouts to get to know these kids. You can have all the tools in the world, but without the right makeup, you'll never get to use those abilities. I played for thirteen years, seven of them in the big leagues, and as you move up a lot of guys move past you that have much better ability. It's one reason: makeup – the makeup of the individual."

2. DON'T DISCOUNT STATS, BUT...

"There's nothing wrong with looking at stats as a tool, but when you go strictly by that then you're saying that anybody can scout," says Clark. "The old school guys, the veteran scouts, they didn't have the radar guns and they didn't have all the stats they have today. But they could tell you who was going to be a major leaguer. They may not be able to put your finger on it, but when they say, 'this is the guy,' you have to listen to them. When you take all that out of the picture, I don't think you're giving credit to the scouts – who deserve it."

The current emphasis on statistical analysis has created the question of whether or not the computer, with all of its glory, is more important than the person – than the scout out getting to know who the person is to see if they have the total package to be a major leaguer. Can a team create a farm system or a roster strictly on stats? Maybe. But the Braves and some other teams prefer to have stats as one piece of a much larger pie – and by no means not the largest one.

"Statistics have always been apart of the game and they always will be," Moore says. "It's a good tool. They tell you something about what a player has done or hasn't done. So it's a tool that you need to use, but you've got to use it correctly. Statistics don't tell the whole story. You can manipulate statistics in any number of ways. But you evaluate tools and makeup. It's about tools, bodies, and makeup. You stay with the tools and be patient. If a guy has ability, you stay with it. Hopefully, at some point in time, the performance will equal the ability."

3. TRUST YOUR SCOUTS

This is the most important trait passed down by Snyder to Moore and Clark. They don't have time to see every player themselves, and they know the area scouts are the ones who get to know the players personally. So they have to be able to listen to scouts like Brian Kohlscheen and trust him when he tells them about an Adam LaRoche or a Donnie Poplin when he tells them about a Charles Thomas.

"I'm a firm believer that scouts are like players," Clark says. "You either have instincts or you don't. I think to be a good scout you have to have instincts. You've either got them or you don't. I don't know how you teach that. I guess it's taught by mom and dad at an early age and that's having a passion for the game and learning about it as much as possible."

4. COLLEGE VS. HIGH SCHOOL

The percentages show that college players make it to the big leagues quicker than high school players. But there is no concrete evidence that a college player will be a better major leaguer than a high school draft pick. The Braves prefer to raise their own players, to get the players before they've developed bad habits. If they get the players when they're young, right out of high school, they're able to imprint their philosophies so the players know what to expect, what is expected of them, and how to play "The Braves' Way."

That doesn't mean the Braves and other teams like them aren't interested in college players. Kevin Barry and Sean White are two solid pitching prospects who were college players, while James Jurries, Billy McCarthy, and J.C. Holt were college position players taken early by the Braves. Sometimes they might need a player at a certain position to play at a higher level in the minor leagues, or if they have a weakness at a position in the system they may want to get a player with a little more experience. But the key is not limiting themselves to the types of players they go after.

The Braves also like junior college players, like Adam LaRoche and current prospects Steve Doetsch and Van Pope, and also draft-and-follow players that go to a JUCO for their freshman year, like Marcus Giles and Nick Green.

"I think there's got to be a good balance in everything you do," Moore says. "There are only a few talent pools: International players and then you draft high school and college players. You have to give your organization every opportunity to acquire talent in different ways. There's got to be a balance with high school and college. It's up to our scouting people to ultimately decide who is ready to come out and play physically and mentally. Our philosophy here is that we like high school players. We like young players. We like to develop our own. When you have young players in your system, you have to be more patient. You have to do more teaching. You have to be an energizer, an encourager. You have to be a dad and everything to these players. But if you don't have a player development staff that reflects that and understands the young player, it's a formula for disaster."

5. SYNERGY BETWEEN SCOUTING AND PLAYER DEVELOPMENT

There are some front offices in baseball that are split right down the middle. Philosophical differences can kill an organization. This is not to say people won't have different opinions, but it's important for the brass to be on the same page on many basic principles. The most common area for division is between player development and scouting. The scouts have to trust the coaches down on the farm will do everything possible to develop a player so he can reach his full potential, while the player development staff must trust the scouts to find the players with the right makeup so the ability is there to reach their ceiling. Synergy is crucial to a successful farm system.

"You have to have people that understand what the processes are that you go through to scout, to sign, and to develop players," Moore says. "They have to respect the process. It's no different than what we expect from the players. We expect the players to trust in the process, trust in the information they are given, and to go out and apply it. Well, the scouting and the player development people have to trust in the process as well."

6. PATIENCE

Since the Braves draft mostly high school players, they have to be extremely patient. They very rarely would ever draft a player so he can be in the big leagues the next season. That's not their idea of replacing players on their major league roster. Instead, they want the player to fully develop. They say the players will tell them when they are ready – not verbally, but by their play on the field.

"If this organization is going to be successful, you've got to be patient with the players," says Moore. "The ones that are most patient with players and believe in their players are going to be successful."

7. THE STRENGTH OF THE DRAFT DICTATES PICKS

The Braves' goal is to have a legitimate big league prospect at every stop in their minor league system. So as they approach every draft, there's a full awareness of every need. However, even if they have depth at a certain position, Clark believes there is nothing more dangerous than going against the strength of a draft. If a draft is pitching-heavy, they'll look at pitchers, even if they have depth at that position.

"You cannot go into a draft saying, 'we're going to take position players this year,'" Clark says. "And then all of a sudden, we're picking seventy-first, and all of the position players are gone or all of the good pitchers are gone. You never know who is going to be there. I like picking thirtieth every year. I want to pick thirtieth every year."

8. PROTECTING PICKS

During Clark's third draft, he learned a very valuable lesson. Tyler Greene, a hotshot prospect out of St. Thomas Aquinas High School in South Florida, was the Braves second pick in the second round. He was a fabulous prospect, and the Braves were thrilled to draft him. But after months of negotiations, Greene decided against signing and instead attended Georgia Tech. The Braves lost out on a top prospect and decided to change their philosophy. They didn't want to waste a spot on their draft board on a player who was only after the money or didn't want to play at all, so they added signability as a key element in the scouting of amateur players. They wanted to find out exactly who wanted to play for them and who didn't. The loss of Greene triggered a more consistent effort in finding out exactly which players they'd be able to sign.

"Tyler Greene has a chance to be an outstanding major league player," Conroy says. "We were on the right guy, but it just didn't finish. There were no red flags there to where you'd look back on and say, 'well, this is what he was really saying.' Everything was a go, but it just didn't work. I don't know if there was anything we could have done different there, but I think it got us to refocus."

The strategy now is very simple. The Braves talk to the players they are interested in drafting before their round comes up. They ask the simple question: Do you want to be a Brave? Then they are very honest with the player in what they can pay him if he is drafted. If the player scoffs, they move on. If the player is agreeable, he becomes a legit candidate to be drafted by the Braves.

"The bottom line with signability is that if he really wants to play pro ball, he'll sign," Clark says. "It all comes down to whether or not the kid wants to play. We pinpoint guys. We've got nothing to hide. If we want to take you in the such and such round, then here it is (money-wise). Yes or no, and if they don't want to do it, then that's okay. But we're honest with them up front. 'If you want to be a Brave, this is what we're looking at.'"

"If a player doesn't think they can be a major league player and help the Atlanta Braves win championships, they shouldn't sign," says Moore. "I tell players all the time that if they're 99.9% sure you want to sign with the Atlanta Braves, then don't sign with us. You've got to be 100% committed to sign with this organization. The minor leagues are not an easy environment, but it's a great environment. If you want to be a baseball player, this is the environment to be in.

We help guys reach their ceilings, and if they want to be a baseball player and grow as a person, this is an environment that I'd put my name on."

9. PITCHING, PITCHING, PITCHING

It all started back in the mid-80's when Bill Wight told Paul Snyder the Braves needed to focus on pitching. Then Bobby Cox came back to the Braves and believed the same thing. When you get "lucky" with guys like Glavine, Avery, and Smoltz, it's usually a good idea to stay with that philosophy. Pitching remains the priority for the Braves. The more pitching prospects they have, the more pitchers they have to rise to the bigs or be used in a trade. The Braves continually test the old adage "you can never have enough pitching."

"In that case, we have a history," Moore says. "We treat these pitchers like they are thoroughbred racehorses. We treat them with tremendous care. We don't need to win ballgames in the minors. It's all about development. That's the difference between the minor leagues and college. We never try to win ballgames at the expense of developing our players. If a guy has a no-hitter in the sixth inning and he's reached his pitch count, he's coming out."

10. DEVELOP TALENT FOR TRADES

The ability of a minor league system to produce talent for the General Manager to use in potential trades is equally important to getting your own talent to the majors. In 2004, as the Yankees were desperately courting Randy Johnson from the Arizona Diamondback, the D-backs were scouring the Yankees' farm system for players to take in a deal and simply didn't see enough they were interested in. Consequently, Johnson remained in Arizona, the Yankees were forced to acquire mediocre right-hander Esteban Loaiza, and the Red Sox won their first World Series in eighty-six years.

The Braves don't draft players specifically to trade them, but they have to build up the depth in the system so even if they do trade a player, it won't weaken a position. The trick is to have a prospect ready to replace a player that you may include in a deal.

"From a scouting perspective, these are our kids," Clark says. "We started scouted them at an early age, and we've seen them over and over. We're with them all the way through. Is it disappointing when they're traded? It is, but you understand why you've got to do it. Our job is to produce enough quality talent through our scouting and player development systems so if we don't have anybody ready, there will be players for John to use in deals to bring in that type of player. I think it's a credit to our player development staff and scouting staff that guys like Jason Schmidt, Odalis Perez, and Jason Marquis have done well. Sure, we'd love to have them. But they were used to help us get players that will allow us to continue this championship run."

"My job is to sign them and get them down there and then hope they get to a point where we want them or other teams want them," says Hep Cronin, the Braves Midwest Regional Scouting Supervisor. "My job isn't to trade. I trust John. He knows what he's doing."

11. REPLACEMENT VALUE

The Braves must have a stable of prospects ready to come up to the major league level to fill out its roster. When Robert Fick left, the Braves had Adam LaRoche ready to take over at first base. When Tom Glavine left, Horacio Ramirez came up to take his spot. If a major leaguer gets hurt, it's good to be able to turn to your farm system to find readied talent. Veteran players can't all be replaced with veteran players. Maybe the Yankees can do it, but it's also important to reinvigorate your roster with youth and enthusiasm. Therefore, the system must develop players that can be promoted and help fill the roster.

"Our goal is to have a premium prospect at every position ready for the big leagues when the time comes when we need that particular player at the big league level," Clark says.

"We want every pitcher in the organization to be a prospect," Moore says. "That's our goal. We want every pitcher we run out there to have the chance to pitch in the big leagues. That means they've got to have ability. We've got to continue to be aggressive in our scouting and sign and develop players. You can never be satisfied with what you've done. You've got to work hard to make good decisions. You can't take a day off."

12. SCOUTING YOUR OWN PLAYERS

This is perhaps one of the most overlooked necessities of having a solid farm system. The Braves' scouts work long hours looking for new talent, but after the draft is over, they also spend valuable time analyzing their existing talent. It's important to determine which players in your system are legit prospects, fringe prospects, or simply roster fillers. The Braves have to have solid opinions on which players they should keep and which players can be sacrificed in deals if necessary.

"Bill Lajoie once said that the most important thing we do in the summer is get our own guys right because the last thing you want to do it to misevaluate one of your own guys and let him come back and be a star with another club," Clark says. "To get quality in a trade, you've got to give up quality. So we fully anticipate Richard Lewis and Bubba Nelson and Adam Wainwright to be successful major leaguers. But in return we got productive major league players."

Lajoie was the General Manager that traded John Smoltz to the Braves in the summer of 1987. The trade worked for him, getting a valuable veteran in Doyle Alexander, but it also may have made him more careful in the future when he later came to the Braves as a scout for John Schuerholz.

"That is no doubt as big a key as anything, not only in acquiring but in who you give up," Lajoie says. "You must evaluate your players properly. I remember we were having a meeting and Al Martin had been on the Richmond ball club. I had gone in there to look at a couple of pitchers. At the meeting in the fall I said, 'How about Al Martin?' Nobody said anything. So I asked again the next day and found out that he had not been properly evaluated by the people in the system. So he had signed a contract with Pittsburgh as a six-year free agent. He went on to become a ten-year player in the big leagues. So that was kind of a sore spot. So you have to make sure you evaluate your own talent."

13. FOLLOW THE PLAN

The plan, the philosophy, has been in place for years. They know it works, so they try not to vary it much at all. Consistency is important – not only with philosophies, but with people, and in this case, the people are the philosophies. They have a lot of momentum in the Braves' organization since they've been winning for fourteen years and the farm system has been spitting out talent regularly for the last twenty. So it's crucial to stay the course and not make any drastic changes that can alter the plan.

14. MAKING AN IMPACT ON THE PLAYERS

The scouts, managers, coaches, and executives are the players' bosses. They are in charge. But the environment they've created is one of family. These bosses know that the players are also people. They are all there to work towards a common goal. So in order to provide the environment which will create those opportunities, it's important for there to be mutual respect that starts with a one-on-one relationship. And to no one's surprise, that all goes back to the Braves patriarch, Paul Snyder. His treatment of minor league players as family members and more specifically, sons, goes a long way to explaining how the rest of the organization treats the talent.

"What I try to do every morning (in spring training) is to go by every one of them and say, 'Good Morning,'" Snyder says. "I tell them, 'If you've got a problem, we can talk about it while you're doing your exercises.' I try to. I know what it meant to me when Roland Hemond (Braves Farm Director in the late 50's) used to do it to me. We had some-300 odd people in Waycross, Georgia. We had sixteen teams at that time. He called everybody by their first name. So I try to walk by them and acknowledge them everyday."

15. THE PHILOSOPHY IS THE PEOPLE

Snyder's actions go a long way in explaining the true reason for the success of the philosophies that have been in place for years with the Braves. It's the people. It's not perfect, nor should it be, but it all starts with the people that are hired to do a job and help youngsters get to the major leagues. From the time a scout first asks a sixteen-year old junior to fill out a player information card, to the time a AAA manager tells a player he's going to "the show," it's all about people. The people in the organization make the philosophies work.

"That's the one thing I think that has made this organization as strong as it has been for as long as it has been," says Brian Snitker, a member since 1977 as a minor league player, major league coach, and minor league manager. "You can find a lot of people that know baseball. It's not that complicated a game. You can always learn from it, and there's always something you can pick up in baseball. You never stop learning. But the basics of the game are real simple. You can find a lot of people that know that and a lot of people that can teach it. But what sets the good ones apart from the bad ones is what kind of people they are. This is an organization of great people. Not only are they blessed to have great people with outstanding baseball sense and feel, but I also think it's the kind of people that are here. To me that pretty much epitomizes the Atlanta Braves."

24
THE MONEYBALL EFFECT

The most recent discussion of how teams scout and develop players and create rosters was brought to the forefront by a book from Michael Lewis called *Moneyball*. It has almost become part of baseball's language. It's managed to spiral so out of hand that teams that follow the Moneyball philosophies are referred to as "Moneyballers."

Lewis tracked the style and beliefs of Oakland A's General Manager Billy Beane, a former player who failed in the majors after being a first round draft pick of the Mets in 1980. Beane uses a heavily statistical approach in his analysis, hoping to maximize the value of his draft picks and potential players. Lewis portrayed Beane as an egotistical man obsessed with statistics and basically unwilling to rely on traditional scouting as a means of finding players.

The book touched a nerve in the baseball world, which is likely what Lewis intended. The author ridiculed scouts as being worthless, chubby, ex-players who did nothing but sit around and chew tobacco, reliving the good-old days. Lewis forwarded the belief that it's better to use a source of information that spits out statistics instead of sunflower seeds as the basis for finding baseball talent- in other words, the computer over the commuter.

At times Beane has tried to back away from the book, but there's little he can do to deny the quotes attributed to him where he mocks his old-school scouts and where he explodes at the realization that his Scouting Director has drafted a high school pitcher.

There are two differences that set the A's and other "Moneyballers" apart from the rest of baseball. First, their use of statistics is extreme, believing that on-base percentage is the primary indication of potential big league success, and that stats override makeup in determining who will make it to "the show." Also, speed and defense are trivial. It's all about OBP.

Secondly, due to their financial restrictions, the A's claim that if they're going to spend money on draft picks, they must not miss. They feel the best way to get a value pick is to emphasize college players and to almost ignore talent from the high school level.

It's the extreme to which the Moneyballers believe in their philosophies that have executives from other teams scratching their heads. The Braves and others also use stats, but simply as one arrow in their expansive quiver.

"I don't think you totally discount stats," says Phillies Assistant GM for Scouting and Player Development Mike Arbuckle. "To me those statistics are of value just like a radar gun is or the stopwatch. I think it is *a* tool, just like the psychological testing is *a* tool. I don't think you ignore it, but I think it's just one more piece of information, as a Scouting Director at draft time, that you *may* want to factor in. I think this stuff is of more value at the professional level in pro scouting than it is in amateur. And I say that because at the amateur level, the competition varies so much from area to area in the country – high school of college. If you want to compare a kid's numbers that plays in a tough high school region in the Los Angeles area, Orange County, you're going to take those and try to compare them to some kid playing in northern Michigan and think that those numbers have any meaning whatsoever when you're comparing? There's no way in the world."

"I think statistics play a role and they do come into the picture," says longtime baseball executive Lou Gorman. "When you get a picture of a player, you want as complete a picture of that player as you can get. Statistics will help you but it can't be the dominating factor. It's got to be the skills of the player and the makeup of the player that is most predominant. I've always felt that way."

Bill Lajoie is another long-time baseball executive. He started as a scout with the Reds forty years ago and now works as an assistant to Red Sox GM Theo Epstein, one of the young "Ivy League types" that now occupy many executive positions in baseball.

"The club I'm with now is into statistical information a great deal," Lajoie says. "But they do put a lot of weight on the player's ability to fit in and a lot of times that becomes a critical issue, especially in a trade. We're very much aware of that also."

Since the Red Sox won the World Series in 2004, many believe they are the first "Moneyball team" to win anything of consequence, since Epstein and Beane share many views. The Red Sox do draft a significant number of college players and do focus on stats. However, several key moves made late in the 2004 season make you wonder how close the Red Sox actually are to being Moneyballers. Michael Lewis portrayed the A's as being very much against speed and defense, but the Red Sox acquired Orlando Cabrera from the Expos and Doug Mientkiewicz from the Twins before the trade deadline. Both players are excellent defensively; Cabrera stabilized the Boston infield with his slick play. Epstein also traded for Dave Roberts from the Dodgers, a speedy outfielder who acted primarily as a pinch runner the rest of the season and was a huge factor in the Red Sox amazing comeback against the Yankees in the American League Championship Series. A philosophy that was at least partly anti-Moneyball actually helped the Red Sox win their first championship in eighty-six years.

"Makeup, as far as I'm concerned, is half the equation," Lajoie says. "Ability will get you to the big leagues and makeup will keep you there."

If not for the makeup of guys like Curt Schilling, Kevin Millar, Mark Bellhorn, Jason Varitek, and Bill Mueller, the defense of Cabrera and Mientkiewicz, and the speed of Roberts, Red Sox fans may still be blaming the "Curse of the Bambino" for their horrific postseason history. The on-base percentages helped, but so did the makeup of that team, which was off the charts.

For nineteen years Dan Evans grew up in the Chicago White Sox organization knowing how important makeup is in the evaluation process. Roland Hemond, a former Braves' minor league administrator when the team was in Milwaukee, was a huge influence on Evans, as were Tony LaRussa, Dave Dombrowski, and Larry Himes.

"Roland taught me to listen to the veteran scouts," Evans says. "They had been around and it was almost like they had been through experiments in the past in terms of 'Does this work?' or 'Does this not work?' 'Can this guy play?' 'Can this guy not play.' I think what he stressed to me was that the veteran scouts have the best answers. You've got to listen to them and give them as much input as you can because they're not going to be fooled by a lot of things."

Evans joined the Los Angeles Dodgers in May of 2001 as a Senior Advisor to Interim GM Dave Wallace. He then assumed the GM position five months later. When he took over the Dodgers, Evans learned a few things. First, the Dodgers no longer had the farm system that was developing talent other teams wanted in potential deals. Second, the Dodgers were stuck with a bunch of bad contracts, like Darren Dreifort, Andy Ashby, and Mark Grudzielanek. That combined with a tighter budget handed down from FOX, the owner of the Dodgers, gave him very little payroll flexibility. One of Evans' goals coming in was to return the Dodgers to the way they use to be: continually churning out prospects like they did in the 70's with the world famous homegrown infield of Steve Garvey, Davey Lopes, Bill Russell, and Ron Cey. The first thing he knew he had to do was find a Scouting Director that would build the organization from the ground up.

Evans says, "When I interviewed people for that position what I wanted was a guy who was going to be committed to growing from within and to not worry about trading prospects, but to be really focused on bringing in guys who could help us."

He found Logan White, who had spent seven years with the Baltimore Orioles as the West Coast Scouting Supervisor. White has a few things in common with Braves Scouting Director Roy Clark: both were minor leaguers in the Mariners' farm system in the 80's (Clark was later a coach on one of White's minor league teams) and both started their scouting careers with Seattle. White also had the same philosophical beliefs as Evans, and for that matter, Clark.

"What I wanted was a best-player-available philosophy," Evans says. "That's what I got in Logan. I didn't want a high school philosophy and I didn't want a college philosophy. His belief was, 'I want the guy who I think is going to be the total package.' He didn't have any issues drafting college players whatsoever. It just happened that the guys available happened to be high school guys."

White and Evans really didn't alter the philosophy that had already been in place. Even though they have had trouble with first round picks through the years, the Dodgers have pretty much always been known as a team that leaned toward high schoolers. However, the ratio of picks used on high school players increased in the first two years of White's tenure as Scouting Director. Here are the percentages of high school players taken by the Dodgers in a few pinpointed drafts: (picks, not rounds)

HIGH SCHOOL PLAYERS

YEARS	1st 10 PICKS	1st 20 PICKS	1st 30 PICKS
1999-01	63%	43.3%	47.6%
2002-03 (White, Evans)	80%	70%	68%

There's a pretty good reason for the increase in high school picks under White's watch. He was able to snag some decent talent, the best available talent, in his first two drafts: first baseman James Loney (first rounder in 2002), left-handed pitcher Greg Miller (first round sandwich pick in 2002), right-hander Jonathan Broxton (second round in 2002), left-hander Mike Megrew (fifth round in 2002), right-hander Chad Billingsley (first round in 2003), and lefty Chuck Tiffany (second round in 2003). All six are very good prospects.

"When you take a look at some of our successes in the first couple of drafts that we had, it just happened that those players were high school players," Evans says. "The first draft was heralded as the fourth best draft and the second one was the best draft."

Despite an uncertain ownership situation in his two years as GM, Evans was able to make some other moves that proved to be tremendously important to the Dodgers. He acquired some very important pieces through trades like Cesar Izturis, Jeff Weaver, Guillermo Mota, Jolbert Cabrera, Dave Roberts, and from the Braves, Odalis Perez. He signed Jose Lima, Wilson Alvarez, and

Olmedo Saenz to minor league deals. And perhaps his biggest decision was endorsing a move to the bullpen for a mediocre starter named Eric Gagne. Evans also came to a contract agreement with free agent outfielder Vladimir Guerrero (who wound up winning the American League MVP award after an outstanding season for the cross-town Anaheim Angels) in the winter of 2004, only to have the Commissioner's Office veto the deal, blaming the unstable ownership.

But like many GM's, Evans was not able to enjoy the fruits of his labor. The Dodgers were finally sold early in 2004 to Frank McCourt, whose grandfather was a minority owner of the old Boston Braves back in the 1940's. Unbelievably, McCourt interviewed candidates for the GM job right under Evans' nose, while he still held the position, and he even wanted Evans to interview for his own job. Billy Beane even publicly campaigned for the post before Evans and McCourt were able to work out an agreement that allowed Evans to exit gracefully.

"When we inherited the organization we were ranked twenty-eighth in minor league talent," Evans says. "When I was let go I think we were second. Over a two and a half year period, I'm really proud of that."

Evans should be proud of his accomplishments. Years earlier, when he was with the White Sox, he had long conversations with Don Drysdale, the late Dodger legend. Drysdale told Evans about the glory days of the Dodgers, when the pride that Branch Rickey installed was still going strong. It meant something back then, to wear Dodger Blue, and that's exactly what Evans was trying to restore.

But McCourt had other ideas. To replace Evans, he hired thirty-one-year-old Paul DePodesta, the Assistant GM of Billy Beane's Oakland A's. DePodesta was portrayed in Michael Lewis's *Moneyball* as Beane's human laptop computer. He's a Harvard Graduate in Economics, which more than anything represents the culture clash of young executives penetrating the game from the outside. DePodesta had only eight years of experience in baseball, but the association with Beane and the popularity of *Moneyball* made DePodesta an even more attractive candidate than he probably should have been.

There is no doubt that DePodesta is incredibly intelligent, but the change of guard in the Dodgers front office pretty much bludgeoned Evans' game plan for returning the Dodgers glory. DePodesta retained Logan White and said the Dodgers would not have an overhaul in scouting practices. However, considering that during DePodesta's five years with Oakland the A's drafted college players 90% of the time in their first thirty picks, you knew the emphasis on high school players would be altered.

The Dodgers had a very solid draft in 2004, rated the second best in the game by *Baseball America*. However, it showed a change in the emphasis on high school talent. Look at the difference in the percentage of high school talent taken in 2004 compared to Evans' two years as GM:

HIGH SCHOOL PLAYERS

YEARS	1st 10 Picks	1st 20 Picks	1st 30 Picks
2004	50%	30%	33%
2002-03	80%	70%	68%

DePodesta also had a much stronger farm system to work with compared to Evans. The improved depth allowed him to make eleven trades in his first season, five after July 30th. After the season, DePodesta fired three of the Dodgers' main scouts, Don Welke, John Boles, and Jeff Schugel. He kept White in his position, but many observers wonder how long it will be before other changes are made to more closely mirror what's going on in Oakland.

Dan Evans was clearly a victim of Moneyball. He was implementing a solid plan to emphasize the farm system and to restore the Dodgers' tradition. But after only two years he was replaced by the flavor of the month. Evans has recovered, joining his old friend Bill Bavasi in Seattle as an assistant. Hopefully, he'll get another chance to mold an organization with his philosophies.

"What we tried to do is get back to a teaching and development organization," Evans says. "What that effectively does is elongate your chances for winning and more importantly brings together a real cohesive group within your minor league system. This is a sport, more than any other sport, where not only is patience rewarded, but patience is front and center of the organization's that have won."

The Dodgers weren't very patient with Dan Evans, but in 2004 they still won to get into the postseason for the first time since

1996. Don't think Evans didn't have a lot to do with that.

DePodesta was chosen over several executives with mountains of more experience, including Pat Gillick, the former GM of the Blue Jays, Orioles, and Mariners. Gillick is one of the many "traditional" baseball people that have been drawn into the debate created by *Moneyball*. Gillick publicly stated after the book was released that it was written in "poor taste." Lewis shot back in an article in *Sports Illustrated* ridiculing Gillick as a leader of the old raccoon club, saying Gillick, Hall of Fame second baseman Joe Morgan, and Tracy Ringolsby, one of the best baseball writers in the country, should be viewed as out-of-touch and unwilling to accept change if they disagree and criticize the thesis of his book.

Gillick has read only the excerpts of *Moneyball* that appeared in magazines, but he came away most upset with the portrayal of scouts as being irrelevant in the evaluation process.

"There are a lot of ways to skin a cat," Gillick says. "If these guys want to use only statistical information, then that's just a prerogative. I have no problem with that. I have a problem with them portraying people who have a love of the game and have committed their life to baseball and who have been very successful. To take shots at them in the book, yeah, I have a problem with that."

Lewis' poke at Gillick was almost laughable. Here's one of the most respected executives in baseball who led the Blue Jays to back-to-back World Series titles in 1992-93, and two appearances in the ALCS for both the Orioles and Mariners under his watch. Gillick believes the debate about the emphasis on stats is worthwhile, and it also allows baseball people who believe in makeup to state their case clearly.

"I frankly think statistics are important," Gillick says. "You've got to use every resource possible. If you look at sports now, hockey, basketball, and baseball, if you look at the sports page all the statistics you see are offensive. There's very little defensive statistics. I think defense is very important. If you look at the Braves the reason they've been there is because of their pitching and defense. But I think people want to be entertained. They want to see offense. They want to see home runs, points, or goals scored. So I don't think walks are very entertaining. But to say I'm not interested in statistics, that's not true. I am interested in statistics. But again, they are a resource and I want to use that resource."

Gillick built most of his teams with a blend of international, high school, and college players. But he warns all those believing in the college player to take a closer look at some of the big numbers those players can put up.

"You know if you look at college players you have to think about their competition," Gillick says. "In the SEC they play on Friday, Saturday, and Sunday. You tell me what the guy's on-base percentage is on Friday (against the competition's best pitcher) and you tell me what his on-base percentage is on Sunday against a number three pitcher. I bet there's a hell of a lot of difference."

"I don't think the game of a player is all about statistics," he continues. "I think the visual observation and the visual evaluation of players is important. You can't just look at statistics and say this player can do this. I think you have to visually evaluate and visually observe a player. To me there are two different things. You want me to cover a player or do you want me to scout a player? In other words, if you want me to go out there and cover a player, I'll go and look at the player and tell you what I think about him. If you want me to scout a player, I have to find out a lot of information about the player before I can make a recommendation to you. That to me, if you're going to do a full scouting job, you have to not only know the player's physical ability, but you've got to know his background, you've got to know his makeup, and you've got to know his motivation. You've got to know what this player is all about if you want to do a full scouting job. You can look at statistics, but as somebody said, 'There's statistics and then there's lies.'"

The inconsistencies in the *Moneyball* book make Gillick question its relevance. Gillick points out that while Lewis takes great pleasure in mocking someone in Beane's draft room known as 'the fat scout,' he fails to mention that the same scout, John Poloni, scouted and signed one of Oakland's best players for the first half of the decade, right-hander Tim Hudson. And with all the college talk, it's also conveniently omitted that Eric Chavez, Oakland's best player, was a first round pick out of high school.

"Look, everyone has their own style," Gillick says. "If they just want to draft college guys, then that just leaves more players for other clubs like Atlanta and Seattle and the other teams that focus on player development. That leaves more high school players. I'm happy that they're only going to draft college guys. That just leaves more for us. But I think the Moneyball philosophy is more on survival than it is on winning. I think it's a new model for a low revenue club, for a small market revenue club so they can survive. I don't think really it's a formula to win. I think it's a formula to survive."

That's a monumental difference.

Harry Minor considers himself a friend of Billy Beane, but for the life of him he can't understand why Beane is so against high school talent. As a scout for the Mets, he was one of the folks who scouted Beane in high school before the Mets took him as a first round pick. Minor knows there will always be stories of players like Beane, a great athlete with bad makeup, who will not fulfill his promise, but the potential of finding a star far outweighs the risks involved in taking a high school player.

"You have to say I'm from the old school," says Minor, who has been with the Mets for almost forty years and in baseball for near a half century. "I've done free agent work, professional work, and been a national crosschecker for the Mets. So I know the high school player is a bigger gamble, but you realize when you get a high school player to the big leagues that his productive years are just enormous. I remember when I saw Dwight Gooden. There was a pitcher at Tampa Catholic (High School) who had been at Dwight Gooden's school and had transferred over and I remember in the meetings when some people liked him. I liked him, but I liked Gooden more. I remember saying, 'You know, that boy is two years older than Gooden and he's graduating the same time. Dwight Gooden is seventeen. By the time he's nineteen, he could be pitching in the big leagues.' I was being very facetious 'cause I didn't think he would be, but by God he was. At nineteen he was striking everybody out in the big leagues."

For many of the years Minor has been with the Mets, they were run by Frank Cashen, who along with Lou Gorman, built a tremendous team in the 1980's. Their preference in the draft was high school players, just like both had stressed with the Orioles in the 1960's. Minor says some critical scouting decisions enabled the Mets to build a consistent winner for many years.

"We just took the best player that we thought was available," he says. "I remember one year our strength was in pitching. We needed middle infielders and hitting in the outfield. So we went into the draft and the first three players we took were pitchers because we felt they were the best. Gooden and Roger McDowell were the first two. Now, there's an example of one high school guy and one college guy. We didn't design it that way. I just don't see how you can come in and say, 'I don't want to take a high school player.' That's stupid. There might be a Mickey Mantle out there or a Dwight Gooden. That's just burying your head in the sand because of the percentages."

The percentages are what the A's and Lewis base their argument on that college players have a much greater chance at making the big leagues. However, research has been done to dispel that theory. Jim Callis is the Executive Editor of *Baseball America*, the premiere amateur and minor league baseball publication in the country. After *Moneyball* came out, he sensed several inconsistencies with the theory of college players being much less of a gamble than high school players. So he decided to do a little research.

Callis looked at every player drafted in the first ten rounds of the drafts between 1990 and 1997. When he did the study in 2003, those were the eight drafts that basically made up most of the drafted talent in major league baseball. Those players had enough time to make it to the big leagues and make an impact. To find out how good the players were he broke them down into six categories – along with separating them by high school or college players at the time of their draft.

He assigned values to the players on a 0-5 scale with the following qualifications: 0 – never played in the big leagues; 1 – a cup of coffee in the big leagues (minimal time); 2 – fringe player in the big leagues; 3 – a major league regular for a few years; 4 – an above average major league player; and 5 – superstar big leaguer.

"I expected the college guys to come out a little bit better than the high school guys," Callis says. "I was actually surprised when I did it to find out that they really didn't come out slightly better; they actually came out the same. If you're just looking to get guys to the big leagues, more college guys are going to make it. 39% of the college players did play in the big leagues, as opposed to 28% of the high school players in those rounds. But if you're actually looking at guys who actually made a contribution, there was no real difference."

Callis found that 8.7% of the college players drafted during that period went on to become major league regulars or better, compared to 8.4% of the high school players. Then, when he looked for players who became above average players or stars, the high school players came out significantly ahead. It was 4.3% for high school players and 2.3% for college players. Callis can't understand why a team hasn't done more complete research such as this to debunk the theories presented in *Moneyball*.

"It's not that hard to put a study like this together," he says. "If you want to quantify it even more, you could use win shares or you could use the value of a replacement player. Yet this belief persists with some of these clubs that the college players are much better players to pursue in the draft."

Callis believes part of the reason for this is the worry by some GM's and Scouting Directors that they may not last long enough in their jobs to see their talent make it to the big leagues, so, since college players do get to the big leagues quicker, they'll have a better chance to prove to their owners that the work they are doing in scouting is working. The impatience level with ownership is out of control, and many executives try to compensate for this by rushing talent to the big leagues.

Callis continues, "I also do think that just with the hype of *Moneyball*, you do have owners out there who believe that college is the way to go from reading the book, even though there is nothing to demonstrate in the book that what the A's were doing was any better than anybody else's philosophy. I do think if you're looking at the big picture, which I think would really be your job if you are the Scouting Director, you're trying to find the best long-term talent for your team. I'm not saying you should necessarily draft all high school players. I really think what you want is a blend. Take some college guys, who may get there a little bit quicker, but you also don't want to ignore all the high school guys. If there's thirty good players in the draft, it's not going to be twenty-five from college and five from high school. It's going to be pretty much fifteen from high school and fifteen from college. If you ignore the high schools completely, you're ignoring half of the ultimate good players in the draft."

Yet that's exactly what the A's do, and Lewis ridicules anyone who questions their philosophy and puts Beane on a pedestal for supposedly knowing something everyone else doesn't. The one time that Lewis documents the A's taking a high school player, Jeremy

Bonderman, Beane supposedly throws a chair through a wall. But Callis says that even that information was incorrect.

"He threw the chair, but he threw it before the draft started," Callis says. "Michael got his timing off a little bit there. Beane was mad that a player they were going to get was going to go and that was going to lead them to Bonderman. It wasn't quite the way Michael Lewis depicted it in the book."

Thirteen months after he was drafted, Bonderman was traded by the A's to the Detroit Tigers, where he is now one of the best young pitchers in the American League. Bonderman surely would look good on the A's pitching staff now, particularly with Hudson in Atlanta and Mark Mulder in St. Louis. Critics say Hudson, Mulder, and Barry Zito, Oakland's 'Big Three' in the starting rotation, were the main reason for the A's success over the last five seasons, even more than any college oriented or statistical philosophies. But the "Big Three" were barely mentioned in *Moneyball*.

"They brought those three into the organization at the same period of time where they could overlap for five consecutive years where they'd control the contracts before they're ready for free agency," Callis says. "And that's really been the trick of keeping the payroll down – to have three pitchers like that who if they were on the open market would be making $10 million or more per year. They didn't have to pay anywhere close to that. Looking back, yes, they drafted those guys, and they deserve credit for that, but Mark Mulder was the number two pick in the country. He wasn't like some guy they found under a rock somewhere that nobody knew about. Barry Zito was played up in *Moneyball* like he was a shocking pick at number nine, but there were teams that liked him. That year they took Tim Hudson, they took college pitchers in the first round, Chris Enochs and Eric Dubose, who have done next to nothing."

And then there's Jeremy Brown, the catcher from the University of Alabama that caught the eye of Paul DePodesta only because his on-base percentage was sky high, despite the claims of the scouts who actually saw him play that Brown was nothing but a bad-bodied catcher who could be had in the range of the fifteenth round. Beane used a first round pick on Brown so he could sign someone below market value, but how much value does a catcher have when in two years he's become a mediocre AA player (.256 average, 6 home runs, 49 RBI, but a .361 OBP) that is now not only being called "bad-bodied" but outright "fat" by some scouts? It all points to another fallacy in the book and the philosophy, that drafting college players has saved the A's money. College seniors have zero leverage, since they can only take the team's offer or not play, so some teams do choose college talent to balance out their budgets. But despite an almost exclusive approach to college players, the A's are still spending tremendous amounts of money on their draft picks, with usually one of the largest budgets for draft picks in the game.

"I think there's a misconception out there, again from people reading *Moneyball*, perhaps that the A's have this system of finding players that nobody else likes and they're saving a lot of money in the draft," Callis says. "You certainly have to tie in that they've had extra picks, but for the most part they've paid pretty much market value for those extra picks. The A's have probably spent more on the draft in the last three years than anybody has. I don't think for all the money they've spent they've gotten more talent than anybody else has."

The scary part is that some teams are actually buying the philosophies pointed out in the book. The Cardinals' owners reportedly read *Moneyball* and revamped their scouting department to go after more college players. When the Diamondbacks, who went from winning the World Series in 2001 to losing 111 games in 2004, brought in a new CEO, the rumor was they were going to the *Moneyball* approach and go after more college players. Is that the best way for a team that has hit rock bottom to rebuild? Or is it just another impatient owner who wants quick results at any cost?

Thankfully, there are some teams trying to build for the long-term and for consistent success. The Cincinnati Reds have always had a dichotomy in their scouting and player development philosophies. For years, they were owned by Marge Schott, who once asked, 'Why do we need all of these scouts? They just sit there and watch games.' Jim Bowden was a GM who believed in scouting and player development, but tight finances handicapped him. When Bowden left, Dan O'Brien came in as General Manager determined to return the Reds to an organization built from within.

"I think right from the beginning in talking with ownership about this franchise and all the tradition it's not difficult if you look back and see the zenith of this franchise in the 70's with the 'Big Red Machine' the vast majority of players on that club were homegrown," O'Brien says. "And so there's no secret here as to how and why that's the path we have to take."

In O'Brien's first year on the job, he took several pages from the Braves' blueprint from the late 80's when they were developing a winning team. In every deal that he traded a veteran pitcher, he got back quality young arms (like Bubba Nelson and Jung Bong from the Braves). O'Brien did not go for the quick fix by signing free agents, which could have cost his team valuable draft picks. Instead, he gave young players like outfielder Wily Mo Pena and pitchers Ryan Wagner, Aaron Harang, Brandon Claussen, Luke Hudson, and Josh Hancock (acquired from the Phillies) valuable playing time. O'Brien's game plan: get quality out of quantity, even if it may take some time.

"As an organization, we're continually working and striving to add depth to our system," he says. "We know the importance of it. In all of the transactions we contemplate, we look for pitching. If there's a position player and a pitcher let's say of equal ability, we'll probably lean toward the pitcher if we have the choice."

O'Brien also took the long-term approach in the draft, where he had the seventh overall pick in the first round in 2004. Despite calls from Reds fans to take a college player that could possibly contribute in the next season or two, O'Brien and his scouting staff went with *Baseball America's* High School Player of the Year, a tall right-handed pitcher out of Texas named Homer Bailey.

"All we're trying to do in the draft, and I think the Braves have done this very well, is take the best player available," O'Brien says. "While you may lean toward getting pitching, it's never at the expense of getting the best player available. We're not going to limit ourselves to the talent pool of a particular type, be it college, junior college, or high school. Patience doesn't just manifest itself in making decisions in the draft. It comes into play as far as your development process in your minor league system, and this is the thing that gets frustrating for the fans, it also has to permeate what you are doing at the major league level. Major league starting pitchers that you develop from within are going to have the inevitable peaks and valleys that are part and parcel of the learning process. There's the inevitable learning curve and I know fans can get frustrated with that. If you look and study the good organizations in the game, they have that requisite of patience with starting pitching at the major league level."

Count O'Brien as one of the GM's inclined to follow the

Braves' way over the sensationalism portrayed in *Moneyball*. He knows the job security for GM's is slim. Owners want to win now, and often scoff at any long-term planning. But O'Brien believes he has the Reds on course to not only eventually win, but to consistently win in the future.

"We've had a lot of internal discussions about what our overall game plan is going forward for this organization," he says. "The one thing that we all agree on is no matter what we may encounter, whether it be on the plus side or the negative side, we are going to continue to stay the course. We knew that was the only way that we were inevitably going to achieve success in the long term."

The Oakland A's didn't re-invent the wheel with their emphasis on statistical analysis, even though *Moneyball* and Lewis want you to think they did. While it can't be called a "fad," it may be better to compare it to the Atkins Diet. There might be a short-term benefit, but just like diet and exercise, the traditional scouting approach is still the best way to construct a consistent winner. Short-term success is the easy way out. It takes guts to build a team for the long haul.

John Schuerholz has often said that scouts are the lifeblood of the game of baseball. He knows that without them, there's no way the Braves could have achieved such success. *Baseball America* has ranked the Braves as having one of the top seven farm systems in each of the last fourteen years. There's a simple reason for that unprecedented recognition. It's the scouts. When you see someone like Paul Snyder walking around with a cigar hanging from his mouth, a funny hat on his head, and a radar gun in his hand, you know he is doing more than just watching games. He's slowly and methodically finding the pieces of the puzzle that make up a major league baseball player – the complete circle. And that is the bravest way to build a winning team.

ACKNOWLEDGEMENTS

For me, a broadcaster, this has been a labor of love. I've loved the Atlanta Braves for as long as I can remember. It's been a pleasure to talk about them, and it's been even more of an honor to write about their story and that of others.

The first thank-you goes to my mother, Charlotte Williams, who encouraged me to follow my dreams. Our summer vacations were spent driving up I-75 to Atlanta Fulton-County Stadium, leaving South Georgia in the wee hours to get autographs. It was unfathomable to walk into that stadium to watch the Braves in person, and it wasn't always easy for us to make the trip. Who in the world could have had it better? And she let me stay up late to watch the west coast games. For that and so much more, I thank you. You're the best mother in the world. This book is for you.

Ted Turner had Bill Tush, and over the last five years my SportsCom partner has been Skip Seda, an awesome videographer. Words can't express my gratitude to you for being a true friend, a brother, and I wouldn't trade the last few years for anything. To you, Kathy, and Tripp, thanks for being there through everything and being my family.

Randy Sharpe started me on this dream in 1998 when we talked about a sports production company. Your friendship means a lot, and your confidence in me even more. No one has ever showed more faith in me professionally than J.R. Wright. Thank you for believing in me and in SportsCom Network.

To get to know members of the Atlanta Braves organization has been a lifelong dream for a kid from Waycross. The friendships I have made are more valuable than anything. To Roy Clark, Dayton Moore, and Paul Snyder, thank you for sharing your stories. And to John Schuerholz, Bobby Cox, and Stan Kasten, I thank all three of you for fixing my team.

I've known Brian Snitker longer than any other Brave. Snit, Bill Champion, Randy Ingle, Pat Kelly, Rocket Wheeler, Franklin Stubbs, Guy Hansen, Bruce Dal Canton, Kent Willis, Bobby Moore, Mel Roberts, and Mike Alvarez have all become friends and it's an honor. The friendships I have made with the players are very special as well. Telling your stories is a privilege, and each of you have no bigger fan than myself.

Anne McAlister, the glue in the Braves PR office, is simply a jewel of a person. Mike Dunn and Dick Balderson gave me "The Braves Show" in 2001. I'll be indebted to both of you for life. And to Ernie Johnson, Pete Van Wieren, and Skip Caray, thanks for making me a sportscaster.

Heartfelt thanks to my publisher Drew Nederpelt who believed in my ability to tell this story. Thanks also to Sarah Heath, Charmaine O'Saerang, Don Banducci, Eddie Gaedel and everyone at Sterling & Ross Publishers- you made it happen. Jason Walker helped me edit the book along the way and I will always be grateful for his support and friendship.

Thanks to the many people in Waycross, Georgia who helped me get to this point. Thank you as well to Gary Griffin, David B. Shields, Tommy Tucker, JoAnn Brehm, Lou Essick and Dave Calloway, Mickey Garnto, Southwood School, Ken Holder, Darrell Holder, Ryle Holder, Chris Karle, Dedi Thomas, Dennis Abercrombie, Lee Webb, Susan Brantley, Dr. James Dye, Dr. Alison Alexander, David Hazinski, Bob Mitchell, Bill Davis, Hector Garcia, Bob Young, George Jobin, Krissy "Bailey" Button, Pam Moseley, David Mason, John Townsend, Anne Townsend, Kike Seda, Pat Steed, Lee Douglas, Kyle Hawkins, Trey Wainwright, Fontaine Lewis, Ann Orowski, Jim Jones, Robyn Clarke, Ray Cannon, John and Cathy Nelson, and Scott and Toni Alvarez. Plus Gay McMichael, Ken Hartley, Frank Shurling, Ted Gumbart, Ron Douthit, Doug Fincher, Rick Thomas, and David Wall in Macon.

To Bernice, Wendy, Johnnie, Buster, and Baby Wendy. The best family a guy could ever have. Thanks to Charlie "Rabbit" Williams for giving me the love of baseball. And finally I thank my grandmother, Jean Williams, for loving me more than necessary.

Index

Index

Index

Index

Index

OTHER TITLES BY STERLING & ROSS PUBLISHERS

SPRAWL KILLS, How Blandburbs Steal Your Time, Health and Money, by Joel S. Hirschhorn, PhD. ISBN#09766372-0-0 $25.95

THE OFFICIAL CELEBRITY HANDBOOK, The How-To Guide To Becoming Famous, by Beth Efran and Erin Hiner-Gee. ISBN# 09766372-3-5 $14.95

DOUBLE WIDE: Living Large in a Super-Sized America...and What You Can Do About It, by Chris Katsaropoulos and Dr. John Katsaropoulos. ISNBN# 09766372-2-7 $22.95

THE SUCCESS EFFECT: Uncommon Conversations with America's Business Innovators, by John Eckberg. ISBN# 09766372-4-3 $22.95

MONKEY TO THE STARS: Confessions of a Celebrity Profiler, by Robert Kerwin. ISBN# 09766372-7-8 $24.95

THE WORLD'S BEST GOLF JOKE BOOK, Remembered, Compiled and Told By One of Them, by Ray Welch, Illustrated by Dan Reeves. ISBN# 09766372-5-1 $22.95

THE ONE AND ONLY FLICKHEADS GUIDE TO THE CLASSICS...and Some That Should Be, by The FlickHeads. ISBN# 09766372-6-X $14.95